ALLAN PINKERTON

RHODRI
JEFFREYS-JONES

ALLAN PINKERTON

AMERICA'S LEGENDARY DETECTIVE AND THE BIRTH OF PRIVATE SECURITY

GEORGETOWN UNIVERSITY PRESS / WASHINGTON, DC

Cataloging-in-Publication Data is on file with the Library of Congress.

ISBN 9781647125844 (paperback)
ISBN 9781647125851 (ebook)

∞ This paper meets the requirements of ANSI/NISO Z39.48-1992 (Permanence of Paper).

EU GPSR Authorised Representative
LOGOS EUROPE, 9 rue Nicolas Poussin,
17000, LA ROCHELLE, France
E-mail: Contact@logoseurope.eu

26 25 9 8 7 6 5 4 3 2 First printing

Printed in the United States of America

Cover design by Faceout Studio, Molly von Borstel
Interior design by Westchester Publishing Services

Figure 0.1. Allan Pinkerton in his later years, from *Harper's Weekly*. *Library of Congress*

am Elin

Contents

Illustrations

Acknowledgments

A large amount has been written about the Pinkerton National Detective Agency (PNDA), much of it encouraged by the agency and taking a favorable view. There was a regular output, also, that was hostile in its stance. The subject matter of this book is, then, controversial. The wise course of action in contending with the subjectivity would be to pay heed to primary evidence. However, there is a problem here. Over a period of 130 years, many Pinkerton records disappeared.[1] In 1871 the Great Fire that destroyed Chicago consumed the records of the agency that was headquartered in that city. Thereafter, like other image-conscious organizations, the agency took care to preserve some documents but not others. Notably rare are overviews of the Pinkerton agency's sources of income—information that might have been of use to the PNDA's competitors if published and would have been a source of embarrassment because of the agency's labor work. In the 1930s the La Follette US Senate investigation that focused on the Pinkertons' labor espionage issued a request for evidence that prompted wholesale preemptive record destruction. Finally, in 1999, the agency further reduced its files in preparing them for deposit in the Library of Congress. Jane Adler, the archivist entrusted with bringing order to chaos on that occasion, assured me that the company brought no subjective pressure to bear regarding what was to be jettisoned.[2]

Thankfully the ProQuest company soon thereafter created a digital archive from the records now on deposit in the Library of Congress. These have been of great assistance to me. I had previously worked on the Pinkerton letterbooks that were already held by the Library. In citing them I used the box number system devised by staff at the Manuscript Room in that library. The ProQuest digital collection is organized on different principles, but in this book I use the box numbers assigned by the Library of Congress throughout in the interests of clarity and uniformity. The only exception is a small quantity of material given to me by Jane Adler when she was in the process of arranging the transfer of the residual Pinkerton materials to the public archive. They are identified as such.

I thanked the late Mrs. Adler at the time and would like to reiterate my gratitude here. As my interest in the subject matter of this book goes back to the 1960s, she is not the only deceased person to whom I am indebted. Sidney Fine gave me access to research materials to which he had private access and which he later used in his own publications—it was an inspiring example of collegiality. Oscar Handlin patiently guided the research for the doctoral dissertation on which the present work in a few places draws. Howard Lamar offered wise reflections on residual frontier conditions east of the Mississippi.

More recently others have helped with advice, archival hints, and comments on drafts. I am most grateful to David Barrie, Robert Bartlett, Doug Charles, Bob Cherny, Lorette Deaver, Tom Devine, Owen Dudley Edwards, Neil Evans, John E. Fox, W. Hamish Fraser, Susan-Mary Grant, George Grella, Fabian Hilfrich, Tom Hyry, Les James, Dolores Janiewski, Angela John, Elin Jones, Oliver Kendrick, Michelle Krowl, Val McDermid, Alex Murdoch, Colin Nicolson, Kathy Olmsted, Jim Phillips, Sian Reynolds, David Silkenat, and Michael Woodiwiss.

At Georgetown University Press, Don Jacobs was a perceptive and dedicated editor. There are not many like him, and he has my heartfelt gratitude. On the home front, my wife Mary was as ever supportive—and a reliable distraction. This volume is dedicated to my cousin Elin, who with customary generosity shared her encyclopedic knowledge and understanding of Welsh history in a way that informed my account of events and nonevents in Newport.

Rhodri Jeffreys-Jones
Summer of 2024

Introduction

Allan Pinkerton was the world's most famous detective. Born in Scotland in 1819, he qualified as a cooper, then immigrated to the United States in 1842. His strong physique, ingenuity, and determination propelled him on his new and fruitful career as a private eye. By the time of his death in 1884, he had become a household name in America and beyond. "Pinkertonism," the practice of private detection as advocated by Allan Pinkerton, was one of the notable "isms" of its day. It was a counterweight to communism and socialism and a problem in its own right. As we shall see, it was also a reinforcement to at least some aspects of liberalism.

Pinkerton made his mark not only in his own time but also on posterity. The management of his renowned firm, the Pinkerton National Detective Agency, passed on his death to his sons. The resultant dynasty lasted until the passing of the last of his direct male descendants in 1967. Even after that and despite several mergers, the Pinkertons remained a force on the land, if not so prominently—students today sometimes ask to be reminded who Allan Pinkerton was. In sum, Pinkertonism is a thread that runs through American history from the 1850s to recent times, reflecting great issues of the day and contributing to them. It has fueled past controversies and informs debates within the historical profession.

Especially in the early years of his detective career, Allan Pinkerton was an innovator. For example, immediately in the wake of the emergence of modern photography, he circulated mugshots as a means of identifying criminals who fled from one jurisdiction to another. In terms of practical results, he was responsible for the arrest of numerous counterfeiters, bank robbers, and fraudsters.

Pinkerton's achievements have nevertheless been widely questioned. Adding to the roster of preexisting controversies, this study opens with a new challenge to his reputation. According to previous accounts, Allan Pinkerton fled his native Scotland in 1842 because he was a fugitive from justice: the police wanted to arrest him because of his advocacy of force in the pursuit of universal male suffrage.[1] He was indeed an outspoken adherent of the franchise movement known as Chartism. His admirers have furthermore depicted him as a participant in the last attempt in British history at social revolution. This was an uprising that started in the Welsh town of Newport but succumbed to the bullets and bayonets of militiamen before it could spread to the population at large.

However, the "last rising" claim made on Pinkerton's behalf was fictitious. He was never anywhere near Newport. On the contrary, it is possible that he was a police informer. It may well be that when in 1842 he fled to the New World with Joan, his teenage bride, it was to escape not punishment by the authorities but the condemnation, if not vengeance, of the Chartists he betrayed. In his immigrant baggage a cynical opportunism may well have jostled for space with his vaunted principles.

Once he arrived in America Pinkerton did advocate and uphold liberal principles. The pages that follow highlight, for the first time, the fact that he was a protofeminist. His employment of female detectives and the trust he placed in them marked him as a leader who was well in advance of his contemporaries. Here it must be conceded that Pinkerton remained a gender conservative in his treatment of female members of his own family. Furthermore there are scattered examples of female detectives in nineteenth century Britain, so it cannot be said that his feminism was unique.[2] However his enlightened attitude toward gender is still significant because, whereas private detection had minimal status in the UK except as fiction, the Pinkerton agency was a national institution.

Pinkerton's antislavery views and actions have been more widely acknowledged. Resident in Chicago, he was acquainted with the rebel John Brown and with the future president Abraham Lincoln. The evidence supports his claim that he facilitated the workings of the Underground Railroad, the secret network that in defiance of the law helped runaway slaves on their way to safety in Canada. At the same time, we shall be asking two questions. The first is, where and when did he acquire his abolitionist principles? And the second, did he exploit and even exaggerate his abolitionist reputation in order to advance his business interests?

Allan Pinkerton's contributions at the time of the American Civil War (1861–65) are controversial. Already the nation's leading detective, Pinkerton claimed to have foiled the Baltimore plot, a conspiracy to assassinate Lincoln as he traveled to Washington, DC, to be inaugurated. As contemporaries and later historical critics pointed out, the Baltimore story was brilliant publicity for Pinkerton and his senior female detective, Kate Warne. However, the following narrative suggests that cynicism should stop here. The fact that the Baltimore story lent itself to opportunistic exploitation does not mean that there was no conspiracy to assassinate Lincoln.

Less credible than the Baltimore claim, as confirmed on the pages that follow, are the assertions that Pinkerton established the US Secret Service and performed a vital military intelligence function in the early months of the war.[3] Pinkerton lacked both military experience and the will to stand up to superior officers. He grossly overestimated the strength of the army commanded by the Confederacy's General Robert E. Lee. Overestimation caused Union timidity in the face of Confederate weakness and meant that an opportunity was missed to win, and thus end, the bloody war early. Was this a precedent for the malpractice known as intelligence to please and for the politicization of intelligence?

In the years between the Civil War and the 1890s, the Pinkerton agency expanded, setting up offices in every part of the nation. A private agency thus performed functions that in other nations were the domain of public police forces. There was an important difference between the Pinkerton and public models of policing. The Pinkertons served only those who had the money and inclination to employ them. They were not helpful to the majority of the population. Nevertheless, the Pinkertons comprised nineteenth-century America's best effort at a national police force. And it is here argued that, in being a private police enterprise, they were a distinctive American phenomenon.

The Pinkertons' reach and standing in American society owed much to the imagination, leadership, and organizational prowess of their founder, Allan Pinkerton. At the same time, there were other reasons for their success and expansion. One was the spatial frontier experience. White settlers moved into new areas of the North American continent at a pace that outran the institutions of the early Republic. There were shortages of doctors, teachers, religious leaders, and—giving the Pinkertons an opportunity—sheriffs, courts, and the apparatus of law and order. It is no coincidence that Allan Pinkerton began his detective career in 1840s Dundee, Illinois, a frontier community built on land that an Indigenous tribe, the Pottowatomie, had only recently lost to settlers of Scottish, German, and New England descent.

In addition to the reality of the frontier with its judicial deficiencies, there was the *myth* of the frontier, the tradition of individualism pitted against oppressive authority. The Pinkertons could present themselves as a free enterprise voluntarily commissioned by individuals in their quest for justice, as distinct from public police authorities that imposed order from above. Allan Pinkerton was at pains to stress the corruption of urban police forces and the contrasting integrity, with freedom from political influence, of his agency's operatives.

Yet there was a problem here. When the Pinkertons hired their services to bankers and express companies with the aim of apprehending bank robbers, they took on some of America's most charismatic free spirits. The gunslinging James brothers and the Sundance Kid are prominent examples discussed in this book. However illogically, these outlaws were widely admired as Robin Hood characters who stood up to invidious authority. They did not just engage in gunfights with the Pinkertons; they took them on in a struggle for the soul of America, and the Pinkertons could not credibly claim to have won.

Allan Pinkerton's agency operated not only in the West but also in long-settled eastern and southern areas of the United States, where frontier experiences had receded into memory. In such locations throughout America, certain weaknesses in the US model of federalism contributed to the attractiveness of private police solutions. Urban and state police forces had not yet learned to cooperate and to share data on criminals. Fugitives from justice found safety when they crossed a state line, or even a city boundary. Pinkerton agents had the advantage of freedom to pursue suspects anywhere, even if they had to get local police to handcuff the fugitives they tracked down.[4]

The nation did not entirely lack a federal police and detective force. Just before his assassination in 1865, President Lincoln had established the US Secret Service. Under the umbrella of the Treasury Department, its agents tracked down counterfeiters and illicit whiskey distillers. Then in the 1870s the Secret Service moved temporarily to the Justice Department with the job of identifying the hooded night riders known collectively as the Ku Klux Klan. So well did the Secret Service perform this task that fears welled up, in the white South and beyond, about the possibility of a federal secret police that would suppress citizens' liberties. The story told in this study thus suggests that antifederalism, as well as federalism, restricted public competition with the private Pinkertons.

The profitability of anti–organized labor work was a prime reason for the rise of the Pinkerton National Detective Agency. Although Allan Pinkerton professed sympathy with workers in their struggle for decent wages and conditions, in practice he introduced techniques designed to inhibit and crush labor unionism. His insinuation of spies into the ranks of labor was strongly reminiscent of employers' practices in his native Scotland. Additionally, he and his sons hired out armed guards to protect property and strikebreakers.

Pinkertons were to the fore in some of the great labor struggles of the day. In the 1870s Pinkerton agent James McParland claimed to have penetrated a clandestine labor group in the Pennsylvania coalfields called the Molly Maguires. Twenty alleged Mollies went to the gallows. In 1886, two years after Allan

Pinkerton's death, a labor protest in Chicago in favor of the eight-hour working day came to a juddering halt when a bomb was thrown into a column of policemen with fatal consequences. Five local anarchists—martyrs to their supporters—received death sentences for their alleged complicity. The Pinkertons were accused of manufacturing evidence for the prosecution. Then in 1892, three hundred armed Pinkertons fought a pitched battle with pro-union workers at the Homestead steel works outside Pittsburgh. In the short term, such events swelled the coffers of the Pinkerton agency. Around one-third of Pinkerton agency income came from labor work, making it by far its greatest income stream. But it was at the cost of public notoriety. And in subsequent decades debate raged among historians about the injustices arising from these and other dramatic events.[5]

In light of this, why did the Pinkertons apparently go for the kill, destroying the very unions whose existence gave them an unending flow of profit? The answer stems from the fact that Allan Pinkerton's ideology set him apart from many of his competitors. His fervent belief in private enterprise as distinct from public police services was the reverse of a coin whose obverse was passionate opposition to communism. The Paris Commune of 1871, a socialist experiment that resulted in thousands of deaths, alarmed many Americans. Its bloody demise prepared them for the charismatic detective's message. In his writings Allan Pinkerton gave a powerful fillip to what was to be a recurring American phobia, anticommunism. Whatever his early sympathies may have been and despite having postured as a physical-force Chartist, by the 1870s he condemned labor unions, saying they were tarred with a commitment to violence—violence he associated with the danger of proletarian revolution. No doubt he welcomed the profit to be made from labor work, but my contention is that he was also ideologically committed to it—as were his descendants until they abandoned the practice at the end of the 1930s.

The Homestead gunfight of 1892 was one of the major scandals of its decade. Labor leaders hoped it would result in a congressional ban on the use of Pinkertons in industrial disputes. In 1893 Congress did pass an anti-Pinkerton law. However, this legislation prohibited not the industrial employment of Pinkertons but the hiring of private detectives for federal work.

The anti-Pinkerton law facilitated an upswing in federal policing and detection. The Secret Service played a successful role in suffocating a Spanish espionage effort in the War of 1898. Ten years later President Theodore Roosevelt created the Bureau of Investigation (BofI), which would be known from 1935 onward as the Federal Bureau of Investigation (FBI).

Ironically, in light of Allan Pinkerton's laissez-faire principles, the publicly funded BofI/FBI and Central Intelligence Agency (CIA) drew on the experience and expertise of the private detective industry. The Pinkertons were especially influential. It was the Pinkerton agency that chiefly served as a model for federal detection and security agencies. One example of their relevance to the CIA is the Pinkertons' rendition of suspects. Notoriously in the case of US socialist revolutionary William D. Haywood, the Pinkertons snatched suspects from one state jurisdiction for trial in another without regard for due process. They also ignored habeas corpus rights in capturing prisoners from abroad for delivery to the US courts for trial. History repeated itself in the present century's actions of the CIA—though there was a difference in that the suspected terrorists the CIA kidnapped were never delivered to US courts for trial. Other examples of influence abound and will be discussed in this book.

All this was in spite of a further major discrediting of the private detective industry. For in the 1920s, a series of exposés of Pinkerton agency labor espionage prepared the way for a heavily resourced 1930s investigation by a congressional committee chaired by Senator Robert M. La Follette, Jr. The inquiry caught the agency's new principal, Robert A. Pinkerton (RAP) II, off guard. Not for the first time, the Pinkertons foreswore labor work, with the difference that this time they mainly lived up to their words. RAP II adapted skillfully to the resultant loss of 33 percent of agency income. The last member of the Pinkerton dynasty, he became its most successful businessman when he diversified into private security work.

The events of the 1920s and 1930s swung public opinion behind labor to such a degree that corporate attempts to repeal the Anti-Pinkerton Act with its prohibition of federal work failed in the postwar years. Finally, however, in 1977 the US district court case *Jacob Weinberger v. Equifax* modified the effect of the anti-Pinkerton law. The Pinkerton pause in the privatization of federal security arrangements that had endured from 1893 to 1977 was now, in principle, at an end. *Equifax* combined with other factors to ensure that the surge in homeland security provision that occurred on the wake of the 9/11 terrorist attacks would be achieved largely with the assistance of private enterprise firms. Allan Pinkerton and his legacy had had a long, if interrupted, reach in American history.

The chapters that follow detail the story of Allan Pinkerton: his formative years, the founding of his agency, the Civil War experience, his philosophy, and his controversial clashes with charismatic outlaws and with organized labor. They continue with an account of his legacy. There is coverage of the practices and beliefs of his male descendants and of their agency's role in dramatic episodes such as the Haymarket bomb explosion and Homestead lockout. The text details a clash with the great defense lawyer Clarence Darrow and an internecine rivalry with rival detective William J. Burns. There is an account of attempts to rein in the perceived excesses of Pinkertonism. But as our narrative is chronological, it starts at the beginning—with the circumstances of Allan Pinkerton's birth and upbringing in Scotland's most notorious community, the Gorbals.

CHAPTER 1

The Gorbals Man

Isabella Pinkerton endured the final stages of labor on July 21, 1819. She lay in one of the two rooms of her family's dwelling place. In addition to Isabella and her husband William, the home accommodated four survivors from the seven children brought into the world by William's deceased first wife. The rooms also housed Isabella's own son Robert, the sole survivor from three further children fathered by the persistent William.

Isabella survived the trauma on that summer day, as did the baby boy to whom she gave birth. The child would outlast the endemic diseases of those times. He grew to be strong and talented. Allan Pinkerton became the world's most famous detective.

The Pinkerton apartment was on the top floor of a tenement at the junction of Muirhead Street and Rutherglen Loan in the Gorbals, a district immediately to the south of Scotland's River Clyde. On the opposite bank of the river lay the city of Glasgow, to which the Gorbals would be annexed in 1846. Years later, Allan Pinkerton penned negative recollections of his home district, writing to a friend, "Ah! The misery I think of . . . the misery and wretchedness of the Gorbals."[1]

The Gorbals left its mark on Allan Pinkerton. The struggles of his youth would shape his character and gave him the threads with which to weave an autobiographical narrative. The Gorbals was a dynamic and unsettling environment that belied its ancient pastoral origins. "Gorbals" may have derived from a dimly recalled Celtic place name, its preceding definite article being similarly a practice whose rationale was long forgotten. For most of the eighteenth century, the Gorbals remained a rural village with a population of no more than

Figure 1.1. Allan Pinkerton was born here in 1819 in the Gorbals, Scotland. This photograph is from the 1850s. *Library of Congress*

300. Then came the industrial revolution. Coal mines, factories, pollution, disease, wealth for a few, decent wages for some, and poverty for many ensued. Challenging circumstances drove some of the indigenous population to emigrate to America, but demographic ingress dwarfed that exodus. Workers to turn the wheels of industry poured in from Lowland and Highland Scotland. Many

had been driven off their ancestral lands by the "Clearances." Landowners cleared the land worked by crofters (subsistence farmers) in order to put sheep to pasture—sheep for whose wool the booming textile industry hungered. Hard on the heels of the Highlanders came the Irish. Later, Russian Jews and Asians arrived, though by this time the primary population boom had already occurred. The people of the Gorbals, 5,000 by the time of the 1801 census, numbered 80,000 by 1861.[2]

Such rapid, multiethnic growth was potentially a recipe for disorder, and civic leaders tried to respond to the challenge. By establishing a public police force in 1800, Glasgow showed itself to be one of the world's progressive cities. Eight years later, an act of Parliament allowed the Gorbals to do the same. However, the community to the south of the Clyde supported only a very small force. It was unequal to the task of containing criminality or moderating the area's debauchery. Beyond the reach of the regulatory powers of its neighbor across the river, the Gorbals harbored more than its share of brothels and drinking dens. If you lived in Glasgow and wanted to sin, you had only to cross the river—if you were rash enough to risk robbery and disease.

Like Tiger Bay in Cardiff and the Five Points district in New York City, the Gorbals acquired a terrible, if perversely cherished, reputation. Sometimes that reputation bordered on absurdity. In John Buchan's 1922 novel *Huntingtower*, a gang known as the Gorbals Die-Hards rescue a Russian princess from the clutches of evildoers, while singing songs with the improbable lines "Proley Tarians, arise!" and "Class conscious we are."[3] More grimly, Kingsley Long wrote of the Gorbals' razor gangs in his 1935 work of fiction *No Mean City*. All this has given enduring credibility to Pinkerton's claim to have grown up in a tough neighborhood.

A few things need to be said in mitigation of Pinkerton's characterization of "misery and wretchedness" in the Gorbals. The children of the area received at least rudimentary education. Indeed, young Allan Pinkerton was literate and an avid reader. Some areas in the Gorbals and especially in the neighboring south-of-the-river communities Hutchesontown and Laurieston were less crowded and had good housing. They contained aspiring artisanal and middle-class escapees from the smoky city to the north. One might add that the Pinkertons' dwelling place, unimaginably cramped by modern standards, was not, in its day, exceptionally constricted.

Infant mortality was a tragedy for the Pinkerton family, but high rates were the norm in Scottish society, where if a live birth were achieved, a child had only an 88 percent chance of reaching its first birthday.[4] That was one reason why families had so many children. It was an insurance against death. It was neither a uniquely Gorbals problem nor for that matter a Scottish one. High child mortality was an international phenomenon. Pinkerton did not have greatly improved luck with the children he fathered in America. Most of them died in infancy.[5] Finally, while the influx of Catholic Irish into the Gorbals may have influenced Pinkerton's mentality, the main Irish surge came after the potato famine (1845–1852) caused a mass exodus from the Emerald Isle, by which time Pinkerton had quit Scotland and was living in America.

In characterizing the Gorbals the way he did, Pinkerton may have been influenced by accounts of the area's decline after he left. He also subscribed to one of the tropes of migrant letter writing. Having made the momentous decision to emigrate, Scots who prospered in the New World found it necessary to justify that decision to the relatives, friends, and dependents they left behind, and, in the process, to themselves. It was only natural to dwell on the disadvantages of the Old World and the compensations in the New. For Pinkerton, who was hugely successful in America, the upbeat–downbeat message flowed easily.[6]

Allan Pinkerton came from an old Gorbals family. Some of his relatives had been prominent citizens, for example serving as provosts (mayors) of nearby communities. His grandfather was a blacksmith. Good physique together with strength were hereditary traits. Allan's father, William, was six feet tall, enjoyed a long life by Gorbals standards (1767–approx. 1830), and passed on muscular attributes to his son. According to one admiring account, "Allan Pinkerton was a man of great physical strength. He stood nearly six feet and weighed 200 pounds, with no waste flesh on his solid frame. He was a formidable antagonist in a rough-and-tumble fight."[7] All accounts agree that Allan was endowed with a strong will, nerves of steel, deductive powers, and a shrewd capacity to understand his fellow human beings. His father was a handloom weaver, a trade that survived the initial economic vicissitudes of the Napoleonic wars and their aftermath. Allan's half-brother James was a wastrel who took regular advantage of the local whorehouses and drinking dens, but James's three sisters brought home wages earned at Thomson's cotton mill further along Muirhead Street. Thus did the working classes, as well as their masters, benefit from the unpaid toil of New World slaves who picked the cotton.

By the time Allan was a preteen, the daughters had married and left home, fewer mouths to feed but also fewer breadwinners. William Pinkerton, by now in his fifties, a ripe old age for the times, suffered a loss in earnings due to the vagaries of supply, demand, and mechanization. For a while, he managed to redeem the situation. Exploiting his local connections, he obtained a post as prison officer in Glasgow's City Jail. This was a new edifice just across the Clyde, at the western extremity of a recreational area called Glasgow Green. The prison served three nearby counties as well as Glasgow itself. It was further evidence of the city's progressivism. With hygiene at a premium, the jail had running water and indoor bathrooms, a facility that the inhabitants of the Pinkertons' tenement could only dream of. William Pinkerton had landed a plum job.

Allan Pinkerton did not write an autobiography, and our knowledge of these early years is fragmentary. What we do know about his life before fame comes from his asides in books and correspondence, remarks that can be useful and are supplemented by other sources such as the writings of the popular journalist Edgar L. Wakeman, who stated he had had "repeated opportunities" in the course of his "constant association" with Allan Pinkerton to glean the story of his life. Like other chroniclers of Pinkerton's life, Wakeman could be unreliable. In part, this was because Pinkerton's own orally delivered recollections were embellished or incomplete (which of us, after all, remembers their childhood with unerring accuracy?). Thus Wakeman was in error in saying that Allan's father William Pinkerton was a British army veteran. He may not have been far from the truth, however, in recording, "Finally at an outbreak of prisoners [William Pinkerton] was so savagely set upon that the poor man was disabled for life."[8]

Though his death was never officially recorded, William Pinkerton appears to have died in 1830 or 1831. A certain version of his passing invites scrutiny. According to Allan Pinkerton's biographer Sigmund Lavine, William was not a turnkey, but a serving sergeant in the Glasgow police force "who died as a result of injuries received while trying to maintain order during a Chartist riot."[9] Lavine was simply repeating what had come to be a popular, but unfounded, myth about Allan's father. Unfounded, because the Chartists did not begin their activities until 1838, several years after William's death. The story may have originated with Allan, though there is no evidence for that. It is still a significant bit of mythology as, if true, it would help to explain Allan Pinkerton's motivation in becoming America's leading policeman, as well as some of the conservative sociopolitical views he came to hold. If Allan *invented* the story, it would have been an instance of the liberality with strictly defined truth that characterized some of his later writings. It is possible, too, that Allan (or Wakeman) innocently conflated his father's story with that of his half-brother, also called William. This younger William had been a private in the 42nd Regiment and joined the Glasgow police as a sergeant in the 1830s. Though there is no evidence to confirm it, he may well have been injured in a radical disturbance.

Regardless of the uncertainties, the death-by-riot narrative was a potent message in the hands of those who saw Allan Pinkerton as a consistently conservative hero.

The manner of his father's death may or may not have preyed on Allan's mind in the years to come. What is certain is that William's demise had immediate economic consequences. Allan's life had hitherto been economically stable. There were hints of other troubles, to be sure. For example, although he was baptized in a Protestant church one month after his birth, his parents were atheists, as he would be. The departure from religious observance was radical for those times. It signaled a readiness to step outside conventional bounds in a manner that might well endanger one's career. Family discord was another source of instability. Quite apart from the stresses caused by James's reckless behavior, there were tensions and jealousies between the half-siblings arising from their different maternal parentage. Still, things could have been a great deal worse for the child Allan, as he discovered on the death of his father.

The economic consequences of William's passing meant that, at the age of eleven, Allan had to leave school and contribute to the income of his mother. Isabella still worked at Thomson's Mill but needed additional income. A friend of Allan's late father ran a mixed business in the Candleriggs district of the city of Glasgow. He paid Allan pennies for doing unskilled errands and jobs. The assigned tasks gave the boy no sense of fulfillment or interest. After a year of boredom, he opted to become an apprentice cooper at a concern in the main street of the Gorbals. There he remained until, at the age of 18 in 1837, he received his journeyman's card at a ceremony in a local pub. In keeping with a family history of achievement, he had joined the aristocracy of labor.

Thus qualified, the young journeyman, as was standard in those days, went "on the tramp." Living the life of an itinerant, he picked up work wherever coopers were needed and sent money home to his mother. In an article published in 1985, the Texas psychiatrist and author Sue Chance wrote a "psychobiographical" assessment of his personality that picked up on this supportive behavior. Noting that Allan was close to his mother, Chance suggested that he fell into the "good son" mode of conduct. She also noted that, later in life, he showed remarkable empathy with some of the criminals he tracked down in his capacity as a detective. She traced the origins of this empathy to his father's death at the hands of a criminal. Implying that Allan empathized with that criminal, she referred to the possibility of his having "unconscious death wishes toward his father and guilt over their fulfillment."[10]

However, the story about the manner of William's demise was fictional. A more plausible source of Allan Pinkerton's empathy for criminals was that it reflected his claim to having been personally willing to engage in criminal behavior of the most violent kind. The young man from the Gorbals professed to be a revolutionary ready to defy the rule of law and the authority of the British Parliament.

CHAPTER 2

The Revolutionary

In September 1889 one of Edgar Wakeman's articles about Allan Pinkerton appeared in the *Philadelphia Evening Star*. In a dramatic passage, the journalist stated that Pinkerton had been "a delegate from Glasgow" at the Rising centered in the south Wales town of Newport in November 1839.[1] Biographers would later repeat the story with relish. James Horan, for example, recorded that when soldiers opened fire to restore order in Newport, Pinkerton had to duck "under a hail of bullets." He quoted the great man verbatim: "It was a bad day. We returned to Glasgow by the back streets and the lanes, more like thieves than honest workingmen."[2]

Prominent Pinkerton biographers have devoted key passages to the future detective's participation in the Newport Rising.[3] The Rising was the last attempt at social revolution in the United Kingdom and a turning point in Chartist history. As we shall see subsequently, Chartism was a campaign for universal male suffrage named after a People's Charter drawn up in 1838 and supported by a petition signed by 1.3 million people, which was presented to Parliament in June 1839. The movement was slow to succeed. Never more than 25 percent of adults were eligible to vote in British elections until the Representation of the People Act of 1918.[4] But Chartism was a great upheaval in its day that has attracted the attention of Allan Pinkerton biographers. For Pinkerton was a product not just of locality—of the Gorbals and Scottish society—but also of British politics in his time. The thrusts and ambivalences of Chartism helped to determine his outlook and to some degree explain the seeming contradictions of the stances he took in the course of his controversial career in America.

Agitation for the vote for all had been a longstanding feature of politics in the British Isles. There was stiff resistance to it by the governing classes, whose leaders sought to defend time-honored privilege. The same leaders feared that franchise agitation was a harbinger of bloody, republican revolution of the kind witnessed first in America and then in France in the last quarter of the previous century. Britain's wars against the expansionist Napoleon made it possible to descry the apostles of change as traitors aligned to French ideology. Prominent advocates of the universal franchise were regularly imprisoned on rotting hulks in the Thames estuary or sentenced to transportation, ending their days in the wilds of the far-off continent of Australia.

Since the creation of England, Ireland, Scotland, and Wales in premedieval times, only a few entitled men were allowed to vote, and women played a limited role in politics. In 1831 Lord John Russell led a parliamentary campaign to widen the franchise, and in the following year the Great Reform Act entered the statute books. It enabled a greater number of men to vote if they met certain property qualifications and meant that more members of the urban middle classes would now be able to participate in democracy. The great majority of men were still excluded from the ballot. And for the first time in its history, parliament formally limited the right to vote to men. In spite of its limitations, the Reform Act raised expectations of further moves toward democracy.[5] However, one of Russell's arguments for the 1832 bill had been that it would be the "final" solution for British social and political problems. Ably assisted by another rising politician, Benjamin Disraeli, "Finality Jack" now led the opposition to further reform. These men did not trust popular democracy. They could count on the support of the newly enfranchised affluent middle class that, in a status-conscious society, was keen to pull up the ladder it had recently been permitted to climb.

In the wake of 1832's arousal of democratic aspirations, the less fortunate subjects of the British monarch demanded a further widening of the right to vote. Many laboring men saw the ballot as a means of achieving better conditions at work, and there was some sympathy for feminism, though the Radicals (as they were known, particularly in Scotland) trod warily here for fear of being ridiculed. The British Establishment did not smile on the continuing efforts. In 1833 six agricultural workers in the village of Tolpuddle, Dorset, formed a "friendly society" to try to resist the lowering of their wages. The government reacted with savagery. It invoked an obscure law from 1797 to have them convicted of taking secret oaths, and all six were transported to the Australian colonies of New South Wales and Van Diemen's Land (today's Tasmania). Only after the delivery of a petition with 800,000 signatures did Russell, by now home secretary, authorize their release and return to England, where they have been known since as the "Tolpuddle Martyrs."

In agreeing to the release, the government was being more strategic than sympathetic. In 1834 it repealed the Poor Law of 1601 enacted by Queen Elizabeth I's parliament. The repeal removed poor relief and forced the indigent to abide in workhouses, where conditions were deliberately harsh. The intention was to nurture a hard-working mentality in the rest of the population through the medium of fear. The measure conformed with the Malthusian opinion, then prevalent, that it would be economically inefficient to allow population increase by subsidizing the living standards of the lazy. Outrage over the Tolpuddle episode and opposition to the "New Poor Law" morphed into Chartism, the great resurgence of working-class agitation in which Allan Pinkerton participated.

The People's Charter that gave its name to Chartism was a petition for reforms that included the right of men over 21 to vote, the secret ballot, and an end to property qualifications for members of Parliament. Signed by hundreds of thousands and later by millions, from 1838 onward it was presented to Parliament at regular intervals, but the legislature refused to debate it. Russell and the majority of members of Parliament (MPs) whose support he commanded thought they could afford to ignore the Charter. For the Chartist movement suffered from weaknesses arising from two fissures. Both of these fissures affected Allan Pinkerton. The first fissure was between, on the one hand, skilled workers who thought they could more effectively make material gains by resorting to economic means such as strike action and, on the other hand, the mass of laborers who, with their middle-class allies, saw more hope in the deployment of political means—the presentation of petitions, propaganda, and, if successful, the vote. The second fissure was between adherence to "moral force" (petitions, propaganda) and to "physical force" (culminating, if necessary, in revolution).

The Chartists could not organize formally because of legislation against combination designed to frustrate the rise of labor unions. Instead, they met in "conventions" to which local Chartist groups elected "delegates"—hence Pinkerton's stated status as a delegate from Glasgow. When the conventions that met in London and then Birmingham in 1839 met with police repression, opinion hardened among the physical force elements of the movement. Simultaneous uprisings were planned for south Wales and the north of England. Secrecy was necessary to the enterprise, so records are sparse and the degree of central planning, if it existed, is uncertain. According to one tale, the nonarrival in Birmingham of a coach carrying the Welsh mails was to be the signal that the revolution had started across the border in Wales, giving the cue for a parallel uprising in the English Midlands.[6] This was, however, a time of disinformation and calculated rumor, and the one conclusion that seems clear is that the revolutionaries were amateurs faced by professionalized state resistance to their objectives.

In the event, around 4,000 Chartists from the nearby hinterlands converged in Newport on November 3–4, 1839, under the leadership of John Frost. Despite expectations to the contrary, it was an uprising that was duplicated nowhere else in the UK. Its participants received grim reprisals. When the crowd, armed with work tools and other homemade weapons, gathered in front of the Westgate Hotel, soldiers of the 45th Foot Regiment awaited their arrival. Responding to an order, the riflemen opened fire, killing twenty-two of the protesters. Frost's role in the event is a matter of debate. He was certainly defiant. When Russell warned him that if he continued as a delegate to Chartist conventions he would be stripped of his role as a magistrate, Frost had retorted, "if Lord Russell takes my name off, the people will put it on."[7] Tried for their role in Newport, Frost and two of his fellow leaders were convicted of high treason and sentenced to be hanged, drawn, and quartered. An outpouring of popular protest won commutation, and Frost with his comrades were instead transported. Frost, now a martyr to his cause, did not return from Australia until his pardon in 1856.

In Glasgow and the nearby Gorbals where Pinkerton developed his Chartist sympathies, there had been acute awareness of events in other parts of the United Kingdom. Thirty thousand Glaswegians signed the petition pleading for the Tolpuddle Martyrs.[8] Glasgow was scarred by class conflict. The city's cotton-spinners had gone on strike in 1837–1838 and met with ruthless repression by the Sheriff of Lanarkshire, Sir Archibald Alison. Workers were ready for alternative courses of action, such as those offered by the Chartist movement. Glasgow Green, just a few minutes' walk from the Pinkertons' home, was the scene of demonstrations that hosted speakers from all parts of the British Isles, and it can be assumed that Allan Pinkerton was in regular attendance.

On June 10, 1839, John Frost was due to deliver an address at the Green. The crowds gathered. According to one account, "The Radicals of Gorbals and the surrounding districts were the first body that entered the Green, with music and banners." When all had arrived, 150,000 were present. The Chartist leader rose to speak. Frost said he had insisted in Wales and was now insisting in Scotland that the Chartist conventions had been held strictly in accordance with the law. However, if the convention delegates "are attempted to be laid hold of by the Government, we are determined to lay hold upon some of the leading men in the country as hostages for the safety of the Convention." This terrorist-style idea of hostage-taking marked Frost out, in the eyes of the authorities, as a dangerous radical. According to the contemporary press, it drew forth "immense cheering" from the crowd.[9]

Turning to the first of the two Chartist fissures mentioned earlier, there has been some suggestion that Pinkerton was never really a labor militant and that his aim was purely political.[10] If his outlook was limited in this way, it would make sense of some his actions on behalf of American industrialists in later years. However, we do have vivid evidence indicating his declared sympathy for organized labor. In 1869 he would write to one of his former Chartist comrades, "Capital has invariably preyed upon the labouring classes." He added that the "labouring classes have a right to organize."[11] These were the words of a man who continued to cherish his credentials as a labor radical long after he had arrived in the United States. However, the letter appeared in a Scottish pro-labor journal, the *Sentinel*, that would have had few, if any, readers in America. Pinkerton's words and actions in his adoptive nation would more typically be directed at a different audience, affluent employers who were prepared to pay him for his services.

The second of the two Chartist fissures was the tactical divide between moral persuasion and physical advocates. There can be no ambiguity here about Allan Pinkerton's allegiance. In 1873 he wrote to a Scottish acquaintance living in England, "I was a physical force man. . . . I went down with some others such as my friend John Taylor of Glasgow to attend a meeting in Bermingham [*sic*]. You will probably know the rest the Yeomanry went down and scattered us with drawn swords."[12]

This statement is authentic. Pinkerton spelled "Birmingham" phonetically according to the local pronunciation, strongly suggesting that he was there. The disturbance of which he spoke did take place. John Frost chaired a meeting in Birmingham on July 2, 1839, and two days later there was a riot at the Bull Ring district in that city. Taylor had warned the crowd against violence. He even helped to rescue two policemen from the wrath of the crowd but was nevertheless arrested.[13]

What is striking about Pinkerton's espousal of violent means of reform is that it persisted after the Newport debacle. This set him apart from the great majority of Chartists, who concluded, in the light of Newport, that a hard lesson had to be learned, namely that democracy could not be achieved by means of a revolution.[14] Pinkerton, however, had helped to set up a new Glaswegian venture, the Northern Democratic Association, that took issue with the majority of

Chartists. Its motto reiterated a slogan that had elsewhere lost its popularity, "peaceably if we may, forcibly if we must." The association and its publication, the *Vindicator*, had little faith in petitions. In spite of the setback at Newport, Pinkerton remained a tribune of the direct-action wing of Chartism. In February 1840 he braved the ire of mainstream Chartists by inviting George J. Harney to speak at Glasgow's Lyceum Theatre, a meeting that Pinkerton chaired. Harney was a leading champion of physical force. A future Marxist, he championed labor and is considered to have been on the left of the radical movement of those days.[15]

We opened this chapter with a quotation ascribed to Pinkerton regarding his participation in the Newport Rising and consequent flight from the authorities: "It was a bad day. We returned to Glasgow by the back streets and the lanes, more like thieves than honest workingmen." Pinkerton's presence in Newport apparently set the seal on his revolutionary reputation. However, at this stage in our review of the available evidence, the claim invites examination.

James Horan, a New York *Journal-American* writer selected by the Pinkerton National Detective Agency and given privileged access to its files, deployed the "back streets" quotation in his resultant history of the agency. His notes suggest that the quotation was from Allan's correspondence with his son Robert.[16] James Mackay, a more recent biographer of Pinkerton, apparently relied on that suggestion when he used the same quotation, ascribing it to "Autobiographical letters of Allan Pinkerton to Robert Pinkerton, 1879. Pinkerton MSS, Library of Congress."[17] Neither Horan nor Mackay gave precise dates or specified where precisely the to-Robert letter in question was to be found. Allan Pinkerton did write to his son Robert about family history, and the letters are to be found in the Letterbooks deposited in the Library of Congress Manuscript Room.[18] However, they do not contain the Newport claim or a letter containing the passage in question.[19]

So how did the latter become a staple of prominent Pinkerton biographies and of the detective's revolutionary reputation? It is possible that the letter does exist, perhaps misfiled and for this reason tucked away out of subsequent researchers' sight, or even inadvertently interleaved with a past researcher's notes and removed from the archive. But if Allan Pinkerton did write the letter, it may have been with reference to his departure from Birmingham in the aftermath of the Bull Ring riot. He may also have suffered from faulty memory. The death of John Frost in 1877 may have triggered a false recollection of Newport.[20] Though given to embellishing his narrative, Horan would not have invented the specific text of a letter. However, it was common practice for Victorian writers to invent dialogue, and Horan may have confused one of their accounts with the texts of other letters he had seen in the original.

Whatever the explanation, the idea that Pinkerton was in Newport is fictitious. The Rising and the plotting behind it were conducted in the Welsh language by workers who resented being exploited by local land magnates in harness with English capitalists.[21] As a monoglot Scot unable to speak Welsh at all, let alone the local Gwentian or Heads of the Valleys dialects, Pinkerton would have stood out conspicuously in the crowd, and there is no trace of his presence. The Newport Rising has been studied in minute, almost fanatical, detail. Historians confirm that Pinkerton was not present.[22]

Pinkerton, a master of the art of gilding the lily, may have seen an opportunity to enhance the credibility of his claim to have been a revolutionary by claiming he was at Newport. Equally, that may have been the intention of his devotees, giving rise to the dramatic narrative of the Newport fiction in Horan's book. A compelling story about how Pinkerton partook in the attempt to overthrow the British governing oligarchy was, from a certain point of view, a good counter to the criticism of Pinkerton for having become a prime instrument of Big Business repression of labor in the age of the "Robber Barons." As for less sympathetic observers, they could not but be impressed by his apparent inconsistency and hypocrisy—behold the Radical hero who during his American career proved to be no better than the vile oppressors whom he claimed to have despised.[23] The Newport story had strong appeal on all sides.

Misremembrance of Newport was not the only complexity that arose from Pinkerton's youth. There are other puzzles that invite examination. They concern, in particular, the reasons for Pinkerton's escape to America, and an associated evidential gap in his life story covering the two years prior to his emigration. These are our concern in the next chapter.

CHAPTER 3

Escape to America

On March 13, 1842, Allan Pinkerton married Joan Carfrae in Glasgow Cathedral. As required by the Presbyterian church, the banns had been read on three successive Sundays. In spite of Pinkerton's atheism, he had entered openly into a conventional religious ceremony. The manner of the marriage perhaps illustrates the need for ceremony in all people's lives. It may also have reflected Joan's desire to please the aunt who had raised her in Paisley, near Glasgow—her mother, also called Joan, had died giving birth to her only daughter in Edinburgh, and her father, William, went to his grave three years later. Joan, a well-educated bookbinder's apprentice, was herself a Christian who sang in the choir of a Glasgow Unitarian church.[1]

She was more than a chorister. In an age when singing was highly valued as a form of recreation, Joan was a soprano soloist. It may have pleased Pinkerton to observe that she was in demand as a singer at Chartist meetings—and that she was so young. The Pinkerton–Carfrae marriage was one of considerable age disparity. On their wedding day, Allan Pinkerton was within four months of his twenty-third birthday. Joan Carfrae (born January 7, 1827) had just turned fifteen. She did not have to lie to the authorities about her age, as Scots law followed Roman precedent, and a girl could in those days marry from the age of twelve without parental consent. But it was still rare for a child to marry so young. The age gap is early evidence of how Pinkerton felt the need to control his partner and signaled his approach, in later years, to the rest of his family and a swathe of the working population of America.[2]

Three weeks after their wedding, the Pinkertons headed for the Broomielaw, a thoroughfare running along the quay on the north bank of the River Clyde.

Though the couple by now resided further into the interior of the city of Glasgow, Allan Pinkerton knew it well, as it was directly across the water from his childhood home in the Gorbals.

The Broomielaw was the point of embarkation for transatlantic voyages. Taking advantage of the ebb tide on the evening of Sunday, April 3, a New Brunswick–built 404-ton square-rigged passenger vessel, the *Kent*, cast off from the Broomielaw bound for Canada. The Pinkertons were on board. Passengers, some of whom would never return, gazed at the receding city and hills beyond as the ship slipped down the ever-widening estuary. Thirty-six years later, Allan Pinkerton dictated a letter addressed to Joan recalling the time when "we sailed down the Clyde [and] sights were many and varied of that land and those friends we were leaving." He addressed Joan as "My Dear Little Wife."[3]

The *Kent* sailed past the Isle of Arran. It rounded the Mull of Kintyre into the North Passage with Ireland's County Antrim visible to port. Now, its passengers began to experience the Atlantic swell from which the Kintyre peninsula had protected them. They begin to suffer discomfort of various magnitudes. Allan had a degree of protection, having signed on as the ship's cooper. That meant sleeping with the ship's crew, while Joan was in steerage, the very cheapest form of passenger accommodation. According to one version of events—and much of the Victorian hyperbole surrounding Allan Pinkerton's life needs to be taken with a dose of salt—some of the kindlier passengers, on learning of the Pinkertons' newlywed status, prevailed on Captain James Gardner to give them an upgrade to a man-and-wife cabin.[4]

If so, their luck ran only so far. The Atlantic swell developed into mountainous waves driven by a powerful wind. Two weeks after setting sail, the *Kent* was driven onto reefs off Sable Island, over a hundred miles to the southeast of Nova Scotia, the nearest part of the North American mainland. The copper-bottomed *Kent* survived long enough for its passengers and crew to make it into lifeboats and to the shore. We can dispense with the myth that a party of "Indians" now set upon the survivors, for there is no record of an Indigenous population on the island.[5] The rough and perilous nature of the Pinkertons' journey to the New World is in need of no such embellishment.

The couple managed to continue their journey to Montreal. After some months plying his cooper's trade in that city, Allan Pinkerton decided to strike for the West in pursuit of greater opportunities. Arriving in Chicago, he sought and found Robbie Fergus, a former Chartist comrade from the Gorbals who was plying his trade as a printer in the dynamic new city. Fergus helped the

Pinkertons to find their feet. Allan and Joan must have realized that their emigration story had ended and that a new passage in their lives was about to begin in the United States.

Some 20 years after he arrived in Chicago, Allan Pinkerton gave an account of his reasons for leaving Scotland:

> The country of my adoption is now engaged in Civil War. . . . It is not the country of my birth, but to it I owe all that I have as the foster mother of my natural energies. . . . In my native country I was free in name, but a slave in fact. I toiled, in and out of season, and my labor went to sustain the government, yet I was allowed no voice in the direction of that government. . . . You will recollect the Bull Ring Riots of Birmingham and the fate of Frost. . . . I had contravened the strict letter of the law and I found it advisable to leave my country for my country's good. . . . For me to remain in Scotland was to risk an indefinite term of penal service in the colony of Van Demans Land.

Pinkerton added:

> I found, after a brief time, that, although [America] was said to be a Republic, there was a class existing here similar to the one against which I had rebelled across the ocean, and before whose tyranny I was forced to flee. . . . Then it was, thank God, that our noble President [Abraham Lincoln] proclaimed a war begun. . . . That the Union will stand firm and slavery die in this terrible struggle there is no question.[6]

What did Pinkerton mean when he used the phrase "advisable to leave my country for my country's good"? The words are of sixteenth-century origin but appeared again in reference to transportation, now used satirically by the victims.[7] Was Pinkerton saying that he had become a menace to the stability of his native land, and if so, why? The words are ambiguous.

The storyline that Pinkerton, a hunted Chartist, fled Scotland to escape official retribution became gospel for the emigrant himself, for his family, and for his admirers. The notion survived into the years immediately following his death. The journalist Wakeman stated that after the disturbances in Birmingham and Newport there was a price on Pinkerton's head, that he was driven into hiding for months, and finally escaped to America in company with his "noble wife."[8] Shortly after that *The National Cyclopedia of American Biography* agreed that

Pinkerton "would have been taken into custody (had he remained in Great Britain) for participation in the Chartist raids in which he was associated with John Frost."[9]

Widely accepted though it may be, the idea that Allan Pinkerton escaped to America because he was in imminent danger of arrest and of deportation to Australia is open to question. He himself suggested one alternative motive, the principled desire to live in a free country—excepting the slavocracy in the American South. There is also circumstantial evidence that leaves a question mark over the theory that he was a hunted man. The reading of the marriage banns over a period of weeks and then the openly conducted wedding in Glasgow's premier church was hardly consistent with the behavior of a man who was hiding from the authorities. There is a strong case for exploring alternative motives for Pinkerton's flight to America.

Pinkerton may have been an economic migrant. Tired of being "on the tramp" as a traveling cooper, he may have sought a more settled and remunerative lifestyle across the ocean. Rather than being a hunted man, he may have been simply disillusioned by the failure of the Chartist crusade. He would have had company in both respects. As the example of his friend Robbie Fergus shows, emigration to the United States from the Gorbals was not a novel course of action.

Any convincing explanation of Pinkerton's decision to emigrate must heed a hiatus in his radical activities, indeed a gap in his biography. It will be recalled that early in 1840, Pinkerton chaired a meeting at the Lyceum Theatre, Glasgow, addressed by the revolutionary Chartist Julian Harney. After that, according to a leading historian of Scottish Chartism, Pinkerton "disappears from Chartist reports in Scotland."[10] What happened to Allan Pinkerton between March 1840 and his departure for North America on the morning tide of April 3, 1842? Could he really have been in hiding from the authorities for a period as long as two years, or is there another explanation?

One such explanation is romance. Allan Pinkerton fell in love with Joan Carfrae and may have transferred his energies from radicalism to courtship. It does happen, and the frustrations suffered by the Chartists may have been a contributing factor. Allan may have decided to keep a low profile not just out of self-preservation but also for Joan's sake and to preserve their relationship. But while Pinkerton offered recollections of the courtship, he was vague about the chronology (he kept no diaries at the time, and his dates were awry on a number of events). Joan was barely 13 years of age at the start of the hiatus. Their courtship probably started closer to the end of the two-year period we are discussing.

It could only have been a supplementary cause of Allan's uncharacteristic period of silence.

We turn now to another account of what Pinkerton may have been doing in the mysterious two-year interval. In 1908 his older son William wrote to a distant relative in Oklahoma: "My father . . . was prominently identified in the Chartist Movement in Glasgow nearly seventy years ago. His prominence in this movement made him an object of suspicion to the government there, and he left Scotland when about 17 or 18 years old and made a trip to Africa on a ship as the ship's cooper. Returning from Africa he married my mother in 1841 and almost immediately they sailed for America."[11]

Disregarding the errors (Pinkerton would have been in his 20s and did not emigrate until 1842), what do we make of William's remark? Jane Adler, appointed Pinkerton archivist at the time when the agency was transferring its records to the Library of Congress, took a close interest in the family and observed: "The reference to the trip to Africa occurs nowhere else in the archives [or] in any biographical material about Pinkerton. It's entirely possible that William made it up—he had on occasion a fairly cavalier approach to fact. But why invent such a story in a letter to a stranger?"[12]

If Pinkerton made the trip to Africa, it would help to explain his disappearance from Scottish records. It would further be of interest because of his later declaration of opposition to slavery, especially if he grew to like and respect the dark-skinned people whom he met on making landfall on the African continent. Those Africans would certainly have told him about the iniquities of the slave trade.

However, while shipping records from the time did list crew members, they indicate that no ships left Scottish ports for Africa in the years in question. Pinkerton may have sailed from a non-Scottish port, but there is no supportive evidence for that. He did not have to visit Africa to detest slavery. He could have become an abolitionist prior to his departure for America for other reasons. His sentiments may well have stemmed from the impact of the antislavery crusade. A party of radical American abolitionists arrived in Scotland in 1841, and escaped slaves such as Moses Roper regularly told of their experiences in venues such as Glasgow Green. To be antislavery in late 1830s and early 1840s Scotland would not have been dangerously radical, as the Westminster parliament had abolished slavery in 1833 and manumission then took place gradually throughout the Empire.[13] Pinkerton did not have to have visited Africa to be antislavery prior to his American experience.

Another consideration had a more pressing bearing on Pinkerton's low profile in 1840–1842, and on his decision to pursue a new life across the ocean. This was the phenomenon of informing. At a time when he was well established in America, Pinkerton expressed an emphatic view on the subject. He denounced the "'Stool Pigeon' system of England and America."[14] His view on the matter was sufficiently pronounced to make an impression on his son Robert, who in the 1880s denounced US police departments' practice of utilizing the "'stool pigeon' (an informer)."[15]

The informer had played a prominent role in Scottish history, a circumstance that had a bearing on Pinkerton's escape to America. The ever-present Scottish informer very likely gave Pinkerton both a motive for emigration and ideological baggage on his journey to the United States.

Informing and revulsion against it were deeply imbedded in the cultures of the British Isles. The story of William "Oliver" (apparently a Welshman named Richards) is imbedded in English history—or, at least, in English mythology, for official secrecy meant it was never easy to verify accounts of informing. Oliver, a government spy, was held to have provoked unrest in Derbyshire and then betrayed the ringleaders to the authorities. In 1817, three radicals, convicted of treason, were hanged and posthumously beheaded, while 23 of their comrades were deported.[16]

Scotland was no different from other nations in having its own, painful experience of informing. In the year when Oliver plied his trade in Derbyshire, Alexander Richmond was performing similar services among the weavers of Glasgow. A Glasgow uprising declared a "Provisional Government" in April 1820, but officialdom's agents were at the heart of the conspiracy and were instrumental in the securing of ensuing arrests and prosecutions.[17] One outcome of Richmond's work was the execution, in September 1820, of James Wilson, who had been accused of "Compassing and imagining to put the king to death," as well as, more credibly, "striking work and compelling and persuading others to do the same."[18] Indignation about the work of Richmond and similar spies lasted well into the next century. Tom Johnston, a Labour Party politician who would serve as secretary of state for Scotland, complained of Lord Liverpool, Tory prime minister 1812–1827, that his government "busily engaged appointing spies and *agents provocateurs* who should go about among leaders of the militant section of the working class, encourage them in treasonable oaths and acts and generally provide victims for the scaffold."[19]

At the time of the events of 1817–1820, Allan Pinkerton was unborn, and then a mere babe in arms. However, the spy scandal again came to the boil at a time when he was an impressionable teenager interested in radical causes. In 1832, when Pinkerton was thirteen, Peter Mackenzie published an exposure of the Richmond spy scandal. The editor of *Reformer's Gazette* and a moderate Whig, Mackenzie had served in the Glasgow yeomanry that helped to crush the 1820 rising. He was a respected and credible journalist. His exposure of Richmond's activities annoyed radicals because it made them seem naïve, and it enraged Tories because it laid bare their deceitful and ruthless tactics in maintaining the power of their own governing class. The case remained prominent in the years when Pinkerton considered his political options, for Richmond sued the Scottish publishers of Mackenzie's disclosures. The ensuing trial at London's Court of the Exchequer only increased Richmond's infamy as testimony confirmed he had been an agent provocateur as well as a spy. The outcome was a vindication of the radicals of 1820. Those who had been transported received a pardon. This was in 1835, when Pinkerton was sixteen.[20]

Spies were not to be trusted. They exaggerated threats in order to remain in employment. They could play both sides (Richmond began to testify against his employers when they did not pay him enough). Also, the authorities must have been aware that radicals could make political capital out of their espionage practices. Moreover, in the wake of exposures, radicals were very wary of spies, a circumstance that limited spies' effectiveness. One of the reasons that Scots other than Pinkerton shunned physical-force Chartism was that they wished to deny a point of ingress to provocateurs. The Newport debacle of 1839, widely seen as an example of how spies could wreak damage on worthy causes, reminded Scottish radicals of their own hurts at the hands of spies and deepened their desire to dissociate themselves from violence.[21]

Tory magnates showed no sign of relinquishing espionage as a tool of repression. If Pinkerton or anyone else in Scotland were in danger of forgetting about the practice, they were shaken out of their complacency by the activities of Sir Archibald Alison. Born in Shropshire in England, Alison was an Edinburgh-trained lawyer. A member of the "sugar aristocracy," he had profited from the unpaid labor of his slaves in the Caribbean. When he received compensation upon the British abolition of slavery in 1833, he invested the money in the coal and iron industries. Alison became sheriff of Lanarkshire in the following year. A Tory who believed that the French Revolution and its aftermath were a threat to civilization, he wrote a history of Europe with that principle in mind and entertained fears that the French contagion would spread in the United Kingdom.

On April 14, 1837, 32,000 cotton spinners and weavers in Glasgow and surrounding areas went on strike. According to Alison's posthumous autobiography, edited by his wife Lady Jane Alison, the sheriff had little faith in the impartiality of the Glasgow police. He offered a £500 reward for information about the murder of a strikebreaker named John Smith—"shot through the back," his wife recorded on his behalf, "by two assassins employed by the united cotton-spinners." He subsequently received information furtively delivered in a vault of the University of Glasgow. According to his widow, Alison believed the claims of his informers that a "secret committee" ran the spinners' strike, and that it organized intimidation culminating in Smith's murder. No proof was forthcoming—according to Lady Jane's narrative, this was because the secret committee had paid for the assassin to escape to America. But the demoralizing story contributed to the defeat of the strike.[22]

Alison's deployment of spies at this time was no secret to contemporary radicals. The Chartist *Scots Times* recorded how Alison met his informers "in an obscure place on Glasgow, where he took their depositions."[23] Pinkerton must have been aware of the story.

We can go further than this. Could Pinkerton have been an informer at the time of the Chartist campaign? He had police contacts through his father and his half-brother. Some twentieth-century biographers stressed that point. At least one of them ignored his radical activities, lionizing him as a pro-law-and-order conservative from the outset.[24] That aspirational assertion ignored the fact that Pinkerton did at least play the role of a radical. The role he played meant he was close enough to John Frost to be useful to the authorities, should they have wanted him to inform on the Chartist leader's contacts. It was a saying at the time that the "marshals" of revolt were sometimes the first to inform, and Pinkerton was such a marshal.[25] There is an indication that his dark secret was known and kept within the family. Family secrets are not always openly articulated and are sometimes hinted-at truths that make their way down through generations. Perhaps letting his guard slip, Robert A. Pinkerton II would state that his grandfather escaped to America because "the Chartists were breathing down his neck."[26] Was that poor historical literacy on the part of the Harvard-educated descendant, or was it the plain truth? If his fellow Chartists were "on to" Allan Pinkerton, it would explain his absence from radical activity in the years 1840–1842 culminating in his "escape" to America.

Pinkerton may have been a spy, or he may have been betrayed by a spy. Whatever the truth of the matter, and whatever the true cause of his escape to America, he must have had a deep consciousness of spying, of betrayal, and of informing. That consciousness shaped his career choice and conduct in the years to come.

CHAPTER 4

Pinkerton & Co.

Not many Chartists made it as far as the frontier town of Chicago.[1] That may have been an attraction if Allan Pinkerton feared the wrath of some of his former comrades. Yet not all such erstwhile associates hated him, for it was his old Chartist colleague from the Gorbals, Robbie Fergus, who welcomed the Pinkertons into his home until Allan found paid employment. Once Pinkerton had found coopering work in Lill's brewery, he and Joan were able to afford their own residence, a clapboard house on Adams Street.

Chicago was exciting, a boom town. It offered opportunities to the enterprising and the strong. In other ways, it was no great improvement on the Gorbals. Public services were prominent by their absence, as evidenced in the rutted roads and sidewalks. Unregulated animal offal and human excrement scented the air by day and by night. Untreated sewage flowed into the drinking water supply. Child mortality was as prevalent as it had been back home. The Pinkertons' house, like Allan's childhood home in the Gorbals, had just two rooms, a recipe for mutual infection. For the time being, nevertheless, the still-childless Allan and Joan remained unscathed.

Like many skilled workers, Allan Pinkerton aspired to be his own boss. He saw an opportunity in a community thirty-eight miles to the northwest of Chicago. Dundee nestled on each side of Fox River. Scottish settlers had given the place its name when they arrived on the Fox's banks in 1839, sponsored in part by the Aberdeen North American Investment and Loan Company, a concern that imported Scottish capital to buy up land in the northern counties of Illinois. Irma Dupré, who published a history of the community based partly on oral history, stated that, with "the skirmishes with the Indians once ended"

Figure 4.1. Allan with his wife Joan Pinkerton. *Library of Congress*

in the early 1830s, the agricultural potential of the land became evident. Allan made a scouting visit to the new community, after which he and Joan arrived in Dundee in 1843. Dupré recorded how they "hailed the prospect of a new home in the verdant rolling hills of the Fox River Valley, green-spreading and lovely."[2]

Pinkerton recalled that there was "one rough bridge across the river, built of oaken beams and rude planks, in a cheap, common fashion; and at either end of this were clustered, each side of the street, all the stores and shops of the place, save one." That one exception stood three hundred yards away facing the main road and on the "crest of a fine hill."[3] The Pinkerton log cabin doubled as a cooperage. Now the master of his own fate, Allan grew the business, attracting customers from beyond Dundee's small population of 300. He took on eight employees. To find these workers, he looked to a particular ethnic group, noting that "nearly all my hands were German."[4] The Germans may have worked for lower wages, or possibly Pinkerton was not entirely comfortable with his fellow Scottish settlers.

West Dundee was the section favored by New Englanders. They looked down on immigrants like the Scots and Germans. The fabled frontier "melting pot" had not produced universal harmony on the banks of the dividing river. When Pinkerton ran as a Liberty Party candidate for the Illinois constitutional convention in 1848, he represented the view that the US Constitution was an antislavery document whose abolitionist tenets should be applied. He encountered the wrath of anti-abolitionist New Englander elders of the local Baptist Church. Despite his stated atheism, Pinkerton attended that church, perhaps to propitiate Joan, but more likely to make business contacts and establish his respectability. It must have been painful when M.L. Wisner, his own minister at the Baptist Church, denounced him as a drunkard and an atheist. Pinkerton received the lowest vote of the nine candidates.[5]

The setback did not deter Allan Pinkerton from seeking new opportunities. Already in the previous year he had had an accidental encounter that would change his life and draw him back to Chicago. Running short of timber for his barrels, he poled a raft along the Fox, reaching an islet where he set about cutting wood for the staves and hoops that he needed. Stumbling on the remains of a fire, he suspected that the island was being used for illicit purposes. Further surveillance confirmed his suspicions. He now teamed up with Sheriff Luther Dearborn of Kane County and a posse. They caught a band of counterfeiters red-handed, in possession of a bag of bogus dimes. The humble wooded islet became the locally famous Bogus Island, and Pinkerton acquired a new reputation. Counterfeiting was a menace to the fledgling banks that issued legal currency, and Pinkerton found himself in demand as a detective.

Soon thereafter, Pinkerton received a tip-off about John Craig. A farmer from Vermont, Craig had a lucrative sideline in laundering forged bank notes. Pinkerton ingratiated himself with Craig, posing as a person who would be interested in quick gain.[6] He arranged to meet Craig in Chicago to receive a number of forged ten-dollar bills. By prior arrangement with the sheriff of Cook County, Craig was arrested in possession of the incriminating false funds. A local banker, George Smith, paid Pinkerton for his work. It had been a form of entrapment straight out of the informer playbook back in Scotland and would be repeated many times in Pinkerton's career—pretend to be a confederate, encourage an illegal deed, arrange an arrest.

Pinkerton's cooperage business was a success. According to one account he finally employed 25 men and "was counted one of the most prosperous men in Kane County."[7] Joan enjoyed her Dundee years. It was there that she gave birth to a son, William, in 1846. Then in 1848 she delivered twins, Joan (named after her) and Robert. But Allan was not at ease with the Dundonian population. He dreamed of a wider canvas than that offered by the Fox River hamlet and had become infected with the detective bug. When William L. Church, sheriff of Cook County, offered him a deputyship, he accepted the post. The Pinkertons moved back to Chicago, a city that continued to enjoy an economic boom but whose embryonic police force was in no better shape than the local sidewalks. After a short time, Pinkerton accepted an even more congenial job. He became Chicago's first official detective.

Pinkerton remained a public employee for a year. However, in the meantime, he set himself up as a private detective, initially on a modest basis in 1850. The "Pinkerton & Co." detective agency was not a unique idea.[8] In the 1840s, there had been attempts to establish private detective agencies in St. Louis, Baltimore, and Philadelphia.[9] More famously, Eugène-François Vidocq (1775–1857), a French ex-convict, had become a private detective before helping to set up a state security police force. Vidocq was a source of inspiration for the American poet and short story writer Edgar Allan Poe, whose tales "The Murders in the Rue Morgue" (1841) and "The Purloined Letter" (1844) were set in Paris. They presented the private detective C. Auguste Dupin as a model of intrigue and rationality in a way that no doubt prepared the American public for the emergence of their very own detective, Allan Pinkerton. When in 1854 Pinkerton was being considered for a new public policing role, that of city marshal of Chicago, the *Chicago Tribune* supported him because "he has not been equaled in the West, as a real genuine thief catcher," and "is to Chicago what Vidocq was to Paris."[10]

They may not have been the first of their kind, but Pinkerton and his evolving agency established a distinctive and continuous American model. Relinquishing the role of a "thief-taker" who hunted down wanted criminals just for the reward money, he insisted on receiving a daily retainer. With the intention of indicating his probity and that of his investigators, he emphasized to prospective clients the importance of record-keeping and transparency. His new venture took on an increasing number of employees. Pinkerton's gift for branding was another feature of the model that he developed. Several of his rivals used a "wide-awake" human eye as their emblem, giving rise to the phrase "private eye." Recognizing that this was an effective symbol, Pinkerton adopted the emblem for his own agency, along with the motto, "We Never Sleep."[11]

Though now in the private sector, Pinkerton continued to combat counterfeiting under contract to public agencies. He looked beyond Chicago to take on work for the US Treasury Department. That department had the duty of protecting currency but the disadvantage of having very few agents of its own. However, Pinkerton revenue flowed mainly from private sources. The railway boom of the 1850s was a lucrative source of income, and Pinkerton's association with Chicago was advantageous. For although Atlanta, Georgia, was geographically well placed to become the hub of transcontinental railroad travel, traffic through that city was limited by the different track gauges insisted upon for states' rights reasons. Chicago had the advantage of a universal 4′8.5″ gauge. Though at a wider point than Atlanta in the continental expanse, Chicago would become the nation's railway hub when transcontinental lines began to operate after the Civil War. Meantime, the Illinois Central and other railroads already snaked out great distances from the midwestern city. Taking on work for the railroads and their clients, Pinkerton found his business extending far beyond the confines of the place he now called home.

Railroads offered a variety of opportunities. Once a train left an urban setting where there was at least some semblance of law enforcement, its passengers and corporate clients were vulnerable to robbery. Pinkerton's agency offered protection against raiders. In 1852, Wells Fargo became the first of several express companies to deliver their goods, including sums of money, in special coaches attached to the trains. These fortified coaches lent themselves to improved protection. Pinkerton found himself working for Wells Fargo and other express companies as well as for the railroads.

One controversial activity for Pinkerton's agency was "testing" the honesty of railroad employees. Pinkerton would insinuate his spies onto trains to ensure that conductors did not keep the money paid for on-board tickets or fail to collect such money from their friends. In November 1855 Pinkerton welcomed the publicity attached to the role it played in the arrest of Oscar

Caldwell. Formerly a Michigan Central employee, Caldwell had taken a pay cut to work on the Burlington Railroad, apparently because he could see that there were opportunities for embezzlement. Caldwell went on trial in Chicago. A nascent labor movement saw in the prosecution of Caldwell an instance of overbearing management. However, the discovery of stolen ticket receipts in Caldwell's possession—he had retained both the receipts and records of the fares that they represented—led to a sentence of one year in prison.[12]

In 1855 Pinkerton rebranded his firm the North West Police Agency. "North West" referred to the area once referred to as the Old Northwest territory, comprising lands that were to make up the states of Ohio, Indiana, Michigan, and Wisconsin, as well as Pinkerton's adoptive state of Illinois. His detective activities now embraced this wider area. Rising to the geographic challenge, Pinkerton resorted to a recent development in technology. The Frenchman Louis Daguerre had in 1839 invented an early form of photography that came to be known as the daguerreotype. Pinkerton used the process to build up a collection of images, face mugs of wanted criminals. The result was a "Rogues Gallery" database. When photographic improvements superseded daguerreotypes around 1860, Pinkerton moved with the times. Chicago's Great Fire of 1871 destroyed the records, but the Pinkertons would start over again.[13] Public police forces by the 1890s had their own local rogues galleries. But for out-of-town images, they had recourse to the Pinkertons'.

Pinkerton had a gift for spotting talent and began to hire individuals who would become pillars of the agency. He called them "operatives," a throwback to his Scottish days when workers were thus described. The first man he hired was George Henry Bangs, a smartly dressed New Englander who boasted descent from the voyagers on the *Mayflower*. Bangs became his general superintendent. Soon thereafter, he took on Timothy Webster, who had arrived in New Jersey from Sussex, in England, at the age of twelve. Establishing a practice that was to endure, Pinkerton charged his clients flat rates for hiring such individuals instead of working for reward money. To hire an operative cost $3 a day. It was $8 for a supervisor and $12 for Pinkerton's own services. A few years later in 1860, the US Department of Commerce estimated that laborers cost an average of $1.03 a day to hire, and skilled workers $1.61. The figures suggest that the demand for detective services was buoyant.[14]

In 1855 Pinkerton hired the nation's first demonstrably successful female detective. He remembered Kate Warne as "a commanding person, with clear-cut, expressive features, and with an ease of manner that was quite captivating at times [who] was calculated to make a favorable impression at once."[15] He

Figure 4.2. Kate Warne, 1866. *Chicago History Museum*

had not intended to employ a woman. A slim, brown-haired 23-year-old of average height, Warne had taken the initiative to approach him in search of a post. She announced herself as a widow in search of employment. When Pinkerton told her he had reservations about taking the unheard-of step of employing a woman, Warne made a persuasive pitch. She said that women could sometimes induce a suspect to talk who would hold out against a male interrogator. Pinkerton sent her away to give himself time to think. The next day, he awoke believing that Warne would make a good detective. He told her she was hired. When she justified his faith, he put her in charge of a female division of his agency. He later explained his decision to take on a woman saying, "we live in a progressive age, and in a progressive country."[16] He consistently sang the praises of his female detectives.[17] Pinkerton and Warne would enjoy an intimate relationship, and the inevitable rumor circulated that they were lovers. Whatever the truth of the matter, Warne headed a corps of female detectives whose existence placed Pinkerton's agency ahead of its times.[18]

While these were heady days, there were downsides. Once back in disease-infested Chicago, Joan and Allan Pinkerton lost three daughters. In 1854 their toddler daughter Mary died at age two. In 1855, the year when Pinkerton announced his expanded North West Police Agency, seven-year-old Joan died. A new daughter arrived in 1857 and, observing the custom of the times, she too was named Joan, though as a child she was known as Belle within the family. She, too, was sickly and a source of constant worry for her mother but lived. Only three of Joan's many children survived to adulthood.[19] With her husband often away on business, it was a tough life for Joan Pinkerton, a traumatic transition from the healthier climate of Dundee, especially as her husband now worked away from home.

In the second half of the 1850s, Allan Pinkerton confronted a challenge to his professional status and to his income that was less upsetting than family tragedy yet was a harbinger of things to come. For there were those who questioned the desirability of private police. In February 1857 Representative John V. Eustace of Lee County, a polity some distance west of Chicago, introduced in the Illinois state legislature An Act to Suppress Police Agencies of a Private Nature. This bill, which was endorsed by the relevant legislative committee, would have made illegal the kind of contract work awarded to Pinkerton's agency. A debate raged between the supporters of "independent" (private) police and the public police. The *Chicago Tribune* thought that the debate was itself a problem. The paper had in 1855 attacked the idea of a uniformed public force as contrary to the principle of freedom, but by the summer of 1857 it saw competition between public and private police as the cause of what it depicted as a booming crime rate. The *Tribune* urged cooperation as the answer. Pinkerton opposed the abolition bill, and it did not enter the statute books.[20]

In 1858 Pinkerton had mixed success in another quarter. There was a plague of break-ins and robberies that affected Chicago businesses, especially at night. The Chicago public police were prone to corruption and political control, so businessmen seeking the protection of guards and night watchmen turned to the private sector. Noting that other private detective agencies were cashing in on the opportunity, the proprietor of the North West Police Agency founded his own Pinkerton's Protective Patrol. This branch of his agency needed to cooperate with the public police if it was to make arrests. Given the nature of the Chicago police, this was difficult. Moreover, in other cities Pinkerton had even less influence with the police, and the possibility of seeking police help or having his guards deputized was sometimes remote. For the time being, Pinkerton's Protective Patrol remained a limited concern. In future years, Pinkerton would be at pains to seek cooperation with the public police in different locations, but still with mixed results. His Protective Patrol would expand to be a source of both income and political turmoil.

Difficulties notwithstanding, Pinkerton's fame as a detective spread beyond Chicago and its Midwest hinterland. His handling of a robbery of the Adams Express Company is one illustration. The New York–based Adams Company handled cash sent to agents in the Southern states to pay for shipments of cotton. One day in 1859, $40,000 went missing from the firm's office in Montgomery, Alabama. Officers of the corporation suspected a certain employee. Nathan Moroney's extravagant expenditures on horse-track betting and on "low" companions were at odds with his modest salary, but Adams Express could not pin the theft on him. Edward S. Sanford, a vice president of the company, had learned of Pinkerton's reputation and sent him a telegram: "Can you send me a man half horse and half alligator? I have got 'bit' once more. When can you send him?"[21]

When George Bangs found that Nathan Moroney was ordering duplicates of Adams Express keys from a New York locksmith, Pinkerton sent a talented operative to work on the case. Kate Warne befriended Mrs. Moroney and waited for unguarded remarks. This paid off when Moroney, panicking in the wake of Bangs's discovery, was duped into getting his indiscrete wife to dig up the pouch containing the money. Arrests followed, and the entire hoard was recovered, barring a modest $400. It was a result that further enhanced Pinkerton's reputation and opened the door to ever more lucrative contracts with express companies and bankers.

Meanwhile Pinkerton remained politically active. It will be recalled that he had been a candidate for the Liberty Party. That small entity was dedicated to achieving the emancipation of the slaves by constitutional means, through the ballot. However Pinkerton later declared himself, in a rerun of his Scottish political stance, to be in support not of democratic means or moral persuasion but of direct action. This meant breaking the law. The 1850 Fugitive Slave Act made it illegal to assist any African American slave fleeing servitude. It made it even more perilous than previously for Black escapees seeking their freedom. In contravention of the 1850 law, the network known as the Underground Railroad existed to help the freedom seekers. With the assistance mainly of free Black "conductors," fugitive slaves would head for Chicago, where there were safe houses as well as transport links to Canada, where they would be secure from bounty-hunting slave catchers. The Pinkertons, the hard-pressed Joan as well as her husband, appear to have harbored Black refugees in their home. Allan may well have known the legendary John Brown, who used violence to protect fleeing slaves from their pursuers.

Confirmation of Pinkerton's willingness to defy the Fugitive Slave Act is to be found in an account by a Black man who, together with Brown, organized a party of fugitive slaves to flee to Canada via Chicago early in 1859. H. O. Wagoner, who later lived in Denver, recalled meeting the already renowned detective in Chicago, recognizing him at once as Allan Pinkerton. Wagoner, a law-breaking abolitionist, at first feared that Pinkerton would arrest him. Instead, Pinkerton made available "over three hundred dollars, which he said he had raised to pay the transportation of the whole party, bag and baggage, to Detroit by the Michigan Central Railroad." No doubt Pinkerton's knowledge of the railways helped the party to travel by this "underground line," arrive in the Michigan town, and thence cross the Detroit River to Canada and to freedom.[22]

Biographers have highlighted Pinkerton's abolitionist activity.[23] Their emphasis echoes the claims made by Pinkerton. However, while his expression of pride in his antislavery record was genuine, it was not entirely devoid of calculation. In cultivating the friendship of Abraham Lincoln, whose presidential Emancipation Proclamation would set the seal on abolitionism, he appreciated the patronage benefits that friendship conferred. When the antislavery cause triumphed in the Civil War, Pinkerton saw the business advantage to having been on the winning side. In the period known as Reconstruction following the Civil War, a combination of Republican antislavery advocates and northern industrialists held the strings of power, and Pinkerton profited by sharing their political outlook and hunting down their enemies. Such business opportunities help to explain why Pinkerton, while posing as America's policeman, was still keen to tell of his antebellum lawbreaking.

In truth there were limits to Pinkerton's enthusiasm for that law breaking. In October 1859 John Brown and a party of supporters attacked the federal arsenal in Harper's Ferry, Virginia (today West Virginia). It was meant to prefigure an uprising against the Southern slavocracy, but Colonel Robert E. Lee's local militia crushed the insurrection. Brown ended on the gallows, one of American history's martyrs. As in the case of the Newport Rising, Pinkerton was not present at the insurrection. It is doubtful that he approved of the Harper's Ferry raid. Equally, there has been no corroborative evidence in support of the legend that he offered to deploy his detectives in a bold attempt to rescue Brown from the gallows, only to have the plan vetoed by the martyr himself.[24]

Pinkerton conveyed a flavor of his developing stance in a letter penned in 1856. Southern politicians were speaking of secession from the Union. In ambiguous language, Pinkerton seemed to say, let them do it, and take the consequences: "This may be considered ultraism . . . I admit it is not a very bright picture to look at." However he added "This is more politics than I have ever talked or written since I left Dundee."[25]

There would be limits to Pinkerton's sympathy for Black Americans. This became evident when Radical Reconstruction of the defeated South drew to a close and with it the momentum of the fight against racism. In 1877 Black sanitation workers struck in Louisville, Kentucky, in pursuit of higher wages. Pinkerton unleashed a torrent of abuse at the "childish and ignorant race," referring to "Sambos who clambered out of the sewer" to participate in a solidarity march to the "infinite delight of a multitude of Dinahs and pickaninnies" who lined their route.[26]

Pinkerton was by no means alone in his apparent change of heart concerning racial matters. Others had supported abolition for political reasons, or self-fixatedly to save their souls and redeem white America—but then tired of, or lost patience with, racial radicalism after the Civil War. As Harriet Beecher Stowe recognized in her novel *Uncle Tom's Cabin* (1852), non-Southerners who espoused the Black cause at a distance and in the abstract could be frigid when it came to social contact, revealing an innate racial prejudice. By comparison, Pinkerton did have direct contact with fugitive then freed slaves and maintained abolitionist principles up to a point. However, pragmatism and the prospect of gaining an advantage drove his actions, too.

CHAPTER 5

The Baltimore Plot to Assassinate Lincoln

It was one of history's greatest publicity scoops. Pinkerton claimed to have saved president-elect Lincoln from assassination.

That was in 1861. The Pinkerton–Lincoln story had started six years earlier. In 1855 Pinkerton agreed to a security contract with the Illinois Central Railroad. Abraham Lincoln had drawn up the contract. The future president had risen from his log-cabin childhood to be a successful lawyer and was thus—like Pinkerton—a self-made man. Politically, too, he and the detective were fairly well attuned. Lincoln would not endorse abolitionist policies that might tear the nation asunder, but he did condemn slavery. The detective later recalled that the two men got along together. Lincoln's friend Norman Judd confirmed that view. He said, "Lincoln liked Pinkerton—[he] had the utmost confidence in him as a gentleman, and a man of sagacity."[1]

In 1856 Lincoln joined the newly formed Republican Party, with its policies of opposing the extension of slavery to the west and of supporting the admission of Kansas to the Union as a free state. Four years later the Republicans adopted him as their presidential candidate. On November 6, 1860, Abe Lincoln was elected the sixteenth president of the United States. It was by a decisive margin across the nation, but only a sprinkling of Southerners voted for him (slaves, were, of course, disenfranchised). The white leadership of the slave states had for decades feared they would be politically outflanked. Now in spite of Lincoln's moderate approach, they felt alienated. On December 20, 1860, South Carolina seceded from the Union. Six other Southern states followed suit.

Against the inauspicious background of a divided nation, Lincoln's entourage planned his inauguration in the federal capital, Washington, DC. The president-elect's route there from Springfield, Illinois, would take him through Maryland and the city of Baltimore. There he would have to change trains, traveling over a mile between one depot and another. Probably he would be surrounded by crowds whose enthusiasm for the newly elected chief executive was uncertain. For Baltimore was a hotbed of pro-Southern feeling.

The state of Maryland was actively debating the possibility of secession, and proslavery sentiment among its citizens was rife. There were many predictions of plots to assassinate Lincoln, some of them specified in letters sent to the president-elect in Springfield. One correspondent indicated that, thanks to Lincoln's election, the slaves were in a state of incipient revolt, and consequently terrified white Southerners were desperate to see the incoming chief executive killed. The *New York Sun* reported that a pair of New York detectives had discovered in Baltimore a 5,000-strong "secret organization with oaths, grips, secret signs, &c., and each member, after passing through a most horrible and trying ordeal, took a solemn oath to kill Mr. Lincoln at the first opportunity."[2]

At the time Pinkerton was contracted with the Philadelphia, Wilmington, and Baltimore Railroad (PWBRR) to supply security. The company's tracks traversed Maryland. Pinkerton later spoke of how his work for the PWBRR enabled him to detect a plot to assassinate the president-elect and of how he foiled that plot. Timothy Webster helped him to achieve that end. Forty-year-old Webster was working for Pinkerton on the PWBRR contract. A polite and elegant man, he had immigrated to Princeton, New Jersey, with his English parents when he was twelve. He had given up his profession as a machinist to apply for a post with the New York police. Rejected in that quarter, the well-spoken Englishman became a Pinkerton detective. In an attraction of social opposites, he and Pinkerton were close and effective colleagues.

Webster succeeded in infiltrating secessionist circles in the small community of Perrymansville (today's Perryman), around thirty miles northeast of Baltimore. The president of the PWBRR, Samuel Morse Felton, had heard that plans were being hatched there to tear up tracks and destroy railway property. Learning that a local cavalry company was implicated in these schemes, Webster enrolled in the company. He won secessionist trust by posing as an extremist. Pinkerton's words might have come right out of the Richmond trial back in the 1830s when he described how his agents acted the part of "fire-eaters" who gave vent to "blatant expressions of the most rebellious nature."[3]

Webster claimed to have won the confidence of local cavalry officers and to have attended a secret meeting they held with three men from Baltimore. In a later account, Pinkerton drew on Webster's narrative to recall how, sitting at a long table in a cavalry captain's home, lit only by the subdued flames of a few lanterns, the plotters decided on their course of action. Lincoln was to be killed when he disembarked from his train at the Calvert Street depot in Baltimore:

> When the train entered the depot, and Mr. Lincoln attempted to pass through the narrow passage leading to the streets, a party already delegated were to engage in a conflict on the outside, and then the policemen were to rush away to quell the disturbance. At this moment—the police being entirely withdrawn—Mr. Lincoln would find himself surrounded by a dense, excited and hostile crowd, all hustling and jamming against him, and then the fatal blow was to be struck. A swift steamer was to be stationed in Chesapeake Bay, with a boat awaiting upon the shore, ready to take the assassin on board as soon as the deed was done, and convey him to a Southern port, where he would be received with acclamations of joy and honored as a hero.[4]

When Webster sent a coded telegram to Pinkerton warning him of the murder conspiracy, Lincoln had already departed Springfield on his inauguration journey. Pinkerton rushed to intercept Lincoln, who was stopping in Philadelphia in the course of his triumphal, speech-punctuated journey to Washington, DC, the venue of his upcoming inauguration. At first Lincoln was reluctant to accept there was a plot and did not want to disrupt the plan for his triumphal procession. However, Pinkerton was persuasive, and his advice prevailed.

To foil the assassination plot, Pinkerton laid plans to smuggle Lincoln through Baltimore 36 hours earlier than expected. Lincoln had intended to traverse Baltimore on February 23, 1861, a timetable that had been openly announced. Now he canceled his meetings in Philadelphia in order to advance his schedule. Pinkerton arranged for him to leave Philadelphia incognito, traveling in a privately hired coach on the Baltimore train. To prevent news of this ruse from reaching the plotters, Pinkerton climbers cut the telegraph wires running along the railroad track leading to Baltimore.

Lincoln boarded the train with his friend, fellow Illinois lawyer Ward H. Lamon. Lincoln refused Lamon's offer to equip him with a Bowie knife and pistol (the imposingly large Lamon was an anti-abolitionist, but still Republican, and regarded himself as Lincoln's bodyguard). The train, guarded by

Pinkerton men deployed at regular intervals along its route, pulled into Baltimore's PWBRR terminal on the 22nd at 3:30 a.m. The arrangement in those days was that horse-drawn carriages would carry passengers through the streets of the city to Camden Station, the Baltimore & Ohio depot. Taking a circuitous route to deceive any would-be assassins, Lincoln's carriage arrived at its destination under cover of darkness. His sleeping cabin attached to the onward train was one of two commissioned by the Pinkertons for the president-elect and his security escort consisting of Pinkerton, his assistant Bangs, Lamon, and Kate Warne—Warne had spent the last few days befriending the wives of would-be plotters in a quest for useful information. After a nail-biting two hours' delay caused by the late arrival of a connecting train from the West, Lincoln proceeded safely on his way to the capital.[5]

News of the Baltimore precautions met with scorn in the South. It also provoked mirth, disdain, and disbelief in sections of the northern and midwestern press. Lincoln had hardly begun to achieve the stature that history has given him, and the contemporary satirists treated him as fair game. The *Chicago Tribune* gave credit to Pinkerton for his lifesaving endeavor, but its rival the *Chicago Democrat* asked, "How much longer will the people of this country be the dupe of these private detectives?" The proprietor of the *Democrat*, former Chicago mayor "Long John" Wentworth, was an old friend of Pinkerton's and was by now a Republican despite his newspaper's title. Casting aside past friendship, the son of the Gorbals was unforgiving of the *Democrat*'s skepticism. The two men engaged in fisticuffs after an encounter on a Chicago street. Elsewhere there were all kinds of versions of how Lincoln had disguised himself in preparation for his brief journey from one Baltimore terminal to another. Pinkerton's own account had the six-foot-four politician improbably disguised as an old lady. The *New York Times* dressed him in a "Scotch plaid cap" and Confederate sympathizers would lampoon him for having worn a "Scotch cap and cloak." *Vanity Fair* ran a cartoon depicting the tall traveler in a kilt and feathered hat, dancing the "MacLincoln Highland Fling."[6]

There was widespread incredulity about the existence of the plot. Herman Melville's novel *The Confidence-Man* had appeared four years previously and reflected Americans' suspicions of fake-it-to-make-it individuals. There was a belief in circulation that Pinkerton could not be trusted, and that citizens needed to be protected from the wiles of private detectives. For the politically motivated, there was a delicious link between supposition that Pinkerton had invented the Baltimore plot and the notion that Lincoln had acted in a cowardly manner.

For the rest of his life, Pinkerton was at pains to protect his version of events and, with it, his professional reputation. Interest in the Baltimore plot intensified in the wake of President Lincoln's assassination in 1865. William Herndon, Lincoln's former law partner, collected documents relating to the Baltimore plot in a compilation that supported Pinkerton's story. Because of his initiative, they survived the destruction of other Pinkerton records in Chicago's Great Fire of 1871. Pinkerton, however, did not greet Herndon's enterprise with unalloyed joy. On August 5, 1866, he wrote to him requesting confidentiality regarding certain portions of the records of the PWBRR pertaining to the Baltimore plot. His stated reason was that, with magnanimity in short supply in the wake of a bitter war, he wished to protect the identity of a certain former rebel who was now working as a broker for the PWBRR.[7] His real motive may have been to conceal evidence that might cast doubt on his version of events.

In a letter to the historian Benson J. Lossing in 1864, Lincoln supplied a statement of his own regarding the plot. He recalled how he had disguised himself in Philadelphia, well before his arrival in Baltimore, by wearing a "soft wool hat . . . I had never worn one of the latter in my life." He credited "Mr. Pinkerton, a skillful police detective, also from Chicago," for uncovering a potential threat to his life and taking proper protective measures. At first he had doubted Pinkerton, but then he received word from Assistant Secretary of State Frederick Seward (the son of Secretary of State William H. Seward) that some non-Pinkerton detectives were sounding alarm bells about a Baltimore assassination plot. He decided to go along with Pinkerton's deception plan.[8]

John A. Kennedy, superintendent of the New York Metropolitan police, wrote to the *New York Times* to complain that Pinkerton was seizing too much credit over the Baltimore plot, the discovery of which was due to Kennedy's own diligence. Kennedy and another New York detective had in 1861 agreed to perform a security sweep in preparation for Lincoln's inauguration. They had given the nation's capital a clean bill of health but regarded Baltimore as dangerous. Kennedy had his own independent suspicions about the dangers Lincoln faced on his journey from Philadelphia to Washington. He claimed that his report to that effect had helped persuade Lincoln to accept the subterfuges devised by Pinkerton.[9]

By the end of 1865 the Pinkerton–Kennedy relationship was sour. Pinkerton opened an office in New York in November of that year. It resulted in a public–private feud of the type that had previously occurred in Chicago. Shortly afterward, Pinkerton rejected the public policeman's claim to have helped save Lincoln's life. He and his supporters depicted Kennedy's account as an effort at self-inflation. The private detective was sufficiently agitated to launch what would be the first step in a considerable literary career. Pinkerton's compilation appeared in 1866, titled *The History and Evidence of the Passage of Abraham Lincoln from Harrisburg, Pa. to Washington, D.C., on the 22nd and 23rd of February, 1861.*[10]

When preparing that volume, Pinkerton wrote more than once to Ward Lamon asking for a corroborative statement. Lamon never replied. The reason became apparent in 1872 when, with the help of a shadow writer, he published his biography *The Life of Abraham Lincoln*. Lamon's *Life* referred to the Pinkerton's role in the Baltimore plot: "Being intensely ambitious to shine in the professional way, and something of a politician besides, it struck him that it would be a particularly fine thing to discover a dreadful plot to assassinate the President elect; and he discovered it accordingly." Commenting on Pinkerton's folio of evidence on the 1861 assassination plot, Lamon remarked: "These documents are neither edifying nor useful; they prove nothing but the baseness of the vocation which gave them existence."[11]

There was no love lost between Lamon and Pinkerton, who had at one point commented bluntly on Lamon's stupidity in offering Lincoln a Bowie knife with which to defend himself against an assassin. Lamon's skepticism irritated anew an already raw nerve, and in 1883 Pinkerton, sensitive to belittlement even in the final year of his life, published a riposte, *The Spy of the Rebellion*.

Encouraged by Pinkerton's descendants, future writers and historians would favor the detective's version of events. Examples from the later nineteenth century are Cleveland Moffett writing for *McClure's Magazine* about "How Allan Pinkerton Thwarted the First Plot to Assassinate Lincoln," and loyalist William Herndon's biography of Lincoln that recorded how "the noted detective of Chicago" averted "tragedy" and ensured Lincoln's safe arrival in Washington.[12] In 1950 the PNDA helped and guided journalist James Horan in his research for a study of the Pinkerton "dynasty." Allan Pinkerton's grandson Robert A. Pinkerton II read the chapter on the Baltimore plot and wrote to Horan's assistant stating, "It has our approval."[13] Following the assassination of President John F. Kennedy in 1963, there was a surge of interest in the Baltimore plot. Then and since, Allan Pinkerton's account has been accepted.[14]

All these endorsements notwithstanding, Lamon was right in hinting that the Baltimore plot was a meal ticket for Allan Pinkerton. The detective continued to see assassination plots as one of his agency's raisons d'être for some years after 1861. In November 1862, he wrote to the Union army's General George B. McClellan warning that a group of the commander's friends were planning to kill Lincoln. McClellan dismissed the idea as "conspiracy nonsense."[15] Pinkerton saw Lincoln's violent death in 1865 as a vindication and a further opportunity. He wrote to Secretary of War Edwin Stanton: "This morning's papers contain the deplorable intelligence of the assassination of President Lincoln. Under the providence of God in July 1861, I was enabled to save him from the fate he has now met. How I regret that I had not been near him previous to this fatal act. I might have been the means to avert it. If I can be of any service please let me know."[16] Stanton did not take up his offer.

In spite of partisans' attempts over a century and a half to massage history, the significance of the Baltimore plot story is plain. Yes, the case for its existence was purely circumstantial. There was no way of confirming or denying the story that Pinkerton told. Yet the detective can be defended for his precautionary approach. It is entirely credible that fire-eaters spoke of killing Lincoln in 1861. It would have been irresponsible for Pinkerton, Webster, and Lincoln to ignore the dangerous talk. We have Lincoln's own testimony to the fact that Pinkerton was neither gullible nor overstating his case. The president-elect stated, "He was well informed as to the plan, but did not know that the conspirator would have pluck enough to execute it."[17]

Three observations may be made in conclusion. First, Pinkerton was wise to take precautions when president-elect Lincoln passed through a largely hostile Maryland. Second, Pinkerton can be credited with having had the vision to see that the president of the United States needed a professional protection service. Third, the private detective exploited the Baltimore plot to advance his career.

Pinkerton's first career advancement would be immediate, with unfortunate results in America's unfolding tragedy.

CHAPTER 6

A Secret Service

On February 4, 1861, a month before Lincoln's inauguration, delegates from the seceded states met in Montgomery, the capital city of Alabama. Here they adopted the newly drafted constitution of the Confederate States of America. Their action placed US Army Major Robert Anderson in a predicament. The commander at Fort Sumter, an island fort off the Charleston, South Carolina, coastline, he found himself surrounded by what had become potentially enemy waters and territory. Brigadier General P.G.T. Beauregard of the Confederacy gave Anderson an opportunity to evacuate the fort, but the major refused. Early in April, President Lincoln sent a small fleet to resupply Sumter. Confederate forces responded. At 4:30 a.m. on Friday, April 12, their shore batteries opened fire on Anderson's garrison, continuing their bombardment for 34 hours. The gunners' action marked the start of hostilities in what would be one of the world's most serious conflicts in the century, stretching from the final defeat of Napoleon at Waterloo to the opening salvoes of World War I. By the Civil War's end, 620,000 men lay dead.

On Saturday, April 13, Major Anderson surrendered Fort Sumter and was allowed to take his men north. Immediately after this, Allan Pinkerton offered his services to President Lincoln:

> I have in my Force from Sixteen to Eighteen persons on whose courage, Skill and Devotion to their country I can rely. If they with myself at the head can be of service in the way of obtaining information of the movements of the Traitors, or Safely conveying your letters or dispatches, on

> that class of Secret Service which is the most dangerous, I am at your command.
> In the present disturbed state of affairs I dare not trust this to the mail . . .
> Secrecy is the great lever I propose to operate with . . .
> My Force comprises both Sexes—all of good character and well skilled in their business.[1]

As the war progressed, the need for an intelligence capability became increasingly evident. The Confederates were fighting on home soil, a terrible experience for the seceded states, but also an advantage in terms of motivation and knowledge of local topography and defensive layouts. The Union had a need to penetrate the South's secrets. In offering to meet that need early in the conflict, Pinkerton was aware of a commercial opportunity.

The Union's war machine was in its infancy in the early months of 1861. Lincoln lacked the military experience to hasten its reform. In spite of the pressing need, the president did not appoint an intelligence chief. Instead, he left intelligence collection to his military commanders. One of these was General George McClellan. Just 34 years old at the start of the war, this ambitious officer had been educated at the University of Pennsylvania and at West Point military academy, New York, and had been an observer at the Crimean War (1853–1856). He first met Pinkerton when serving as a vice president of the Illinois Central Railroad. They were not ideological soul mates. McClellan was no abolitionist. However, Pinkerton with his working-class origins became enamored of McClellan with his polite manners, just as he had fallen for the similarly polished Timothy Webster. When the general asked his old acquaintance to set up a military intelligence capability, Pinkerton accepted the invitation.[2]

At this point, McClellan was in command of the Department of the Ohio, charged with the defense of several Middle Western states. Accordingly, Pinkerton moved his headquarters to Cincinnati in May 1861. Change came when, on July 21, Union forces suffered a major defeat at Bull Run, Virginia. Known as "Manassas" to the Confederates, Bull Run was just thirty miles from Washington, DC. McClellan had meantime enjoyed some success in operations in the western part of Virginia (today's West Virginia). Lincoln decided to place him in command of units responsible for the defense of the capital, units that McClellan soon forged into the core of what would eventually become the Army of the Potomac, the Union's chief fighting force. In November, Pinkerton's patron was promoted to be general-in-chief of all Union armies.

Figure 6.1. At Antietam, Maryland, site of the 1862 Civil War battle. From left to right, Allan Pinkerton, President Abraham Lincoln, and General George B. McClellan. *Library of Congress*

Pinkerton's status rose accordingly. In August, he made Washington, DC, the center of his operations. He later recalled, "This was the first real organization of the secret service. How much benefit was rendered to the country by this branch of the army will probably never be known—the destruction of nearly all my papers in the great fire of Chicago preventing their full publication—but that our operations were of immense practical value to the Union commander is a fact attested to by every one connected with the leading movements of our forces."[3]

General McClellan affirmed, in an official report, the provenance and nomenclature of Pinkerton's unit: "Immediately after being assigned to the command of the troops around Washington I organized a secret-service force, under E.J. Allen, a very experienced and efficient person."[4] Pinkerton had adopted that cover name. He was too well known to remain entirely anonymous, but the use of a nom de guerre in correspondence was an effort to achieve at least some secrecy. In similar vein he insisted that his employers remained in ignorance of the identities of his spies, giving security as his reason but also in the knowledge that he was an independent contractor in control of his own lines of command. For Pinkerton ran not a federal secret service but a private bureau contracted to perform intelligence functions for the Union's armed forces. His services did not come cheaply. On the eve of the Civil War, his daily rate for work undertaken by his agents was six dollars. While freelance contracts do not guarantee continuous employment, those per diems still converted into high salaries by the standard of the day.[5]

The Pinkerton men and women engaged in four forms of intelligence activity. First, they conducted counterintelligence, or spycatching, especially in the nation's capital. This was a challenging task. North–South borders were porous. Confederate spies spoke the same language as their opponents, and there was no need for disguise, as they had the same mannerisms and appearance as northerners. Their accents might give them away if they originated from below the Mason-Dixon Line, but the Confederacy also had at its disposal northerners who spied for the South, a problem for Pinkerton agents who tried to root them out.

Second, the Pinkertons collected intelligence. They did so by interrogating prisoners, deserters, and refugees from the South. Third, a chosen few undertook proactive missions. Five of the twenty-four agents at the director's disposal attempted the dangerous task of operating behind enemy lines and gleaning information within the Confederacy's capital, Richmond, Virginia. Finally, Pinkerton and associates like Timothy Webster produced estimates of the enemy order of battle based on intelligence they had gleaned.

The most celebrated example of the Pinkertons' spycatching prowess was their apprehension of Mrs. Rose O'Neal Greenhow. Married to a Virginian who enjoyed a career with the US State Department prior to his death in 1854, Greenhow was one of Washington, DC's society ladies. In her late forties on the Civil War's outbreak, she was a woman of charm and persuasiveness who made it her business to remain intimately acquainted with men of influence in the nation's capital. She was a personal friend of Lincoln's predecessor in the White House, the Pennsylvanian Democrat James Buchanan. Pinkerton referred to her use of "almost irresistible seductive powers" in the Confederate cause. Greenhow sent coded messages via a string of couriers to the Confederate military leadership. Her reputation blossomed. For example, prior to the Confederate triumph at Bull Run she was believed (though on no good evidence) to have sent alerts of Union plans to General Beauregard's adjutant, Colonel Thomas Jordan.[6]

Assistant Secretary of War Thomas A. Scott asked Pinkerton to place Greenhow under surveillance. On the night of August 22, 1861, a pair of Pinkerton agents tailed an army officer, referred to as "Captain Ellison," whom they had seen leaving Greenhow's house. Blunders now occurred on both sides. Arriving at his quarters, the captain summoned help, then turned on his pursuers and had them arrested. They were released the next day on the intervention of Secretary Scott, but in the meantime the allegedly treasonous army officer had plenty of time to destroy evidence. Undeterred, Pinkerton arrested Greenhow on the 23rd. Mrs. Greenhow recalled, "the man Allen, or Pinkerton (for he had several aliases) . . . mumbled something about verbal authority from the War and State Department," then marched her into her house with another man (probably from the local police) on her other side: "I was made a prisoner in my own house and subjected to an ordeal which must have been copied from the days of the [Revolutionary] Directory in France."[7] In case her detention had not yet alerted her clandestine contacts, her daughter made sure by climbing a tree and shouting, "My Mother's been arrested."[8]

Greenhow had kept copies of the reports she sent to Jordan. Like Captain Ellison, she was anxious to conceal evidence. "I . . . put into my mouth," she recalled, "a very important note, which I destroyed."[9] But she had insufficient time and oral capacity, so incriminating evidence was found in abundance. It included coded messages and a few decodes, a combination that gave clues about the structure of the codes being used.

The federal authorities naïvely decided to leave Greenhow under continued house detention under the supervision of Lieutenant N.E. Sheldon. The lieutenant was no match for her guile, and she continued to transmit Union military secrets to her Confederate comrades. However, with the assistance of the aforementioned clues Pinkerton operatives had mastered the codes supplied to her by her controllers, and the Union military thus had the advantage of knowing what Greenhow was telling the enemy.

In January 1862 Greenhow, together with her daughter and a maid, were transferred to the vermin-infested Old Capitol Prison (the by-now crumbling building had temporarily housed Congress in the wake of the burning of the Capitol in the War of 1812). Allowed rubber balls for her daughter to play with, the irrepressible spy gouged them open, packed them with messages, and threw them through the prison windows at prearranged times for her couriers to catch.[10] These activities ceased only when, in a prisoner exchange, mother and daughter were transferred to Richmond. Greenhow then left the Confederate capital to make a triumphal tour of Europe, where she promoted the South's cause.

On her return journey aboard a British blockade-busting vessel, the *Condor*, a Union gunboat gave chase and closed in on its hapless prey off the coast of North Carolina. When the fleeing *Condor* ran aground on October 1, 1864, Greenhow took to a rowboat. A wave capsized it. Dragged to the bottom by the weight of the gold sewed into her underclothes, the former spy breathed her last at the age of 51.[11]

Though in the final phases of her life she had passed beyond Pinkerton's purview, prior to her demise Greenhow made one more contribution to the detective's fame. In an 1863 memoir that consolidated her status as a Confederate heroine, the reputed courtesan attacked Pinkerton's character. She denounced him as "a German Jew" who "possessed all the national instincts of his race in an exaggerated degree besides having these inherent characteristics sharpened by Yankee association."[12]

Pinkerton had some success in the business of counterespionage. Offensive espionage—spying on the Confederate enemy—posed different challenges and opportunities. Pinkerton's son William commented on the peculiarities of the civil conflict. Enrolled at Notre Dame University and just sixteen at the time of the war's outbreak, William had volunteered for military service. However, Allan secured his discharge and took him on as a wartime operative, giving him an opportunity to observe espionage at first hand. In 1898 when the United States was at war with Spain and spying was once again to the fore, William offered his Civil War recollections to the *Chicago Evening Post*: "The secret service of the war of the rebellion was cast upon wholly different lines from that of today. This is mainly owing to the fact that we are at war with a foreign country in which an American is at a disadvantage. On the contrary, a man in the [18]60s could be transferred to this kind of work from one section of the country to another without attracting particular attention."

Continuing his recollections, William Pinkerton delivered a verdict from which few have differed: "Timothy Webster was unquestionably one of the most brilliant of the pioneer secret service men who gave great aid to the federal government during the war of the rebellion."[13]

It will be recalled that Webster had spied, in Baltimore and its outlying communities, on Confederate sympathizers allegedly plotting to assassinate president-elect Lincoln. The married father of four (two deceased in childhood and another about to die fighting the Confederates) did not operate under an assumed name. Having through his Baltimore infiltrations established his credentials as a Confederate sympathizer, Webster clung to the identity that equipped him to gain entrance to Southern political and military society. In need of marital respectability to achieve that end, he spied in tandem with a woman in her twenties who posed as his wife. Hattie (aka Carrie) Lawton (aka Lewis) was herself married and had been taken on as a Pinkerton operative in 1860.

In the dead of night on October 25, 1861, Webster crossed the Chesapeake Bay to Virginia, traveling thirty miles aboard a dugout canoe equipped with three sails. Continuing his journey to Richmond, he obtained information on Confederate military dispositions. He requested an audience with Judah P. Benjamin, the Confederate acting secretary of war. Benjamin was in the event too preoccupied to meet Webster as he had just received accurate intelligence of an impending Union naval attack on Port Royal Sound. However, Webster's request and its consideration illustrated the spy's audacity and connectedness in Confederate circles. Those same qualities obtained travel passes for the enterprising Webster, enabling him to visit, for example, sensitive military installations near twice-fought-over Bull Run. He gained information both by visual inspection and by interviewing unsuspecting Southern personnel. Relying on his capacity for smooth talk to cross military lines, he finally made it back to Washington to report his findings to Allan Pinkerton on November 15.

Webster made further trips to Virginia, where he convinced Confederate leaders that he was running secret missions on their behalf. Double agents are, however, in double jeopardy, and his luck ran out. His several wintry crossings of the Chesapeake took their toll on his rheumatic physique. In the early spring of 1862 he succumbed to this condition and had to confine himself to his quarters at the Monument Hotel in Richmond. His apocryphal wife Hattie Lawton nursed him with the help of John Scobell, who posed as her manservant. Pinkerton had earlier hired Scobell as an operative. Scobell just happened to be versed in Scottish songs, which must have appealed to Pinkerton. On a more practical note, the detective chief realized that an African American freedman from Virginia would be an asset.[14]

Webster's period of convalescence dragged on, and Pinkerton began to worry because he had been away from Washington for longer than the usual three to four weeks. Pinkerton sent two further agents, Pryce Lewis and John Scully, to check on his welfare. A Welshman born in Newport, the scene of the 1839 Rising, Lewis appealed to a perceived Southern weakness for aristocracy and no doubt pleased Pinkerton by posing as an English lord. However, Rose Greenhow knew both Lewis and Scully from her Washington days and warned her Confederate friends that they were spies. Lewis and Scully unwittingly alerted the Confederate authorities to Webster's whereabouts and confirmed his likely treason when they visited him in the Monument Hotel.

The Confederates arrested all five spies. Four were spared, but Webster had made fools of leading Confederate figures and could not be forgiven. On April 29, 1862, the English immigrant became the first Union spy to be executed. It took two attempts and a replacement rope to complete the deed, and then Webster was buried locally. After the war Pinkerton arranged for his reinternment at a well-tended plot in Graceland Cemetery, Chicago. There, by special arrangement, his remains lay alongside those of Kate Warne and members of the Pinkerton dynasty.[15]

To the names of Webster, Lawton, Scobell, Lewis, and Scully might be added that of Samuel M. Bridgeman, another operative who served as an offensive spy and was singled out for his valor by William Pinkerton. A native of Fairfax County, Virginia, Bridgeman had served in the US Marine Corps at the time of the Mexican War, rising to the rank of sergeant. He had been one of the Pinkerton agency's intake of 1855. In his early forties by the first year of the Civil War, he posed as Pryce Lewis's coachman and helped the Welsh poseur obtain military information about the Confederate forces in western Virginia.[16]

Notwithstanding William Pinkerton's claim that it was easy to pass as a southerner, Pinkerton supplied only a handful of such penetrative spies to the Union cause. In spite of pro-Union sympathy in Richmond and elsewhere in the South, the private detective recruited no "agents in place." He preferred to rely on the interrogation of prisoners of war and refugees. The testimony of such individuals was often unreliable. In a civil war with families torn asunder, loyalty to the Union cause was often professed but could not be taken for granted.

There was an exception. The Union loyalty of African Americans who had fled the tyranny and carnage of the Southern slavocracy could be relied upon.

Pinkerton's operatives referred to such escaped slaves as "contraband." W.H. Ringgold was one example. He had been a steward on a river steamer that the Confederates impressed into military service at the start of the war. The vessel transported gray-clad troops on the York River. One day, a storm damaged the boat. Released from his duties as a steward, Ringgold was sufficiently trusted to receive a travel pass. He made it across the Chesapeake. His reports concerning the northern side of the Virginia peninsula were the only intelligence of that kind that General McClellan received before starting his campaign there in March 1862. Ringgold's reporting was, however, far from comprehensive, and Black Americans could be forgiven for having subjective views on the military strengths and weaknesses of the Confederacy.[17]

Southern military strategists did their best to encourage inaccurate, especially inflated, estimates of their strength. They may have dropped their guard in the cases of Webster and Lewis, but in the opening phase of the war their counterintelligence was a match for Pinkerton's efforts. They also engaged in deception. An example occurred during the Peninsula Campaign of March–July 1862, when McClellan's forces landed in southeastern Virginia with the aim of marching north to attack Richmond from the rear. The Confederates painted logs to resemble cannon, slowing McClellan's advance—though it took the military flair of General Lee finally to halt the blue tide on the approaches to Richmond.[18]

For whatever reason, McClellan consistently overestimated Confederate strength. It later became a widespread perception that Pinkerton was responsible for the exaggerations that blighted the general's decision-making. The publication of Confederate and Union war records between 1880 and 1901 contributed to that perception. For example, the *Boston Globe*, though it repeatedly published stories in praise of Pinkerton and his agency, remarked on "the worthlessness of the supposed accurate information that Allan Pinkerton innocently supplied to Gen McClellan."[19] The verdict of numerous historians has been that Pinkerton was responsible for McClellan's errors.[20]

In 1996 Edwin Fishel attempted a more nuanced contribution to the historiography of Pinkerton's Civil War estimates. Fishel's job until 1968 had been with the US National Security Agency (NSA). In his retirement he pursued twin passions. In the Washington, DC, area he was a well-known pianist with professional jazz groups like the Bull Run Blues Blowers. His other passion was historical research. At first, he did so on behalf of the NSA, but his own enthusiasm strayed to another field culminating in his formidable work of the mid-1990s, *The Secret War for the Union*.

Fishel argued that Pinkerton was at fault, but McClellan was to blame. The NSA veteran predicated his argument on data from order of battle estimates. McClellan was cautious about engaging the enemy, afraid of humiliation through defeat and ambitious to go into one decisive battle with overwhelming strength. So he plucked figures out of the air to show that the Confederates' forces outnumbered his, intending to buy time and to pressure Union politicians into giving him more men and military equipment. Fishel focused on McClellan's exaggerations. On August 8, 1861, McClellan told a skeptical Winfield Scott, whom he was soon to displace as commanding general, that the Confederates in Virginia had 100,000 men. A month later, he was telling Secretary of War Simon Cameron that the Confederates would be able to put 170,000 into the field at Bull Run to oppose his paltry 81,000. In the event, the Confederates were able to muster no more than 35,000 for the end-of-August 1862 second battle of Bull Run.[21]

Crucial to Fishel's argument was his contention that Pinkerton was probably not responsible for the original 100,000 estimate. This was because "on the day it was written he had just begun setting up shop, with only three of his detectives on hand."[22] This indicated that McClellan was responsible for his own inventions. Subsequently, however, Pinkerton did play along with the inflationary general. He found it difficult to invent credible figures that matched McClellan's but did his best to oblige. On October 4, 1861, he gave the game away when writing to his employer that his latest estimate, "was founded upon all the information then in my possession, derived from my own operatives, deserters from the Rebel service, 'Contrabands', &c, &c; *and was made large*, as intimated to you at the time."[23]

Did Pinkerton, to quote the *Boston Globe*, "innocently" supply false estimates to General McClellan?[24] Fishel summarized his view on this matter as follows: "The necessity that mothered Pinkerton's statistical inventions was McClellan's conviction of being outnumbered. But sycophancy does not necessarily imply insincerity; evidently Pinkerton honestly absorbed his chief's conviction."[25]

A more critical view is in order. Often credited with mastering the psychology of the criminal, Pinkerton was even more ardent in his character-reading of potential employers. In peacetime the Pinkerton firm would become infamous for inventing imaginary proletarian threats to frighten employers into hiring detectives. In the case of McClellan, fear already existed, and Pinkerton simply had to feed it. There is no plausible exculpatory interpretation of the detective's actions. He helped McClellan to justify delay after delay in attacking the enemy in the months when the Union might have inflicted a knock-out blow, ending earlier the war that cost so many lives. Pinkerton would not be the last intelligence chief who saw advantage in failing to speak truth to power.

The whole matter came to a head at Antietam. This monumental battle occurred in the wake of General Robert E. Lee's crossing of the Potomac River into Maryland at the head of the Army of North Virginia with a view to winning a peace deal favorable to the Confederacy. In mid-September 1862 McClellan received an unexpected intelligence coup. Wrapped round a consignment of cigars in an abandoned camp, Union forces discovered Lee's plan for an attack on Harper's Ferry that, if successful, would have facilitated the general Confederate advance. The jubilant McClellan told Lincoln that "no time shall be lost," adding "[I] will send you trophies."[26] But even now the young general did not act quickly. Lee's forces took Harper's Ferry and on September 17 met McClellan's forces at Sharpsburg on the banks of Antietam Creek.

In the ensuing battle McClellan's men secured, if marginally, an advantage. The northern general had started the engagement with 75,000 troops at his disposal compared with 36,000 on the enemy side. In this bloodiest engagement of the Civil War, the Confederates lost 12,400 killed, wounded, missing, or captured, a huge proportionate reduction of Lee's fighting strength. However, cautious as ever, McClellan refrained from giving chase to his vulnerable foe as Lee organized a strategic withdrawal. Pinkerton and a group of operatives that included George Bangs and John Babcock were at McClellan's side for the campaign but produced no intelligence to persuade their employer to advance more expeditiously than he did.[27]

CHAPTER 7

The Secret Service

Though the Confederacy's desire to preserve slavery was the underlying cause of secession, thus far Lincoln's war aim was preservation of the Union, not abolition. Yet how could such desiccated reasoning possibly excuse expenditures of human life on the scale of Antietam? On September 22, 1862, Lincoln gave the Union a higher cause. He issued a Preliminary Emancipation Proclamation. As of the first day of 1863, "all persons held as slaves within any state, or any part of a state, the people whereof shall then be in rebellion against the United States shall be then, thenceforward, and forever free." Though a tiny minority as the war's beginning, abolitionists like Allan Pinkerton could now rejoice. The impact on Union soldiers' morale of the Proclamation, reissued in final form on January 1, is open to question. However, the Proclamation arguably created one of history's few examples of a just war.[1]

Lincoln responded further to Antietam by questioning General McClellan's competence. McClellan lost his post as commanding general in October 1862, and on November 5, 1862, was relieved of all command. In the preceding months, Pinkerton had acted as McClellan's spy within the Washington establishment. He wrote letters reporting on the political scene and had them confidentially couriered to the general in his various field locations. Some three weeks before General Lee's Maryland operation, Pinkerton had written to McClellan, "unless some other military genius appears soon they cannot do otherwise than appoint you to the command." However, in the meantime he reported that General Henry W. Hallek, who had in July 1862 replaced McClellan as general in chief, now had the president's ear. He warned that Lincoln, Hallek, and Secretary of War Edwin M. Stanton would all prefer if

McClellan were not entrusted with command of the effort to stop Lee's threatened advance.[2]

In the wake of Antietam, Lincoln summoned Pinkerton to the White House. The president was more than capable of using someone else's spy. Pinkerton later impressed on McClellan that he had not really wanted to see Lincoln but was called in regardless. Lincoln was "very friendly," disarmingly referred to Antietam as a "great and decisive victory," and said he would be forever indebted to McClellan. But he wondered if the general "had not advised him" of any details deemed "not sufficiently worthy of notice," details that Pinkerton might now wish to impart. Lincoln then asked specifically about the order of battle in Antietam. Pinkerton told the president a clear untruth, that Lee had 140,000 men and McClellan 90,000. Even more bluntly, the president asked, "why the Army did not fight on Thursday," the day after Lee's reverses on September 17. Pinkerton parroted the McClellan line about troop exhaustion, the need to bury the dead, and shortages of ammunition. Lincoln responded less than convincingly with an assurance that he was sure that McClellan had fought well.[3]

Though Pinkerton continued for a while in his role as a kind of political double agent, he remained primarily loyal to McClellan. That Pinkerton could thus support an unwavering anti-abolitionist is a reminder of the detective's pragmatism when it came to principles. He was no doubt swayed by the facts that the general had been his patron and offered what to the socially untutored Pinkerton seemed attractive, a relationship with a cultivated man.

Early in October Lincoln delivered a speech at Frederick Junction, a few miles north of the capital. Pinkerton had a "considerable conversation" with him on the special train that carried the presidential party back to Washington. Pinkerton reported the exchange to McClelland, reassuring him that the president remained effusive about the general and his performance at Antietam and "at the present time is friendly." Of Stanton and his assistant secretary of war Peter H. Watson, Pinkerton wrote, "General I do not believe they are or ever will be your friends." Watson had had the temerity to challenge Pinkerton's accounting. He had not paid Pinkerton's bills for the July-to-September period. The assistant secretary of war may have had doubts about Pinkerton's effectiveness and loyalty, or about the desirability of secret service operations. Whatever his reason, he gave as the justification for his nonpayment Pinkerton's refusal to give him the names of his operatives.[4]

A month later Lincoln's doubts about McClellan led to the general's dismissal. McClellan's continuing reluctance to move preemptively against Lee was at the root of the decision. Lincoln waited until after the mid-term elections of October 4 to make the announcement. Command of the Army of the Potomac passed to General Ambrose E. Burnside on October 5, spelling the end of Pinkerton's service as chief Union spy.

John Babcock took Pinkerton's place. Before the war, Babcock had helped design some of the "millionaires' row" mansions along Michigan Avenue in Chicago. In 1861 he enlisted, still aged only twenty-five, as a rifleman in the Union army prior to his transfer to Pinkerton's unit, where he distinguished himself by scouting and mapping enemy positions. The only one of Pinkerton's operatives to survive the October purge, the former Private Babcock continued to work in an intelligence capacity until the end of the war. He was referred to as "Captain Babcock" and later "Colonel Babcock" yet in reality remained, like Pinkerton, a civilian in service to the armed forces. He was not, however, involved with a private agency. Pinkerton's idea that a private detective agency could be the nation's secret service had died.

Pinkerton did not suffer financially by serving the Union. In his twilight years, he told his son Robert that, when with General McClellan, he had "amassed considerable money, which was all invested in property of one kind or the other in Chicago."[5] In all the government paid him $38,567 between September 1861 and November 1862.[6] Thereafter, while resuming his trade in the civilian field, Pinkerton continued to contract to the federal government. Following the Union army's occupation of Louisiana, he investigated civil suits brought against the federal government by local people. Pinkerton continued his federal contracting until after General Lee's April 9, 1865, surrender at Appomattox (an event that his former operative, John Babcock, helped to facilitate). Toward the end of May, he was still sending Brigadier General George L. Andrews reports on the alleged malfeasances of soldiers and cavalrymen, such as the looting of tobacco and other provisions.[7]

Five days after Appomattox, John Wilkes Booth, an actor and Confederate spy, shot Lincoln from behind as the president watched a play at Ford's Theatre, just five short blocks from the White House. The man who had done so much to facilitate the emancipation of the slaves, not just by issuing the Emancipation Proclamation but also by steering the crucial 13th Amendment through a divided Congress, died the next day. On April 19, Pinkerton sent his previously mentioned coded military telegram from New Orleans to his old nemesis Secretary of War Stanton suggesting he might have (again) saved Lincoln's life and offering the services of his "whole force." The message reflected Pinkerton's usual eye for an opportunity. It testified also to his pique at being sidelined. To some degree, the detective was the author of his own lack of prominence, as the telegram's ciphered "signature" showed. For Pinkerton, consistent in his adherence to the principles of security, did not use his own name. He appended, instead, his wartime nom de plume, "E. J. Allen."[8]

Stanton replied to Pinkerton stating that Booth was still at large and might be heading for Texas or Mexico: "You will please take measures to watch the western rivers and you may get him. The rewards offered for him now amount to One Hundred Thousand Dollars or over."[9] Gallingly for Pinkerton, most of the reward money in the event went to his rival Lafayette C. Baker, a colorful character who made no effort to conceal his identity. Baker was a veteran of the 1856 San Francisco Vigilante movement, the Bay City elite's attempt to put the Irish-Democrat element in its place. He was in his mid-thirties at the outbreak of hostilities. Early in the war, he undertook an espionage mission in Virginia for Secretary of State William H. Seward, a mission whose success he was to exaggerate. Switching to become a protégé of Secretary Stanton, Baker became a "Special Provost-Marshall" in the employ of the War Department and undertook counterintelligence work in Washington, DC. Headquartered in 217 Pennsylvania Avenue, his unit rounded up Southern sympathizers and war profiteers. Among his achievements was the arrest of Isabella Maria Boyd, the "Siren of the Shenandoah." Belle Boyd, as she liked to be called, was a spy who repeatedly delivered intelligence to the Confederates' General Thomas J. "Stonewall" Jackson. Though arrested, she slipped through Baker's fingers, just as she had earlier escaped the clutches of the Pinkertons.

Baker claimed to have set up a "National Detective Bureau" just before McClellan's removal. Both the terminology and the entity were figments of his imagination. After a year the War Department dismissed him for tapping Stanton's telegraph lines. Recalled to Washington immediately after Lincoln's assassination, Baker put a military unit onto Booth's trail, and the assassin was tracked to a barn south of Port Royal, Virginia, where he was killed. After the war, Baker again fell out of favor, this time for forging letters in an attempt to incriminate Lincoln's successor in the White House, Andrew Johnson. In 1867 he published a book that was as unreliable as its author but whose title threatened Pinkerton's narrative: *History of the United States Secret Service.*[10]

Baker was, however, a mere flash in the pan. A greater challenge to Pinkerton's private enterprise came from public institutions. According to the historian Edwin Fishel, "Pinkerton's wide reputation as the author of strength estimates that damaged the Union's war effort has cast a bad odor over the whole subject of Civil War intelligence," but, he insisted, the malodorous reputation was undeserved. Union intelligence on Lee's forces improved as the war wore on.[11] General John Pope utilized daring cavalry incursions to find out what was going on behind enemy lines. General Joseph "Fighting Joe" Hooker, remembered for his defeat by Lee's forces at the Battle of Chancellorsville (1863), made an important contribution, that same year, by establishing a Bureau of Information. The bureau operated until the end of the war, serving the intelligence needs of Generals George G. Meade and Ulysses S. Grant.

The Bureau of Information lacked the institutional continuity of Pinkerton's agency and was terminated at the war's end. US military intelligence did not achieve continuity until 1882. In that year a campaign by Rear Admiral Stephen B. Luce culminated in the creation of the Office of Naval Intelligence. The Military Intelligence Division followed in 1885. In short, there was no national military intelligence between 1865 and the 1880s. There was, however, one Civil War–era government agency that endured in the intervening period and posed a continuing challenge to the Pinkertons. It was the United States Secret Service, *the* Secret Service.

Hours before his fatal wounding at Ford's Theatre, President Lincoln approved the creation of a Secret Service that would operate under the umbrella of the Treasury Department. The arrangement reflected the fact that counterfeiting and its inflationary effects had threatened the economic management of the war effort. The service's first director, sworn in on July 5, 1865, some weeks after Lincoln's death, was William Wood, who had already served the Treasury Department as a counterfeiting investigator. The service's original mission thus called time on private investigations of counterfeiting, the activities that had drawn Allan Pinkerton into the world of detection in his days at Dundee, Illinois.[12]

The future history of the Secret Service would have a bearing on the business opportunities available to the Pinkertons. After the war, in the early years of Reconstruction, Secret Service "operatives" (as they were then called, perhaps in homage to the Pinkertons) branched out to investigate the illegal and tax-evading production of moonshine whiskey in the Carolinas and other Southern states. The defeated secessionist states were at the time under military occupation by the Union army. From the beginning, then, the federal agents of the Secret Service risked alienating segments of the white population of the region.

In May 1869 President Grant appointed Hiram C. Whitley to be the second chief of the Secret Service. There was serious lawlessness in several of the Southern states. Local terrorists refused to accept the Reconstruction-era US constitutional amendments that gave former slaves benefits of citizenship such as the right to vote. African Americans who attempted to use such rights were being beaten, used for target practice, tortured, hanged, and burned alive. The federal government responded by transferring the Secret Service to the newly formed Justice Department with the mission of stamping out terrorism. Whitley knew the South well, in part because he was a former slave catcher who had fleetingly sympathized with the Confederacy before joining the Union Army in Louisiana. Now, he told his operatives to "ascertain as far as possible the aims and objectives of the different secret sects of the South, known under one general head as the Ku Klux Klan."[13]

Backed by US marshals with powers to arrest and by the presence of the US Army, Whitley's agents moved against the Klan and similar terrorist groups. Local freedmen as well as sympathetic whites risked their lives to inform on the whereabouts and activities of their night-riding white neighbors. Former slave John Good, a blacksmith in Union, South Carolina, shoed the horses he suspected were used by the Klan. By using a bent nail, he ensured the riders would leave distinctive tracks for the military to follow, tracks that led to their arrest. Although the Klan killed him in revenge, Good was one of those who ensured that convictions of Klansmen and the like reached a peak in 1872, effectively destroying the Klan's power at that time.[14] Unlike the Pinkertons, who served only private individuals who paid them, the publicly funded Secret Service had achieved a policing goal on behalf of society.

The Secret Service promised to deliver a national detective service. Additionally, most large cities had police forces by the 1870s, with crime-detection functions of varying capabilities. Yet these public challenges to Pinkertonism were still weak. Local police forces lacked the national networking that the Pinkertons supplied. On the federal level, the Secret Service declined after its spectacular success in 1872. There were few federal laws for it to enforce, a problem that would still affect the fledgling FBI after its founding in 1908. There was ideological antipathy to the idea of a government secret service. Hostility was particularly strong in the South, where the seceded states were gradually allowed back into the Union culminating in the completion of "Restoration" in 1877. The Secret Service moved back into the Treasury Department, where it remained, operating on an ungenerous budget with strenuous objections raised whenever it strayed beyond its original mission of catching counterfeiters.[15]

Potentially, then, there remained in the 1870s an opportunity for the PNDA to become a national, privately run crime-busting unit that looked after society's interests. Instead, it would engage in profit-making in the pay of wealthy industrialists.

CHAPTER 8

Labor Violence a New Source of Income

The Civil War changed the industrial landscape of the United States. With the agrarian-minded Southern states excluded from the Union until the 1870s, businessmen were able to pursue newly available opportunities, such as the displacement of much Mississippi river trade with a Chicago-to-the-Gulf Illinois Central railroad consolidation controlled by northern capital. Transcontinental railway construction proceeded with Chicago, not Atlanta, as its hub. Northern business protected its interests by securing tariffs on imported manufactured goods, a policy that had been anathema to the now-defeated South. The nation's industrial takeoff was obvious to all in the wake of the Civil War.

With the South temporarily dormant, an incipient challenge to business hegemony came from a newly militant labor movement. Labor shortages in the Civil War had strengthened workers' bargaining power, and wartime inflation had encouraged expectations of higher wages. Organized labor was far from being a revolutionary force. It had interests in common with the new capitalist class, for example regarding higher tariffs that protected jobs as well as profits. The National Labor Union, an attempt at national unification launched in Baltimore in August 1866, vacillated between the pursuit of economic and political goals. Nevertheless, some employers were alarmed at labor's challenge to their hegemony.

These developments prompted Allan Pinkerton to express his philosophy on labor–capital relations. In the fullness of time he did so at length, addressing an American audience. But it was in a missive to his former Scottish comrades that he initially—and seminally—expressed his views. On January 27, 1869, Pinkerton wrote a letter that would be published in the Glasgow *Sentinel*. This was four months before the stroke that had a debilitating effect on his physique and, arguably, on his literary reliability. He addressed the letter to Alexander Macdonald. Having achieved prominence as the leader of an 1842 Lanarkshire miners' strike, Macdonald was by 1869 president of the UK-wide Miners' National Association. He was destined to be one of the first two working-class individuals elected to the British Parliament. The *Sentinel,* with its socialist tendencies was the most widely read Scottish labor newspaper of the nineteenth century. It had campaigned for the abolition of American slavery and supported the UK franchise movement.[1]

Pinkerton's letter was an endorsement of labor unionism, a validation that might seem hypocritical considering its author's actions against workers' combinations over the years. The key to the apparent contradiction is that in the same letter Pinkerton rejected the "physical force" doctrine to which he had subscribed both in his Chartist days and in his espousal of John Brown–style abolitionism. In the letter he stated, "Capital has invariably preyed upon the labouring classes," so the "labouring classes have a right to organize." However, he urged his former Scottish comrades to embrace the "new idea" of arbitration. Pinkerton argued that the use of force, by which he meant strikes as well as physical violence, was a losing game for workers, as "the law will step in then, and the law will be powerful enough to suppress violence in the end." It was "scarcely possible" that he would ever return to Scotland or see his radical friends again, but he wished "to convey to them [his] ardent and strong sympathy with them, and [his] desire that the resort to force may, if possible, be avoided by all unionists in the future."[2] These views expressed by Pinkerton in 1869 would be repeated time and again in justification of his agency's behavior in the 1870s and thereafter.

In the event, labor relations in America as compared with other countries would not be characterized by violence to any exceptional degree. Allegations of violence were, however, frequent. They were sometimes based on reality, sometimes on ignorance, and often made for partisan reasons.[3] Allegations of violence would increasingly lead to the introduction of Pinkerton men. Such deployments were already observable by the time of Allan Pinkerton's declaration of philosophy. An example occurred when, in September–October 1866, coal miners went on strike in Braidwood, Illinois. The Pinkerton agency supplied the employers there with armed guards to counter alleged threats and violence by the striking miners—according to Pinkerton's sons, this was the first time the agency engaged in such work.[4]

In 1868, the Irish-born John Siney led a successful strike to enforce a recent eight-hour-day law in Schuylkill County, at the heart of the Pennsylvania's anthracite coal region. He and his fellow workers then formed a Workers' Benevolent Association (WBA) to promote sickness and death benefits and the arbitration of industrial disputes. Here, and in their belief that strikes were not anti-employer but a means to force up prices to the benefit of both labor and capital, the WBA's members followed the precepts of Pinkerton's correspondent Alexander McDonald. It was in disregard of the WBA's peaceful philosophy that the impending conflict in the coalfields came to be defined, in the public eye, by violence.

The extent of union violence was exaggerated, but such violence did occur. One example, as related by a source that was prejudiced yet well versed in local tensions, occurred in Shenandoah and Hazleton on June 3, 1875:

> Striking miners . . . openly threatened the destruction of some of the larger coal operations in Schuylkill County . . . strikers made elaborate preparations for a picnic and dance. . . . In the evening of June 2nd fires blazed from the hillsides surrounding the collieries. Seven or eight hundred persons attended the picnic . . . the county's roughest characters [each carried] as many as three revolvers. . . . A mob estimated to number three hundred from Hazleton and vicinity appeared in the neighborhood of Mahoney City early in the morning of June 3rd and stopped the men working [at a number of collieries]. . . . When [Pierce] Walker's mob reached Mahoney City, it numbered two thousand men . . . the rioters took over the city. . . . The collieries were all blocked and the workers sent home.[5]

A smaller but more extreme example of physical force occurred later that summer when James Gomer was tending bar at a charity event just outside Schuylkill County's Shenandoah Valley. Gomer was the son of Welsh immigrants. There were tensions between miners of Welsh heritage and those of Irish heritage, with the latter accusing the former of being complicit in a discriminatory Protestant ascendency in the mining regions. As Gomer dispensed drinks, his mother stood nearby, no doubt admiring her son's community spirit. Perhaps she did not realize that, having been acquitted of the murder of an Irishman, he was a marked man. A group of men walked up to Gomer's bar and asked for a beer. While he was drawing it, one of the men leveled a gun and shot him dead. The assassin melted away into the crowd. He was never apprehended. Such violence was diminutive on the scale of the recent Civil War's bloodshed in the Shenandoah Valley but was shocking nevertheless.[6]

Figure 8.1. Welsh miners attack an Irish workers' meeting near Scranton, Pennsylvania, 1871. From *Frank Leslie's Illustrated Newspaper,* this sketch runs counter to the Pinkerton narrative that blamed such disorders on a supposed Irish terrorist group, the Molly Maguires. *New York Public Library.*

A further fifteen men were killed in circumstances that arose from the coalfield conflicts, most of them in Schuylkill County. Six of the murders had already taken place when Pinkerton articulated his views in the *Sentinel,* the earliest case having been the beating to death of mine foreman F.W. Langdon in 1862. The killings continued until 1875, a year in which Gomer was one of a final six victims to be dispatched.[7]

The employers in the coalfields blamed these various incidents on what they said was a terrorist secret society run by an unprincipled "inner circle." That society was called the "Molly Maguires." Reblazing a trail cut by UK employers and one that future US employers would follow, the coal magnates equated terrorism with unionism in the hope of asserting their right to manage their businesses without heeding the demands of their workers.

So, who were the Molly Maguires of eastern Pennsylvania? Whoever they were, if they existed at all in the form outlined by their enemies, they left no trace of their identity. They would have been unskilled and, unlike their detractors who left an ample and biased record of events, they would have been largely illiterate in the English language. Their point of origin would have been Donegal and adjacent counties, an Irish-language speaking part of Ireland.

We do know a little more about the *name* Molly Maguire. In poverty-stricken Donegal and the surrounding areas, a group thus named was one of several that resisted rural injustice and foreign exploitation. A modified version of the 1832 Reform Act applied in the Celtic island as, following the Act of Union of 1800, Ireland had been governed by British laws. The terms of the Reform Act allowed only 90,000 propertied Irish men to vote—out of a population of well over eight million reduced by two million when famine and emigration took their toll. The Molly Maguires and other, similar groups arrived at a conclusion that should have been familiar to Allan Pinkerton—where there is no redress through democratic means, it is justifiable to resort to force. Aggrieved workers attacked stores, ploughed land that property owners had grassed over for pasture, and dug shallow graves for oppressors who sometimes ended up in them. By occasionally dressing as women, hence the "Molly Maguire" tag, the Irish Mollies conformed to a European agricultural tradition—emulated in Wales, for example, by "Merched Beca" (Beca's daughters), known in English as the "Rebecca rioters." The reasons for the cross-dressing are as obscure as the inner histories of such movements. Perhaps the aim was to frighten because, according to a rationale that then obtained, women are irrational and capable of anything. More probably, cross-dressing by European protesters was simply a means of disguise.

This brings us to the year 1873 in the United States. It was the year in which Pinkerton condemned the "'Stool Pigeon' system of England and America."[8] It was also a desperate year. A financial crash had spurred a panic that devastated many businesses. Pinkerton was forced to borrow to stay in business and mortgaged some of his properties. The economic downturn caused employers to reduce costs by squeezing workers and labor unions. It spawned desperate measures, including Pinkerton's resort to the "stool pigeon" practice he had only just criticized. In pursuit of restoring profitability, the PNDA would evolve an approach that might suggest an ideological turning point for a former radical. Yet the language used in one of its fliers is so reminiscent of Scotland's informer system as to intimate that there may have been some continuity and that Pinkerton remembered more than he chose to confess about the country he left behind:

> when there is so much dissatisfaction among the laboring classes and secret labor societies are organizing throughout the Unites States, we suggest whether it would not be well for railroad companies and other corporations, as well as individuals who are extensive employers of labor, to keep a close watch on designing men among their own employés, who, in the interest of secret labor societies, are inducing their employés to join these organizations and eventually to cause a strike.[9]

On May 18, Pinkerton confided to his firm's chief administrator, George H. Bangs, concerns about his agency's profitability at a time of industrial recession. He asked Bangs to approach Franklin B. Gowen, who was president of both the Philadelphia and Reading Railway and the Philadelphia and Reading Coal and Iron Company. By shrewdly manipulating freight rates for the transportation of coal, Gowen had made himself the dominant businessman of the anthracite region. At first, he had propitiated John Siney and the WBA. But, like Allan Pinkerton, he really belonged on the other side of the fence. In 1871 he had complained to the Judiciary Committee of the Pennsylvania State Senate that the WBA had organized "nearly the entire laboring population of the anthracite coal region" and that its aim was "to secure employment for all its members, and prevent the reduction of wages which every other class of labor had to submit to at the close of the war." Pinkerton saw Gowen as a likely client. "Suggest some things to Mr. Gowen," he urged Bangs, "about one thing or another which would be feasible and I have no doubt he will give us work."[10]

Pinkerton already had preconceptions about Gowen's labor problem. His detectives had been investigating dishonesty among Philadelphia and Reading Railway conductors since 1863. Early in 1873 they turned their attention to social disorder in Schuylkill County, where Gowen had suffered frustration when he worked as a district attorney during the Civil War and made little impact on the region's soaring crime rate. On October 9, following an apparent arson attack on a mine tipple in Glen Carbon a little west of Pottsville in that county, local Pinkerton superintendent Benjamin Franklin wrote to Gowen warning of "the rumored existence" of "a band of roughs" known as the Molly Maguires.[11]

The touch paper having been lit, Pinkerton and Gowen conferred. There is no surviving official record of what the two men said to each other, but Pinkerton recorded a version of the dialogue in his book *The Molly Maguires and the Detectives* (1877). His colorful paraphrasing was an indication of both the pitch he was making and the nature of Gowen's propaganda:

> Early in the month of October, 1873, I was in Philadelphia, and received a note from Mr. F.B. Gowen . . . saying that he desired to see me at his place of business. I immediately responded to the invitation, accompanied by Superintendent Franklin, and met the gentleman in his private apartment, in the [Philadelphia and Reading] Company's elegant building on Fourth street. [Gowen stated], "the coal regions are infected by a most desperate class of men, banded together for the worst purposes—called, by some the Buckshots, by others the Mollie Maguires. . . . sheriffs of counties are powerless, and the usual run of detectives are of . . . little value . . . Now, if you cannot disperse the murderous crew, or give us grounds upon which to base prosecutions, then I shall believe that it never will be effected . . . As far as we can learn, the society is of foreign birth, a noxious weed which has been transplanted from its native soil—that of Ireland."[12]

Gowen's ascribed remarks referring to the uselessness of other detectives may well have been the invention of Pinkerton or his shadow scribes.

Pinkerton accepted the commission to investigate the Mollies. He later offered a comparison, saying he "had heard of many assassinations by these Mollie Maguires, and also about those performed by the Ku-Klux and similar political combinations in the Southern States."[13] The US Secret Service had already assumed the police/detective function of penetrating the Klan, a goal accomplished with the help of local African Americans and of "pukers," Klansmen who informed on their own in return for lenient treatment. The Klan commission had afforded less opportunity for profit and would thus have been of no interest to the Pinkertons. (Nevertheless, one private detective, Captain Seymour Barmore, had earlier contracted to the governor of Tennessee to penetrate the Klan. He met a premature end with a bullet hole in the back of the head and a noose around his neck).[14] The Molly Maguires case looked more lucrative, as the well-resourced coal mine owners were willing to finance an anti-union effort. Pinkerton sent two detectives, identified in reports as S.M. and W.R.H., to Glen Carbon to investigate. This first initiative drew a blank. The locals had clammed up and would not talk.[15]

According to his memoir on the subject, Pinkerton had by this time told Gowen that he needed an operative who could penetrate the conjectured inner circle of the Molly Maguires: "He must be an Irishman, and a Catholic, as only this class of persons can find admission to the Mollie Maguires. My detective should become, to all intents and purposes, one of the order."[16] The word "order" referred to the Ancient Order of Hibernians, a charitable organization whose local chapters Pinkerton, Gowen, and their supporters held to have been suborned by the Mollies, in a similar manner to their alleged involvement in the by-now-ailing WBA.

Pinkerton found his man in James McParland. McParlan (he added the letter "d" to his name after arriving in the United States in 1866) was born in 1844 in Armagh, a county some distance from Donegal but just as liable to social turbulence—young McParlan's local priest had fulminated against "the assassin, who, unprovoked, and with cool and calculating premeditation, waylays his fellow-man, and sends the victim to an unmerited and untimely grave."[17] A bespectacled bachelor of average height with a slight stoop, red hair, and a florid complexion, McParland had several jobs in Ireland, England, and the United States before working for the Pinkertons between April 1872 and January 1873, and then rejoining in August 1873 to commence what would be a long career with the agency.

McParland was a Catholic whose slight accent, Pinkerton noted, "betrayed his Celtic origin," and made it possible for him to pass as a member of Irish immigrant society. McParland deplored lawlessness, especially when it was of a type that gave the Irish a bad name. There was yet another factor that would facilitate his mission. McParland was a prodigious consumer of alcohol. It was a habit that Pinkerton officially deplored. But it would be an advantage to McParland's inquiries that he was a "cold soak" who kept his wits about him when his fellow drinkers lost theirs and might confide their innermost secrets.[18]

Once he had interviewed McParland for what he indicated would be a major assignment, Pinkerton asked his candidate to submit an assessment of Molly Maguirism. On October 10, 1873, McParland submitted his report. He pointed to the Irish background of the Mollies, saying that they had their origins in secret societies dedicated to violence that had been formed to oppose the Protestant Orange Order in Ireland.[19] There had been a redistributive element to the societies' thievery at the time of the Famine. But they soon abandoned the idea of helping the poor and resorted to behavior "something after the fashion of the Ku Klux Klahn [*sic*], . . . shooting down Landlord's Agents Bailiffs or any unoffending neighbor who might not coincide with their views." He reported that in the United States they assumed a new name, the Ancient Order of Hibernians.[20] Later he was to modify that view, telling Gowen that the "Ancient Order of Hibernians had no affiliation, pro or con with the Molly Maguires, notwithstanding the fact that at times . . . the Molly Maguires had represented in a secret manner that they were really members of the Ancient Order of Hibernians." In all his commentaries on the Mollies, McParland insisted that the Catholic Church was steadfastly opposed to the Mollies' violence.[21]

Though he mentioned the oppression that originally spawned the Mollies in Ireland, McParland skirted the oppressive conditions in the anthracite region that helped history to repeat itself on the other side of the Atlantic. Miners suffered from uncertain wage rates, child labor, dangerous work, and poor provision for sickness and old age. Here the unskilled Irish immigrants had grievances in common with other miners who supported the WBA, but they also suffered from discrimination. The Irish had been imported to supply cheap labor. Established, English-speaking miners saw them as a threat to their wages and living standards. As the Irish saw it, established workers kept them out of good jobs, rich coal seams, and pivotal positions such as check-weighing, the assessment of the weight of coal coming up and how much the miner would get for it. McParland was not acquainted with these problems at the time he wrote his report. Historians who later had the opportunity to study the events of the 1870s came up with ever more sophisticated explanations of who the Mollies were, whether they existed and, if they did, what explained their violent behavior.[22]

Setting aside later insights acquired through historical research, McParland must have seemed remarkably informed and perceptive at the time when he submitted his report. Pinkerton saw the commercial advantage to believing McParland and, in any case, he had no other frame of reference for understanding the Mollies. He instructed McParland to enter the coalfields.

CHAPTER 9

McParland Tilts at the Molly Maguires

McParland spent the first two weeks of his new assignment in Philadelphia. There he constructed a new identity. Taking the name of a man who had sponsored his sister Rose for baptism back in 1835, he became James McKenna. Fleshing out this McKenna, he invented two lives, each with its own level of depravity. He designed the lower level to satisfy the generality of the local population. It made him out to be a disreputable crook, a man who fraudulently obtained a US Navy pension by claiming that he had been wounded fighting the Confederacy's Mississippi River fleet. The lower-level McKenna also claimed to be a counterfeiter, a profession requiring visits to Philadelphia to deal with his partners in crime—in reality, of course, to confer with Pinkerton and coal magnate Franklin Gowen about his anti-Molly mission. The pension fraud and counterfeiting stories conveniently explained the availability of the funds that enabled him to be so generous buying the drinks that would loosen local tongues.

The second life story was reserved for the conjectured inner circle of the Mollies once his first story had made him seem a promising recruit. This tale of higher-level depravity told how he had murdered a man in a Buffalo grain elevator and was now seeking to hide in the coal patches of Pennsylvania. The fact that he was already a killer was supposed to have a special appeal to the Molly leadership.[1]

Notably absent from the McKenna story was any suggestion that he was a union man. The omission helped the propaganda line that he was able to gain access to the Mollies' inner circle purely because of his projected image as a violent criminal, and not because he was a comrade in the struggle against the injustices of the local employing class.[2] Only when he attributed to the Mollies the motive of "revenge" did McParland hint at a deeper motive for his postulated opponents' alleged actions (revenge for what? Could it have been for employers' oppressive treatment and actions?).[3]

On October 27, 1873, McParland made his first foray into the anthracite region. Dressed as a tramp and traveling by train, he toured its communities and drank at the "shabeens," illicit drinking dens in private homes. When this approach yielded no result, he returned to Philadelphia. A change of plan was agreed. He would now abide in Pottsville, whose population of 13,000 made it the region's largest town. There he was to attempt to operate from within.

Once in Pottsville, he lodged at an East Norwegian Street boarding house run by Mary O'Reagan. One of O'Reagan's tenants took him to a tavern, Sheridan House. The tavern's proprietor, Patrick Dormer, was rumored to be a Molly. Undeterred by Dormer's imposing 6′4″ physique, McParland returned later the same evening and impressed by dancing an Irish jig, buying whiskeys all round, and singing the Donegal ballad, "Make Way for the Molly Maguires."[4]

At this and later encounters, McParland learned to issue recognition signals, for example by raising a glass to "the power that makes English landlords tremble."[5] Most of the examples he gave of such "goods" or passwords were hostile to the British government and monarch. For example:

Here is that every Irishman
May stand to his cause,
And subdue the British Government
And its coercion laws,

and

Gladstone's policy must be put down,
He is the main support to the British Crown.[6]

Such words conveyed a sense of general injustice, running counter to the Pinkertons' claim that an evil conspiracy brewed by a secretive inner circle accounted for grievances and disorder.

By March 1874 McParland had come to realize that not all violence stemmed from the Mollies. Assaults and murders could be attributed to any one of a number of feuding gangs. The Chain Gang, for example, was also known as the Kilkenny Men, indicating their origin in southeast Ireland and distinctiveness from rivals like the Mollies who were associated with Donegal and other northerly counties.

In addition to inter-Irish gang rivalry, there were also non-Irish gangs in competition with the Irish gangs. Gang grievances did not center exclusively on matters of ethnic status. They sprang, for example, from antipathies between competing fire companies. Ever since the Jacksonian era in the 1830s, such rivalries had produced disorder. Like policing, firefighting as a public service was in its infancy. Towns and cities would instead fund volunteer companies. These private crews would race to be the first at the scene of a fire and would sometimes be at each other's throats before arriving at their destination.[7] In Mahoney City in the 1870s the "Modocs" were a predominantly Welsh and Protestant fire company who operated in rivalry with an Irish Catholic company. On October 31, 1874, they engaged in their habitual brawl with the Irish when rushing to a city-center fire. A city burgess, George Major, tried to restore order and was shot dead. There ensued a trial, on a charge of murder, of one of the Irish company, Daniel Dougherty. On the basis of ballistic evidence, Dougherty was found not guilty.

McParland was not interested in combating all the factions that generated violence in the coal patches. His remit was solely to prove the existence of the Molly Maguires and their links to efforts to unionize the miners. By the time of the foregoing disturbances, he was lodging with an acquaintance he had made at Sheridan House's bar in Shenandoah. Proprietor Michael "Muff" Lawler ran this tavern. McParland was able to report that Lawler was a supporter of strike action. The Pinkerton spy told Lawler that he wanted to join the Ancient Order of Hibernians. Informed that he would need to get a job first, McParland became a miner. He now learned he would have to join the union, the Workers' Benevolent Association (WBA), to keep his job.

At this stage in his investigation, McKenna equated the Ancient Order of Hibernians with the Molly Maguires.[8] He aimed to be able to establish the link between the Hibernians, the closed shop, strikes, and the Mollies. The WBA had already been penetrated by other Pinkerton operatives. One of these, P.M. Cummings, had ingratiated himself with WBA leader John Siney and became vice president of that union's St. Clair local. Cummings reported that a former secretary of the branch, Thomas R. Nash, had murdered his stepfather, who was rumored to be a Molly. McParland, however, conceded that there was nothing to link the WBA to violence and that the union's policy was to expel known criminals. It was an inner circle within the "Body-masters" or leaders of the Ancient Order of Hibernians that he accused of directing a reign of terror.

In December 1874 the WBA launched on what became known as the "long strike." The WBA strike was a desperate response that was doomed to fail in the face of the tactics that Gowen employed. Anticipating trouble, Gowen had organized the coal mine employers into a united front that imposed a uniform reduction in wages of between 10% and 20%. The employers' tactics included the launching of a benefits scheme to undermine the scheme already run by the WBA, and the precautionary amassing of reserve stocks of coal in preparation for a strike. After six grim months, the strike collapsed. In the bitterness that followed, "coffin notices" were delivered to senior personnel at the Philadelphia and Reading Coal and Iron Company. These were crude images of coffins drawn on a sheet of paper on which was inscribed a threatening message. There were also attacks on property. Gowen exploited the upsurge in violence when he submitted "A List of Outrages" to a committee of the Pennsylvania legislature that was investigating his company. His list implied a link between the Molly Maguires and the WBA.

According to McParland's account, John "Black Jack" Kehoe had by this time commissioned the detective's alter ego, McKenna, to commit a murder. Just as every conspiracy needs an inner circle, so every inner circle needs an evil mastermind. In Kehoe McParland had found his man. When Kehoe finally went on trial, Gowen denounced him as "the chief conspirator, murderer and villain." He added rather vaguely that Kehoe was guilty less of the crime of "killing of the body, but the crime of the killing of the soul." He held that it was Kehoe, sometimes referred to as the "King of the Mollies," who had led the young men of the anthracite fields astray.[9]

Kehoe seems an unlikely candidate for the royal title. Born in County Wicklow in 1837, he had migrated to the United States with his family at age 13. Drawn by the coal boom, he settled in Schuylkill County and after working as a miner went into the tavern business and prospered. Six feet two tall with jet black curly hair, Kehoe was an imposing and charismatic figure. He was elected Girardville's high constable and was the leader of the Irish community in the town. What condemned him in McParland's eyes was his election to be the Schuylkill County delegate of the Ancient Order of Hibernians. McKenna got himself elected secretary of his local branch of that order, giving him the opportunity to socialize with Kehoe and watch him closely.

McKenna, having sidestepped his contract to kill, attempted to implicate Kehoe in Molly-attributed 1870s violence but failed. However, Kehoe then went on trial for a murder that had taken place in 1862. From Gowen's perspective, the story of the murder showed that the Mollies has been an insidious force for many years, explaining Gowen's failure to bring successful prosecutions at the time when he had been a local district attorney. The Kehoe story hinged on the fate of Frank W.S. Langdon, a mine foreman. Langdon's job was to check the weight of coal brought to the surface by miners and to separate dross from the real stuff, a task that did not endear him to workers who were paid by the weight of what they produced and who had their pay docked whenever Langdon decreed that some dross had to be removed from the scales.

Allegedly Kehoe one day addressed several expletives at Langdon, then said, "I will kill you before long because you are robbing me and robbing the men by your docking."[10] Not long afterward, on June 14, 1862, miners in Carbon County gathered to prepare for forthcoming July 4 celebrations. At the meeting Langdon denounced Kehoe, saying he had insulted the American flag. A group of angry miners responded by beating the checkweighman to death. At Kehoe's trial a decade and a half later, the prosecution used data painstakingly amassed by the Pinkertons, including the charge about Kehoe's threat to kill Langdon. The jury found Kehoe guilty of first-degree murder, and he was hanged at the Pottsville jail on December 18, 1878.[11]

By the time of Kehoe's arrest, "McKenna" had fled the coalfields. Kehoe had suspected McKenna of being a detective, and McKenna, according to his version of events, received a tip-off about this. His informant, Bodymaster Frank McAndrew from Shenandoah, indicated that Kehoe feared McKenna's testimony would "hang half the people in Schuylkill County." Within the Hibernians, McKenna demanded a trial before the Bodymasters of Schuylkill County. The request was granted and the date of the trial set for March 2, 1876. McKenna stated that Kehoe arranged for the Pinkerton spy to be dead before this event occurred. Alerted to these intentions and noting that Kehoe ominously had laid no plans to attend the trial, McKenna decided the time had come to board a train for Philadelphia. There he became once again James McParland, Pinkerton operative.[12]

By this time, the arrests of suspected Mollies had begun. Gowen had at his disposal a private force, the Coal and Iron Police, whose law-enforcement powers had been approved by a Pennsylvania legislative statute in 1866. This constabulary made the arrests in tandem with Pinkerton operatives, who supplied much of the narrative used as evidence in the resultant trials.

At the trials, defense attorneys charged that McParland had been an agent provocateur, encouraging murder and other outrages in a ruthless effort to tarnish the images of those who challenged the hegemony of Gowen and his confreres. A pro-labor publication in Pottsville protested that in the seven years preceding McParland's sojourn in the mining patches, there had been little violence, but during his two-and-a-half years undercover, eight assassinations were laid at the door of the Molly Maguires.

The evidence does not support the provocateur contention. However, McParland is open to another charge, of having been a silent harbinger of death. By his own admission he failed to give timely warnings to intended murder victims. In the case of two murders, he accepted he could have saved lives, but only, he claimed, at the cost of his own as he would have been exposed as an informer. A more severe judgement has been that McParland allowed himself to become "contaminated" by immersing himself in the criminal mentality of his chosen associates in the mine patches—and that he allowed the killings to take place in order to blacken the names of those who challenged the might of Franklin Gowen and his fellow coal barons.[13]

The alleged Mollies were subjected to unfair trials. The prosecution deployed well-paid lawyers who were employees of the mining and railroad companies. These attorneys secured the barring of Irish Catholics from jury membership. The judges allowed free rein to Franklin B. Gowen to express views in court that were prejudicial to fair trial, some of them converted into inflammatory pamphlets.

The trial of County Mayo-born Thomas Munley is a case in point. Munley was charged with being a Molly Maguire and with the murder of Thomas Sanger, a Cornishman and skilled miner who worked in a junior management capacity at Heaton's Colliery near Gerardville. Sanger received several coffin notices before being shot dead on his way to work along with a colleague who was killed because he had witnessed Sanger's murder. McParland admitted to knowing

Figure 9.1. An "eye" letterhead above a note covering the report of a Pinkerton spy operating amongst Pennsylvania miners in 1879. *Hagley Museum and Library, Wilmington, Delaware*

of the impending murder by Munley. But he took no steps to prevent it and was then a key witness at Munley's trial.

Disregarding such nuances, Gowen stressed the Pinkertons' integrity when he addressed the court during Munley's trial. He upheld the Pinkerton system of regular payments to detectives as a way of preventing provocations to murder: "The detective who operates for rewards, who is only paid upon his conviction of the offender, has a motive to incite him to action which I would be the last man in the world to arouse." Gowen announced that he knew from previous experience that the Pinkerton's National Detective Agency (PNDA), "established by an intelligent and broad-minded Scotchman," was trustworthy. Allan Pinkerton had assured him that the agent he would deploy against the Mollies would work only for regular stipends: "I will secure an agent or an officer to ferret out the existence of this society. Whoever I get is to be paid so much per week no matter if he finds nothing."[14]

A jury dominated by German Americans and containing no Irish took just an hour to convict Thomas Munley of first-degree murder. He was sentenced to death and hanged, one of 20 alleged Molly Maguires to suffer that fate.

A mantle of martyrdom settled inexorably on the memory of the executed presumed Mollies. In 1979 the state of Pennsylvania would grant a posthumous pardon to the so-called King of the Mollies, John Kehoe. In the following year, a new plaque outside Schuylkill County prison, located in Pottsville, justified Kehoe's pardon on the ground that it stemmed from "the judgement of many historians that the trials and executions were part of a repression directed against the mineworkers' union of that historic period."[15] The erection of the plaque followed in the wake of a movie, *The Molly Maguires*. In the film Sean Connery, a Scottish actor of part-Irish descent famed for playing James Bond roles, had taken on the role of Kehoe. Connery played Kehoe sympathetically, but it was a subtle performance that portrayed the alleged Molly as neither villain nor hero. It was this hint of guilt that injected power into the cult of Molly Maguire martyrdom. Behind the claims of injustice, there lurked intimations of an iron fist.

The historian Paul O'Hara has written that the Molly Maguires "seemed to exist because undercover agents said they existed."[16] The evidence about the complicity of the Mollies in the sixteen murders attributed to them is certainly unconvincing, not least because the literary abstinence of the accused working-class men meant that the court and posterity heard one-sided narratives. In the absence of contravening evidence, it was left to the employers, the Pinkerton operatives, and their supervisors to construct a version of what happened and of the Mollies' identity.

Allan Pinkerton developed a proprietorial interest in his version of events, which came to be ingrained in the Pinkertons' own identity. The first of several editions of his book *The Molly Maguires and the Detectives* appeared in 1877. That narrative impressed an array of sympathizers, including Arthur Conan Doyle of Sherlock Holmes fame who wrote a novel, *The Valley of Fear* (1915), that was based on the McParland/Pinkerton account of what happened in the 1870s.

The narrative was central to the Pinkertons' new antilabor raison d'être. So vital were the Molly memories to Allan Pinkerton's son William, that he took issue with Conan Doyle. William A. Pinkerton and Conan Doyle had previously been friends and had discussed the Mollies story. But when James McParland died in 1919, William gave vent to his feelings. He told C.V. Hatter, who headed the Pinkertons' Denver office, that Conan Doyle "had stolen the story of the Molly Maguires literally and published it as an original story of the Valley of Fear." He was indignant that Conan Doyle had depicted McParland (John McMurdo in the novel) as a heavy drinker. On another occasion he complained that his old, now former, friend should have had the courtesy to consult him about the text of the novel before using information that William had confided in him. William's complaints had an intensity that belied the ideological affinity between the Pinkertons and Conan Doyle. They show how Allan Pinkerton's legacy of having concocted a particular image of the Mollies was still sufficiently vital to be strenuously defended many years after the events of the 1870s.[17]

The Molly Maguire episode assumed a role in the iconography of US industrial violence. This was even though the Pinkerton narrative convinced neither a majority of Americans at the time nor historians in the longer run. When Pinkerton and McParland tilted at the Mollies it was not quite quixotic, as there was an undeniable thread of violence in the coal patches. But the two detectives did construct a largely fake image of labor violence. That became an ingredient in US antiradicalism—a great irony, for the Mollies (if they really existed) were Catholic and politically conservative in the American context, even if resolutely opposed to British tyranny in Ireland. Over the next two decades, the detectives and the employers continued to stress the violent conspiracy theme. It influenced American labor to steer a more conservative course than it might have in order to protect its respectability and command public support. This was part of Allan Pinkerton's legacy—as was the well-grounded perception, reinforced by dramatic future events, that the Pinkertons were antilabor.

CHAPTER 10

Inventing Anticommunism

Allan Pinkerton was an architect of what would be a defining feature of American life, anticommunism. To be sure, he is not always singled out as a leading progenitor of that phenomenon. Some historians see anticommunism as starting later, notably in 1917, the year of the Bolshevik take-over in Russia.[1] Yet one of Pinkerton's most prominent books was *Strikers, Communists, Tramps, and Detectives*, published many years earlier in 1878. *Strikers, Communists* did not make its mark on intellectual history. However, it was significant for its outreach. Pinkerton was an assiduous promoter of each and every one of his eighteen cloth-bound books.

In the days before radio, television, and illuminated billboards, leafleting was a prominent way of advertising. Pinkerton took advantage of his railroad contracts to organize the distribution of illustrated leaflets advertising his books, which sold affordably for between a dollar and one-fifty each. He arranged for such leaflets to be placed on train seats. Unsuspecting passengers who boarded trains departing cities all over the nation had to pick up the leaflets in the act of sitting down, and it would have taken a conscious denial of curiosity to ignore them. The leaflets sought to boost the reputation of the detective's works. They described them variously as "the best-selling books ever issued from the America press" and the "most wonderful books since *Uncle Tom's Cabin*."

Pinkerton backed up the leafleting campaign by supplying copies of his books to the news agents who plied their trade on trains. While distributing their newspapers, the agents would invite passengers to sample Pinkerton's writings. Some of his books were narratives bordering on fiction, for example *The Expressman and the Detective* and *The Murderer and the Fortune Teller. Strikers,*

Communists did not fall into this category, but the appeal of Pinkerton's thrillers enhanced the sales potential of his nonfiction anticommunist book.[2]

While the Molly Maguire episode had been an opportunity to depict labor unions as violent and undemocratic, the Mollies were neither revolutionary nor left wing. However, two other upheavals from the 1870s encouraged Pinkerton to equate, in *Strikers, Communists*, the triple evils of labor militancy, violence, and communism.

The first event was the Paris Commune of March 18 to May 28, 1871. When the Franco-Prussian War of 1870–71 exposed the weakness of the French government, working-class members of the National Guard who had recently defended Paris against the Germans seized control of their city and established a "commune." For a period of two months, the world watched as the Paris Commune experimented with the abolition of child labor, worker control of businesses, secularism, and feminism. Communist, socialist, and anarchist rhetoric fueled the experiment.

Pinkerton's account of the communards' "sanguinary reign" was a straightforward condemnation: "The city fell an easy prey to a horde of bad men, the worst of its vile elements, and human beings so devoid of all conscience, pity, or consideration, that it is hard to look upon them as possessing the least of human attributes. But this is the class, the world over, who are at the bottom of all troubles of a communistic nature."[3]

Pinkerton conveniently forgot that the real violence in the history of the Commune occurred during its repression. When the opportunity arose, France's chief executive Adolphe Thiers ordered the army to crush the communards. The army achieved this goal at the cost of thousands of lives. Thiers then oversaw the execution of a further 20,000 revolutionaries. As in the case of the United States, if on a vastly larger scale, the violence of repression far exceeded the violence of those who rebelled from below.

The communards had few sympathizers in the United States. Labor unionists, like the rest of their compatriots, looked aghast at the Parisian uprising. Pinkerton was attuned to popular feeling and turned that popular feeling to his advantage by fanning fears that communists might cause an upheaval in the United States. Pointing to the international reach of the communist theorist Karl Marx and to the existence of a branch of the Communist International in America, he postulated some alarmist conclusions.[4]

The second episode that agitated Pinkerton was the Great Strike of 1877. After the third of three wage reductions, railroad workers throughout the United States embarked on a series of shutdowns commencing on July 20 of that year.

They attracted widespread sympathy. For while railroads generated great wealth for the nation in the years of America's industrial take-off, they were natural monopolies. Prior to the age of interstate highways and of air travel, if you owned the tracks, you owned the people in the sense that you had power over consumers, workers, and neighborhoods.[5] Opposition to the pernicious effects of railroad hegemony was widespread. The crowds of 1877 who turned out to support striking railroad workers throughout the land were evidence of that.

In Maryland sympathizers demonstrated in support of Baltimore and Ohio Railroad workers who had refused to move freight wagons. Of the ten people killed when state militiamen opened fire on the angry mob in Baltimore, none were railway workers; all were there in sympathy. This was an alarming indication of the widespread nature of the unrest, leading to fears of a general uprising. Newspapers next focused their frenzied attention on events on Pittsburgh, where the Pennsylvania Railroad had its headquarters and extensive marshaling yards. There, militiamen drawn from the local population refused to shoot at the antirailroad men, women, and children who gathered in support of the strikers. The authorities therefore drafted in 600 alternative militiamen from Philadelphia, strangers who were more willing to use their bayonets and guns on 'Burghers. Their bullets having killed twenty, the ensuing revenge of the mob terrified America's propertied classes. Angry demonstrators torched and smashed railroad assets. By the end of the disturbances, 2,000 cars and 40 buildings lay in cinders, while 40 locomotives had been reduced to scrap metal.

The story of the uprising varied from city to city. In St. Louis, there was a general strike. In San Francisco, federal troops entered the fray on the command of President Rutherford B. Hayes. In Chicago, twenty died in disturbances. The events of 1877 conjured up memories, if in miniature, of the Paris Commune. Would America be prone, after all, to the social tensions that had caused so many people to find refuge on its shores?[6]

Pinkerton fanned such fears. But could he have been all that sincere? After all, he had aligned himself with the revolutionary wing of the Chartists, supporting the idea of proletarian revolt. His contemporary Karl Marx (1818–83), the inspirer of modern communism, similarly regarded the working class as the vehicle for revolution. Marx had, further, denounced religion as the "opium of the people," and Pinkerton was an atheist.[7]

Where once he had established his credentials with his Chartist comrades by adopting a revolutionary stance, by the 1870s Pinkerton endeared himself through his equally militant anticommunist rhetoric to a new set of comrades, to be found in the boardrooms of America's corporations. To a degree, he did so with an eye to advantage. But there is also the question of whether he had been a Chartist or a Chartist poseur. Perhaps his 1870s anticommunism was not so far removed from his view in the 1830s.

Writing of the Great Strike, Pinkerton left little doubt about the threat and its underlying cause. He emphasized

> the immediate connection of the Internationale, as the great international bodies of the communists are called, with our great strikes of '77. . . . On every railroad that was held by lawless men, in every city where violence reigned, and through every excited assemblage where law had been trampled under foot, this accursed thing came to the surface. If its members did not actually inaugurate the strikes, the strikes were the direct result of the communistic spirit spread through the ranks of railroad employees by communistic leaders and their teachings.[8]

There was, in Pinkerton's account of the communist menace, what might seem a puzzling inclusion. The Brotherhood of Locomotive Engineers, founded in 1868 with roots in the 1850s, was a benevolent society that doubled as a labor union. Its leader Peter M. Arthur and his colleagues presented the Brotherhood as a safe and respectable alternative to violent or radical unionism. In the aftermath of 1877 many railroad managers would come to see the Brotherhood as a stabilizing influence in their industry. Pinkerton took a radically different view. He wrote that while communists had been the instigators of "arson and murder" in 1877, "the great moral responsibility for the strikes and their vast train of disastrous effects is certain to rest upon the Brotherhood of Locomotive Engineers." It was an improbable charge. But a promise to crush unions, no matter how conservative those unions' tactics, was a staple of Pinkerton's business model and essential to his agency's profits as well as a reflection of his political beliefs.[9]

There was a notable omission from Pinkerton's tirades. In the 1870s there was a widespread tendency to link feminism and communism. Misogynists and others who opposed women's rights portrayed the feminists of the day as loose, communistic misfits who posed a threat to traditional American family values. For example, the celebrated journalist E. L. Godkin opposed socialism and feminism, arguing that the introduction of "sexual passion" into politics would lead to a "deeper and darker" corruption.[10] Because of the barbs directed against it in the 1870s, the American women's movement, like similarly besieged American labor, took a conservative turn. Feminist leaders agitated only for narrow, political reform.[11]

Misogyny cannot, however, be laid at the door of Pinkerton. He stood apart from those detectives who profited from family breakdown. Other detectives engaged in the divorce business with its opportunities for the paid surveillance of partners suspected of infidelity. Pinkerton and his agency eschewed all that. It may well have been out of respect for women. After all, Pinkerton had pioneered the hiring of female agents. By the standards of his day, his view of women was enlightened. It played no part in his anticommunist philosophy. It was in marked contrast with his expressed views on organized labor.

CHAPTER 11

Inventing Private Detection

During the last third of the nineteenth century labor work became a significant source of income for the Pinkerton agency. Yet flying in the face of that reality, crime detection remained at the heart of the Pinkertons' cherished and vigorously projected brand. Allan Pinkerton's vision of a private-enterprise detective who upheld the American principle of freedom of the individual and who towered morally over his corrupt municipal counterparts retained its vitality for decades—and lived on, eternally, in detective fiction and its media derivatives.

Pinkerton defined his invention, the virtuous private detective, when setting forth rules for his operatives in a pamphlet (1867, revised in 1873), *General Principles of Pinkerton's National Detective Agency*. The pamphlet painted an uplifting image of Pinkertonism for the consumption of potential employers and the wider public. The uplift was needed, for in some quarters, sleuths were poorly regarded. In the 1867 trial of a conductor on the Philadelphia and Erie Railroad, the jury refused to believe the Pinkertons' testimony that the accused had engaged in embezzlement. Judge John P. Vincent presided over the case. He observed that detectives were unpopular because they were mere spies and people did not like the "deception and deceit" that espionage involved. Judge Vincent's observation was in keeping with sentiments expressed elsewhere. A speaker at the 1870 meeting of the American Social Sciences Association opined that detectives were "moral scavengers."[1]

Allan Pinkerton's *Principles* extolled the virtues of private detection as a profession but also distinguished sharply between the probity of his own operatives and the delinquencies of his competitors. His tract elevated private over public detection. In the aftermath of the Civil War Pinkerton had called his enterprise the "National Police Agency," suggesting that he thought the whole of US law enforcement could be privatized.[2]

Pinkerton excoriated the French and English public police for pursuing only small-time criminals and for showing more interest in drawing their salaries than in doing their jobs. It was a strange point to make, as he also argued that his operatives were dependable precisely because they drew regular salaries—they were not mere bounty hunters who would do anything, perhaps even inventing evidence, to grab the reward some client might offer for the apprehension of suspects. Taking no notice of such subtleties, the opening sentence of his *Principles* hammered home the virtue of the private: "This agency is an individual and private enterprise, and is not in any way connected with, or controlled by, any Municipal Corporation or Governmental authority."[3]

Pinkerton's views may be compared with those of George S. McWatters, a detective with New York City's Metropolitan Police. Like Pinkerton, McWatters was born in Scotland, though he had then been raised in Northern Ireland before emigrating to the United States, where he studied law, dabbled in socialist-inspired cooperative living, raised a family of six children, and served with New York's police force from 1848 to 1870. In his 1871 autobiography, McWatters, like Pinkerton, spoke of criminal detection as a high calling and gave a similarly immodest account of the cases he had solved.

Unlike Pinkerton, McWatters believed that "society creates, for the most part, the crimes which it punishes." He blamed crime on America's swindling upper classes. When he used the term "railroad robbers," he alluded not to gunmen on horseback but to the businessmen who exploited their fellow Americans. McWatters stated that the police detective faced pickpockets and counterfeiters who had been made by the system. These criminals were often more intelligent than their oppressors. Police detectives performed the essential task of hunting them down and saving the nation from "anarchy." The alternative would be private vigilance committees with little experience of policing, who would "run riot themselves at last." In light of New York's Tammany Hall politics, one might conclude that Pinkerton was correct in saying that public police forces were susceptible to corruption. McWatters's account is, however, testimony to another form of corruption, that practiced by the rich, the very people who paid Pinkerton and other private detectives for their services.[4]

Pinkerton expected his detectives to "possess clear, honest, comprehensive understanding, force of will, and vigor of body." The expectation was consistent with his belief that "The profession of the Detective is a high and honorable calling. Few professions excel it." He declared that the good detective had to be able to keep a secret. A further requirement was that "he" (Pinkerton employed the masculine pronoun in an androgynous manner) should present regular expense accounts that were both honest and restrained. Pinkerton devoted two pages of his pamphlet, about a fifth of its main text, to exhortations against drink. His investigators did not need to be teetotalers, but it was the mark of a poor detective if they drank heavily.[5]

Pinkerton's ideal detective would be philanthropic. He subscribed to the view that the American penitentiary system failed to recognize the humanity of criminals. There should be a greater effort to reform and rehabilitate the nation's prisoners—"perhaps, if they could be taught some handicraft, whereby they might secure an honest livelihood." Pinkerton conceded that a detective's opportunities for reforming criminals were limited by the need to remain unknown to those whom they surveilled, "but kindness and justice should go hand in hand, whenever it is possible, in the dealings of the Detective with the Criminal." His remarks might be dismissed as the subjective words of someone who had defied Scottish law in his youth and was rationalizing his own criminality. However, they attested convincingly to his philanthropic instinct, an instinct that Allan Pinkerton's sons would inherit.[6]

Pinkerton claimed that "the character of the Detective is new."[7] Rarely are such claims to originality entirely true, and in some ways the Pinkertons were unexceptional. Edgar Allan Poe's *Murders in the Rue Morgue* had popularized the detective profession as early as 1841, the year before Pinkerton's arrival in the United States. The Pinkertons used a stylized image of an eye as a logo, and their slogan was "the eye that never sleeps." This was not novel initiative, for the "private eye" trope was already widely in use in the detective world. Yet Pinkerton's claim to uniqueness gained some traction in being so often repeated and publicized, and because the agency was a commercial success.

Principles was not a comprehensive guide to Allan Pinkerton's practices, or indeed to the principles behind them. For example, there was no mention of the agency's unwillingness to undertake divorce work. Pinkerton realized that his business depended on public respect—and other detective agencies that were beginning to make money out of matrimonial collapses were anything but respectable. Between 1867 and 1886 there was a 157 percent increase in the annual number of divorces, which reached 25,535 in the latter year. Private eyes offered to spy on errant partners and in several high-profile cases simply invented evidence of infidelity. The *New York Times* protested that because of perjuring detectives who were "the average of their order . . . innocent women would be put away and stamped with infamy."[8]

Divorce became yet more frequent by the twentieth century, but the Pinkertons still refrained from the associated business of tracking errant partners. That business remained a mainstay of other detective agencies. As late as the 1970s, when attitudes to promiscuity had softened and infidelity was less frequently cited as a prime cause for divorce, eleven out of thirty-five detective-agency advertisements in the Manhattan yellow pages offered "matrimonial" services.[9] Yet Pinkerton's axiom that principled private eyes did not take on that kind of work had by this time taken root, not least in fiction. Accused of indiscriminately taking on "all kinds of detective work," the iconic private eye Philip Marlowe retorted, in a 1944 Raymond Chandler novel, "Only the fairly honest kinds. . . . For one thing I don't do divorce business."[10]

Another omission from *Principles* perhaps suggests that Pinkerton's contempt for divorce work was not entirely a quest for respectability but may also have reflected a different facet of his character. Not in *Principles* but in later works, he discussed his policy of hiring female operatives. Snooping into extramarital sex more often aimed to liberate men, not women, from the matrimonial tie, and Pinkerton, who had been so devoted to his mother, was more sympathetic than many of his contemporaries to women's need for greater standing in society. In his 1875 book *The Somnambulist and the Detective*, he refuted the notion that it would be immoral for women to undertake clandestine detective work, which was "no different from that of any other position where women are thrown upon their own resources." Most "great criminals" confided in their wives and mistresses, and only female operatives could so befriend those women that they divulged their partners' secrets. The *Boston Daily Globe* noted approvingly that Pinkerton had "a good word for female detectives, whom he vindicates from the imputations made against them, and asserts that the profession for a lady possessing the requisite characteristics, is as useful and honorable employment as can be found in any walk of life."[11]

Pinkerton's high regard for Kate Warne had been evident from antebellum days. He placed her in charge of her own corps of female detectives and deployed her to good effect in several investigations. After her death in 1868 he arranged for her to be buried in the special plot at Graceland Cemetery, Chicago, that was reserved for his family. Such commemoration was important to Pinkerton, as it was to those who remembered the fallen on both sides in the Civil War—and would be to the CIA, which today commemorates those killed in the service of their country with anonymous stars on a dedicated wall at its headquarters in Langley, Virginia. In Pinkerton's will, filed on July 10, 1884, he left a sum to provide for the upkeep of the graves of the Pinkerton agency's chosen ones, in whose ranks Warne was prominent.

It is claimed that there is another side to this story. The historian Frank Morn wrote, "On several occasions critics, even within his own family, claimed that Pinkerton kept concubines and was having a love affair with Warne. After his death women vanished from the agency, probably because of the overt policies of his sons, who suspected their father's philandering." However, there is no documentation in support of such contentions about Allan Pinkerton's infidelities. Nor would proof of the allegation, were it to exist, detract from the conclusion that Pinkerton was in advance of his day—and of his sons—when it came to the practical implementation of women's rights.[12]

As to the principles that *were* enunciated in Pinkerton's pamphlet, his opposition to drink formalized a view that he often expressed about individuals. For example, he recorded a low opinion of George H. Bangs's fondness for alcohol. Pinkerton had talent-spotted this drinker in the 1850s, when Bangs was making a name for himself first as an investigative journalist for the New York *Era* weekly newspaper and later as a detective with the New York police. Bangs then worked as a Pinkerton detective and Civil War spy but, more importantly, spent the twenty-five years prior to his death in 1883 serving in an administrative capacity as the general supervisor of the Pinkerton agency.[13] When informers reported that Bangs had emerged from a saloon in an intoxicated state at 9 a.m. one morning in 1872, Allan Pinkerton wrote, "This thing has almost driven me mad. I feel like coming to New York to ask Mr. Bangs to tender his resignation at once."[14]

The archivist Jane Adler asserted that Pinkerton drank incurably himself and was a hypocrite when he condemned the habit in others.[15] There is no corroborative evidence of the former assertion, and perhaps Pinkerton, ever the pragmatist, was more tolerant than his words suggest. He lived in an age of temperance crusades, so his antidrink stance was politically advantageous and good for business. But he could be flexible when the need arose. George Bangs stayed in post. So did the "cold soak" boozer James McParland, who was allowed to exploit his drinking talents to trap alleged Molly Maguires into drinking themselves into a state of indiscretion. Pinkerton's sons in 1892 rewarded McParland with the directorship of the Western division of the PNDA.

Pinkerton's disquisition on the principles of private detection contributed to his legendary status and helped the PNDA's reputation to at least partly survive the labor scandals that dogged it from the 1870s on. At the time of his death in 1884 the media were in no doubt about the nature of those principles. An obituary in the New York *World* highlighted his policy of working for stipends, not rewards, and his refusal to take on divorce work.[16]

Pinkerton had invented an image of detection that, no doubt as he had intended, inflated his prestige. The American public feasted on a diet of adulatory biography and history, much of it first appearing in monthly journals. *Harper's* had published a biography of Allan Pinkerton in 1873, but the real spate of boosterism came after the detective's death. When the journalist Edgar Wakeman launched a series of syndicated articles about Pinkerton in 1889, the *Springfield Republican* aptly headlined it as a "Tribute Paid by an Ardent Admirer."[17]

In 1894 the PNDA gave Cleveland Moffett privileged access to surviving records. The Yale graduate and author wrote a series of articles for *McClure's Magazine*. They applied a heroic gloss to events like Pinkerton's thwarting of the assassination plot against Lincoln and the "overthrow" of the Molly Maguires, as well as recounting the stories of the thwarting of several bank heists.[18] In 1897 a selection of the articles appeared as chapters in Moffett's book *True Detective Stories from the Archives of the Pinkertons*. The focus this time was entirely on the cracking of bank and express company robbery cases. There was no mention of the Lincoln assassination or Molly Maguires—these controversial episodes were omitted in a book that played into the Pinkertons' strongest suit.

Yet by the early years of the twentieth century the Pinkertons were losing control of their image. The popularity of detective tales as a genre and the sheer proliferation of such stories made lasting control unfeasible, while the actions of the agency in labor cases remained an ineradicable stain on its reputation. The Chicago *Sunday Herald* had noted how the Pinkertons were supplying armed guards to employers and "largely supplanting the authorities in many of the departments of ordinary police work."[19] In a nation chronically opposed to standing interstate armies, the service that Pinkertons offered was controversial.

Those who approved of the Pinkertons by now emphasized Allan Pinkerton's conservatism. This literary tendency had the effect of strengthening the perception that he was no friend of working people. In 1905, for example, the journalist Charles Francis Bourke started a new series telling "the story of the Pinkertons" in *Leslie's Monthly Magazine*. His subtitle might have been mistaken for self-parody in light of the increasing number of biographies: "The History of the Most Remarkable Detective Agency in the World, Taken from

Original Sources and Now Told Comprehensively for the First Time." Bourke retold semi-mythical Pinkerton stories drawn from the usual repertoire. Strikingly, he subscribed to a myth about Pinkerton's father's occupation and from it drew the conclusion that the young Pinkerton was motivated by anti-Chartism:

> It will be interesting to believers in heredity to note that Allan Pinkerton's father was a sergeant of police at Glasgow. . . . [W]hile he was still a young lad, the "physical force" men of the revolutionary Chartists killed Sergeant Pinkerton. . . . The young Allan learned the trade of a cooper,—which some wag has pointed out is the next thing to that of a copper.[20]

The attempt to portray Pinkerton as a prolabor radical had all but disappeared.

Internationally, writings about the Pinkertons and their principles continued the adulatory trend. In an article on the occasion of Robert Pinkerton's death in 1907, the semi-official *London Gazette* expressed its admiration. It remarked that whereas in the UK "the private inquiry agent dabbles in the baser whirlpools of sordid wrongdoing," leaving serious detective work to Scotland Yard's public police, the Pinkertons had a higher strategic role and had "not touched divorce cases."[21] The Pinkertons' reputation would a few years later be reflected in Arthur Conan Doyle's *The Valley of Fear*, serialized in the *Strand* magazine in 1914–15, then published as a novel. Conan Doyle must have been aware of the agency's labor difficulties since the 1870s, but he still portrayed its performance against the Mollies in heroic terms.

By this time, Conan Doyle had staked a British claim for the invention of the *fictional* private detective (though Poe's much earlier detective, C. Auguste Dupin, had also been unofficial). Despite the dominance of public detection in the United Kingdom, the Irish–Scottish story writer made Sherlock Holmes, an English private detective, world famous. The Holmes mystique took hold in the United States. Conan Doyle's lone-figure detective stories helped boost the popularity of US monthly magazines and thus, incidentally, their capacity for influencing politics. The British author lectured widely in the United States and invested $1,000 of his earned fees in *McClure's Magazine*.

In December 1893 Conan Doyle published his story "The Final Problem" in *McClure's*. It introduced Professor James Moriarty, the Napoleon of crime. There followed a spate of articles in *McClure's* representing the captains of industry as Napoleonic figures. As the tides of Progressivism gathered strength, the Moriarty-style Napoleons became "Robber Barons." The era of the "muckraker" had arrived. The word—derived from John Bunyan's theological tract *Pilgrim's*

Progress (1678)—described journalists who penetrated veils of secrecy to rake up information about the misdeeds of businessmen like John D. Rockefeller and J. Ogden Armour. By 1902 muckraking in *McClure's* and its competitors was in full spate. Investigative journalists had assumed their status as private detectives acting in the public interest. The principles jointly enunciated by Allan Pinkerton and Conan Doyle had come full circle to be applied against precisely those big businessmen whose interests the Pinkertons had promised to serve. The private detective invented by Allan Pinkerton had contributed by accident to an unforeseen consequence.[22]

On a more censorious note, some scholars have asserted that Pinkertonism was at the root of a developing surveillance society. Proper accounts and reporting, two of Allan Pinkerton's cardinal principles, were prerequisites of effective surveillance.[23] The Pinkertons and their competitors in the private detective industry did saturate many a union with spies looking for evidence of disloyalty, militancy, and radicalism.

Workforce surveillance was not confined to Pinkertons and the like. Employers had other means of keeping tabs on their workers, ranging from watchtowers erected to oversee company-owned towns to the use of the stopwatch to ration work-shy bathroom visits—one of the many intrusive practices associated with the "scientific management" movement of the early twentieth century.

Furthermore, the credit assessment business, pioneered in 1833 by dry goods merchant Lewis Tappan (famous for his abolitionism) and then taken forward by R.G. Dun and company, furthered surveillance in a way that had nothing to do with Pinkertonism. Tappan and his later competitors undertook the surveillance of those who wanted a good credit rating. By 1880 R.G. Dun was gathering data on 800,000 traders.[24] It was a much more prevalent form of surveillance (and a more benevolent one) than that marketed by the Pinkertons.

The records that Pinkertons and their imitators amassed on workers did encourage the development of one particularly oppressive facet of American life. This was the blacklist. Spied-on workers suspected of union activity would be fired and placed on a roster, the blacklist, that was circulated widely among potential employers to deny employment to militant individuals. The invention of carbon paper—increasingly in use by the 1880s—enabled the more efficient dissemination of such reports, by now neatly produced on typewriters.[25] The blacklist would be another reason for the decline in popularity of Allan Pinkerton's real detectives, even as his concepts of private detection soared in American fiction.

CHAPTER 12

Jesse James as Robin Hood

A little girl hovered near the ticket office. It was September 26, 1872. Ten thousand people were enjoying a warm day at the Kansas City fair. Suddenly, the ground trembled under the child's feet. She heard the drumbeat of approaching hooves, just as three horsemen swept into sight. Their purpose was to make off with the day's takings at the fair. To deter any opposition, they fired a wild fusillade of gunshots. The little girl felt a searing pain in her leg. It is not recorded whether she ever fully recovered from the effects of the robber's bullet.

The three horsemen departed with less than a thousand dollars. Although they were never charged with the crime and officially their identities remained unconfirmed, it is universally believed that they were Jesse James, his brother Frank, and a confederate. The event commanded the front page of the *Kansas City Times*. Major John N. Edwards supplied the text. He wrote that the September 26 heist was "so diabolically daring and so utterly in contempt of fear that we are bound to admire it and revere the perpetrators." The event reminded Edwards of the fabled days of King Arthur of the Round Table:

> It was as though three bandits had come to us from storied Odenwald, with the halo of medieval chivalry upon their garments and shown us how the things were done that poets sing of. Nowhere else in the United States or in the civilized world, probably, could this thing have been done.[1]

Edwards had helped found the pro-Democrat *Kansas City Times* after his experience of fighting for the Confederacy. The major had sought out Jesse James in 1870, seeing in him a former comrade-in-arms who opposed the Radical

Republicans' imposition of pro–civil rights rule in Missouri. He had previously written to his sister that the South "must either submit to the greatest possible degree of social and political degradation, or appeal again to the sword." Jesse James either shared the sentiment or found it a convenient justification for his campaign of outlawry. When nobody believed his alibis for his bank robberies, he wrote to the *Kansas City Times* blaming them on the "degraded Radical party."[2] The outlaw appreciated Edwards's support, describing the *Times* as "a paper that has never been afraid to speak its mind on any subject, and to say a kind word even for a dog if he deserves it."[3]

To the James gang robbers, the little girl's injury was just collateral damage. For them, it was nothing new. To take another example of mindless violence, on February 13, 1866, the brothers had led a dozen horse-backed raiders in an attack on the Clay County Savings Bank, Liberty, Missouri. Their venture allegedly yielded $60,000 in cash together with other loot estimated to be worth $2 million (such post-robbery estimates were, however, chronically unreliable). In the course of the raid, an undisciplined bullet had killed a bystander, 17-year-old Jewell College student George Wymore.[4]

Jesse James wrote to the boy's mother saying how much he regretted the "accident." Celebrating that gesture more than a century later, *Boston Globe* scribe William A. Davis departed from the sectional trope and claimed James had shown "a sensitivity that contributed to his Robin Hood-like reputation."[5] The Republican President Theodore Roosevelt (1901–09) noticed the emergence of that new emphasis. He remarked on the similarities between American and English medieval "ballad growth," with "Jesse James taking the place of Robin Hood."[6] One such ballad contained the well-known lines:

Jesse James was a lad who killed many a man
He Robbed the Glendale train
He took from the rich and he gave to the poor
He'd a hand and a heart and a brain.

The image attached not just to the James brothers, but also to another band of robbers we shall discuss in more detail in a later chapter. The Sundance Kid–Butch Cassidy outfit operated between Texas and the Canadian border at the end of the nineteenth century. One magazine writer saw Sundance as operating in the "best Robin Hood tradition." When the Pinkertons helped hound Butch and Sundance out of the United States, the duo resumed their bank robberies in Brazil. There they were said to distribute, from their ill-gotten proceeds, "small sums to poverty-stricken Indians," in this way cementing their reputation as the "Jungle Robin Hoods."[7]

In truth neither the James brothers nor the Sundance crew were philanthropists. Even if they did give to the poor, as Jesse James appears to have claimed in a letter to the *Kansas City Times*, proof would be a rare thing—citizens are not in the habit of blabbing about stolen money they may have received.[8] If the knights on horseback did give to the poor, it may have been with a view to secure practical support or to buy witnesses' silence.

The Robin Hood myth testifies not to reality but to the unpopularity of the bankers, expressmen, and railroad companies that the robbers targeted—and to the detestation felt by many toward the Pinkerton men who served those big-business interests. Consumers, farmers, and urban workers could be forgiven for reasoning that their enemy's enemy must be their friend.

Glowing nineteenth-century depictions of the James gang in the long term prompted disapproving reactions. The *Kansas City Times*'s awestruck approval of gun-toting criminals and its lack of sympathy for an innocent child inspired reprimand in more than one biography of Jesse James.[9] In the aftermath of race riots in America's cities in the 1960s, the National Commission on the Causes and Prevention of Violence commissioned a historical study of violence in the American past. The resultant book's opening passage set the volume's tone when it quoted the *Kansas City Times* report of the 1872 James raid. It claimed that the raid and the canonization of its perpetrators were evidence of an ingrained, deeply regrettable trait of violence in the nation's character.[10]

At the time, nevertheless, the nineteenth-century depictions of the James brothers as heroes of the oppressed South or as Robin Hoods fighting the excesses of modern capitalism presented the Pinkertons with an image problem. Against the background of the bank robbers' depredations, the Pinkertons launched a moral counteroffensive. Allan Pinkerton was determined to appear in a superior light. He and his sons waged a propaganda war that would stretch forward over the years. Yet his campaign overlooked an incongruity in his philosophy. Where convicts were concerned, the Pinkerton family saw themselves as philanthropic criminologists.[11] However their views did not properly address motivations like Confederate defiance, a factor in the psychological makeup of the James brothers and other borderland bandits. The Pinkerton family's conviction that poverty caused crime and that vocational training could reform convicts had little relevance to the criminal careers of Jesse James and his brother Frank and even less relevance to violence arising from labor disputes.

The young Jameses were a poor fit for Allan Pinkerton's notion of good men being driven to crime by economic adversity. They experienced only relatively minor economic vicissitudes. Their father, the Baptist preacher Rev. Robert James, earned at least some economic reward as a farmer in Missouri. When Jesse was just a toddler he took off for California, a "forty-niner" who hoped to return with funds to pay for the boys' education. When the preacher died out West, his widow Zerelda remarried. Her new husband, Dr. Reuben Samuel, drew an income as a physician and was a farmer whose wealth could be measured in terms of the seven African American slaves he possessed.

In 1850s Missouri, as in neighboring "bleeding Kansas," slave owners and abolitionists struggled for ascendancy, and the Civil War started early. For some, the James brothers included, it never ended. It was war, not poverty, that brutalized the Jameses and helped to determine their post-1865 robbery targets. Both brothers were "bushwhackers." These were irregular pro-Confederate guerrillas who fought under the command of ruthless men like William Quantrill and "Bloody Bill" Anderson. Sometimes these poorly disciplined cavalry units dressed in a way that heralded the garb later associated with the Ku Klux Klan. Jesse was just fifteen when he took part in an 1863 massacre in the abolitionist stronghold of Centralia, Kansas. Close to 200 were killed. The safes of two local banks were incidentally relieved of their contents, a flourish that heralded the Jameses' subsequent vocation. Jesse witnessed other events not fit for the eyes of a man, let alone a boy, and when peace officially descended on the land following General Lee's surrender at Appomattox, Jesse and his brother were among those who never dropped the sword of rebellion.

Like others whom the war had traumatized, they may well have suffered from stress for which the only accessible antidote was further danger. The postwar anarchy in Missouri contributed to their disorientation. Confident of Confederate victory early in the conflict, the planter class had invested in war bonds and had agreed to make unsecured loans to further the cause. Because the North was victorious, those of the planter aristocracy who had survived the warfare of 1861–65 were economically ruined and in no position to heal society with cohesive leadership.[12]

The James brothers launched on their careers of robbing trains, stagecoaches, and banks. They teamed up with other rural gangsters, the composition of their gang varying over the years, depending on who had been killed and who was in prison. Their association with the four Younger brothers led by the oldest, Cole, would be an enduring one. According to James sympathizers, they preferred to rob banks owned by Northerners and Unionists. Given the war's ruination of

Figure 12.1. Jesse James in his Bushwhacker days, 1864. *Library of Congress*

Southern wealth, that meant that virtually all banks were legitimate targets. The notion that the Jameses targeted the new capitalist elite was a potent one in the competition for the sympathy of egalitarian citizens.

Various attempts have been made to catalog the Jameses' crimes and their takings.[13] Any narrative can be no more than provisional because of the denials of the perpetrators and the exaggerations of their victims. But the Jameses did steal enough to enable them to enjoy a luxurious lifestyle. They dressed in fine clothes, carried state-of-the-art guns, and rode expensive horses. Jesse, renowned for his piercing blue eyes, exhibited narcissistic tendencies. At the conclusion of a raid, he would rear his magnificent mount, fire shots in the air, and announce his identity in defiance of caution. Their supporters in Missouri sheltered the Jameses from arrest for seventeen years but did not save them and their confederates from every mishap. "I am not exactly a lead man," Cole Younger told the readers of his 1903 autobiography, "but [I] am now carrying over a dozen bullets which have never been extracted."[14]

Attracted by the prospect of retainers from express companies and banks, the Pinkertons entered Missouri in 1874. William took a contingent of half a dozen operatives to establish a branch in Kansas City. It took a brave and skilled sleuth to operate in Missouri's former slave districts in those bitter years of Reconstruction. John W. Whicher was the first to try. He arrived in James country disguised as a farm laborer. He asked naïve questions about the whereabouts of the wanted brothers. He found them soon enough when they ambushed him. They asked him why a self-proclaimed laborer had soft hands and carried a pistol with the Pinkerton emblem. A local journalist found Whicher's body on the road leading to the Blue Mills ferry on the Missouri river.

Next to die was fellow Pinkerton agent Louis J. Lull. He and his Pinkerton partner John Boyle were more experienced operatives. Under assumed names they posed as cattle merchants. Lull and Boyle had the misfortune to encounter the Younger brothers on a stony bluff called Chalk Hill. In an exchange of fire John Younger and Lull were hit, later dying of their wounds. Boyle fled unscathed. The scene was now set for a feud between the Pinkertons, who had lost two men, and the formidable James–Younger gang.

The PNDA had meantime embedded a fourth and rather more effective detective. Jack Ladd, alias Daniel Askew, had found work as a farm laborer not far from the James/Samuel property near Kearney, Clay County, Missouri, about an hour's ride from Kansas City. He ingratiated himself with Dr. Samuel and with his wife, the James brothers' mother, Zerelda. Ladd placed their house under surveillance. Its white walls and blue-shuttered windows would soon be famous for infamous reasons. James and Frank visited briefly, and Ladd reckoned they would be home again on the evening of January 25, 1875. The detective rounded up other Pinkertons to form an attacking force.

Unfortunately for the perpetrators of the deed that would follow—and for the reputation of the PNDA—the James brothers were absent from their mother's home on the evening of the 25th. Believing them to be present, at 12:30 a.m.

on the morning of the 26th the Pinkerton squad smashed the blue-shuttered windows of the dwelling place and threw two flaming missiles through the resultant apertures, possibly with the intention of illuminating the interior. The second of these exploded. The blast injured an African American servant child. It blew away one of Zerelda's arms. It killed Jesse James's half-brother, 8-year old Archie Payton Samuel.

Had Jesse and Frank been present, the public reaction might have been different. But they were not, and people interpreted the attack as an instance of the Pinkertons' violence against innocent victims. Stung by the outrage expressed in what he termed the "Conservative" Kansas City press, Allan Pinkerton adopted a defensive stance. His men had been "positively assured" of Jesse and Frank's presence. When her house had come under attack, Zerelda had "used anything but polite language." He implied that any assault on the house would in any case have been justified, for, he claimed, it was the location where "Whicher, my detective" had been kidnapped prior to his murder. He added that he was "disheartened" by his men's failure to apprehend the James brothers and did not know what to do next.[15]

There was no doubting the strength of feeling in response to the raid on the little blue-and-white house. The Missouri legislature, with former Confederates to the fore in the debate, considered a measure that would grant amnesty to the James and Younger brothers. The resolution's sponsor, former Confederate General Jefferson Jones, failed only narrowly to gain the majority needed to give forgiveness the force of law. The attack on Zerelda's abode remained a touchy subject decades after the event. In 1898 Robert A. Pinkerton listed the various murders laid at the outlaws' door. He emphasized a key point that the Pinkertons made in their own defense: "It has also been repeatedly stated that it was not a bomb that was thrown into Mrs. Samuels' house, but a cotton ball saturated with turpentine or some combustible, which, on being thrown onto a hot fire-place, caused it to explode."[16] That exculpatory version of events took hold in some quarters and according to one report Frank James agreed with it. But what one New York newspaper called the story of "That Sad Old Bomb Fake" never quite faded away, testimony to a widespread desire to believe the worst of the Pinkerton Agency.[17]

Encouraged by public sympathy, the James brothers resumed operations. Their successful evasion of the Pinkertons was not a good advertisement for private policing, especially when compared with the effectiveness of the US Secret Service which, by 1872, had wiped out the Ku Klux Klan and similar night riders who had sought to revive racist mores in the Southern states. When luck turned against the Jameses, it was not because of the efforts of the PNDA.

In 1876 Jesse and Frank teamed up with their old partners, the Younger brothers, in an attempt to rob the First National Bank in Northfield, Minnesota. It seemed to be a good target for the erstwhile confederate raiders. Cole Younger, the oldest of his brood, had heard that Benjamin Butler was making a substantial deposit of funds in the bank. Butler had been a major general in the Union army. In Congress after the war, he led the successful impeachment proceedings against President Andrew Johnson, who had shown sympathy for the predicament of white southerners in the early years of Reconstruction. Congressman Butler was also responsible for the (anti-) Ku Klux Klan Act of 1871 and had co-sponsored the Civil Rights Act of 1875. Ben Butler's money seemed a rightful target.

The population of Northfield was mainly Swedish American and firmly Unionist in political persuasion. When the James–Younger boys and their confederates rode into town with their Southern accents and fine horses, they stood out a mile. The elegant equestrians fired a bullying fusillade. But the citizens of Northfields were well armed. They opened up from behind windows and other concealed positions. Cole Younger later gave his account of proceedings: "The street was full of flying lead, coming from all directions. . . . Dr. Wheeler, from an upper floor of a hotel, got a bead on [fellow desperado] Miller, so that he soon lay dying in the middle of the street." There were mortalities on both sides. Only the Jameses escaped.[18]

Jesse and Frank laid low for a while before resuming their career by robbing a train in Glendale Station, Missouri. That was in 1879. Two years later they once again killed, shooting two men who got in their way. The climate of opinion was by now changing. Residents of the "Show Me" state had not suddenly become fans of the PNDA, but they were tiring of disorder and carnage. Governor Thomas Crittenden defied residual sympathy for the Jameses and put a reward of $5,000 each on the heads of Jesse and Frank. Jesse was by this time living in St. Joseph, Missouri, using the alias Howard. A former gang member, John Ford, visited Jesse on April 3, 1882. He shot his comrade in the back as he was hanging a picture. Ford then collected the reward. He would forever be remembered by a line in the ballad, "Jesse James":

That dirty little coward
That shot Mr. Howard
Has laid poor Jesse in his grave.

Six months later, Frank James gave himself up. He told the journalist Frank O'Neill, "I am tired of this life of taut nerves and night-riding and day-hiding, of constant listening, for footfalls, cracking twigs and rustling leaves and creaking doors; tired of seeing Judas in the face of every friend I know."[19]

Frank James went on trial in Missouri on a charge of murder. The jury acquitted him. Removed to Huntsville, Alabama, he was tried for armed robbery and again acquitted. Returned to Missouri, he again faced a charge of armed robbery, but the jury's verdict was the same. He lived out the rest of his life in a quiet and orderly manner.

Public sympathy of a different quality was present in the later treatment of the Younger brothers. At first escaping Northfield empty-handed, they had been caught and, in the ensuing gunfight, captured. Pleading guilty to avoid being hanged, they received life sentences. After 22 years in the Minnesota state penitentiary, the legislature in St. Paul considered an amendment to the prisoner parole act that would have led to the release of Cole and Jim Younger, their brother Bob having already died in prison. The move sparked some comments that would have pleased Allan Pinkerton. A Chicago journalist argued that prison should be a means of correction, not punishment.[20] When parole was duly granted, a former Minnesota state attorney general agreed: "Reformation is now accepted as one of the most important objects to be achieved in dealing with offenders."[21]

The Youngers had been unfortunate in being arrested in Minnesota, where there was no pro-Confederate feeling. In other parts of the nation, the Robin Hood interpretation of Jesse James and his ilk had greater appeal. It is at this stage that we can again address the question, was Jesse James a latter-day Robin Hood?

In England Robin Hood had many incarnations in and after the thirteenth century. According to a recent study he did not exist as a physical entity. The closest fit was "a Yorkshire outlaw called Robert of Wetherby [who] was hunted down by a group of men employed by a former sheriff of Nottingham and financed by the government of King Henry III."[22]

There is no evidence that, as in countless pieces of folklore, a real Robin Hood gave money to the poor. The Robin Hood myth is encapsulated in the words of an English historian: "What matters is that one of England's most popular literary heroes is a man whose endearing activities to his public were the robbery and killing of landowners, in particular church landowners, and the maintenance of guerilla warfare against established authority represented by the sheriff."[23]

We can talk in terms of two Jesse Jameses. The first was all too real, a callous thief and murderer molded by his terrible experiences of a civil war and by social calamity on Missouri. The second was a figment of literary imagination. As Teddy Roosevelt remarked, there was an Anglo-American similarity in "ballad growth." And it was not just ballads. Jesse James inspired just as many hagiographical biographies as Allan Pinkerton.[24] As in Pinkerton's case, James was a favorite topic for the dime novelists of the late nineteenth century—there was even a book series called *The Jesse James Stories: A Weekly Dealing with the Detection of Crime.* James has been a favorite of movie makers since 1908. The title of one 2007 film indicates where sympathies still lay: *The Assassination of Jesse James by the Coward Robert Ford.*[25] According to many a fictional reconstruction, Jesse James was a latter-day, wealth-spreading Robin Hood. The Pinkertons thus failed on three counts. Their criminological philosophy left no room for comprehension of the sectional underpinnings of the bandit's violence. They failed to lay a hand on the real Jesse James. And in the battle for American sympathy, they came off second best to the Jesse James incarnation of the Robin Hood myth.

CHAPTER 13

Death of the Founder

The stroke that Allan Pinkerton endured in 1869 affected an entrepreneur in his prime. His family and his firm played down the episode's significance not just out of a desire for privacy, but also because it would have been bad for clients' confidence in his business to admit that its presiding genius had been disabled. Details of the misfortune and of Pinkerton's recuperation are therefore hard to confirm. However, historians who dismiss the stroke as a minor episode do appear to have taken the family version of events at face value. Pinkerton was paralyzed down his right side and unable to speak for a year. He would forever remain prone to shaking fits, especially when upset or angry, and his handwriting was now a spidery testament to the pain he still endured. However, the determined convalescent took to walking, short distances to begin with, then several miles a day, to improve his condition. To a degree he succeeded. While he was no longer able to stand for hours dictating letters in faultless prose, he did author missives that enabled him to rule his professional domain, and he supplied his shadow writers with the information on which his several books were based.[1]

The psychological impact of his stroke is a matter for speculation, but it must have been real. Pinkerton did become more irascible and intolerant. His responses to the Molly Maguire and Jesse James challenges were not inconsistent with his prestroke philosophy and reflected his drive to succeed commercially. Yet in his treatment of these opponents there may also have been a strain of vengeful extremism that was absent in the first half-century of the founder's existence.

Allan Pinkerton's life in the 1870s was enriched by his purchase of a summer estate. The decision made sense as an aid to recuperation. It also signaled that the ailing entrepreneur was conspicuously displaying his wealth in a manner typical of the Gilded Age. Finally, it reflected the desire of a recovering invalid to prove that he was still a force to be reckoned with.

Pinkerton had already bought from the Illinois Central Railroad a 254-acre tract of land near Onarga, Illinois. There, in 1873, he built a plantation-style "Villa." Square in shape with an all-round veranda, it was surmounted with a cupola and shaded by a grove of larch trees, 85,000 of which he had imported from Scotland to remind him of home. Beyond lay outbuildings at the heart of a landscaped farm with rolling lawns and thoroughbred livestock.

The development, management, and use of The Larches became a source of pride for the recuperating detective. Its smartly dressed African American servants, its resident Scottish artist imported to paint Civil War and Scottish historical scenes, its extensive agricultural staff, all demanded and received Pinkerton's loving attention. So did the armed guards stationed at strategic points strung between the decorative pond and the wine pavilion—a sign of Pinkerton's anxiety that he might be assassinated in retaliation for his Molly Maguire crusade. By private Pullman car running on the Illinois Central line that bisected the estate, a procession of influential men arrived to be feted and courted. They included President Ulysses Grant, Chief Justice Salmon P. Case, and former Secretary of State William H. Seward, as well as uber-capitalists like Henry Sanford of the Adams Express Company and railroad magnate Cornelius Vanderbilt. The Larches was a relaxed counterpoint to his Chicago office, itself recently rebuilt in the aftermath of the fire, which was all about business and visually dominated by a single picture of "The Eye."[2]

Meanwhile, Pinkerton's urge to control his offspring verged on the tyrannical. His feminism evaporated in the case of Joan, the second of his daughters to carry that name and the only one to survive. In the summer of 1876 the 21-year-old Joan, a favorite whom he addressed as "Pussy," fell in love. William Chalmers was like herself the offspring of a Scottish immigrant who had made good in America. William became a regular caller at the Pinkertons' Chicago mansion at 554 West Monroe Street. But when it dawned on Pinkerton that he had a rival for Joan's affections, he dispatched her on a tour of Europe. He fondly imagined that this would blunt her liking of a young man whose intellect Pinkerton thought was distinctly inferior to his own. The opposite occurred. On her return to Chicago, Joan asked her father for permission to marry William Chalmers. Pinkerton refused that permission.

A sulky truce ensued. Then one bitterly cold night matters came to a head. On the evening of January 19, 1877, Pinkerton went to bed at his accustomed hour of 8 p.m. At 1 a.m. the next morning, three hours before his usual rising hour, he heard sounds that caused him to creep down to the living-room to investigate. There he found Joan and William ensconced together on a sofa. The furious father ejected William and barred him from future visits. The defiant daughter said she would marry William anyway. Pinkerton retorted that he would not attend the wedding. Joan thereupon walked out of the family home.

When Joan left she had to find somewhere respectable to stay. Robert, the younger of her two brothers though still nine years her senior, took her into his New York home. He tried to act as a peacemaker. His diplomacy succeeded up to a point, for when Joan's mother (also Joan) fell ill under the strain of the rift, the rebellious daughter returned to Chicago. This was not enough for Allan Pinkerton. He refused to mellow and continued to vent his spleen, which by now was taking on the whining tone of self-pity. He wrote to Robert noting the presence of Joan at her mother's side, saying she looked "pale" but claiming she would soon return to her senses. The unforgiving tyrant reminded his son (as he did with unsparing regularity) what a struggle life had been for his parents. He recalled the time when he had moved back to Chicago from Dundee: "there 'Pussy' was born many children we lost by death, until only William, 'Pussy,' and yourself were left." He instructed Robert to "look back and think what trouble you have given your mother and me." Unable to control his anger at Robert for taking in Joan, he ordered his son to cease communicating with him on private matters. In future Robert was to write only about official business and should address his letters to the agency's Chicago office.[3]

Undeterred by all this, Joan did marry William. She gave birth to two children and became a society hostess in Chicago. In defiance of Pinkerton's misdirected scorn, William became a successful businessman through the family's Fraser and Chalmers engineering company. In the early years of the twentieth century the company, now known as Allis-Chalmers, hired private detectives in their determined effort to counter the rise of a labor union, the International Association of Machinists.[4] Joan's rebellion had been not against her father's values but against his control.

Outside the family Allan Pinkerton retained, into his final years, some of the feminist principles of his younger days. In 1880 he wrote to his superintendent George Bangs strongly urging him to hire a female detective. Possibly because of ill health, Bangs, who would die in 1883 at the age of 52, had been slow to take that step. Pinkerton stipulated the kind of woman he had in mind. His description might have fitted Kate Warne in the 1850s—unmarried or a widow, discreet, of average height and appearance, dark hair ("I don't think a blonde would do"), and capable of "assuming a character." Pinkerton's faith in women's expertise was more than an unconsciously remembered infatuation. Two years later, he wrote to the UK's prime minister, William Gladstone, offering to help track down Fenian assassins and explaining that he would deploy "men and women."[5]

Inside his family, Pinkerton continued to rule not just his daughter but also his sons' business careers. He vetoed new ideas offered by Robert and his older brother William and would not afford them the means to try their hand at an alternative line of business.

By now in the penultimate year of his life, Allan asserted his authority when visiting his son Robert in New York. Robert surprised his father with the news that he proposed to leave the agency. He had received an offer to go into partnership with a certain Richard O'Connor, who, he explained, had valuable connections with the local police. Allan Pinkerton hated the idea. He took steps intended to direct proceedings even from the grave. In his will as well as through prior direction, he required his sons to carry on the family business. This inconsistency in the cult of the self-made man was by no means confined to Allan Pinkerton. Fathers who boasted of having fought their way to the top through hard graft and superior ability routinely denied their offspring the privilege of a similar ascent and sought to confer on them the sometimes-unappreciated fruits of paternal labor.

Once back in Chicago the senior Pinkerton wrote to reiterate his opposition to Robert's plan for independence. He opened with yet another recapitulation of family history and tribulations. He reminded Robert of his personal virtue: he never squandered money "nor do I drink." The PNDA was a family business, built up to be cherished: "The name of Pinkerton shall always be connected with the detective business and shall be in existence long after I am dead. Pinkerton's Agency is bound to stand, its reputation is too well built and has too firm a foundation. Its principles and rules are well defined."

Robert should be aware that "Dick" O'Connor was the kind of man who was likely to betray his ideas to the competition. The father insisted that it was mandatory that Robert should remain in the agency with his brother "Willie" to protect what Allan Pinkerton had achieved. The outcome was that Robert stayed on, as his father wished.[6]

In the late spring of 1884 Allan Pinkerton slipped on a sidewalk. As he fell, he bit his tongue. Gangrene set in. The 65-year-old showed his usual determination to prevail, but his hitherto resilient body this time did not respond. He began to drift in and out of consciousness. By mid-June, it was evident he was

Figure 13.1. William A. Pinkerton and Robert A. Pinkerton. *Library of Congress*

not going to recover. The family gathered at 554 West Monroe Street. When he died on the first afternoon of July, his son William was at his side, as was his daughter Joan, decorously referred to in the obituaries as Mrs. Will Chalmers.

The atheist's body was laid out in the double parlor room of the family home. There were extravagant floral displays, including a bank of white flowers with forget-me-knots interlaced to spell the name "Allan." The coffin was silver-plated and draped in black velvet. A heavy silver plate bore the inscription, "ALLAN PINKERTON. Died July 1, 1884."

There was no church ceremony. Lawyer and family friend Luther Laflin Mills read out a lengthy eulogy to the assembled mourners. According to a later press account, Allan's widow Joan remained a Christian, yet had been "unable to attach herself to any particular church."[7] She nevertheless was an admirer of the Rev. Dr. Thomas—whom she entrusted to read from the "family Bible" at the celebration that substituted for a religious service.[8]

Upon completion of the commemorative rituals, a cortege of several carriages accompanied Allan Pinkerton's hearse to Graceland Cemetery on Fair View Avenue. It halted at a well-kept lot identified by the inscription, "Pinkerton's National Police Agency." In the southwest corner of the plot were two graves. Plaques identified their occupants, "Timothy Webster, the patriot and martyr" and "Kate Warne, . . . superintendent of the female detective department . . . a brave, true, woman, and possessed of rare merits." In the main section of the plot lay seven deceased members of the Pinkerton family, now joined by the remains of the dynasty's founder.

According to a Chicago dispatch to the *New York Times*, Allan Pinkerton left an estate of £100,000, having spent "a large sum in maintaining a luxury in the shape of a model farm some miles south of this city." Another New York newspaper put the annual cost of maintenance at The Larches at $10,000.[9] In the era that Mark Twain labeled "The Gilded Age," evidently it was necessary to explain away relatively modest inheritances in terms of the extravagance of the deceased. In reality, however, the sums Allan Pinkerton bequeathed were more ample. When his widow Joan, crippled by rheumatism, died at her daughter's house on Ashland Avenue in January 1887, her estate amounted to $300,000, consisting of Chicago real estate and two farms, as well as liquid assets.[10]

Pinkerton's will left Joan comfortably well-off, but that was not all. It also provided for the long-term upkeep of the Graceland cemetery. Pinkerton made provision for George Bangs's widow to receive a pension of $15 a week. To his daughter Joan, Pinkerton bequeathed the royalties from his books. Perhaps he wanted to concentrate her attention on his directive philosophy, or perhaps he did not expect husband William to provide for her properly. The books did continue to sell well, but William's business success meant she did not need the money. Insistent though he may have been on the professional promotion of women, Pinkerton gave Joan no share in his agency. There is no evidence that she would have wanted that. He conferred the PNDA, the chief source of his wealth, equally on his sons. Robert took charge of the New York office, where he was already working. He administered the eastern division of the agency. His older brother managed the Chicago headquarters and the agency's remaining operations.[11]

In the United States, there were numerous obituaries of and tributes to Allan Pinkerton.[12] They observed the convention, speak no ill of the dead. Nevertheless, what they chose to include and omit is of interest. They still remembered his claim to a radical past. There was praise for his Chartist and abolitionist principles, and for his saving of Lincoln from assassination in 1861. He was credited with upholding the law, yet also with a criminal past—fleeing the authorities in Scotland and contributing to the Underground Railroad in Chicago. In its garnished account, New York's reform-minded *Sun* newspaper justified Pinkerton's pursuit of the James brothers by saying that Jesse James was out to assassinate him. It explained his demolition of the "Molly Maguires" saying that they were a "band of murderers." The paper praised his promotion of Kate Warne.[13] If they had been so inclined, readers might have looked in the contemporary press for references to Pinkerton's campaign against organized labor. They would have found none.

CHAPTER 14

Odyssey of the Sons

As William and Robert Pinkerton embarked on the journey that now lay before them, they brought different personalities to the task. William, whose imposing 200-pound frame and emphatic black mustache made him impossible to miss in a crowd, had been his father's least respected surviving offspring. Allan kept him working in Chicago, where he could keep an eye on him. Yet William was in some ways quite like Allan Pinkerton. When William died in Los Angeles in 1923 leaving an estate of $15 million, the *Buffalo Evening News* echoed a widely held sentiment in saying "his life story has in it all the thrill and color of the dime novel." The *Kansas City Times* recalled that Allan Pinkerton had in the Civil War used his 15-year-old boy to carry messages through enemy lines:

> "They used to write the messages on tissue paper which I hid between my toes," he related in later years. "If I feared capture I could wiggle my toes into the soil and lose the messages."
>
> "Couldn't your father have given those dangerous errands to someone else?" he once was asked.
>
> "My father wasn't the kind of man to try to get anybody else as long as he had a son of his own," was the reply.[1]

"Big Bill" Pinkerton briefly attended Notre Dame University at the war's end and took some business courses in Chicago, but he was much more an on-the-ground detective than a bookworm. Known as "The Eye," William was a keen observer and an action man. For example, still aged only age 22 in 1868, he captured the notorious Frank Reno and his gang after they had looted trains and banks in Iowa.

Allan Pinkerton fretted because William frequented saloons where he mixed with low life and the betting fraternity. Beyond his gaze, William was learning quickly at the university of life, but the anxious father took him to task for his bibulous inclination. He had himself "taken a drop now and then" until the age of forty, he confessed to his son, and it had made him cantankerous. William must have wondered whether giving up the drink had made his father even more difficult. He took no notice and continued with his accustomed lifestyle. In vain did Allan Pinkerton complain to Robert about his brother's excessive drinking and keep William in Chicago under his watchful eye. He could not understand that William sought the society of friends because he needed their companionship.[2]

Though William was not a committed administrator, his talent with people was an asset for the agency. In 1872, he visited Europe in pursuit of a band of robbers who had burgled the Third Bank of Baltimore. His father fretted when stories filtered home about William having a grand time and sampling local beverages. Yet during the visit William established contacts in France's *Sûreté* and in Scotland Yard, the kind of recognition that his father craved even as he denounced public police forces. After Allan Pinkerton's death, William would prove to be a continuing public relations boon for the PNDA.

In August 1907 Robert A. Pinkerton boarded the steamer *Bremen* to attend his daughter's wedding in Germany. In the course of the voyage, he suffered heart failure. There was a subdued tone to some of the obituaries: "not a spectacular detective," not a "dime novel" hero.[3] Robert's talents lay in administration and empire-building. Unlike his father and his brother, he had little contact with working-class people and would steer the PNDA on a direction of travel that brought it onto conflict with labor. He systematized the approach to strike breaking that his father had pioneered.

Robert's experiences of the Civil War had been less dramatic than his brother's but instructive nonetheless. A biographical note in the Pinkerton records states that he "served in the United States Secret Service, Department of the Gulf, from 1864 till the close of the Civil War."[4] At the age of fifteen Robert therefore experienced his father's profession—and witnessed Allan's pretensions to be still involved in an official secret service. It was not a dangerous assignment, and at war's end he was packed off to study—more assiduously than his brother—at Notre Dame. He then served an apprenticeship under George Bangs at the New York office of his family's firm. By 1874 he was beginning to annoy his otherwise doting father by pressing for new offices to be opened in New Orleans and San Francisco even amid an economic depression.

The empire-building Robert exploited opportunities to expand into the armed guard business. Seeing profit in horse and dog racing, he began to supply security at racing tracks. He took a similar approach to industrial relations. He was at his father's side during the Molly Maguire operation and one of the few who were privy to McParland's secret identity and activities. Robert Pinkerton asked his "detectives" not just to infiltrate the ranks of labor unions but also to carry rifles in the cause of employers.

Freed of his father's cautious restraints in 1884, Robert set about achieving expansion. Summing up his career in 1907, the *Chicago Examiner* characterized him as a Sherlock Holmes for whom the "world of crime was a chess board." He was a man who "held himself somewhat aloof from the throng [and] affected none of the haunts or friendship of his brother." Instead, he was an "Intimate of Magnates" and "Bulwark of Bankers."[5]

In 1893 Robert began to supply protection to members of the American Bankers' Association (established in 1875). In pitching for such contracts, he exhibited a keen eye for publicity. For example in June 1904 he asserted his claim to be speaking for American law enforcement by addressing the annual convention of the International Association of Chiefs of Police, meeting that year in St. Louis. His subject was "hobo" bank burglars. The pioneering movie director E.S. Porter read his speech and saw an opportunity to make a sequel to his popular film, *The Great Train Robbery*. Robert Pinkerton and a senior agency detective, George S. Dougherty, advised on the making of the resultant *Capture of 'Yegg' Bank Burglars*, with dramatic scenes of robbers escaping across a lake after a shootout.[6] The Pinkertons' claim to be protecting banks against robbers was valid. In an age of professional "yeggs" or safebreakers, banks outside the Bankers' Association lost more money to robberies than those within it who benefited from the Pinkerton contract. Partly for this reason, membership of the Bankers' Association rose from 1,742 in 1894 to 10,682 in 1909. Robert Pinkerton had been instrumental in delivering the lucrative bank-protection business. Two years after his death, the Pinkertons lost their bank role to the rival William J. Burns agency.

Jewelers who were paid-up members of the Jewelers' Security Alliance (established at the urging of Robert Pinkerton in 1883) benefited from the Pinkerton protective contract and could feel more confident that their safes would remain unviolated. Jewelry salesmen who belonged to the sister association, the Jewelers' Protective Union, likewise benefited. They now traveled on the nation's railways with diminished fear that they might be robbed of what the *Chicago Examiner* called their "miniature cargoes of the worth of a king's ransom."[7] Jewelers, like bankers, appreciated that the Pinkertons could operate and pursue their prey across state lines, unlike municipal or state police forces.

The Pinkertons diversified into still more areas, politics included. In 1888, twenty of the agency's operatives supplied security at the presidential inauguration ceremony of the Republicans' triumphant candidate, Benjamin Harrison. The agency grew. In the mid 1870s, it employed between eighty and a hundred personnel. By 1892, the number was 800 spread over eight offices. Five of those offices were still under the nominal control of William Pinkerton and his Chicago office, but Robert was the agency's prime moving force in the realms of expansion and profit-making. On the death of Robert Pinkerton in 1907 one newspaper reported he had co-headed an agency that now employed "2,000 sleuths."[8]

While Allan Pinkerton had pioneered labor work, Robert's efficiency took it to a new level. Another change in emphasis stemmed even more clearly from the passing of management to the sons. Possibly because of their views on Allan's alleged love life, the employment of women ceased to be a cardinal principle. Because the PNDA still eschewed divorce work, the temptation to deploy women in such cases did not exist for the Pinkertons. Women were occasionally taken on for other tasks, but in a subordinate role. Thirty years after Allan Pinkerton's death, for example, his agency supplied female cashiers and ticket collectors to the organizers of the Panama-Pacific Exposition, a world fair held in San Francisco. Their job was to look out for thieves. However, these women turned on their male supervisors, accusing them of persecution. If Allan Pinkerton left a legacy of antimisogyny, his agency proved to be a poor vehicle for its transmission.[9]

Allan Pinkerton's technophobia made one change overdue. When comparatively young, he had embraced technical advances in photography and communications. In the 1860s he had linked his Chicago, Philadelphia, and New York offices using the nation's developing telegraph system. But his enthusiasm waned. Although a fellow Scottish immigrant, Alexander Graham Bell, helped develop the telephone and in 1876 Allan witnessed Bell giving a demonstration of his latest model, the detective was by this time displaying the rigidity of advancing years and ill health, and he never took to that invention. His sons were free of such inhibitions. They made the most of the telephones that the old man had installed but refused to use. The invention of the typewriter similarly increased office efficiency for the PNDA as for other corporations. The introduction of carbon paper and resultant dissemination of carbon copies meant that detailed information on suspects could be exchanged between different colleagues and offices. Businesses came to expect the Pinkertons' clear and efficient-looking uniform reports.[10]

There was, however, much that remained unchanged after the founder's death. The agency's administrator George H. Bangs having died the year before Allan, his son George D. Bangs, who had experience overseeing the New York Office, took over as general manager. He helped to preserve the PNDA's founding principles. In response to Robert's death in 1907 he dictated a memorandum stating, "When the elder Mr. Pinkerton died in 1884, William and Robert succeeded to the business and have studiously conducted it on the same principles as laid down by the founder:—a legitimate detective business only, avoiding divorce cases or such matters as would interfere with the marriage relations and scandalous matters."[11]

There was lifestyle evolution from one Pinkerton generation to the next. The continuing story of The Larches farm illustrates the point. In his will, Allan Pinkerton had made provision for the upkeep of The Larches and expressed the wish for it to remain in the family in perpetuity. Robert and Allan continued to manage the estate, and the PNDA records contain many files to attest to their continuing attention. Much of the land was rented out to a tenant farmer, yielding an annual income of $1,084.50 in 1906. In that year William was outraged to learn of an initiative by the farmer, a Mr. Risser. The farmer had on his own authority felled twenty-three larch trees on the ground that they were dying. He had used any good timber to make fence posts. William complained that Risser had no right to do so and had acted in a "sneaky manner." He would on no account agree to further felling unless obliged to do so by law. He demanded compensation and talked of ending Risser's lease.

Still the diplomat and efficient micromanager even as his heart was failing, Robert arranged for an inspection of the farm and made recommendations to defuse the situation. Addressing his brother by letter, he noted that his father had arranged for the planting of various trees that were unsuitable for the local climate. Regarding the larches, he was in favor of "considering the incident closed" so long as Risser promised never to transgress again.[12]

Even if William had a sentimental attachment to trees planted by his father, the brothers by now managed the estate at a distance. In terms of their lifestyle, the male descendants were moving on. Unlike their father both William and Robert had an interest in dogs, horses, and racetracks. The brothers' interest in horse racing, the "sport of kings," was part social aspiration, part hobby, but also a business proposition. The PNDA helped the jockey clubs springing up in the state of New York to protect the good name of their sport by rooting out illegal betting such as typically took place in the poolrooms of the day. In 1887 Albany legislated against pool rooms, and these dens of assumed iniquity remained targets for reformers over the next twenty years. The enforcement of the new legislation was contracted out to the Pinkertons. In 1896 the New York Steeple Chase Association paid the Pinkertons $480 for policing one of their three-day events, and several New York Jockey Clubs similarly paid the agency to protect their good name. When Robert died, the local obituary notice declared, "Race Track Patrons Lost a True Friend in Pinkerton."[13]

As for William, his interest in "dogs and horses" was not confined to race tracks but extended also to the animals themselves.[14] In March 1905 he wrote to his son Allan Pinkerton. Born in 1876, Allan was one of the three surviving children born to William and his wife Elizabeth and was serving an apprenticeship as assistant general manager at the firm's New York office. William urged: "Will you please have a lookout for that English Bull bitch of mine and, when she comes in season, have her bred to an A. No. 1 dog."[15] His feelings ran deep in the matter of dogs. In 1908 he wrote to the PNDA general manager in Los Angeles complaining about a "vetinerary" who was trying to "blackmail" him into returning a dog he had bought for $50 as a gift for his subordinate: "I would see him in hell before I would give him a puppy or anything." William Pinkerton had inherited his father's irascibility but in second-generation style had found a place in his life for interests with no direct link to profit or social climbing.[16]

The Pinkerton brothers nevertheless developed their taste for the elite lifestyle. Knowing the right people brought them more money-making opportunities, but it not just that. It was the mark of a second generation reaping the benefits of the first and beginning to relax into the role of the rich. William's sister Joan had married into a major engineering enterprise. A member of the third generation who would display continuing symptoms of dynastic privilege, William's daughter Margaret (born 1870) married George M. Pullman, the manufacturer whose luxury railway cars had carried the rich and famous to The Larches—and whose hostility to labor unions would spark a nationwide strike in 1894.

When they managed to find and return her stolen jewels, the Pinkertons found themselves mixing with American royalty in the person of actress (and women's franchise advocate) Lillian Russell. Across the Atlantic, they served more traditional royalty, supplying security at King George V's coronation. They advised the Bank of England how to protect itself from robbers.

All this was a far cry from the principles associated with Allan Pinkerton at the time of his upbringing in the Gorbals. Yet some of those principles remained.

For example Allan Pinkerton had been interested in carceral reform. In his *General Principles of Pinkerton's National Detective Agency* (1873), cowritten with George H. Bangs, Pinkerton had argued that every criminal had an inner urge to confess. It was an urge that a detective could exploit in securing a conviction. But it also meant that the penitentiary where the convict suffered punishment should build on the potential for redemption. Prisons should be reformed so that they could train their inmates to pursue honest professions once released. Pinkerton also unleashed a broadside that might have endeared him to a wider range of sympathizers had his actions toward labor unions been less hostile. The broadside lashed the practice of leasing convict laborers to employers who cared greatly about their profits and but little for the reform of the involuntary toilers who enlarged those gains. Pinkerton admitted his detectives were in no position directly to reform the suspected criminals they pursued, but he urged every operative to keep in mind the fact that every citizen had a potential for good.[17]

The philanthropic instincts of the Pinkerton dynasty did not disappear with the founder's death in 1884. In 1887 Robert Pinkerton penned several articles that reflected the work of Zebulon R. Brockway. A penologist who introduced vocational training at New York's Elmira Reformatory, Brockway was an influential reformer. In one of his admiring articles, Robert proposed the creation of a National Prison Reform Society that would help to take care of released criminals. He urged major employers, such as the railroad corporations, to take the risk of employing ex-convicts, to give them a chance to pursue honest livelihoods.

Robert Pinkerton's argument was not devoid of artifice. Using language reminiscent of his father's, he attacked urban police forces for using "stool pigeon" and "informer" tactics. The use of such tactics meant that "circumstantial" offenders—those, for example, who stole to feed their families in times of economic stress—might be led on the path to becoming "professional" practitioners. Robert charged that the police blackmailed ex-convicts who might otherwise have had a chance at redemption. Reenter the criminal fraternity and inform on it, police officers insisted, or we will charge you and you'll go back to prison. Over the years, Robert Pinkerton stuck to his critique of such practices, for example in a lead article for the *New York Post*'s *Sunday Magazine* in 1898, titled "Do Professional Criminals Reform?"[18] However, his argument was opportunist in that it aimed to vindicate private policing. It also ignored the corrupting effects of the PNDA's own infiltration practices.

After Robert Pinkerton died in 1907, his older brother kept the spirit of philanthropy alive. In 1912 William revealed to the journalist Frank P.

Stockbridge his "philosophy of crime." Stockbridge began his account by remarking on the detective's seriousness and his modesty in refusing to sensationalize crime or talk about his Civil War heroism: "The close-cropped gray head would shake a slow negative, the thin lips under the close-cropped mustache press themselves more tightly upon the big, carved and blackened meerschaum cigar-holder, the keen gray eyes fix themselves on some point beyond the distant Jersey shore, and after a vigorous puff or two the answer was always the same: 'It would serve no good purpose to print that.'"

Stockbridge was impressed by his subject's thoughts. He wrote of how the PNDA chief had "reached certain conclusions which do not agree with the theories of some eminent scientists." Robert Pinkerton rejected the opinion of the late Italian criminologist and phrenologist Cesare Lombroso (1835–1909) that some individuals were genetically predisposed to crime. He recited his experience of a pickpocket, Jimmy the Nibbler, who was forced into crime because of environmental circumstances, and who managed to reform. He attacked American prison authorities who claimed to educate their institutions' inmates but trained them only for professions that made them unemployable.[19]

The Pinkertons, father and sons, were not cutting-edge thinkers. They are not cited in serious works on criminology or the history of crime.[20] They did, however, latch on to and help popularize some progressive ideas. Their views won them some admirers. When Robert Pinkerton died, the *Denver News* noted that he had been a great reformer of criminals and had always given to beggars. William's demise inspired similar eulogies, evidenced in the following headlines: "Ex-Crooks Mourn for Pinkerton," "Relentless in Pursuit of Criminals, He Helped to Reform Many of Them," and "Noted Criminologist."[21]

On Robert's passing there was an extravagant funeral in Brooklyn, New York, attended by prominent citizens ranging from August Belmont to a former head of the US Secret Service—but reports also indicated that the crowds were a cross section of society. The *New York Telegraph* hinted at the reason: "Both these men [Robert and William] have been something more than mere thief-takers. They have been reformers without tincturing their philanthropy with hysteria: public benefactors who believed in the development of any latent good strain they might discover in a habitant of the underworld."[22] The reputation of the Pinkertons as robber-hunters who remained benevolent criminologists remained intact in the eyes of their admirers, even if their views did little to explain the behavior of Jesse James—even less the allegedly violent labor leaders they continued to hound after the Founder's death.

CHAPTER 15

Pinkertons in the Haymarket Trial

On May 1, 1886, Chicago Knights of Labor leader Albert Parsons led a march of 80,000 people down Chicago's Michigan Avenue demanding an "eight-hour day with no cut in pay." It was the first modern May Day parade. In the next few days, 350,000 workers went on strike nationwide in support of the eight-hour day demand. Three days later, the movement suffered the Haymarket catastrophe.

The bomb explosion on May 4 at a protest meeting called by local anarchists at Haymarket Square killed seven Chicago policemen and wounded many more. The casualties seemed to indicate that public order, if not democracy itself, was in peril. The slaughter sparked the nation's first Red Scare. The press fulminated against anarchism and communism, depicting them as un-American creeds fostered by immigrants. A wave of antiforeign sentiment swept America. Recently arrived immigrants feared for their lives. In Chicago the police arrested dozens of workers thought to be anarchists. They barred public meetings. Without waiting for warrants and confident in their belief that they enjoyed public support, they raided the offices of radical organizations and suspects' homes.

The police built a case that resulted in the indictment of eight anarchists on the charge of having conspired to murder Police Officer Mathias J. Degan. The force of the blast had propelled the unfortunate Degan into the arms of his comrade John McDonald. The wounded policeman had then managed to take a few steps away from the carnage before dropping dead, the first mortality of the infamous explosion.

Five of the indicted anarchists were German-born. These were August Spies, Michael Schwab, George Engel, Adolph Fischer, and Louis Lingg. Samuel Fielden came from England. The remaining accused were Oscar Neebe and Albert Parsons, both American born.

The indictment of Albert Parsons had special political significance. He seemed an unlikely revolutionary. A native of Alabama descended on his mother's side from a veteran of George Washington's Continental Army, he had moved to Texas as a child. There at the age of thirteen, he had enrolled as a Confederate soldier, and thereafter he served with Texan units until the war's end. In a dramatic switch after the war, he aligned himself with the Radical Republicans who supported Black rights and for this incurred the wrath of the Ku Klux Klan.[1]

So far so good, and so American. But by the 1870s Parsons had moved to Chicago, where he developed socialist and anarchist views. He was a prominent prolabor orator at the time of the 1877 railway disturbances. As editor of the anarchist paper *The Alarm*, he advocated peaceful revolution but allowed contributors to advocate violence. What made him a key target for anti-union propagandists was his prominent role in the leading nationwide workers' movement, the Knights of Labor, of which he had been a member since 1876. His involvement in the Haymarket atrocity meant that his name could be used to discredit both the eight-hour-day campaign and the labor movement.

There was little prospect of a fair trial for the Haymarket eight. For a start there was the inbuilt antilabor bias that characterized the corporation-lawyer-dominated American courts in the days before diversification of the legal profession. As if that were not enough, the whole nation was in the grip of Red Scare hysteria. The state's attorney for Cook County was Julius S. Grinnell, formerly general counsel for the Chicago City Railway Company.[2] His opening words outlining the prosecution's case to the jury were: "Gentlemen, for the first time in the history of our country are people on trial for endeavoring to make anarchy the rule, and in that attempt for ruthlessly destroying human life."[3] He thus equated anarchism with murder; if the accused were "guilty" of espousing anarchism (as they certainly were), they must be guilty of murder.

Critics of the Haymarket trial variously accused Judge Joseph E. Gary of allowing too much latitude to the politically freighted arguments of the prosecution, of permitting the selection of jury members who expressed hatred of anarchists, and of paying too little attention to the proceedings. Only two of the eight arrestees had been present at the time of the explosion. These two, Spies and Fielden, having addressed the assembly, were stepping down from the speakers' wagon in full sight of the crowd at the time of the detonation and could not have thrown the bomb. Parsons had spoken for an hour but had left the scene, as had Fischer. The other accused anarchists had been at no stage present. The crowd was dispersing at the time when the bomb was thrown. Yet few at the time believed that the jury would find the accused innocent. They were right. On the basis of circumstantial evidence and an assumption of self-evident guilt in the case of anarchists, all eight were convicted—not of throwing the bomb but of being accessories before the fact, meaning they had conspired to facilitate the massacre. Judge Gary sentenced three defendants, Fielden, Neebe, and Schwab, to fifteen years in prison. He condemned the remaining five to death.

Louis Lingg managed to defy the hangman. This good-looking native of Mannheim, Germany, a "lion of the ballroom" according to his fellow carpenters, had not been present at the Haymarket on the night of the explosion.[4] But when the police raided his home they found bomb shells, with chemical traces they claimed were similar to those found at the murder scene.[5] Lingg had resisted arrest by pulling a revolver, but the police took him alive. On November 10, 1887, he finally escaped the clutches of Chicago's authorities. This was the day before he was scheduled to hang. His fellow prisoners received cigars as gifts from friends and families. Lingg used the wooden cigar cases to produce carvings. Only when it was too late was it realized that bomb-making equipment had been smuggled into his cell in these cases. Lingg detonated a blasting cap that he had placed in his mouth. It blew a chunk out of his head. On November 11, Spies, Parsons, Engel, and Fischer were duly executed by hanging as Lingg lay writhing in his death throes. By now opinion was beginning to turn. The novelist William Dean Howells called the executions "judicial murder."[6]

The Pinkerton National Detective Agency was intimately involved in the Haymarket affair and its aftermath. It had a putative role in the causation of the bomb atrocity. The accused depicted Pinkertonism as part of the oppressive system that weighed down on working people and made them turn to radicalism. August Spies saw the agency as a relic of feudalism. George Engel stated that strikes and boycotts too often met with "the deadly bullets of the Pinkertons," illustrating how the "oppressing classes always maintain their tyranny by force and violence." Samuel Fielden saw Pinkertonism as an integral part of judicial oppression: Pinkerton "murderers were allowed to have able lawyers who bull-dozed the coroner and all the witnesses," while judicial officials fraternized all too readily with Pinkerton attorneys.[7] The testimony of the accused was eloquent in its denunciation of the role of Pinkertons in industrial relations.

Such testimony carried a danger, the danger that the anarchists might be seen as subscribing to the view that oppression justified violence. The discovery of bomb components in Lingg's home gave force to that perception. In fact even peaceful anarchists could be less than dewy-eyed about the innocence of the accused. Benjamin R. Tucker wrote to his fellow individualist/pacifist anarchist comrade Joseph Labadie warning him not to believe allegations that the police had "planted" evidence in the office of August Spies's anarchist paper, the *Arbeiter Zeitung*:

> I notice a communication in the last Labor Leaf signed "Free Speech" from Chicago. I don't know who the writer is but he is badly at fault in his premises. I don't doubt that the police have manufactured evidence, but the particular piece of evidence referred to—the finding of dynamite in Spies' desk—was not manufactured, *and I know it*. I tell you this simply for your own information. I should not like to have you say that I said so. Under no circumstances would I tell I know it, and consequently I do not wish to be asked to tell. But it is certain that the identical package of dynamite seized in the office of the Arbeiter Zeitung office was sent there long ago.[8]

Inconsistently with such doubts—and with the anarchists' aspiration to be potent revolutionaries—partisans of the accused men insisted that the Pinkertons had engineered an unfair trial of innocent people. The *Arbeiter Zeitung* had long pointed to the role of Pinkertons in planting evidence, such as quantities of dynamite that were far too small to cause real damage to employers' property.[9] According to an extreme version of this view, the Pinkertons were so keen to win court convictions conducive to their profits that one of them took it on himself to throw the fatal bomb on May 4.[10]

In the months preceding the bomb incident, the Chicago Citizens' Association, worried about labor unrest and radical influences in their city, had decided to hire Pinkerton agents to penetrate suspicious-looking organizations. Lyman J. Gage, vice president of the First National Bank, engaged five seasoned Pinkerton operatives. The most prominent of these by virtue of his pivotal testimony at the trial was Andrew C. Johnson. The *Chicago Tribune* described Johnson as "a sandy-haired, thin-faced Scandinavian, born in Copenhagen about thirty-five years ago." He had been in the employ of the Chicago branch of the Pinkerton agency for the last three years.[11]

Albert Parsons, during his trial, pointed an accusing finger at the Pinkertons. He believed that the private detectives had from the first "contracted to" big business to prevent the achievement of the eight-hour-day, a prevention that was worth "hundreds of millions annually" in extra profits.[12] As for the fatal explosion, "I say that a Pinkerton man, or a member of the Chicago police force itself had as much inducement to throw the bomb as I had."[13] After he was sentenced to death, Parsons appealed against his conviction. His appeal was widely circulated in a leaflet that took its place in the literature of left-wing martyrdom.

In his appeal, Parsons questioned the prosecution's most damaging vein of evidence. In general, the prosecution case made little advance on the postulation that the anarchists were in fact anarchists and ipso facto guilty of murder. Some of the evidence, however, was more concrete, purporting to show that the anarchists in question had specifically advocated and planned for violence, right up to the point when the bomb was thrown. The prosecution bolstered the credibility of that assertion by stressing that Parsons, the former Confederate soldier, had been an officer in a revolutionary group, the International Rifles. Parsons stated in his appeal that contrary to charges made in court, the International group had never carried out drills involving weapons and had long since disbanded. He continued, "The Pinkerton man, Johnson, says that dynamite bombs were exhibited in the presence of the International Rifles. It will take corroborative testimony before the American people will credit the statement of such a man engaged for such a purpose."[14]

According to their accusers, several of the defendants issued exhortations to violence in the course of their speeches to laboring people. In his appeal, Parsons questioned the ways in which the speeches were reported: "Again, concerning the alleged speeches, they were reported by the Pinkerton detective, Johnson." He stated that Gage had hired Johnson on behalf of corporate business to discredit Chicago's militants.[15]

After a difficult search for lawyers who were prepared to risk notoriety for meager reward, the Chicago eight retained four defense attorneys. William A. Foster was one of these. A native of Iowa, Foster had fought for the Union against Parsons' Confederates and had served in the Iowa state senate. He argued that the Haymarket prosecution was based on manufactured evidence.

The *Chicago Tribune* described Foster's cross-examinations as "damaging to the State witnesses." However, the newspaper clung to the idea that the anarchists must be guilty of murder: "Johnson suffered most [from Foster's cross-examination] and at one point was put in conflict with several of the city detectives and the reporters as to the character of the speeches made by Parsons and Fielden. . . . This, however, does not seem to be as important as the defense tried to make it appear."[16]

The *Tribune*'s unforgiving stance was far from unique. Its view of the Chicago anarchists echoed a widely expressed sentiment about the left, and the Knights of Labor also took its share of opprobrium. For example, the German American Thomas Nast, a famous caricaturist with a weakness for puns, published a cartoon in *Harper's Weekly* titled 'What's in a Name?' It depicted Knights Grand Master Powderly sitting on and about to ignite a barrel of "Powder" adjacent to a building labeled "United States Magazine."[17]

In evidential terms the Haymarket trial proceedings were inconclusive, proving neither guilt nor innocence. Johnson's testimony was supposed to underpin the prosecution case, but under cross-examination by William Foster the Pinkerton detective was unable to give definitive answers. Take this example. Johnson said he had attended an anarchist meeting at Turner Hall on Chicago's 12th Street on October 11, or it might have been October 12, 1885—the Pinkertons' vaunted record-keeping seemed to have gone missing. On that occasion one anarchist in particular had advocated the use of force. When Foster countered with the suggestion that the man might have been another Pinkerton detective posing as an anarchist, Johnson was unable to identify the individual to prove or disprove Foster's theory.

Foster quizzed Johnson on the latter's contention that Parsons favored the murder of police inspector John Bonfield:

Q: Was that a speech or a private conversation with you?
A: That was a speech.
Q: Mr Parsons simply was giving his opinion, was he not, of what in his judgment would have occurred [in a recent teamsters' strike], provided things had happened differently from what they did happen?
A: I don't know what was his opinion. I only know what he said.

* * *

Q: Did he say he intended to shoot Bonfield in the future?
A: No, he did not say so.[18]

The exchange resembled many similar in the field of labor relations: if a radical or labor leader predicted that that there might be violent consequences if certain demands were not met, was it a threat, a warning, or simply a responsible prediction?[19] In the Haymarket case, the jury did not give the defendants the benefit of the doubt.

In 1893 Governor John P. Altgeld of Illinois pardoned the three Haymarket anarchists who remained alive in their prison cells. A progenitor of the Progressive movement, the Democrat Altgeld supported legislation that restricted child labor and imposed workplace safety rules. He was not an admirer of the presiding officer at the Haymarket trial. Justifying his pardon, Altgeld questioned the impartiality of Judge Gary. He held that the jury had been packed and challenged the reliability of prosecution evidence. Altgeld believed the Pinkertons had made up evidence:

> At the trial a number of detectives and members of the police swore that the defendant, [Samuel] Fielden at the Haymarket meeting, made threat to kill, urging his hearers to do their duty as he would do his, just as the policemen were coming up; and one policeman swears that Fielden drew a revolver and fired at the police while he was standing on the wagon before the bomb was thrown, while some of the others testified that he first climbed down off the wagon and fired while standing by a wheel. On the other hand, it was proven by a number of witnesses, and by facts and circumstances, that this evidence must be absolutely untrue. A number of newspaper reporters, who testified on the part of the State, said they were standing near Fielden—much nearer than the police were—and heard all that was said and saw what was done; that they had been sent there for that purpose, and that Fielden did not make any such threats as the police swore to, and that he did not use a revolver.[20]

Over time the Haymarket affair became a chapter in the history of labor martyrdom. Eugene Debs, a union leader and future socialist candidate for the US presidency, wrote in 1899 that the Chicago anarchists were "the first martyrs to a cause which, fertilized by their blood, has grown in strength and sweep and influence from the day they yielded up their lives and liberty in its defense." In a 1925 novel by the more politically mainstream Willa Cather, one of the book's sympathetic characters "brooded on the great injustices of his time; the hanging of the Anarchists in Chicago, which he could just remember, and the Dreyfus case."[21]

Subsequent commentary on the Haymarket anarchists has followed a similar line. By the second decade of the present century there were over 1,500 publications devoted to the Haymarket affair. Most of the major works subscribed to the unfair trial/martyr trope. Beyond academia, in 2004 the Illinois state legislature made a subvention of $300,000 for the commission of an artwork to commemorate the "martyrs." The resultant sculpture depicts the wagon and the anarchist orators at the spot, on North Desplaines Street, where they were at the time of the explosion.[22]

The Haymarket affair was a setback for the eight-hour day movement and discredited the Knights of Labor, whose membership plunged. It encouraged the rise, in the Knights' place, of the American Federation of Labor (AFL). Organized in Columbus, Ohio, in December 1886 under the leadership of cigar-maker Samuel Gompers, the AFL rejected as being too utopian general reform movements like the Knights of Labor. It took a more cautious, pragmatic line, emphasizing "job consciousness" and rejecting the concept of class consciousness. Recruiting mainly white, male, skilled workers, it aimed to develop the bargaining power of those operatives who were difficult to replace with competent strikebreakers. Unions affiliated with the AFL embraced the strike as the main weapon in their armory. They publicly eschewed violence even if, as we shall see, dynamite and guns did not disappear from the scene.

Employers grew more confident of their ability to resist the demands of labor. The railroad magnate Jay Gould, an archetypal robber baron of the Gilded Age, is reported to have remarked that he could "hire one half of the working class to kill the other half."[23] Emboldened first by the Mollies triumph and now by their vindication at the Haymarket trial, the Pinkertons engaged with greater determination in labor work. They continued to supply labor spies and, in ever greater numbers, armed guards who would protect property and strikebreaking workers.

The result was ever-greater labor bitterness toward the Pinkertons. The now rapidly declining Knights of Labor complained in 1889 that the Reading railroad was ignoring a stipulation in the Pennsylvania constitution that prohibited the use of Pinkertons. In the following year the Knights condemned the Pinkertons for firing into a crowd during a strike in Albany, New York, where the detectives had allegedly been agents provocateurs. The Knights depicted Robert Pinkerton, the son of the agency's founder, as an "agent of the railroad company." Powderly accused the same detective of operating under a "pirate flag." There were several calls for Congress to outlaw Pinkertonism once and for all. Allan Pinkerton's claim to be a champion of labor had been challenged in his lifetime; within a few years after his death, his agency had become anathema to the American worker.[24]

CHAPTER 16

Homestead Lockout and the End of Legitimacy

In the summer of 1892 the Pinkerton agency was center stage in a labor dispute that became a political scandal. Already in wide disrepute in labor circles, the agency would emerge from the affair a pariah, with many citizens questioning its legitimacy.

The crushing of the steel workers in Homestead, Pennsylvania, asserted business supremacy in a way that helped move the vocabulary of political debate. It was the outcome of a pivotal struggle in a key industry. Together with the railroads whose tracks it supplied, the steel industry was the driving force behind US industrialization and prosperity. By the decade's end, the output of the Monongahela Valley steel plants of the Carnegie Steel Company—mainly in Homestead, Duquesne, and Braddock—exceeded by 35 percent the 1885 world record established by *all* the steel plants in the United Kingdom.[1] Steel was an essential ingredient in America's rise to be a world power. Armor plating, ranging from four to twenty inches in thickness, rolled off the Homestead mills to encase the US Navy's new fleet of warships. A dispute that affected Homestead affected the nation and its destiny. Politicians could not afford to ignore it.[2]

Andrew Carnegie, the dominant figure in his eponymous steel company, had much in common with Allan Pinkerton. He was born to a poor weaving family in Dunfermline, on the east coast of Scotland. The Carnegie family moved to Pittsburgh in 1848, when Andrew was just twelve years old, too young to have made a contribution to Scottish radicalism. Yet he was already politically conscious. He was acquainted with the writings of the egalitarian poet Robert Burns.

He remembered how, as a boy in Dunfermline, he had been barred from setting foot in the privately owned laird's park across from the cramped cottage—today a museum—where the Carnegies lived. He was a firm republican who would in due course buy a chain of UK newspapers and instruct their editors to advocate the overthrow of the British monarchy. Once established in the United States, he came to be seen as conservative not because he had changed, but because Americans had already achieved the reforms that he, like Allan Pinkerton, extolled.

Until the dire events of 1892, Andrew Carnegie was a national hero. He was a self-made man who had a transforming impact on the prosperity of his adopted nation. Like Pinkerton, he had voiced support for workers' collective action. His 1886 essay endorsing labor unions was republished in a book that served as the seminal expression of the philosophy of America's Gilded Age capitalists. *The Gospel of Wealth* (1900) reiterated Carnegie's declaration: "The right of the workingmen to combine and to form trades-unions is no less sacred than the right of the manufacturer to enter into associations and conferences with his fellows."[3]

Opposed to Carnegie and representing Homestead's skilled workers was the Amalgamated Association of Iron and Steel Workers. Like the Carnegie Steel Company, this labor union was a giant. When its nationwide membership reached a peak of 24,068 in 1891, it was the world's largest steel union. Its members hoped for a partnership of equal trust with Carnegie and his firm, but it turned out to be a vain ambition. The Knights of Labor's Terence Powderly would articulate a widespread view as to Carnegie's hypocrisy in making use of "black sheep" or strikebreakers. During the 1892 conflict, union workers were accused of intimidating imported strikebreakers. When questioned about this during a US House of Representatives inquiry, Powderly replied: "We agree with Andrew Carnegie—'Thou shalt not take thy neighbor's job.'"[4]

Like many who professed a belief in laissez-faire, Carnegie in real life aimed to eliminate competition and to achieve profit-maximizing monopoly. He lobbied for protective tariffs. Here, he and others in the successful protariff movement courted the political support of workers, arguing that tariffs gave them job protection.

Ruthless and cunning in his business affairs, Carnegie was rarely outwitted. He used organized labor as a lever to put his competitors out of business. When in 1889 Amalgamated struck the Homestead plant, Carnegie's management team made concessions. Competing firms found it difficult to match the generous wages that Carnegie now paid. A few of them, for example the future Jones & Laughlin and Bethlehem Steel concerns, survived. Others went to the wall or were bought out by Carnegie in his quest to dominate the industry.[5]

Over the next three years, changes took place. Improvements to the Bessemer process and the introduction of open-hearth steel furnaces enhanced productivity at the Homestead plant and made it the world's most advanced steel mill. It meant greater profits but also eroded the bargaining power of skilled workers whose labor had been indispensable prior to the technical advances that made their expertise redundant. Another change in the months leading up to 1892's fateful summer was a falling off in demand for steel because the nation's great rail construction boom was slowing down. The price of rails fell, and workers were laid off at some steel mills.

The Carnegie firm took advantage of the economic downturn. It built up a supply of steel so that any backlog in the order books could be rapidly cleared after any production stoppage. All this meant that if the mills had to shut in the coming dispute, the losses would be less.[6] With the competition by now largely ruined, the time had come to cash in on the outcome of previous wage generosity. Carnegie decided to destroy Amalgamated. First, though, he took a step that would feed the charges of hypocrisy leveled against him. He detailed his deputy to face the music.

Henry Clay Frick was already in charge of the day-to-day management of the Carnegie mills. Mindful of Frick's previously established hostility to labor unions and of his determination in crushing strikes, Carnegie entrusted him with handling the situation that arose upon the ending of the three-year labor contract agreed on in 1889. Having made this arrangement, the steel magnate saw advantage in taking his usual annual vacation in Scotland. There, like Allan Pinkerton at his Illinois retreat at The Larches, he could live the life of the country gentlemen he had once despised. On this occasion the special advantage of his absence in Scotland was that he would be able to argue that he was out of contact during the forthcoming Homestead confrontation. That, at least, was what he hoped.

In the event, Carnegie would emerge from the 1892 confrontation victorious but with a tarnished reputation. While Amalgamated lost an unequal struggle, the indications are that many Americans believed it had justice on its side, especially because of the role that Pinkertons played. Amalgamated's ethical qualifications do, however, merit inspection. Amalgamated was a craft union that represented skilled workers. It embraced a conservative philosophy like that of the American Federation of Labor, to which it was affiliated. Its president, William Weihe, had served as a vice president of the American Federation of Labor (AFL). Amalgamated's founding declaration of principles predated the formation of the AFL. They were less than revolutionary: "In all countries and at all times capital has been used by those possessing it to monopolize particular branches of business until the vast and various industrial pursuits of the world have been under the immediate control of a comparatively small portion of mankind. Although an unequal distribution of the world's wealth, it is perhaps necessary that it should be so."[7]

Amalgamated pursued the cautious strategy of organizing only those it considered to be organizable. Its leaders considered "New Immigrant" arrivals from southern and eastern regions of Europe to be unfit for membership. It applied the same attitude to African Americans. Quite apart from the ethical issue, it was a dangerous stance. If the union in your industry rejected you and excluded you from prime jobs, why should you respect appeals for solidarity? Employers could exploit such sentiment in recruiting strikebreakers. In the 1889 Homestead strike the management had deployed New Immigrant and Black "scabs." Amalgamated members chased them out of town on that occasion without intervention by the official forces and law and order. Such outcomes could not be guaranteed in the future.[8]

Amalgamated represented just 800 of the 3,800 workers employed at Homestead. Amalgamated men took home the highest wages. They were organized into eight "lodges," each of which represented specialists like rollers, screwmen, and shearmen. The remuneration of these "tonnage" workers depended on the weight of steel they produced and related, on a sliding scale, to the market price of the commodity. On the eve of the 1892 dispute, R. Hotchkiss, a roller, earned $279.30 for 23 days' work. J. Banks, a laborer excluded from Amalgamated, settled for $44.35 as remuneration for 34 days' work.[9]

Divisions in the workforce signaled troubled times ahead, especially for race relations in the industrial northern cities, cities to which displaced descendants of slaves were migrating in the tens of thousands. However, at the time of the 1892 confrontation, the workforce and almost the entire Homestead community was solidly behind the Amalgamated leadership. For a time, class solidarity and communal togetherness prevailed. It was for a reason. Union-excluded laborers, no less than the more privileged Amalgamated men, resented a company that so exploited them in the name of profit.

Enter the Pinkertons. Their deployment in Homestead was a prominent part of the oppressive establishment against which workers struggled unsuccessfully. It had long-term effects. Unfolding events at Homestead would destroy community solidarity, at least until a new union, the United Steelworkers of America, opened its door to all ethnic and race groups in the 1930s. But those unfolding events would also result in a further casualty. In the eyes of many Americans, the Homestead episode stripped from Pinkertonism the remaining shreds of its legitimacy.

In January 1892 Carnegie began a war of words about the Homestead plant. He initiated a survey of all wages paid in Pittsburgh's steel mills and in light of its findings stated that the Homestead workers were overpaid. This prepared the way for Frick to make a series of demands, including substantial wage cuts. These were unacceptable to Amalgamated. Weihe, basing his confidence on precedent, treated Frick's demands as bluff and waited until the expiration of the three-year contract on June 30. This time, however, Carnegie's intention was not to negotiate a new contract but to dispense entirely with a union that he regarded as a drag on the efficiency and profits of his enterprise.

In preparation for the coming showdown, Frick fortified the Homestead steel works. The mill rested on the banks of the Monongahela River, seven miles from Pittsburgh's center. The substantial waterway was a means of transit for the mill's supplies and products. Frick extended and heightened the plant's hitherto sporadic fencing so that it formed a loop enclosing the mills on the landward side. He had barbed wire strung along the top. Locals who soon christened the edifice "Fort Frick" wondered whether the slit holes hollowed into the wall at intervals were gun ports. At longer intervals, Frick's construction team erected a series of watchtowers.

When the old contract expired, Frick announced new terms of employment without consulting Amalgamated. The union rejected them. On June 25, Frick responded to a letter from Robert Pinkerton. In addition to this written communication, he spoke to the detective several times by telephone. The transcripts of the phone calls do not exist, but the text of Frick's letter would be published in a US Senate report: "We will want 300 guards for service at our Homestead mills as a measure of precaution against interference with our plan to start the operation of the works on July 6, 1892. The only trouble we anticipate is that an attempt will be made to prevent such of our men, with whom we will by that time have made satisfactory arrangements, from going to work and possibly some demonstration of violence."

Frick instructed that the Pinkerton men should assemble in Ashtabula, Ohio, before being taken to McKees Rocks on the Ohio River whence they could be transported by boat to and along its tributary the Monongahela for disembarkation within the recently built steelworks compound.

Frick stated, "We are not desirous that the men you send shall be armed unless the occasion properly calls for such a measure." He knew that a Pennsylvania law barred the importation across state lines of bodies of armed men for the purpose of breaking strikes. He therefore arranged with Pinkerton that 250 Winchester rifles together with quantities of pistols, ammunition, and truncheons should be imported separately from Chicago, the intention being to unite men and guns once the state line had been crossed. He promised the PNDA chief, "As soon as your men are upon the premises, we will notify the sheriff and ask that they be deputized either at once or immediately upon an outbreak of such a character as to render such a step desirable."[10]

With these plans in place, Frick ordered that the furnaces be fired down. Production ceased. The workers, once they had left their shifts, found that they could not reenter the plant. The Homestead lockout had begun. It was time to report on progress to Andrew Carnegie. The steel magnate was with his wife, Louise, in Rannoch Lodge. This Scottish fishing facility was ten miles from the nearest railway access at Rannoch Station but not quite as remote from the proceedings in Pennsylvania as Carnegie and his apologists later made out. On an inauspicious Fourth of July, Frick wrote to his boss, "We expect to land our guards or watchmen in our property at Homestead without much trouble."[11]

The locked-out workers were ready to picket the landward entries to the plant but suspected there would be a waterborne attempt to reassert management control. In the wake of the construction of Fort Frick, they guessed that "black sheep" would be imported via the Monongahela. William and Robert Pinkerton maintained that the workers had no idea that, instead, their firm would be involved. The brothers were proud of having sprung a surprise. Arthur G. Burgoyne, a Pittsburgh journalist who sympathized with the union cause, made a similar observation about the workers' lack of anticipation. It is distinctly possible that Pinkertons did indeed spring a surprise. Perhaps the Homesteaders should have been more alert. Both Carnegie and Frick had on earlier occasions used Pinkertons, and the PNDA had supplied "guards" to help break at least 70 strikes since 1874.[12]

Just before sunrise on July 6, union scouts discerned the approach of a tug towing two barges. The *Little Bill* had in tow the *Iron Mountain*, converted into a floating dormitory, and the *Monongahela*, newly fitted out as a dining hall equipped with its own kitchen. The 300 "detectives" aboard the company barges by now had their weapons, but some of them had never handled Winchesters, and the majority did not know they were destined for armed confrontation with a large force of alienated workers.

At 4 a.m., the local union man Hugh O'Donnell pulled a steam whistle. Its piercing screech warned the community of the imminent invasion. Men, children, and women, some carrying babies, flocked toward the anticipated point of landing. The Frick palisade blocked their progress briefly but was no match for men accustomed to hard labor. O'Donnell realized that things were getting out of hand and pleaded for the crowd to disperse, but it was too late. A welcoming party of several thousand surged onto the company landing site. It was as unprepared for systematic warfare as were the Pinkerton men on the barges. Yet the throng had or quickly imported some firearms of Civil War vintage, fireworks left over from July Fourth, sticks of dynamite, and even a small cannon, though that would never find its range as the barges lay below its firing trajectory.

On board the barges but keeping a low profile was Colonel Joseph H. Gray. He was deputy to Alleghany County Sheriff William H. McCleary and notionally had the power to deputize the Pinkerton men. Lacking, as he saw it, a mandate to do so, he took no action. Despite the resultant lack of legal authority, the commanders of the invading force, Captains Charles Nordrum and Frederick H. Heinde, ordered their men to disembark. The workers had by this time erected a makeshift barricade using steel components from their workplace. As in so many combustible scenarios, it is unclear who fired the first shot. A gunfight ensued, and all kinds of missiles descended on the stoutly built barges. As the battle progressed and the sun rose to its summertime zenith, the besieged Pinkertons nursed their wounded in confined spaces that became stiflingly hot.

After drawn-out exchanges during which the land-based force released oil to start fires on the barges, at around 5 p.m. the Pinkertons finally displayed the white flag of surrender. They were allowed to file, unarmed, onto the shore and walk toward their liberty through a waiting throng of local citizens. As they did so, individuals in the crowd abused them, especially women whose men had been casualties in the gunfight. The detectives emerged relatively unscathed from that experience. However, in the preceding battle there had been scores of casualties. They included seven mortalities among the Pinkertons and three dead workers.[13]

The disorder played into Frick's hands. Sheriff McCleary had tried to set up a conciliatory meeting in the course of the day, but Frick refused to see Weihe. He knew that if chaos continued the public authorities would need to intervene to restore order, giving him an opportunity to resume production using nonunion labor. However, Pennsylvania's Governor Robert E. Pattison stalled. He was sympathetic to the workers' cause and feared that there would be bloodshed if he sent in the state militia.

Meanwhile Frick had briefed Carnegie. On July 8, Carnegie cabled a reply: "Never employ one of these rioters. Let grass grow over works. Must not fail

HARPER'S WEEKLY
A JOURNAL OF CIVILIZATION
NEW YORK, SATURDAY, JULY 16, 1892

Figure 16.1. Pinkerton mercenaries run the gauntlet of union sympathizers as they retreat from their invasion barges following their surrender to locked out steel workers in Homestead, Pennsylvania, in 1892. Illustration from *Harper's Weekly*, 36 (July 16, 1892). *Library of Congress*

now."[14] On July 11, a subcommittee of the House of Representatives Committee on the Judiciary was due to descend on Homestead with a mandate to investigate. Frick began to feel uncomfortable and appealed to Carnegie for support. Another cable arrived from Rannoch: "Have not spoken, written or cabled one word to anybody. Shall continue silent. Am with you to end whether works run this year, next or never. No longer a question of wages or dollars." After his appearance before the House subcommittee, Frick told his boss that things had gone well but revealed nervousness about Carnegie's reliability in again pressing for support, which he received.[15]

Carnegie's disappearing act was not wholly convincing. On July 12, a reporter from the *New York World* interviewed him at Rannoch Lodge, eliciting the remarks, "I have nothing whatever to say. I have given up all active control of the business and I do not care to interfere in any way with the present management's conduct of this affair."[16]

At 9 a.m. local time that day, Governor Pattison having relented, the troops entered Homestead. They disembarked near the steel mill. In all, 6,000 militiamen arrived for a stay that would last for 95 days—at a cost to the public of $22,000 a day. Their commander, General George R. Snowden, conceived that he was dealing with a "communist" uprising and did all he could to support Frick in the manager's successful effort to reset the furnaces using non-union labor.[17]

On July 23, Henry Frick was at work on the second floor of his Pittsburgh office building when Alexander Berkman entered. Of middle-class Russo-Jewish heritage, Berkman had immigrated to the United States four years earlier. In his adopted land, he had continued to promote an extreme version of anarchism that derived from the struggle against tsarist tyranny and embraced "propaganda of the deed." When his eyes fell on Frick, whom he had identified as the villain of Homestead, he fired two pistol shots, each of which found its mark. Despite the brave intervention of Frick's colleagues and a nearby carpenter, Berkman then stabbed Frick several times using a sharp file. He would serve twenty-two years in prison for the attack.

Frick bled profusely but lived. The watching world learned that he was recuperating in Clayton, his mansion in the Homewood district of Pittsburgh. He was not the only invalid in Clayton. His baby son Henry Clay, born on the day of the Homestead shoot-out, lay dying just as his grief-stricken father was making a physical recovery. Perhaps his tragic circumstances contributed to the effect on opinion of Berkman's attack. Looking back on the events of 1892 at the time of the 1930s revival in steel unionism, a *Boston Globe* journalist reflected on "An anarchist's attempt to kill [Frick that] turned public opinion to his side [and] defeated labor's greatest struggle in steel."[18]

The tide had turned against Amalgamated. It was forced to recognize Carnegie's victory by sanctioning its members' return to work. Its power had been broken permanently. The consequences were dire for the Homestead workforce. The twelve-hour shift returned. Workers sometimes had to work a double shift in taxing and dangerous conditions. Rollers, shearmen, and other skilled workers found their wages more than halved by February 1894. The profits of the Carnegie Steel Company remained static in that period at $4 million but had reached $21 million by 1899. "Ashamed to tell you profits these days," Carnegie confided to a friend in the latter year.[19]

On one level it was a gloating remark. On another the shame was real. Homestead was traumatic for Carnegie, not so much in itself as because of the opprobrium that showered on his head—in his beloved Scotland as well in the United States—for being, as critics of the fallen idol charged, a hypocrite and a coward.[20] The post-Homestead opprobrium was Carnegie's epiphany. The capitalist who had profited from the construction of warships became an ardent anti-imperialist. Carnegie had long shown an interest in philanthropy, but especially after the sale of his steel interests to US Steel in 1901, he became a benefactor on a massive scale, notably funding libraries and peace research. He emphasized his regrets about the confrontation of 1892 in his posthumous autobiography: "Nothing I have ever had to meet in all my life, before or since, wounded me so deeply."[21]

As for the Pinkerton agency, its Homestead exploits inspired *New York Sun* journalist William W. ("Willie Wildwave") Delaney to pen the words of a song that became legendary:

> God help them tonight in the hour of their affliction
> Praying for him who they'll ne'er meet again
> Hear the poor orphans tell their sad story
> Father was killed by the Pinkerton men.

The Pinkertons had on many occasions provoked hatred in working people, especially in the union movement. This time it was different. The attempted assassination of Frick may have created a temporary wave of sympathy for the steel magnates, but the events on the banks of the Monongahela led to a sharp and longer-term rise in popular disgust toward the Pinkertons. The US Congress would act accordingly.

CHAPTER 17

Anti-Pinkerton Legislation

Allan Pinkerton had advocated private detection as an antidote to the corruption of public police forces. Yet much as they strove to achieve this goal, the Pinkertons instead provoked opposition to private policing. In the wake of Homestead, that opposition found expression in the federal Anti-Pinkerton Act of 1893.

That effort to nullify the perceived excesses of Pinkertonism had antecedents. Some states had already debated their own anti-Pinkerton bills. In 1857 the Illinois general assembly had considered, only to reject, a bill to "Suppress Police Agencies of a Private Nature." When in subsequent decades the Pinkertons increasingly intervened in industrial disputes, the agitation for such legislation increased. For example, the New Jersey Democratic convention meeting in Trenton in May 1888 endorsed Grover Cleveland for president and demanded legislative action to make it "unlawful to maintain an armed band of a drilled and uniformed army in private hands for hire as a menace to the people." The *Boston Globe* offered the event under the headline, "The Pinkerton System Condemned." The following year the legislature in Allan Pinkerton's home state of Illinois once again considered without favorable outcome a bill hostile to the Pinkertons. It aimed to forbid the importation of armed men across state lines. The frustrated attempt at legislation also reflected concern regarding court decisions that had allowed railroad corporations to deputize private detectives with a view to suppressing strikes. The proposed Illinois law would have banned the deputization of men from out of state.[1]

Legislation aimed at regulating Pinkertons had fared better in other states. Prior to the 1890s, five states had passed laws imposing licensing conditions on private detective agencies.[2] By the time the Homestead scandal erupted in the summer of 1892, Kentucky, Massachusetts, Montana, Minnesota, Missouri, New Mexico, Washington, and Wyoming had legislated with more apparent success than Illinois to restrict the use of out-of-state armed guards, even if their statutes were easily evaded by ruses such as importing men and weapons separately.

The story of a further initiative in the major industrial state of New York illustrates the contested nature of pre-Homestead anti-Pinkerton legislation. The deployment of Pinkertons during an 1890 strike on the New York Central Railroad had stirred indignation in that state—on one occasion Pinkerton guards who had stones thrown at them by young boys in Albany retaliated by firing live rounds into the crowd.[3]

In early 1891 the New York Assembly debated a bill that had been under consideration ever since the mid-1880s. The Democrats had promised that the bill would be enacted as soon as they won majorities in both chambers of the New York legislature, a goal they had by 1891 achieved. The Democrat-sponsored bill of that year prohibited the use of Pinkertons in railroad labor disputes. Governor David B. Hill backed the measure. The state legislature had recently elected him to the US Senate, a post he would take up in January 1892. Hill was ambitious, hoping to displace Glover Cleveland as the Democratic candidate in the 1892 presidential election. The *New York Times* accused him of courting the labor vote by promoting an extreme anti-Pinkerton bill—"Under the advice and guidance of Hill, the demagogue, every demand made by the most unconscionable Anarchist was granted and planted in the measure." The *Times* averred that Hill acted in the sure knowledge that the bill would be severely amended and that Republicans would be blamed for this.[4]

The Knights of Labor, American Federation of Labor, and local labor unions criticized the diluted wording of the resultant, modified bill. They said it contained too many loopholes. The Republican *New York Tribune* gleefully reported the dilution as a "funeral ceremony." The Assembly had amended the bill to such a degree "that its own father cannot recognize it."[5]

On February 4, 1892, the anti-Pinkerton bill passed the New York Assembly by a vote of 90 to 27. The bill did not prohibit corporations from hiring private security guards. But it did require that any deputies sworn in had to be qualified to vote in New York, resident in the county concerned, and chosen by the local sheriff. The *Tribune* had by this time adopted a gloomy stance: "The Democratic Assembly today tore down one of the defences which property in this state had before."[6]

A year later there were hearings on the Pinkerton bill before the Judiciary Committee of the New York Senate. The *Tribune* depicted the proposal as partisan—the "measure has been part of the Democratic stock-in-trade for many years." The Judiciary Committee's chairman questioned the credentials of labor witnesses pleading for the amended bill. His Republican colleagues queried the power of a state legislature to interfere with the right of employers to import security personnel. There were bitter exchanges over the charge that opponents of the new bill had accepted bribes. After the adoption of an amendment that excluded racing associations from its provisions, the bill passed with a vote of 25 to 4. The *Tribune*'s judgment was that it was not a genuine product of the labor movement but a political gimmick by Richard Croker, the Democratic "Boss" of New York City (and horse racing enthusiast) whom the Republicans wanted to indict for corruption.[7]

In the nation at large the Republicans, who cited the McKinley Tariff of 1890 as evidence for their claim that they were protecting American jobs, were apparently in danger of losing the labor vote. Criticism of high tariffs on industrial imports had hitherto seemed sectional or agrarian in nature—why should the southern farmer pay higher prices for imported machinery and risk foreign tariff retaliation against US agricultural exports? Now resentment at the Republican industrial hierarchy had broadened. The Republicans' support for big business and labor espionage was threatening to become a liability.

William Pinkerton nevertheless exuded confidence bordering on bravado about the resultant New York law: "The law is not aimed at us any more than at any other detective agency. I am not at all sorry that it passed. We can stand it as long as the railroads can. That is a branch of our business we have not been running after, and I won't put crape [*sic*] on my hat if it is stopped altogether."[8]

Like state legislatures, the US Congress came under pressure, though it was not at first compelling. In 1890 the Senate tabled a memorial from the American Federation of Labor (AFL)–linked Women's National Industrial League calling for the suppression and punishment of "armed assassins known as Pinkerton detectives." Other petitions reached out to the House of Representatives, one, for example, signed by 142 workingmen. These workers from Fort Wayne, Indiana, denounced the use of private armies, armies that were deployed exclusively against labor and were "made up of the lowest, most vicious class, thugs and ex-convicts."[9]

Anti-Pinkertonism found a champion in Thomas E. Watson. A congressman from Georgia, Tom Watson was a leading figure in the newly formed People's Party. The party's followers, the Populists, embraced issues that appealed to both rural and urban laborers. The curtailment of Pinkerton activities against working people was one of those issues. Watson's fellow Georgian Charles Crisp was Democratic speaker of the House. He at first blocked attempts by his recently elected colleague to present a bill restricting the use of Pinkertons. On February 9, 1892, Watson at last succeeded in that goal. For a while the resultant bill languished in committee. William Pinkerton meanwhile denounced, in what Watson described as "the foulest and most brutal manner," the Populist politician's "foolish" proposal.[10]

Though he was a rising presence in American politics who would achieve both fame and infamy in the coming decades, in the first few months of 1892 Watson was too minor a figure to make an immediate impression. Nevertheless, in mid-May the Georgia representative made better progress when he proposed that there should be a House investigation of the Pinkerton agency. His resolution was referred to the Judiciary Committee.

At the Judiciary Committee, Congressman William C. Oates was in principle in favor of Watson's bill. A Democrat from Alabama, Oates had lost an arm in combat while fighting for the Confederacy. Though he had favored abolishing slavery as a war measure, he was by the 1890s a white supremacist, whereas at this early stage on his career, Watson was an advocate of racial equality. A defender of the existing order, Oates had opposed Populism in his own state. However, for ex-Confederates like Oates, the Pinkerton agency seemed to be an instrument of corporate tyranny that operated with little regard for states' rights. He therefore shared common ground with Watson.

Agreeing on a form of words that resulted in a favorable reporting of the May 12 amended resolution, Watson and Oates cited the interstate commerce clause of the US Constitution. The railroads engaged in interstate commerce, so Congress had the power to investigate an agency that worked for them. In support of his resolution, Watson delivered an address, applauded on the floor of the chamber, describing the Pinkerton agency as "an armed force of 35,000 men" who enforced employers' policies "by the use of force and bloodshed." He reminded colleagues of the 1890 incident when the New York Central railroad chose to ignore public law enforcement forces, preferring to engage Pinkerton men who "shot down in the streets of Albany men, women, and children, who were noncombatants."

Congressman William Bynum (Democrat, Indiana) was one of those who opposed Watson's resolution. He objected to "these indiscriminate investigations by Congress." With other critics on the floor, he thought that if the Pinkertons had committed crimes they should be tried under the laws of individual states and that the interstate commerce argument was untenable. However, Watson prevailed, and the House adopted the resolution.[11]

The People's Party was by this time primed to take advantage of the Pinkerton issue. At its organizing conference in St. Louis in February 1892, it adopted a preamble that condemned the Pinkertons as an instrument of oppressive plutocracy.[12] On July 4, the day when Frick wrote to Carnegie saying he expected the introduction of Pinkertons would occasion no trouble in Homestead, the party's founding convention in Omaha demanded the "abolition" of the "maintenance of a large standing army of mercenaries, known as the Pinkerton system."[13]

Abolition was now the official policy of a political party, albeit a young and untried one. In retrospect it is clear that the People's Party never threatened to change America's two-party system, but at the time it was sufficiently well supported to command attention. In the 1892 presidential election, the Populist candidate James B. Weaver would poll over a million votes, 8.5 percent of the ballots cast.[14] The challenge to the traditional two-party system seemed potent in the immediate aftermath of Homestead.

The Democrats, like the Populists, benefited politically from the post-Homestead fallout. The Republican President Benjamin Harrison was running for reelection but already had problems with discontent in the West and South. In the mid-term elections of 1890, the Republicans had lost control of the House of Representatives. Demoralized by the illness of his wife, Caroline, who died on October 23, Harrison ran a low-profile campaign in 1892. The incumbent president failed to detach his image either from Homestead or from another violent labor dispute. Just weeks after the carnage on the banks of the Monongahela, President Harrison dispatched federal troops to quell an uprising of metalliferous miners in Coeur d'Alene, Idaho. It cemented his image as a friend of employers. His challenger in the fall 1892 presidential election, Grover Cleveland, projected himself as a friend of labor. The Democratic campaign mercilessly vilified and bracketed together Carnegie, Frick, and Harrison. Cleveland had already served as president, 1885–89. He now won a decisive victory that installed him in the White House for a second term. Frick and Carnegie contended (as have some subsequent historians) that Homestead killed the Harrison reelection campaign—though both industrialists also asserted that their interests would not be unduly affected by the Democratic triumph.[15]

When the Homestead confrontation occurred, the nation's legislators were already debating the Pinkerton issue with a view to changing the law. In the aftermath of the gun battle, Congress immediately intensified its attention to the matter. Congressman Watson denounced this upsurge in interest as typical of the opportunism of the two major parties. He said they had taken up the issue simply because of its sudden prominence and because a presidential election was looming in the fall of 1892.[16] That was, of course, the American political system. The two major parties have long survived by taking up popular issues and proposals proposed by third parties, thus denying the third parties any opportunity to prosper.

The July 6 Homestead debacle caused both houses of Congress to consider resolutions that would set up inquiries. In the House, where the Democrats had a solid majority, David B. Culberson chaired the Judiciary Committee. The Texas Democrat had served as a Confederate soldier and opposed big government. In relation to the Pinkerton problem, he hesitated because of worries about the over-extension of governmental intervention: "Is there a Federal question involved?" Culberson nevertheless concluded that war and peace powers conferred by the Constitution justified potential action.

Tom Watson complained that no such action had been taken earlier. He said Congressman Oates had been wrong in saying that there were no witnesses ready to testify against the Pinkertons. Watson insisted that Terence Powderly had been ready from the start. He weighed in with a bitter attack on William Pinkerton. Oates tried to calm his Georgia colleague. He had had a reasonable discussion with the detective boss. Pinkerton was willing to testify, and the inquiry could proceed.[17]

A subcommittee under the chairmanship of Oates traveled to Pittsburgh and held hearings. Among those who testified were Henry Frick, Sheriff William McCleary, and William Weihe. Democrats were keen to show that the McKinley tariff had not protected wage levels but was part of a Republican-cum-Robber Baron conspiracy to crush American labor with the help of Pinkerton mercenaries. Frick poured cold water on this high-flown partisan rhetoric. It was not a question of the tariff, but of "whether or not the proprietors or its workmen will manage the works." Samuel Gompers, the president of the AFL to which the Amalgamated Association was affiliated, did not give evidence. Despite the post-Haymarket decline of the Knights of Labor, Terence Powderly was accorded the privilege of representing the view of the labor movement. As usual he inveighed against the Pinkertons. He predicted that their continued use would result in civil war. The one-armed veteran in charge of the subcommittee reflected the alarm of the day when he responded, "I agree with you as to that."[18]

The House published its hearings on July 12, and its subcommittee commenced work on a report. On August 5, the debate resumed. Kansas's Jeremiah "Sockless Jerry" Simpson, the People's Party's leader in Congress, denounced the Pinkertons for being in league with Carnegie and the "plutocrats." However, on the floor of the House at large, a note of caution was by now evident. The House adopted an interim measure that would prohibit the federal use of Pinkertons. Though it would have long-term repercussions, this measure seemed, at the time, to be chiefly symbolic. Still, the symbolism mattered. Summarizing the day's work, Indiana's Congressman Benjamin F. Shively stated that the House had "enacted a provision of law which places the seal of Federal condemnation on the Pinkerton armed detective system."[19]

In the Senate the Republicans were in the majority, and the reaction to Homestead was more sympathetic to big business. During the upper chamber's debate of July 7, there was universal condemnation of the behavior of the Pinkerton invasion of Homestead the previous day. However, Republican senators exculpated their party and expressed sympathy with the nations' industrialists. Eugene Hale, of Maine, insisted "the Republican party is not responsible . . . for the employment of the Pinkertons. The mercenaries . . . have no lodgment except in detestation in the hearts of the American people." Responding to a colleague's assertion that Carnegie "skulks" and is not present when this great trouble occurs, Hale said it would have been better had Carnegie been present. But Carnegie was still the head of a "great establishment," and the Republican Party was not responsible for his location at a particular moment. The Democratic senators were also cautious. John M. Palmer of Illinois, another candidate in the running to replace Cleveland as the 1892 presidential nominee, said the deployment of Pinkertons was an error, but he expressed his admiration for Carnegie and his support for "the right of the capitalist to the control of his property."[20]

Colorful attacks on the Pinkertons did occur in the Senate. There were charges that the detectives had committed "treason" at Homestead. Senator George G. Vest thundered that ever since the enactment of the McKinley tariff, "manufacturers have been deliberately planning the present dastardly raid on honest labor." Vest delivered a further speech that confirmed his identity as a Missouri Democrat. The PNDA had "long since ceased to be a detective bureau and is now a standing army." Its operatives were little better than gangsters. He recalled the time when a Pinkerton gang had entered his home state on a specially chartered train. They had then attacked the home of the James family, resulting in the death of Jesse and Frank's infant half-brother.

Despite such pleas, resistance to a general prohibition on the use of Pinkertons persisted. Senator John Sherman, from Ohio, was a Republican without being an admirer of industrial monopoly—it was he who had in 1890 sponsored the eponymous Sherman Anti-Trust Act (he had not then foreseen that, in the event, the act would be used against labor and not, as promised, capital). Sherman opposed an inquiry because the House was already undertaking one and because—while he condemned the behavior of the Pinkertons—to legislate against them would be an infringement of "state sovereignty."[21]

Sherman was not alone in having such reservations. On August 5, the Senate sought unity with the House in approving not an interstate prohibition but a resolution banning only the federal employment of Pinkertons. John J. O'Neill, Vest's Missouri colleague in the lower house, expressed his dismay: "I read the proceedings of the Senate. I saw the shuffling, evasive way in which they treated this proposition [to prohibit the interstate movement of armed guards] . . . this miserable makeshift is practically a backdown by the representatives of the people."[22]

The House published its report on the Pinkertons and Homestead on February 7, 1893, and the Senate, having held its own hearings, followed suit three days later. The House report introduced an element of sobriety into the heated Pinkerton debate. For example, it gave the number of regular Pinkerton employees as between six hundred and eight hundred. The PNDA was not an army of thousands, as its critics maintained. The report was scathing only about the conduct of some small fry in the Pinkertons landings—Colonel Gray had dithered on the subject of deputization and left the scene (in charge of a boatload of wounded) "at first opportunity." The House report was lenient toward the big fish. It found that Frick was "somewhat autocratic" and his hiring of Pinkertons was "unwise"—but the latter act had been lawful in the state of Pennsylvania. Resort to the use of Pinkertons was a recipe for violence—but alternatives were absent because of the "sloth and dilatoriness" of local law enforcement authorities. The states were constitutionally empowered to regulate private armed forces such as the Pinkertons—but Congress was not.[23]

The Senate report concluded that it would have been illegal to send an armed force into Pennsylvania but agreed with Robert Pinkerton, who pleaded that because the guns were dispatched in advance of the men, no law had been broken. It noted that in emergencies the Pinkerton agency had to hire rapidly and could not guarantee the good character of those selected. The Senate committee devoted some consideration to the problem of sheriff's deputies and concluded that in some mining and manufacturing communities the posse comitatus system was inadequate. It refrained from considering the democratic deficit that would flow from the abandonment of the sheriff system.

Still in thrall to Andrew Carnegie in the face of widespread reservations in wider society, the Senate report cited with approval Carnegie's condemnation of strikebreakers. Apparently, its authors intended no irony. Partly because its southern Democrat members remembered why the Civil War was fought, the Senate determined, through its report, that it was "not clear" whether Congress could legislate to ban the interstate trade in armed men. In summary it concluded that the deployment of Pinkertons was wrong, that the states were empowered to act, that it was to be expected that they would all do so, and that such universal state legislation would make the federal question redundant.[24]

Congress did approve one long-lasting limitation on the activities of the Pinkertons. The Sundry Appropriations Act of 1893, effective from March 3 of that year, made permanent the restriction first imposed as a temporary measure on August 5 the previous year. Known as the Anti-Pinkerton Act, the new law provided "That hereafter no employee of the Pinkerton Detective Agency, or similar agency, shall be employed in any Government service or by any officer of the District of Columbia."[25]

As anticipated in the Senate report, many states—though not all of them—passed their own anti-Pinkerton laws. By 1899, twenty-six states plus the District of Columbia had legislated to prevent the importation of armed guards across their boundaries. Additionally, Maine, Colorado, Pennsylvania, and Massachusetts enacted licensing laws for private detective agencies.[26]

The Anti-Pinkerton Act had little bearing on labor relations and was at best an indirect rebuke to the Pinkerton agency. The law did, however, have consequences. This became evident in World War I. In that conflict Robert Pinkerton's son, Allan Pinkerton II, served with the rank of major in the American Expeditionary Force. On the eve of his embarkation to fight in France, he approached the US Shipping Board on behalf of the PNDA to ask that the agency be awarded a contract to "supply and supervise the protection and detective service in all shipyards and plants and in all departments" of the board. He had two meetings with the board's chairman Edward N. Hurley. However, Hurley, who had formerly been a labor union official in the railway industry, cited the 1893 Act in telling the future head of the PNDA that his agency was barred from working for the federal government.[27]

The Anti-Pinkerton Act of 1893 did deprive the agency and its emulators of a potential source of income. For that reason, the act would be subjected to legal scrutiny in the decades to come. Arguably the income deprivation had an unintended, accidental effect. With the federal income stream closed off and because of its self-denying ordinance regarding divorce work, the PNDA could not fully diversify and in its search for income was obliged to continue with its labor work. It was able to do so for the further reason that state-level anti-Pinkerton legislation proved to be ineffective. The Pinkertons and their peers in the private world of anti-unionism found ways of circumventing the state laws. For example, to engage in labor espionage or strikebreaking, a detective agency had only to open a local office, recruiting and arming men without the need to cross state lines.

In the mid-1890s the leaders of the Pinkerton agency had no intention of giving up labor work. But in the aftermath of Homestead and then of humiliating congressional hearings during which hardly a voice was raised in their defense, they needed a distraction that would restore their image. The war against Butch Cassidy and the Sundance Kid promised to be one way of achieving that distraction.

CHAPTER 18

Sundance and the Setting of the Western Sun

In June 1903 Kid Curry entered the penitentiary in Columbus, Ohio, having been sentenced on a charge of robbery. The man whose real name was Harvey Alexander Logan was a quiet-spoken native of Ohio who had earlier made a living by breaking horses on the Cross L ranch in north-central Texas. He inhabited a body that spoke to his later profession—it was covered with the scars left by bullets and knives.

Until his arrest one day in Knoxville, Tennessee, Curry had been the leader of the Hole in the Wall Gang. Hole in the Wall was a basin in the Big Horn Mountains of northern Wyoming, approachable through a niche in the Great Red Wall, a line of cliffs to the south. From its natural ramparts, strangers could be spied in good time to arrange retreat or defense. At the end of the nineteenth century, the Hole was known as a refuge for western outlaws. The loosely constructed gang that found refuge there was otherwise known as the "Wild Bunch" and could number up to a hundred at any given time.

A certain boldness in action complemented Curry's quietness of demeanor. The boldness had been evident in the latest of his robberies, on July 3, 1901. He and three confederates learned of a consignment of $40,000 in new bank notes on its way by rail from the Treasury Department in Washington, DC, to the First National Bank in Montana's state capital, Helena. When the Great Northern Express stopped at Malta on its way to Helena, a member of the gang boarded the engine tender and hid there. As the train steamed out of town, the outlaw crawled over the tender's grimy load of coal to reach the engine cab. The engineer and fireman found themselves staring down the barrel of a Colt revolver. The gunman ordered them to stop the train at a prearranged spot. The locomotive ground to a hissing halt three miles out of Malta. The time was 2:30 p.m.

The remaining outlaws emerged from their concealment in nearby bushes and joined their coal-dusty comrade. The united desperadoes forced the two locomotive platemen to form a human shield as they approached the express car, a fortified carriage used to transport cash. An application of dynamite blew a hole in the side of the car. The express messengers within opened fire but dropped their guns when they saw that they were in danger of killing the two hostages. A measure of nitroglycerin proved sufficient to expose the treasure within a small safe. The robbers mounted their horses and made off with the proceeds. Using their customary relay system, they mounted new horses after a while and outran the pursuing posse.

As of June 1903, little of the stolen money had been recovered. However, by this time, Curry was in prison. So was one of his fellow outlaws, Ben Kilpatrick. The "Tall Texan" had used a woman called Laura Bullion to courier stolen bank notes. When she was caught in possession, a numbered key on her person led law officers to the hotel room, where they captured their lofty prey.

After some weeks of searching for the culprits, the Great Northern Railway had offered a reward of $10,000 for arrests and asked Robert Pinkerton to take on the case. The PNDA issued a circular offering its own reward of $6,500 for information. This poster bore the usual stationary heading of the PNDA, showing that Robert and William Pinkerton were the firm's principals and that George D. Bangs remained the agency's general superintendent. It further listed three regional assistant superintendents. In charge of the Western Division, based in Denver, was James McParland of Molly Maguire repute.[1]

Two of the Montana suspects remained at large. Both had reputations that suggested they were participants in the Great Northern robbery. One was Robert Leroy Parker, better known as Butch Cassidy. The Pinkertons had already been hunting for Cassidy. He was the supposed perpetrator of an earlier Union Pacific railroad holdup near Wilcox, Wyoming. In the wake of that earlier heist, too, railroad magnate Edward H. Harriman had called in the Pinkertons. In the wake of Logan's arrest, Cassidy became the leader of the Hole in the Wall gang.

The other man still at large and wanted for the Montana robbery was the Sundance Kid, whose birth name was Harry Alonzo Longabaugh. Sundance was a much-romanced gunman, perhaps because he was thought to be less of a homicidal "butcher" than Butch Cassidy, or maybe because he showed a human side through his love affair with a woman called Etta Place.

Harry Longabaugh was born in Pennsylvania in 1867. When a teenager, he traveled West in a covered wagon and worked at a horse breeding ranch in Colorado. Laid off in hard times in 1887, he moved to Wyoming, where he stole a cowboy's horse, saddle, and gun. For this felony he received a prison sentence of eighteen months, spent in the jail in Sundance—hence the most popular of the many aliases he would use.

In the Pinkerton criminal files there is a physical description of Sundance dated around 1902. It states that he was of Swedish American lineage, 5′10″ in height and slim at 165 to 175 pounds. Commenting on his good looks, it mentioned that his features were of the "Grecian type." The blue-eyed outlaw combed his reddish-brown hair into a pompadour. In a further report a Pinkerton detective noted that he was bow-legged, walking with his feet far apart and his arms straight down with his thumbs sticking straight out. He was very quiet, a good rider, and used a knife and fork awkwardly.[2]

The pursuit of Sundance and the Hole in the Wall gang promised to revive the Pinkertons' reputation. However, the popularity of the western gunman introduced complexity into the battle for the hearts and minds of Americans. An influential newspaper, the *Philadelphia Public Ledger*, offered philosophical comments on the situation. Years had passed since the days of the James brothers and other "'road agents' who infested every sage bush or crossroad" west of the Mississippi. But the *Ledger* was not alone in longing that at least a few vestiges of wildness would survive the changing West. In a long article on the Hole in the Wall gang, the *Ledger* offered a nostalgic reflection about the generality of "desperate men plying the dangerous vocation of train robbing": "Where they fall short in numbers, they far surpass their comrades of past years in daring and in their hauls. Invention has been as much a helpmate to the criminal of to-day, especially those of the train-robbing class, as to the law-abiding citizen."[3]

Concern about the disappearing frontier and the dying West went further than nostalgia. The idea that the frontier was the cradle of American civilization and the crucible in which the American character had been formed was widely held at the time. Contemporary popular novelists like Owen Wister and Zane Grey, even the socialist Jack London, worshipped at the shrine of western individualism.[4]

President Theodore Roosevelt (1901–09) was aligned with them. On March 15, 1903, the *New York World* reported that the president, famous for his advocacy of the "strenuous life," was going to Hole in the Wall "to kill bears and mountain lions." A passage in a novel by an old friend and Harvard clubmate had inspired Roosevelt in his choice of location. Owen Wister's *The Virginian* described the outlaws' eyrie in evocative prose reproduced in the *World* article: "Somewhere at the eastern base of the Tetons did those hoofprints disappear into a mountain sanctuary where many crooked paths have led."

Referring to a surviving member of the Wild Bunch, the *World* reported, "The Wyoming authorities are making a desperate effort to remove 'Laughing Dick' [Sam Carey]" from the scene. Carey had stolen 300 head of cattle from the Medicine Butte Stock Company in South Dakota and was on the run. The *World* journalist dreamed of how "denizens of 'Hole in the Wall' [would] see the President enter their domain. They will hear his rifle shots ring through the solitudes, and they will see the glimmer of his camp fires in the canyons."[5]

The Hole in the Wall gang had become the epitome of American manhood. They were the enemies of private detectives, which in the eyes of some observers made them the friends of working men. A story about William D. Haywood illustrates the point. Haywood was a western labor leader of whom we shall hear more in the following chapter. He expressed his view of Pinkertons on a printed propaganda postcard: "That you may know how small a detective is, you can take a hair and punch the pith out of it and in the hollow hair you can put the hearts and souls of 40,000 detectives and they will still rattle. You can pour them out on the surface of your thumb and the skin of a gnat will make an umbrella of them."[6]

In his desperate struggle against western employers, Haywood was rumored to have turned to Hole in the Wall desperadoes for protection.[7]

A second anecdote further illustrates popular mythology regarding which side the Wild Bunch were on. James Farley, a "detective" who specialized in breaking streetcar strikes with men recruited in New York City, accepted a commission to perform that service in San Francisco. On their way to California, his men were supposed to have stopped off in Hole in the Wall where, to demonstrate their credentials, they "beat up" some "bad" residents. The truth or otherwise of such stories does not matter. The stories' very existence was testimony to the status of Hole in the Wall both as a proletarian redoubt and as an American virility test. In taking on the Wild Gang, Pinkertons like Farley made a point about their manhood.[8]

For the Pinkerton detectives the death throes of the "wild" West seemed to be both a threat and an opportunity. On the one hand, the spectacle of the gradual disappearance of areas of free land to the West and the development in that vast region of civil society with its public law officers threatened to eviscerate the private detective's raison d'être. Meantime, however, the accompanying nostalgic cult of individualism was a good fit for the private detectives' preferred image, that of one man pitting his wits against the odds to achieve arrests. Officially the Wild Bunch was the enemy. Off the record, it was a lifeline.

The western division of the Pinkerton agency had a reputation for ruthlessness. Whether the reality matched up to the reputation is another matter and one that is unlikely to be resolved, as the PNDA's record-keeping did not match Allan Pinkerton's promises of transparency. But the reputation was good for business anyway. Asa Mercer, a western editor and educator, recalled the role the Pinkertons played in the Johnson County "War" of 1889–93. The big ranch owners, through the Wyoming Stock Growers' Association, were squeezing out small-scale farmers whom they accused of rustling their cattle on the free range for which the warring parties competed. Mercer originally sympathized with the ranchers but changed his mind when he witnessed their tactics. He alleged that the stock growers established a $100,000 "Extermination Fund" to hire out-of-state gunmen, and that the "cattle ring" undertook the "systematic and indiscriminate slaughter of their supposed enemies." In a book that the cattle ranchers almost succeeded in suppressing, Mercer recalled President Harrison's dispatch in April 1892 of federal troops to Crazy Woman Creek, which he saw as a display of support for the mighty against the oppressed. This was quickly followed by the arrival of forty-three US marshals from Texas. Mercer said they "took oaths as Pinkerton detectives" (the reverse is more likely, namely that the Pinkertons were sworn in as lawmen). As in the case of the Homestead debacle a few weeks later, the Pinkertons deployed force to assist the cause of those who could afford to pay them.[9]

Tom Horn was keen to emphasize the role of McParland, the Pinkerton mastermind in Denver. Horn had been a US Army scout and claimed to have assisted in the capture of the Apache leader Geronimo. The Pinkertons hired Horn to track down horse thieves and other malefactors. William Pinkerton testified in favor of his character when he was on trial in 1891 on a charge of robbery, saying "he has been in my employ for several years." Horn quoted the alternative verdict of an Arizona newspaper on his character: "liar, cheat, Indian lover, ambusher and bushwhacker, ladies' man, big talker and top tracker. The last proved to be what the 'Eye That Never Sleeps' was interested in." Horn wrote those words in the autobiography he wrote while in prison in Cheyenne, Wyoming, awaiting his execution for murder. Though a bifurcated lawman-criminal accused of many other killings, Horn admired the Pinkertons' role: "They were 'the law' most feared by the guilty throughout all the West." The renowned tracker was proud when he received a commissioning letter "handwrote by Mr. James McParlan, the Denver superintendent."[10]

How effective were the Pinkertons in their efforts to find and arrest members of the Hole in the Wall gang? The surviving files in the PNDA papers are informative on the gang's history and on individual members Butch Cassidy and the Sundance Kid. Yet while they contain local newspaper clippings as well as later speculation by member of the Pinkerton family and their chosen historians, they are bereft of contemporary detective records.[11] There is, however, a memoir that partially remedies the deficit.

Charles Siringo offered a first-hand account in his autobiographical narrative, *Pinkerton's Cowboy Detective*. Born in Texas in 1855, Siringo spent many years as a cowpuncher. He then found himself in Chicago at the time of the 1886 Haymarket bomb explosion. The event shocked him into a hatred of anarchists and prompted him to seek employment with the Pinkertons. In a memoir that the PNDA sought to suppress, he recalled that the Pinkerton detective headquarters in the aftermath of Haymarket "was a large room, separated from the main offices with secret ways of entrance and exit." In a remark that suggested the abolitionist principles of Allan Pinkerton had not been entirely forgotten, he noted that "Africa was represented in the person of a negro familiarly known as 'Black Jim.'"[12]

Like his off-and-on confederate Tom Horn, Siringo was an able tracker, and he succeeded in bringing about the arrest of a number of rustlers. Still working for the Pinkertons, in 1892 he infiltrated the miners' union in Coeur d'Alene, Idaho, under the assumed name of Charles Leon Allison. He secured information that led to the arrest of several labor militants.

Siringo recorded that at the behest of the Pinkerton agency he similarly infiltrated the Hole in the Wall gang in the days when Butch Cassidy was in charge (Siringo spelled the outlaw's name "Casiday"). According to his account, he contributed to the scattering of the gang and to its demise. His narrative is revealing about the reach of the Pinkertons, even if he is critical of the PNDA's managerial style. The agency was striving to be more systematic. It tracked the serial numbers on stolen banknotes—it will be recalled that Ben Kilpatrick's arrest came because of the traceability of the currency he stole from the Great Northern Express.

Bureaucratic though it may have been, the PNDA's interstate reach allowed it to deny to fugitives the cloak of anonymity. In December 1900 Cassidy, Sundance, Kilpatrick, Kid Curry, and a confederate named Bill Carver posed for a group photograph in Fort Worth, Texas. They wore suits and waistcoats complete with pocket watches and bowler hats. It was a gesture of defiance that backfired. The PNDA made multiple copies of the image and circulated it

Figure 18.1. The Hole in the Wall Gang, aka the Wild Bunch, photographed in Fort Worth, Texas, in December 1900. Clockwise from top left, Will Carver, Harvey Logan (Kid Curry), Leroy Parker (Butch Cassidy), Ben Kilpatrick (the Tall Texan), and Harry Longabaugh (the Sundance Kid). *John Swartz, Denver Public Library Western History Collection, Z-49*

throughout the West, denying the Wild Bunch any chance of obscurity. Siringo was unimpressed by such bureaucratic procedures because he was a loner and a tracker who had low regard for middle-management practices. The PNDA disapproved of his critical tone and forced him to change the title of his memoir *Pinkerton Cowboy Detective* to *The Cowboy Detective*, with all references to the brothers Pinkerton changed to Dickenson.[13]

Siringo's efforts in the event combined with those of his employer—and, increasingly, the maturing regular forces of law and order—to make life hard for the Hole in the Wall gang. Its activities did not survive beyond the first decade of the twentieth century. However, the two most charismatic members of the gang were never apprehended in the United States. These were Butch Cassidy and the Sundance Kid.

Sundance's decision to leave the United States reflected the constant pressures felt by a wanted man. It also stemmed from his romance with Etta Place. This was an attractive woman in her early twenties whom he had met in Texas.

Figure 18.2. The Sundance Kid and Etta Place photographed in DeYoung's New York City studio in 1900. *Library of Congress*

Little is known about Etta Place. Her first name seems to have been an invention. "Place" was Sundance's mother's maiden name. It was the name that they both used when they checked into a New York boarding house in February 1901, Sundance signing himself "Harry E. Place." Butch Cassidy was with them, lodging under the name "Ryan." That Sundance and his girl may have been married by then is suggested by the fact that the couple visited Etta's parents. They had also commissioned a photograph, at the DeYoung studio on Broadway, of themselves as a couple dressed in their finery. The Pinkertons later obtained a copy of the photograph and disseminated it widely.

Various Pinkerton reports speculated that Etta had been a prostitute or that she had been a teacher. They guessed that she was a good horsewoman, that she could handle a rifle, that she dressed as a man while participating in bank raids, and that her role in such raids was to hold the horses in preparation for the outlaws' getaway. More reliably, they reported that Etta was 5′5″ tall and weighed between 110 and 115 pounds.

According to one Pinkerton report, Sundance committed a final US "hold up robbery" while registered at his boarding house on East 12th Street. Shortly afterward, on February 20, 1901, Sundance, Etta, and Butch Cassidy sailed on the Glasgow-built steamer *Herminius* for Buenos Aires.[14]

The foregoing information comes from *subsequent* Pinkerton documents. The agency's detectives had no idea, at the time, that Sundance and Cassidy had left the country. Like the *Philadelphia Public Ledger*, the Pinkertons assumed that Sundance and Cassidy participated in the holdup of the Great Northern train on July 3, 1901. The PNDA issued a poster offering a reward for information leading to their apprehension for that holdup. It disseminated an information sheet indicating that Sundance was "supposed to have participated" in the Montana heist along with Kid Curry and Ben Kilpatrick. Someone in the Pinkerton office later drew neat, straight lines through that information realizing it could not be true, as Sundance had left for South America several months before the robbery in question. The corrected Pinkerton information sheet left intact a paragraph asserting that Sundance had already robbed the Great Northern on an earlier occasion—in December 1892, along with confederates Bill Madden and Harry Bass. It was a muddled piece of misinformation. The Pinkerton detectives were completely at sea.[15]

The assumption that Cassidy and Sundance must have been behind the daring Montana train robbery reflected the awe in which they were held. Their departure added color to their image. In March 1904 the *Denver Republican* announced that Cassidy was in South America. It reported the view of former US marshal Joseph H. Forquer that the Pinkertons and bankers knew where they had gone but were now disinclined to spend thousands on an effort to capture them. Cassidy had been the "smoothest" of the Hole in the Wall gang. The paper recited Forquer's story of how Cassidy outwitted a detective sent to Duncan, Arizona, just after Cassidy's participation in a robbery of the First National Bank of Winnemucca, Nevada. The cowboys and ranchers of Duncan were on Cassidy's side. They spotted the detective and planned to "feather" him. Cassidy took the matter in hand. He had grown a beard since the robbery and was able to fool the detective as to his identity. He took the unwitting not to say witless sleuth aside and said the unruly crowd outside the local saloon were about to lynch him. He, Cassidy, would be willing to guide him to safety. This he did, and the innocent detective never returned to the scene. Even the hard-bitten Forquer, who had run in several outlaws, admired such genius.[16]

From Buenos Aires the party of three continued south along the Atlantic coast by steamboat. They reached Puerto Rawson, on the estuary of the Chubut River. From there, they passed through the Welsh settlement of Trelew, then headed inland on horseback, reaching a ranch they had purchased, still in the Patagonian province of Chubut and a short distance from the communities of 16 d'October and Cholila. The Welsh called the area "Cwm Hyfryd" ("Beautiful Valley"). Etta and Sundance set up in a four-room log cabin on the east bank of the Rio Blanco. Taking advantage of recent dispensations from the Argentine government—and no doubt helped by the proceeds of past misdeeds—they developed their 15,000-acre domain, with Etta owning a share and becoming one of the first female landowners in Argentina. On April 3, 1902, Sundance and Etta arrived back in New York without Cassidy. Possibly Sundance sought further treatment for a stomach ailment that a New York doctor had treated in 1901, or perhaps Etta was already homesick. They then returned to Patagonia without being troubled by the Pinkertons. Nor were the Pinkertons any the wiser when the couple visited New York again in 1903.[17]

But US marshal Forquer had been wrong to assume that the Pinkertons would let things lie. The agency pursued a vendetta against Sundance and his traveling companions, and for good reason. The fugitives were high-profile targets, and success would confer prestige on the PNDA. Furthermore, even if US bankers had given up financing the specific pursuit (perhaps indifferent now that the fugitives were no longer robbing North Americans), the agency was still under general contract to the American Bankers' Association. The First National Bank of Winnemucca was an association member and demanded the return of the $32,640 stolen by Sundance and Cassidy in their noon raid of September 19, 1900.

On March 8, 1903, the New York office of the PNDA cabled Francis P. (Frank) Dimaio. Of Italian heritage, Dimaio was one of the agency's best-regarded detectives. Italian American cases had made him famous. Following the murder of a New Orleans police chief in 1890 arising from a labor dispute involving Sicilian longshoremen, Dimaio had posed as a prisoner and extracted a confession from the murderer, who languished in the same jail. Later, he had displayed ingenuity and courage—if not success—in pursuing the Black Hand, an early manifestation of the Mafia.[18]

When he received the New York cable, Dimaio was working on another case in São Paulo, Brazil. The PNDA told him to go to Buenos Aires to await further instructions. Those instructions directed him to locate Sundance, Cassidy, and Etta. Local US Legation personnel put Dimaio in touch with a dentist called Newberry who said he owned a ranch in Cholila, where Harry Place and his wife and "James Ryan" (i.e., Cassidy) were neighboring ranchers. Newberry warned that the coming rainy season meant the region would be unreachable for some time and that an arrest would be difficult because the wanted men and woman were now accepted locally as respectable citizens. So Dimaio did the next best thing. He circulated details and photographs of the fugitives to all police departments, banks, and shipping companies in Argentina.[19]

Julio Lezana, the governor of Chubut Province, issued an arrest warrant charging Cassidy and company with robbing an Argentinian bank in Villa Mercedes (if that was true—and the case never went to trial—the former American desperadoes had not entirely exchanged their old ways for a more peaceful existence). In April 1905 Milton Roberts, a local rancher-policeman bearing a Welsh surname, set out to assist in the arrest. However, he arrived five days too late. The local sheriff, Edward Humphreys, was a member of the Patagonian Welsh community who remembered that the Welsh had settled in the region earlier in the nineteenth century to escape cultural and religious discrimination in the United Kingdom. Humphreys had befriended, and sympathized with, the American fugitives.[20] Rumor had it that he was enamored of Etta. Instead of arresting the couple, he tipped them off and helped them to escape before the arrival of Roberts and his party—actions for which Humphreys lost his job as sheriff. Cassidy and Etta Place sold their ranch and traveled to Chile. Butch Cassidy accompanied them.

If Sundance and Etta had dreamed of living respectably, that dream had now ended. At some point—the date differs in various accounts, and the fugitives were careful to cover their tracks—Sundance accompanied Etta back to her homeland one more time before returning alone to South America. The couple would never meet again. "Etta Place"—no historian has discovered her real name—disappeared from the record books.

Sundance (now claiming to be Frank Boyd) and Cassidy holed up in Antofagasta, a northern Chilean port town noted for its bordellos. Evidence of a chilling incident that took place there has recently come to light. On August 21, 1905, Sundance got involved in a late-night brawl in a restaurant. Police officer Arturo González, a married man with a two-year-old son, intervened. Sundance shot him dead. It is possibly the first time he had killed a man. He blamed the event on the deficient design of his Smith and Wesson revolver, which was given to premature ejaculation. When arrested for killing González, Sundance had on him almost $70,000 in cash. For whatever reason, the local US consul put up bail for him, possibly unaware that "Frank Boyd" was an alias.[21]

Sundance and Cassidy fled the scene and, covering vast distances as they had during their US life of crime, engaged over the next three years in a series of robberies. The PNDA persisted in its poster campaign. One Spanish-language poster, issued on February 4, 1907, indicated that information could be sent directly to Robert Pinkerton in New York. The poster ignored the by now numerous infractions the famous outlaws had committed in South America. It referred instead to the First National Bank of Winnemucca heist.

But the PNDA could not let go of the Great Northern theme. For its poster had some additions to its earlier picture gallery. One was Etta Place, described as "La esposa de Harry Longbaugh," or Sundance's wife. The other was Kid Curry, the acknowledged perpetrator of the Great Northern robbery. A few pages back, we left Curry in prison having been arrested in a pool room in Knoxville. He escaped. He then robbed a Denver and Rio Grande train near Parachute, Colorado. A posse hunted him down and, on June 19, 1904, there was a gunfight. Wounded, Kid Curry shot himself dead to escape further incarceration. However, the PNDA poster subscribed to the rumor that the Parachute corpse was not Curry's. It further endorsed the myth that Curry had escaped to South America to team up with Sundance and Cassidy. Robert Pinkerton's poster was wrong about this, as it was about Etta's location.[22]

On November 3, 1908, two bandits later assumed to be Sundance and Cassidy robbed a courier for the Armayo Franke silver mine company near San Vicente, Bolivia. They used a pair of mules to carry their booty to their boarding house in the small town. Their landlord Bonifacio Casasola, a miner, noticed that the mules were branded and the property of the Armayo Franke company. He reported his concern to the authorities. Three days later, a small cavalry contingent and several local policemen surrounded the boarding house. The ensuing gunfight lasted until just before 2 a.m. the next day. At that hour the Bolivian law enforcers heard screams followed by two gunshots. On the arrival of daylight, the officers carefully entered the house and surveyed the bloodied scene. They deduced from the body positions and ballistic evidence that both men had been wounded by several bullets. When “Sundance” (if it was he) screamed in agony, Cassidy had shot him in the forehead. He then performed a second mercy killing, shooting himself in the temple.

In a way the Pinkertons could claim to have triumphed. They had flushed out the outlaws, forcing them into ever more risky crimes with the result that they made their inevitable fateful error, using branded mules. But no Pinkerton man had been present to cover himself with glory at the San Vicente shootout. The poster campaign had been badly performed, even if it did oblige Sundance and the others to leave Patagonia and go on the run. It was testimony to the popularity of Cassidy and Sundance that, as in Curry’s case, stories spread that they had never died.[23] In 1943 the PNDA’s research division collected clippings about Kid Curry and the Wild Bunch with a view to boosting the agency’s reputation. But it found scant evidence that the Pinkertons had been credited at the time. It concluded there was “not sufficient material [illegible] to write a brief. Agency not mentioned.”[24]

In his post-presidential autobiography, Theodore Roosevelt devoted a chapter to the “Cowboy Land” where he had spent happy days in the 1880s: “It was still the Wild West in those days, the Far West, the West of Owen Wister’s stories and Frederic Remington’s drawings, the West of the Indian and the buffalo-hunter, the soldier and the cow-puncher. That land of the West has gone now, “‘gone, gone with lost Atlantis,’ gone to the isle of ghosts and of strange dead memories.”[25]

In the case of the Sundance Kid, the Pinkertons had tried to capture some of the final, golden rays of the setting western sun, but to little avail.

A similar lack of success characterized a very different western story, a story that would once again feature James McParland and Charlie Siringo. That story focused on the assassination in 1905 of the fourth governor of the state of Idaho.

CHAPTER 19

The Trial of the Wobblies

It was just days before Christmas, 1905. Frank Steunenberg had performed a Saturday-afternoon chore, the renewal of his life insurance policy. As he prepared to walk home from downtown Caldwell, Idaho, shortly after 6 p.m., the road before him was bleak and white. There was nothing unusual about the frost that crispened the fresh, eight-inch snowfall. It did not unduly worry a forty-four-year-old who still retained the vigor that had driven him to pioneer the development of Caldwell and to serve in high political office—he was still known as "the Governor" a full five years after finishing his term in Boise.

The crunch, crunch of the Governor's steps quickened as his solid, 6′2″ frame neared the welcoming glow of his house on Sixteenth Street. He did not notice the shadowy figure that passed him by in the opposite direction. Reaching his garden fence, Steunenberg performed a small act that would have major repercussions for the whole of America. He pulled back the gate slide.

The blast was so loud, it could be heard sixteen miles away. The Governor's thirteen-year-old daughter Frances was watching through a window for her father's return. The white flash stunned her eyes. With her mother Belle, she rushed outside. Where once the gate had been, there was now a crater. Ten feet away, a sight that no daughter should see. The quick arrival of three doctors was to no avail. What remained of the fond father expired twenty minutes later.[1]

In Caldwell citizens began an immediate search for the bomber. The murder was a national sensation, but long before the arrival of any professional detective, local amateurs formed their suspicions. Registered at the Saratoga Hotel under the name of Thomas Hogan, an out-of-town individual had raised eyebrows because he had a ready supply of dollars but no visible means of income.

The evening of the explosion, he had been playing whist with some local farmers. During an interlude in that game, he had excused himself, returning only minutes after the high-decibel boom. His demeanor then had been calm, but he had shown little appetite for his food later in the evening. As so often happens, individuals in a small community pointed their accusing fingers at an outsider. On New Year's Day, 1906, Judge M.I. Church of the Canyon County Probate Court issued a warrant for the arrest of Hogan on a charge of first-degree murder. At 4 p.m., Sheriff Jasper P. Nichols entered the Saratoga's bar room and arrested the unresisting suspect.

This news was of special interest to the Mine Owners Association (MOA) of Idaho's Coeur d'Alene district. At the time of the district's "labor wars," Governor Steunenberg had upheld the MOA members' right to manage their businesses in their own way and without making concessions to organized workers. What if his killing was more than a casual murder? What if it was a politically motivated assassination performed under the direction of the labor unions? If such could be proved, it would be a propaganda coup for the employers and their political allies. They had lost an old friend in Steunenberg, but the cloud might have a silver lining.

It did not take a genius to realize that given the possibility of discrediting the union movement, the MOA was likely to give generous support to an investigation. Attracted by the prospect of gain, the Thiel Detective Agency was the first on the scene. George H. Thiel had spied under the direction of Allan Pinkerton in the Civil War and later formed his own agency. The Thiel outfit had made only slight inroads on the Pinkerton client base. However, it did have fourteen offices nationwide and had established a footing in the Coeur d'Alene district. There, Thiel's western supervisor, Wilson S. Swain, had deployed an effective undercover agent. Edward L. Zimmerman got himself elected financial secretary of the local union. He supplied the mine owners with the names of union supporters, and they were duly fired and blacklisted.

When Swain turned up in Caldwell with a retinue of Thiel detectives, he persuaded the MOA and judicial authorities to entrust him with the interrogation of the arrested man. Thomas Hogan told Swain that his real name was Harry Orchard. This was not true. "Hogan" had been born Albert Edward Horsley, in Wooler, Ontario, where his parents were impoverished English and Irish farmers. However, Harry Orchard would stick as the name that would go down in infamy.

Swain made little further progress, so the local worthies looked further afield. They approached James McParland. This was an opportunity for the Denver manager to displace Swain and to earn stipends and reputational credit for the Pinkerton agency. However, McParland was by now in his sixties and engaged in directing the activities of others. He was no longer in the habit of doing his own field work. As early as 1901, he had told George Bangs he was not fit enough to travel to Laramie, Wyoming, to investigate the Union Pacific train robbery of 1899 (attributed to the Wild Bunch).[2] Yet in light of the high-profile, strategic nature of the Steunenberg murder case, he now hesitated to say no. Instead, he asked the Pinkerton brothers to decide. Robert and William resolved to commit McParland once more to the fray. They asked the veteran detective to travel to Caldwell and engage with the case, but only if he received an assurance that the Pinkertons would be in sole charge. Governor Frank Gooding agreed to this and dismissed Swain.

At 7 a.m. on Tuesday, January 9, 1906, McParland boarded a train in Denver and traveled to Boise, where he arrived at 6:20 a.m. the following day. He checked in at Idaho's most luxurious hotel, the Idanha. He met Governor Gooding, who briefed him on the murder case. That same day, McParland filed the first of his many reports on the case. Though he had not yet met Harry Orchard, he offered an interpretation of events that that was rooted in his role in the Molly Maguire episode. He suspected the complicity of the Western Federation of Miners (WFM). This was the union that since 1893 had sought to organize the workers in the Rocky Mountains' metalliferous mining and smelting sector:

> I am satisfied that there were other people in this plot besides Orchard, and feel sure that Orchard was the tool of others. . . . I think we will be able to convict the man, but this conspiracy is so wide spread and so well and secretly conducted, that it would not surprise me to find out that the W.F. of M. has one or more men in Caldwell as bona fide residents for [the] purpose of proving an alibi. Such men may have their wives, or women posing as their wives, to help them out in the plot.[3]

McParland now set about his business. He had Orchard transferred from Caldwell to death row in the state penitentiary in Boise. The experienced interrogator was engaging in psychological warfare. In contemporary parlance, he was "sweating" the suspect. After three days in Spartan solitary confinement, Orchard met his inquisitor, who arranged for luxuries such as cigars and a shower. He suggested that a confession would make things still easier for him. Such a confession could be based on the 1870s precedent:

> I then told Orchard who I was and stated that my main reason for interceding for the men who turned states evidence was not because they were innocent but because they had allowed themselves to become tools of the men of the inner circle of the Mollie Maguires, who were more guilty than they who actually committed the crimes, . . . that they did the biddings of the inner circle of the Mollie Maguires just as he had done the biddings of the inner circle of the W. F. of M.[4]

On January 27, Orchard began to talk. Six days later, he signed a confession. It implicated WFM leaders in the murder, namely Charles Moyer, the WFM president; George Pettibone, a former WFM militant; and William Dudley "Big Bill" Haywood, the union's general secretary. McParland sent copies of the 140-page confession to senior PNDA colleagues. He explained to William Pinkerton that he had observed the greatest secrecy in obtaining Orchard's testimony on the "objects and conduct of these cut-throats." When conducting his series of interviews, he had always entered the penitentiary taking a circuitous route via a cigar store and a "natatorium" though he never used its facilities: he quipped that he was "in need of a bath but have not had time to take one." McParland was confident that he had evaded the attention of the "reporters and hackmen gaping at all corners."[5]

A purpose lay behind McParland's secrecy. His intention was to catch Moyer, Haywood, and Pettibone off guard so that they could be captured and brought to trial in Boise. None of them had been in Caldwell at the time of the assassination, but an Idaho statute defined a crime of conspiracy to murder for which the union officials could be arrested. All three of the WFM men were in Denver when Idaho officials arranged with Governor James H. Peabody of Colorado to put the local police at the disposal of the Pinkerton men. On February 17, the miners' leaders were captured, detained without access to lawyers, and removed from Colorado under armed guard on a specially commissioned train. Stopping only for water and fuel in locations selected for their obscurity, the train delivered its cargo to Boise. WFM supporters complained of kidnapping. They challenged the procedure on the ground that their leaders' habeas corpus rights had been violated. The case rose to the US Supreme Court, which decided in favor of the Idaho authorities. Moyer, Haywood, and Pettibone went on trial on a charge of conspiracy to murder.

The Idaho MOA had sound practical reasons to promote the idea that an "Inner Circle" within the WFM was behind the Steunenberg assassination. It gave them an opportunity to smash the union and maximize profits by paying lower wages. The notion of a criminal WFM Inner Circle was satisfyingly plausible. The WFM's leadership seemed to have had a clear motive for murder. Union men hated Steunenberg. In a WFM-led strike in the Coeur d'Alene district in 1899, the then governor had called on President William McKinley to send in federal troops—at the time, the Idaho state militia was unavailable because its members had departed to fight in the Spanish–American War. Washington had sent in a contingent that included African American soldiers. Indignant and racially illiberal local citizens alleged that these men were molesting striking miners' wives. The newly appointed US secretary of war, Elihu Root, promptly withdrew them and threatened to pull out federal troops altogether.[6] The remaining non-Black soldiers remained long enough, however, to imprison pro-WFM miners in "bull pens," stockaded encampments that were evocative of the notorious concentration villages used by the Spanish authorities in Cuba and the British in South Africa. The WFM's bitterness toward Steunenberg is summed up in the reported reaction of one of its publicists to the bomb explosion that killed the former governor: "the gate was completely wrecked."[7]

Orchard charged that the WFM Inner Circle was acting in character when it killed Frank Steunenberg. He maintained it had long engaged in atrocities in the course of the labor wars of the Rocky Mountain region. One such atrocity occurred during the 1903–04 miners' strike in the Cripple Creek region of Colorado, a time when the Colorado MOA, in league with Governor Peabody, had confronted the WFM. At 2:15 a.m. on June 6, 1904, an explosion destroyed the depot of the Florence and Cripple Creek Railroad that served the Findlay mine. Twenty-seven strikebreaking workers who had just come off shift were at the time waiting on the platform for a train that would take them home. Thirteen of them were killed. Four days later, a coroner's jury found that the explosion was the consequence of "a conspiracy entered into by certain members of the Western Federation of Miners."[8] Orchard later stated that he and a confederate, Steve Adams, had set the bomb, on the instruction of Pettibone and with the approval of Haywood. He offered a complex rationale that had to do with an alleged power struggle between Haywood and Moyer. Moyer was supposedly more restrained, and Haywood was seeking to impose his authority.[9]

Thirty men lost their lives in the Cripple Creek struggle of 1904, a high proportion of the fifty-seven violent deaths that occurred in metalliferous mining industrial conflicts between 1892 and 1904. The gold, silver, copper and lead miners were second only to the nation's far more numerous coal miners in their susceptibility to death by industrial conflict.[10] The contemporary scholar

Benjamin M. Rastall argued that the Cripple Creek conflict in the early 1890s reflected frontier conditions, with strikers typically being bachelors who had been itinerant prospectors and were averse to collective work discipline, free of family responsibilities, and prone to anarchic rebellion. Ten years later, the Cripple Creek miners lived in more settled communities and enjoyed family life. Rastall found that they were slow to strike, but, as their families' sole breadwinners, prone to desperation when non-union labor displaced them in a region where other jobs were not on offer.[11] To these characteristics may be added the monocultural nature of the western mining communities, which meant that, as in the mining patches of 1870s Pennsylvania, there was neither an independently minded middle-class citizenry to negotiate peaceful resolutions to disputes nor an even-handed police and judicial system.

PNDA officials were less concerned with these niceties than with the opportunity to defame the WFM and the labor movement generally. Echoing the writings of his former employer Allan Pinkerton, McParland equated unionism and violence. He would unrepentantly stick to this line. In 1915 in the wake of a federal inquiry into labor relations, he sent Pinkerton superintendent George D. Bangs a summary of violent events he said America's unions had perpetrated since 1866, the year from which the Pinkertons dated their involvement in labor work.[12] Anti-union employers joined in the chorus. The Colorado MOA published a "Red Book" of crimes committed by the WFM. The WFM described it as a list of all crimes in the region, whether committed by union men or not.[13]

Labor violence was alarming in the early years of the twentieth century, the more so when viewed in the context of rising fears of social upheaval—fears that encouraged the development of Progressive reform politics. Concern had built up over the years. In the wake of the Paris Commune of 1871, the philanthropist Charles Loring Brace had issued a book pointing a fear-struck finger at "the Prolètaires of New York." Allan Pinkerton had published his *Strikers, Communists* book seven years later. Edward Bellamy's *Looking Backward* (1888) warned of an "impending social cataclysm." The twentieth century dawned with a nerve-jangling reminder of Haymarket, the assassination of President McKinley by a self-proclaimed anarchist, Leon Czolgolz. In the year of the Haywood–Moyer–Pettibone arrests, there appeared a book titled *The Scarlet Empire*. Its author, National Association of Manufacturers president David M. Parry, wrote of a potential revolution led by the American Federation of Labor (AFL), and of the terrors that would ensue. It was a conservative view but was complemented by the output of left-wing writers. The socialist Jack London published his cataclysmic novels *War of the Classes* and *Iron Heel* in 1905 and 1907, respectively. This backdrop of imagined revolution boded ill for the Moyer–Haywood–Pettibone defense.[14]

It did not help the defendants' cause that they had recently rejected American democracy. The suppression of the people's will in Colorado and other western states accounted for their decision. In 1894 the Cripple Creek gold miners had struck for an eight-hour working day and demanded a law to impose that provision. When the Colorado Supreme Court rejected the law on the ground of constitutional incompatibility, the Republican, Democratic, and Populist Parties all endorsed an amendment to the Colorado state constitution. In 1902 a referendum gave force to the amendment with a resounding approval rating of 72 percent. The following year, under pressure from mining corporations (the unions smelled bribery), the state legislature refrained from passing the enabling law, with Governor Peabody openly supporting the mine owners' resistance to it. This was the context, ignored by his critics, for Big Bill Haywood's question, posed frequently in his speeches thereafter, "Do you blame me when I say I despise the law; that I am not a law-abiding citizen?"[15]

On June 27, in 1905, the year before his indictment for the murder of Steunenberg, Haywood addressed the founding convention of the Industrial Workers of the World (IWW, or Wobblies). The convention took place in Allan Pinkerton's adoptive hometown, Chicago. The revolutionary organization rejected not only old-style party politics as practiced by the Democrats and Republicans but also the parliamentary democracy espoused by the more moderate Socialist Party of America (SPA) which had been founded four years earlier. The IWW wanted industry-wide unionism and not the craft-based unionism of the AFL that excluded so many workers. Its aim was to replace America's political system with government that was answerable to "one big union." Vague though this philosophy was, it rang alarm bells and threatened the chances of a fair trial for Haywood—and for Moyer, who had been present in Chicago and who affiliated his WFM to the IWW.

In an indiscreet fillip to the prosecution, President Roosevelt condemned the defendants. His words stood out because the Progressive Republican president was far from hostile to labor. His campaign slogan was "Square Deal." His insistence on arbitration as the solution to the protracted anthracite coal strike of 1902 had been the first federal intervention in a labor dispute that did not favor employers. He disapproved of the undemocratic course of events in Colorado and believed in using his "Big Stick" to discipline plutocrats as well as recalcitrant workers.

However, when, in a much-publicized statement on June 8, 1906, Roosevelt slapped down E.H. Harriman for boasting he could buy any state legislature, he rashly stated it made the railroad magnate "at least as undesirable a citizen as [SPA leader Eugene V.] Debs, or Moyer, or Haywood." It was those last few words that shocked those who hoped for a fair trial in Boise.[16]

From the Pinkerton point of view, the auguries could hardly have been better. McParland was marshalling the case for the prosecution with some skill. He retained Charlie Siringo as his bodyguard. As well as being a long-serving Pinkerton gunslinger, Siringo had been active in the suppression of the 1892 Coeur d'Alene miners' strike. His loyalty could be assumed, and his presence as bodyguard projected the message that McParland faced a murderous foe. Early in 1906 Governor Gooding wrote to William Pinkerton rejoicing that McParland had brought to justice "the worst gang of assassins the world has ever known" and was achieving "great results in his old age." William replied praising McParland's breaking down of Orchard, his "wonderful memory," and his identification of an "inner circle." Later in the year Gooding congratulated McParland on "the crowning effort of a life well spent for the betterment of mankind."[17]

On May 9, 1907, the trial at last began. Haywood's long wait in the Boise penitentiary had deprived the IWW of its charismatic leader in its formative years. Haywood, already a radical, would become further embittered toward the rulers of his native land—on his death in 1928 his ashes would be divided between the Kremlin wall and a spot near the Haymarket Martyrs memorial in Chicago. In contrast the Pinkerton brothers were ever more confident. When the *Cincinnati Enquirer* published an article praising McParland's efforts in Boise, William Pinkerton made sure it was widely circulated. McParland was pleased that the article explained the continuum between the Mollies and the WFM. Robert Pinkerton, now in the final weeks of his life, wrote to McParland from New York expressing his delight at the publicity: "There are very full accounts of the trial being published here, and there is a great deal of comment on it. You see everybody reading it on the railroad trains, ferry-boats, Subway and Elevated cars. So far as I can hear, the general impression appears here that the State is going to be successful in proving their case."[18]

Not everything went smoothly. McParland constantly complained to his employers about his ill health. As the strain took its toll, he wondered whether his sacrifice was worthwhile. He asked for and obtained an increase in his annual salary from $2,200 to $2,300.[19] Orchard was another problem. The prosecution relied heavily on Orchard's testimony, and the killer became problematic in an unpredictable way. Perhaps anticipating his conversion to Christianity, he became ever more eager to reveal his crimes, and he began to over-confess—to a list of misdeeds whose length was a challenge to credulity.

To handle such matters, the prosecution needed a good lawyer. The task fell to William E. Borah. Subsequently well known as a maverick Progressive and as an "Irreconcilable" opponent of US membership in the League of Nations, in 1906 Borah was already a star in the Idaho legal and political firmament. Famed for his oratory, he had just been elected to serve in the US Senate. He was a lawyer of some standing. His partnership in Idaho's leading law firm, Borah and Blake, made him an annual income in the region of $30,000.

It looked like an old story. A mistrial was on the cards. When working men were pitted against the rich and powerful in America's twisted legal system, the odds were stacked against them. The WFM and AFL nevertheless raised money for the defense and were able to pay for a team of lawyers, if not for an army of private detectives. The attorney they chose to lead Haywood's defense had experience with labor cases. He had represented the miners in the 1902 anthracite coal strike arbitration for a fee of $10,000. He would earn an estimated $35,000 for his role in the long-drawn-out Steunenberg trial. His name was Clarence Darrow.[20]

CHAPTER 20

The Verdict

The law case *State of Idaho v. William D. Haywood* was called to trial in Boise on May 9, 1907. The venue was Ada County Courthouse, a well-weathered brick construction that housed the local jail in its basement. The third-floor trial courtroom measured 70 by 45 feet. Jury members, witnesses, the accused, journalists, and spectators sat cheek by jowl as 250 people crammed into the limited space. McParland would sit out the proceedings a short distance away in the new and splendid Idanha hotel. He was absent from the courtroom because the prosecution regarded him as too divisive a figure to testify.[1]

Judge Fremont Wood called the court to order. His selection did not bode well for Haywood and his fellow Western Federation of Miners (WFM) defendants. For although Wood's father had been a New England abolitionist, his own record seemed to be one of anti-unionism. In the wake of the Coeur d'Alene strike of 1892, Wood had been the prosecuting attorney when thirteen union men had been convicted of contempt of court and four of criminal conspiracy. George Pettibone, a current defendant, had been one of the latter four. Little wonder that McParland was satisfied with the selection of Wood to be the trial judge. From labor's standpoint, it was the same old, same old story.[2]

John W. Carberry nevertheless anticipated a fair trial. A journalist in the thirteenth of his twenty years' service to the *Boston Daily Globe*, Carberry jostled daily with his fellow reporters for a seat in the crowded courthouse. Two days into the trial, he noted "the tremendous odds against Haywood on account of the President's utterances, the speeches of Gov. Gooding [and others], all interpreted as proclaiming the guilt of the miners to be placed on trial." Yet the experienced newspaperman remarked also on a seeming nervousness on the part of the prosecution, matched by a "confidence of acquittal" that pervaded the Haywood camp. Haywood's lawyers were in a buoyant mood. They were convinced that "the state cannot sufficiently corroborate the confession of Harry Orchard."[3]

Leading the defense team for Haywood, Clarence Darrow was the son of an abolitionist father and a feminist mother and was a determined, talented fighter for righteous causes. In the Steunenberg murder trial, he failed in one respect. To prove that Orchard did not act at the behest of the WFM, he needed a convincing alternative explanation of the assassin's motive in killing the former governor of Idaho. He found none. Darrow suggested unconvincingly that Orchard might have had a grudge against Steunenberg. He argued only slightly more persuasively that the killer simply worked for whoever paid him, meaning that he could have been an agent provocateur acting at the behest of mine-owners. There was no proof of the latter contention. However, for the purpose of defense, there did not need to be. All that Darrow and his defense team had to prove was that Orchard's account was unreliable and lacking in corroboration.

Behind the scenes though in plain view, as he held forth to journalists with his bodyguard Siringo at his side, McParland continued to search for corroborating witnesses. His search was in vain. More than this, McParland became a target for the defense. Despite the detective's strategic absence from court, Darrow directed a stream of defamation at him. He poured scorn on the story that McParland was a principled Catholic who had persuaded Orchard to become a Christian and do the right thing, confess. He threw vitriol at the private detective profession with its alleged lack of integrity. Orchard's tendency to over-confess did not help the prosecution case. He admitted to being a bigamist, an insurance fraudster, a sheep stealer, a saboteur, and the killer of at least seventeen victims. He testified that the WFM, Haywood especially, had commissioned his recent spate of dynamiting and killings as well as some unfulfilled missions, such as the assassination of Governor Peabody of Colorado. But how much of this could be verified?

If Darrow failed to supply a convincing explanation of Orchard's murder of Steunenberg, he was blessed with ample evidence of the motives of James McParland and his Pinkerton associates. On June 29, John Carberry filed a report on the issue under the heading, "Detective Spies in Miners' Union." It concerned the testimony of Morris Friedman. A young Russian American of striking appearance and a slow, careful manner of speaking, Friedman stated that he had been McParland's stenographer since 1901. He had seen the reports that crossed his employer's desk. These had shocked him, and he decided to be a whistleblower. He testified that McParland had waged a long and unscrupulous war on the WFM. He supplied examples. One of these was the story of Operative No. 42.[4]

When the Cripple Creek miners were expelled from the region for going on strike, they settled in a Denver suburb called Globeville. One A.W. Gratias, whom they had earlier elected as a local union president, accompanied them. Unknown to the miners, Gratias was in reality Pinkerton operative No. 42. He had been insinuated into the WFM on McParland's instructions. In Globeville Gratias was directed

> to be very liberal in the relief to the union miners and to make his bills as large as possible. He was told the purpose was to deplete the treasury of the Western federation by extravagant relief charges.
>
> When it was ascertained that this plan would not operate quickly enough he was ordered to give very little relief, and if the men complained to say that Mr Haywood had cut down his allowance because the work was costing too much.
>
> The agency thought this would dissatisfy the miners, disgust them with the federation and drive them back to Cripple Creek to work upon the terms of the mine owners.[5]

McParland's record of trying to destroy the WFM implied he had a motive for trying to pin the Steunenberg murder on Haywood, and this undermined Orchard's credibility.

In his peroration in Haywood's defense, Darrow did not try to prove innocence. He pointed to weaknesses in the prosecution's case and, famously, to social context. He told the jury of Idaho farmers that but for the labor union movement, "you today would be serfs instead of free men." The nation's unions, "despised and weak and outlaws as they generally are—have stood for the poor. . . . I don't care how often they fail, how many brutalities they are guilty of. I know their cause is just."[6] These were hard words for Darrow to utter, as he was a pacifist. Turning to Haywood, he did not push the character reference too far. "I don't claim that this man is an angel. The Western Federation of Miners could not afford to put an angel at their head. Do you want to hire an angel to fight the Mine Owners' Association and the Pinkerton detectives, and the power of wealth?"[7]

Darrow's appeal to social justice in the Haywood court case challenged the methodology of a legal establishment that had habitually depended on their knowledge of the finer points of law to advance the cause of the rich and powerful. The *Muller v. Oregon* case the following year, in which the US Supreme Court upheld the rights of female laundry workers after hearing arguments about their poor working conditions, would be a further example of Darrow's social approach to legal issues and would contribute to wider acceptance of his courtroom methodology. The outcome of the Haywood trial owed much to Darrow's innovatory tactics and oratorical skill.

Judge Wood's instruction to the jury also contributed to the outcome, as it showed none of the prejudice that WFM and Industrial Workers of the World (IWW) members had come to expect. He cautioned the jury that no man should be convicted on the basis of uncorroborated evidence. As John Carberry had foreseen, reliance on Orchard as its sole witness would be problematic for the prosecution. On July 29, the jury acquitted Haywood. Another jury later acquitted Pettibone, and the charges against Moyer were dropped.[8]

After the verdicts, leading protagonists in the trial experienced different fates. The courtroom drama enhanced Borah's national profile, and he would enjoy a stellar if controversial political career. Already respected as a labor lawyer, Darrow now enjoyed celebrity as a defense counsel and became ever more famous for cases such as the Scopes trial of 1925, which challenged the position of fundamentalism in the classroom. Haywood became a celebrated Wobbly revolutionary leader and even enjoyed a spell as the darling of fashionable New York salons before his exile to the Soviet Union. Orchard's conversion to Christianity helped save him from the noose and won him the support of the widowed Belle Steunenberg, who wanted him pardoned, but both McParland and William Pinkerton turned against him, and he spent the remainder of his long life in the state penitentiary in Boise.[9] McParland continued to insist on the guilt of Haywood and his WFM associates as he declined into self-pitying hypochondria and alcohol-fueled ill health until his death in 1919.

The reputation of the PNDA had already suffered because of previous involvement in labor cases, and the Haywood trial cemented its ill repute. Americans began to wear "I am an undesirable citizen" buttons, referencing President Roosevelt's injudicious intervention in the Haywood trial and showing solidarity with the WFM and IWW. Morris Friedman reinforced the impact of his testimony at the trial by writing a book about his recent employer, a publication that appeared before the year was out. In *The Pinkerton Labor Spy*, Friedman identified three types of PNDA operative: temporary per diem men, general, and labor spies. The latter were "the main source of revenue at every branch of the Agency." He identified by name and code number the operatives that he knew were working against labor unions in the West. He denounced as cosmetic the PNDA's anticrime publicity and its high-profile tactics such as the "Rogues' Gallery" of top wanted criminals originally established by Allan Pinkerton in 1855.[10]

With the trial still under way, Friedman published a portion of his forthcoming book in *The Industrial Union Bulletin*, an official publication of the IWW. Because it was "good business," he stated here, figuratively the Molly Maguires were "still being tried and hanged." Detectives had been at the back of some of the Cripple Creek dynamiting attributed to the WFM. The Moyer–Haywood–Pettibone trial was "a thrilling chapter of conspiracy, knavery and persecution; a chapter in which we find governors, sheriffs and famous Pinkerton detectives acting to perfection the infamous roles of rascals and kidnappers, in brazen defiance of laws and statutes." The misdeeds of the PNDA were "hidden from the public gaze by brilliantly painted lettering proclaiming the fact that the Agency represents the American Bankers' Association, the Jewelers' Protective Union, the Jewelers' Security Alliance, and the Railway Ticket Protective Bureau."[11]

Friedman's testimony and publications were a blow to the PNDA. It redoubled its efforts to cleanse its image. This was unfortunate for Charlie Siringo, who at the conclusion of his stint as McParland's bodyguard decided to revive his literary career and expand his cowboy recollections to embrace the full span of his years with the Pinkerton agency. He mortgaged his farm to help with publication costs. When the PNDA insisted he should not mention the agency or any of its personnel by name, he reluctantly agreed to use pseudonyms in an early edition of the work. The enforced changes embittered him. Aiming to get even, he worked on a hundred-page update titled *Two Evil Isms: Pinkertonism and Anarchism*. William J. Burns, a private detective who was the Pinkertons' arch-rival, assured Siringo it would sell a million copies.

The new book carried mixed messages. Old-style, it referred to the "Molly Maguire" mindset among the miners in Coeur d'Alene in 1892. It boasted of Siringo's pursuit of Butch Cassidy and the Sundance Kid. New-style, however, Siringo recanted in his account of Haymarket, the event that first inspired him to join the Pinkerton company. He now claimed that during the Haymarket affair the PNDA benefited from a million-dollar "slush fund," that it organized perjury, and that it continued to make "hay while the sun of anarchy shone." Turning to more recent events, Siringo wrote of a Pinkerton "inner circle" that orchestrated the "kidnap" of Haywood and his colleagues leading to the Boise trial.

With some success, the PNDA used legal stratagems to delay publication of this version of Siringo's book. When *Two Evil Isms* belatedly appeared, the agency bought up most available copies and acquired the printing plates. For Siringo the venture was a disaster. As for the PNDA, its behavior indicated it was an agency on the back foot.[12]

No amount of massaging the message could restore the standing of the PNDA. The Wobbly trial verdict was damaging and contributed to the loss of an opportunity for the agency. It failed to inspire the kind of presidential patronage that had stood it in good stead in the days of Abe Lincoln. A golden opportunity was missed when President Roosevelt, who had favored the prosecution of Haywood and company when it looked likely to succeed, decided to set up a new federal detective agency instead of relying on the private sector.

CHAPTER 21

The BofI: Challenge and Succession

President Roosevelt had expressed support for the prosecution case managed by McParland. But for the verdict, he might conceivably have taken that support further. As a Republican president contemplating the expansion of federal detective services, he could have challenged or attempted to disregard the Anti-Pinkerton Act of 1893 that forbade the federal employment of sleuths from the private sector. In the event, the verdict in the Haywood case, a blow to the prestige of the Pinkertons, removed any potential temptation to change the status quo. Roosevelt refrained from contesting the post-Homestead settlement, giving implicit bipartisan support to the 1893 legislation.

Roosevelt wanted an increased detection capability for the federal government. The need most recently arose from the fact that the president was a conservationist. With the Scottish-born naturalist John Muir, he campaigned for the preservation of Yellowstone National Park, the eastern edge of which was just a few miles west of Hole in the Wall territory. He was shocked to learn that land fraudsters were acquiring and despoiling tracts of irreplaceable western forest, with the assistance of some corrupt politicians—prosecuting attorney Senator William E. Borah came under investigation even as the Haywood trial was in progress, though he ultimately was acquitted. Roosevelt was convinced he needed a force of federally directed detectives to ferret out wrongdoers. There was a problem here, as Congress was wary of expanding the role of the US Secret Service, lest it snoop into the affairs of congressmen and senators on Capitol Hill, thereby establishing the trappings of a police state. It was one reason why the Pinkertons had been potentially an alternative option for Roosevelt.[1]

The Pinkertons had already tried to displace the Secret Service. The assassination of President McKinley in 1901 gave them an opportunity to press their case. A week after that tragic event, William Pinkerton asked, "how the secret service men could allow the assassin to approach the President with his hand wrapped in a handkerchief. . . . When my men are watching a distinguished person they allow no one to approach who carries a bundle or package of any description."[2]

Robert Pinkerton agreed with his brother about the concealed handgun and took the argument further. He reminded the readers of a popular journal of the PNDA's prowess in the Molly Maguires and Haymarket cases. Overlooking the success of the Secret Service in destroying the 1870s Ku Klux Klan and then a Montreal-centered Spanish spy ring in the war of 1898, he declared that the federal unit was not equipped to operate outside its original sphere of anticounterfeiting. He added a flourish that was reminiscent of the way in which the UK government had transported Chartist leaders to Australia in his father's radical days: "Let the government set aside one of the islands of the [recently acquired] Philippines, . . . then to this place send everybody who wants anarchy."[3]

Such was the opposition both to Pinkertonism and to the notion of expanding the remit and funding of the Secret Service that the Roosevelt administration proposed the founding of a separate federal detective agency that would help fight land fraud and crime generally. There was vociferous opposition in Congress to this idea. Roosevelt accused his critics of protecting the law breakers in their ranks. Opponents of his scheme advanced civil liberty arguments that have resonated through the ages. In the wake of the Haywood trial, nobody on Capitol Hill proposed that the Pinkerton agency should step into the breach as an alternative institution. However, some congressmen argued that, when the need arose, additional detectives could by hired on an ad hoc, per diem basis.

Congressman John J. Fitzgerald of New York warned that if twenty more detectives were added *permanently* to the federal roster, "then we will have in time a Federal secret police." His New York colleague William S. Bennet reminded him of a point already made by Congressman Walter I. Smith of Iowa, that the alternative was to hire Pinkertons—and that the "government is prevented, and properly prevented," from such a recourse. "Everybody knows what that law is," Fitzgerald retorted. He stated that the existing Secret Service had, in addition to its permanent roster, a list of 304 competent non-Pinkerton detectives it could, if necessary, coopt. Whenever *any* government department needed a detective, it could engage one from that pool on a job-specific basis.[4]

On July 26, 1908, Roosevelt's attorney general, Charles Bonaparte, issued an order that established what would become known as the Bureau of Investigation (BofI) and, from 1935, the Federal Bureau of Investigation (FBI). Congressmen had noted how Lincoln similarly established the Secret Service by executive decree and without approval by Congress and how history had now repeated itself. By the end of the year, the significance of the move was apparent in McParland's adoptive hometown. A Christmas-eve *Denver Daily News* headline announced, "Roosevelt Wants Whole Nation Under Watch; Would Vie with Pinkertons in Ferreting Out Offenders Against Law."[5]

The BofI was no immediate threat to the Pinkertons. It captured headlines for its war on "white slavery," as interstate prostitution was called, but that did not encroach on the Pinkertons' domain. The Secret Service, ably led by John E. Wilkie, who had orchestrated the successful campaign against Spanish spies in 1898, was at first a more evident rival. A former newspaperman, Wilkie skillfully projected an image of his special agents as men of good character, often with law qualifications and sometimes having the ability to speak more than one language. The PNDA opened a file on Wilkie noting these things and recording his troubles when the US Senate held hearings on the "Third Degree" methods of interrogation imputed to the Secret Service.[6]

In an age when public policing—and detection—was on the rise, the PNDA began to worry about personnel retention. Hitherto, an appointment to the agency had carried prestige. When Allan Pinkerton traveled east from Chicago to recruit him in the 1850s, George H. Bangs had leaped at the opportunity to leave the New York police in favor of the fledgling Pinkerton agency.[7] But it transpired that the prestige was portable. Over the years, operatives capitalized on the Pinkerton imprimatur to set up their own agencies or to apply for jobs in the public domain.[8] George Thiel left to establish his own private agency. The head of the Pinkertons' Philadelphia office, Robert J. Linden, quit to head the Philadelphia police department for two terms, 1891–97, then set up his own private detective agency. Robert Pinkerton had threatened to leave the agency in the early 1880s, but along with other top personnel had remained. In 1911, however, the PNDA suffered a grave defection. The highly regarded George S. Dougherty, an able detective who supervised the eastern division of the agency, resigned, and not even for a top post. He became second deputy commissioner of police in the NYPD, with responsibility for 150 detectives.

Because the PNDA was a family dynasty, there had been no room at the very top for a gifted individual who had worked his way up. The William J. Burns agency had already tried to poach Dougherty. On that occasion Allan Pinkerton II, the son of Robert who took over executive control of the New York office on his father's death on 1907, wrote to his uncle William expressing pleasure at Dougherty's decision to stay with the firm. He was, however, rattled. He suggested one of Dougherty's two deputies might be planted in the Burns agency, "at the same time remaining in our employ and advise us just what is going on? This is Burns' method of working and I believe in fighting the devil with fire at all times."[9]

When Dougherty intimated his decision to join the NYPD, William Pinkerton expressed his regret in a letter to George Bangs. True to the founder's belief—or assertion—that integrity lay in the private sector, he wrote, "I really and truly believe that Mr. Dougherty will have a hard row to hoe against politicians."[10] He may have been right, because in 1914 Dougherty left the New York police to form his own private detective agency. It remained his vocation until his death in 1924. Dougherty survived some graft investigations into his outfit and applied himself with missionary zeal to the introduction of fingerprinting as a means of criminal identification in the United States. Like Allan Pinkerton and his sons, he took an interest in criminal sociology, publishing a book in that field. A few years after his death, a New York newspaper praised Dougherty's detective work as an example of "Pinkerton persistence."[11]

In World War I the BofI played second fiddle to the Secret Service, which excelled in counterintelligence operations in conjunction with the British secret intelligence service. After being further stalled when mired in the Teapot Dome scandal in the early 1920s, the future FBI began to recover in 1924, when the youthful J. Edgar Hoover became its director. Hoover had been trained in information management at the Library of Congress and was open to new technologies. Dougherty is reputed to have bequeathed his fingerprinting expertise to Hoover's agency, and the PNDA also passed over their database on criminals to the BofI. The era of private criminal detection on a national scale had effectively come to an end.[12]

The Pinkertons left a legacy to the federal bureau that replaced them. Quite how concrete that legacy was is hard to quantify. The bequeathing of records was a straightforward matter, but there were less tangible influences. There is no convenient cache of letters from beyond the grave, beginning "Dear Edgar" and signed "Allan," yet the Pinkerton antecedents of the FBI are not to be lightly dismissed.

To be sure, there were differences. The Pinkertons enforced laws only on behalf of the rich who could pay them, whereas the BofI/FBI was in principle at the service of the whole community. Allan Pinkerton had been more liberal on issues of race and gender than the future director of the FBI. Hoover's BofI/FBI was renowned for its efficient record-keeping and systematized reports on suspects. Although Allan Pinkerton had stressed financial accountability, the Pinkertons were not quite so systematic. Partly because the Pinkertons were against divorce work, they mainly eschewed wiretapping.[13] The FBI became notorious for it and contributed, to a greater degree than the Pinkertons, to fears of a surveillance state.

But there were similarities. Allan Pinkerton and his two sons were determined self-publicists, establishing a cultural tradition that J. Edgar Hoover firmly embraced.[14] Pinkerton's emphasis on the rectitude of his agents had a strong echo in Hoover's insistence that that his special agents displayed white shirts and pure lives. Hoover made no claim to being a criminological liberal like the Pinkertons, but he did follow their example by pillorying the wicked. The FBI's "Ten Most Wanted" posters seemed umbilically tied to the Pinkertons' Rogues Gallery.[15] Conspicuously, Allan Pinkerton had helped to pioneer American anticommunism, and Hoover first made his name as an enthusiastic supporter of the 1919 Red Scare when still a junior official in the BofI. Pinkerton would have been pleased at the way in which Hoover continued to beat the anticommunist drum until he died in office in 1972. Finally, the Pinkerton agency inspired or provoked the actions of whistleblowers like Friedman and Siringo. The whistleblower was to become a fixture of the American political scene, not least when "Deep Throat" (FBI associate director Mark Felt) revealed the Watergate secrets that led to the resignation of President Richard Nixon in 1974.

Similarity is not always the result of influence. The practices of the FBI characteristically stemmed from similar challenges and stimuli, not from conscious imitation and learning. Perhaps it would be an oversimplification to say that the PNDA lost its standing as national crime-fighter to a rival of its own creation. Equally, there is more than a grain of truth in that assertion.

CHAPTER 22

Private Rivals

The Los Angeles Times Building was an impressive edifice. The three-storey structure occupied a downtown block defined by Broadway, Spring, First, and Second Streets. Within its arcaded stone walls, journalists wrote columns boosting their rapidly growing city. They articulated the cult of open-shop Los Angeles business leaders: labor unions were an abomination and a drag on progress.

The first explosion, at 1 a.m. on October 1, 1910, occurred in "Ink Alley," right next to the highly combustible stores of printing ink available to the newspaper's in-house printing presses. Five further explosions resulted in rapid succession. The south face of the building collapsed into Broadway. A fireball tore through the remainder of the structure, engulfing it in four minutes. Second-floor linotype machines smashed their way down to the ground, where they perforated pipes and released gas that fueled the flames. Doors jammed. Engravers on the top floor screamed for help. Twenty-one employees died.

On that very day, the surviving staff brought out an edition. The front-page banner headline announced, "Unionist Bombs Wreck the Times." It was a blatantly biased judgment, based on no immediate evidence.[1]

In this case, though, the evidence did emerge. It turned out that the trigger bomb had been set on behalf of the International Association of Bridge, Structural and Ornamental Ironworkers, or Bridgemen's Union. For some years, the union's leadership—with wide support from its local officials—had conducted what came to be known as the National Dynamite Campaign. The campaign targeted employers in the structural iron and steel industry. These employers subscribed to the "open shop" philosophy that was gaining strength at the time.

Essentially the open shoppers believed, in the words of historian Chad Pearson, that "they alone" had "the right to hire, fire, promote, or demote." It meant they had little time for labor unions.[2] Workers in the industry begged to differ. Improvements in the tensile strength of steel girders and cables had in recent decades made high-rise construction possible, in addition to more ambitious railway bridges. But working on such projects was notoriously dangerous. On behalf of its members, the union wanted a say in the improvement of working conditions and a share of the profits generated by the construction boom.

The Bridgemen's Union leadership as well as many of its members were of Catholic Irish heritage. Those who strove not to employ unionists characteristically bore names, such as McClintic-Marshall, Llewellyn Iron Works, Albert Vanspreckleseln, and Post and McCord, that suggested Protestant lineage. There was another similarity with the Molly Maguire struggle of the 1870s in that the Irish-descended militants were politically conservative and had no revolutionary objectives. They employed ruthless tactics that hearkened back not to the doctrines of Karl Marx but to habits acquired in the dark ages of repression and cultural clash in the far-off Emerald Isle.

The Los Angeles explosion, occurring as it did at a time of alarm about a resurgent IWW, provoked strong reactions. Walter Drew was one exponent of alarmism. A corporation lawyer from Grands Rapids, Michigan, Drew directed the National Erectors Association, an employer's organization founded in 1903. A widower and childless, he threw his considerable energies into anti-unionism. He had for years attempted to counter the National Dynamite Campaign. He saw the problem as criminal violence, not revolution. He declared that "violence is one of the commonest features of our strikes." He equated all unionism with imposition of the closed shop (jobs for union members only) and with an effort to monopolize the labor market. In an attempt to damn the whole labor movement, he linked the actions of the Bridgemen's Union with the policies of Samuel Gompers, president of the AFL. Anticipating that there would be a political reaction to the violent culmination of his struggle against the Bridgemen's Union, he implored Congress to do nothing that would increase the unionists' "ability to use their power for oppression, selfish ambition, civil war and plunder of the public."[3]

The nation's politicians were stirred. "Progressivism," then approaching its apex in American politics, embraced many shades of opinion and appealed to both Democrats and Republicans. It came to be part of the Progressive creed that violence in industrial disputes was not just a business issue but a problem that threatened the fabric of American society (the open shop movement was in this way situated beneath the Progressive umbrella).[4] Despite the innate conservatism of the Bridgemen's Union, there were fears that revolution might be lurking around the corner.[5] Leading Progressives like former President Roosevelt supported the idea that there should be an inquiry into US industrial relations. His successor and fellow Republican President William H. Taft agreed. He authorized a US Commission on Industrial Relations, supported also by the Democratic President Woodrow Wilson, who succeeded Taft in the White House. The inquiry was an example of bipartisan Progressivism. In Congress, Senator William H. Borah, the Republican who had unsuccessfully prosecuted William D. Haywood and his codefendants, sponsored the measure. The resultant major inquiry held hearings at various trouble spots in America. It additionally supported a Research Division that probed into the nation's troubled labor relations.

The Commission had a calming effect in the sense that it unearthed no evidence of a conspiracy to overthrow the republic. However, it did show concern at the provocative behavior of private detective agencies. It found that many a corporation maintained its own "private army" and that this practice was a "menace to public welfare." It regarded private detective agencies as a prime cause of industrial violence. Seeking to meet the unrealized demands of post-Homestead campaigners for a prolabor Anti-Pinkerton Act, it recommended restrictions on the interstate transportation of armed men, whether or not they received their weapons after they entered the state where they were to be employed. It called for the "regulation or prohibition of private detective agencies and private employment agencies" and declared that interstate detective agencies, were they not banned entirely, should be at least "compelled to take out a Federal license."[6]

Circumstances conspired against the enactment of these recommendations. Factional divisions within the Commission diminished its impact. They frustrated calls to publish a series of reports on private detective agencies compiled by the Commission's Research Division. Concerned though it may have been, the US Senate was still, in the words of a contemporary muckraker, a "millionaires' club," of its nature indisposed to enact measures harmful to business hegemony.[7] As the inquiry concluded its deliberations, World War I began, and soon the drumbeat of patriotism would muffle the divided voices of liberal reform.

Research Division staffer Daniel O'Regan uncovered a total of 275 detective agencies engaged in industrial relations work.[8] However, O'Regan and his colleague Inis Weed found it difficult to supply details of detectives' labor espionage and thuggery. They blamed it on concealment. Operatives wore masks when on dubious assignments. O'Regan and Weed also pointed to the reluctance of private detectives to keep written records. One prominent detective wrote to the director of the Research Division in words reminiscent of Allan Pinkerton's: "I render daily reports, and on these reports place the amount of money expended each day, which no other detective agency does."[9] Those who supervised O'Regan's work were disappointed by its lack of specifics.[10]

Such lack of detail was a further reason why the Commission's recommendations about restricting the labor work of private detectives did not find their way onto the federal statute books. The PNDA, like other agencies, had cause to be thankful. However, O'Regan's finding on the sheer volume of private eye involvement in labor work confirmed what had become an issue for the Pinkertons. They now had to contend with serious private competition, as well as with the BofI that blocked their path to federal employment.

Although the PNDA could muster larger numbers for special operations, its regular workforce was modest. In 1893, Robert Pinkerton testified that his agency employed a workforce of 600, a number that included guards, clerks, and stenographers as well as detectives.[11] By 1905 there were (according to the *New York Times*) 4,000 private security personnel in New York City alone, a number that matched the strength of the city's police force.[12] The 1890s was a decade of mushrooming growth in the detective industry, in which the newcomers, taken in the aggregate, dwarfed the Pinkertons numerically. The Commission's *Final Report* noted that some of the more profitable agencies doubled as "private employment agencies." In other words, they supplied strikebreakers as well as spies and armed guards. The most successful of them in the years 1895 to 1907 was the James Farley agency. This specialized in breaking streetcar strikes using agents recruited in New York City and supplied to employers through its "captains" in major US cities. When Farley retired to enjoy his fortune in 1907, Wadell and Mahon, the Bergoff Brothers, and Baldwin-Felts were prominent among those who stepped into the breach.

The greatest single threat to the prestige and profits of the PNDA came from the Burns International Detective Agency. Like Allan Pinkerton, William J. Burns professed support for the principle of unionism: "I believe in organized labor, and believe that it has helped the workingman." He had advanced his career with the US Secret Service by investigating the malpractices of powerful businessmen and their political allies. According to journalist Lincoln Steffens, his success in this regard paradoxically endeared him to enemies who were future clients: "William J. Burns had proved himself to the men he called sons of

Figure 22.1. William J. Burns in 1907, when he was a special agent in the US Secret Service. Portrait by Arnold Genthe. *Library of Congress*

bitches, so that when he organized a national detective bureau they joined it as subscribers."[13]

The competitive threat Burns posed to the Pinkertons became painfully evident when he investigated the *Los Angeles Times* explosion. In his battle with the Bridgemen's Union, Walter Drew had not always relied on private detectives. In New York, for example, he resorted to court proceedings to prosecute Tom Slattery and empty the union's purse. Slattery was a former policeman who became a "walking delegate" (local organizer) for the Bridgemen's Local 35 in Brooklyn. He had at his disposal a number of "Plug Uglies" or tough guys who took care of anti-union individuals. His sense of humor could be grim: in 1910 at the Bridgemen's annual convention, he introduced a motion calling for a cessation of dynamite explosions for the duration of the period when the meeting was in progress. Damon Runyon, who frequented Slattery's bar on Long Island and there soaked up material for his "Guys and Dolls" short stories, would have appreciated that. In a similar vein, when Slattery dropped dead on a Long Island beach in 1929, a *Nassau Daily Review* reporter displayed faith in the afterlife and in its possibilities for refreshment. It reported the cause of Slattery's death as a hemorrhage from an old bullet wound brought on by a "temporary" abstinence from alcohol. It reported that "Big Tom" had many enemies, but many more "looked upon him as a 'regular,' as a friend and champion of the weak against the strong." Like the Pinkertons when they took on Jesse James, Drew was up against a David and Goliath if not Robin Hood mythology. He secured a string of convictions of Slattery and others that weakened the union, but he could not destroy a legend.[14]

In March 1907 Drew decided he needed the help of detectives. He proposed to the executive committee of the Erectors' Association that private investigators should be engaged to help track down the Bridgemen's dynamiters. It was no easy task. Developments of fuse technology meant that saboteurs could be long gone before the dynamite bomb they had set exploded and damaged an open-shop structure. Having assessed the situation, Drew's colleagues referred him to the "Pinkerton Agency at Chicago as being most suited to the purpose." In the event, Drew tried several agencies. The result was often disappointing. America's employers were becoming disillusioned about the benefits of hiring private detectives. Writing to Drew three weeks after the 1910 explosion, F.W. Cohen, erection manager for the Pennsylvania Steel Company, agreed

> that no detective agency is to be relied upon; their expenses run up enormously and they will only give you enough to lead you on, and while once

> in a while they will give you information, they will not uncover the man who gave the information, and it is therefore of no legal value as far as convictions are concerned. . . . The men who give secret information as to the doings of the executive boards in the union play both sides and simply strain you.[15]

Drew nevertheless put his faith in the Burns agency. William J. Burns had a stellar reputation as a detective. He was born in 1861 to Irish immigrant parents in Baltimore. Thirty years later he joined the US Secret Service. He helped break Spain's Montreal spy ring in 1898. The following year he achieved the arrest of a would-be assassin of the British ambassador in Washington. It was Burns who secured the arrests of Boss Ruef in San Francisco and two members of Congress on charges of land fraud during President Roosevelt's crackdown. In regard to the Bridgemen's Union, Burns was in a situation comparable to that of McParland when he took on the Mollies—he was an Irish American Catholic pitted against his own kind.

On the day after the *Times* explosion, Los Angeles Mayor George Alexander hired Burns to investigate. After a tip-off from a McClintic-Marshal official, Burns accepted the services as a spy of Herbert S. Hockin, a member of the Bridgemen's executive board who had decided to become in informer. Hockin claimed that he wanted to stop the Bridgemen's program of "wholesale murder," though there was also a suspicion that he aimed to get even with union officials who suspected him of fraud. Drew had already guessed that the brains behind the dynamiting of the Los Angeles Times Building was John J. McNamara, secretary-treasurer of the Bridgemen's Union. He contacted the US Secret Service about it, but the Service advised him to contact Burns. From now on, Drew's National Erectors Association was Burns's employer.[16]

Like McParland in the case of the Mollies, Burns did not arrest immediately but let his targets run. They consequently dynamited eight additional targets before being arrested. His patience was rewarded with a breakthrough. Acting on information from Hockin, a Burns detective joined John McNamara and another Bridgeman, Ortie McManigal, on a hunting trip. The two union men were heavy drinkers who could not hold their tongues when under the influence. Taking advantage of their indiscretions, Burns alerted the police in Detroit about an opportune moment to effect an arrest. He accompanied them on April 14, 1911, when the officers apprehended McNamara and McManigal and in the process took possession of an alarm clock together with blasting caps and dynamite that they had with them.[17]

After further arrests and a number of confessions, the leading officers and numerous local officials of the Bridgemen's Union went on trial. Anticipating a rerun of the Haywood drama, the AFL ran a campaign portraying the accused as martyrs. Reluctantly, for he was unwell and could recognize adversity when he saw it, Clarence Darrow undertook the defense of John McNamara and of his brother James, the man accused of setting the bomb. On December 28, 1912, a jury in Indianapolis found a total of thirty-eight Bridgemen guilty. The *New York Times* declared Burns to be "the greatest detective certainly, and perhaps the only really great detective, the only detective of genius whom this country has produced."[18]

This was bad news for the Pinkerton brand. Burns made matters worse by burnishing his own reputation. Where McParland had warned of "inner circles," Burns fueled contemporary fears by speaking of a secret insurrection. His book on the Los Angeles tragedy, *The Masked War: The Story of a Peril the Threatened the United States*, appeared in 1913. Here, he claimed that James McNamara told Burns's detective William S. O'Callaghan, "There will be a great and bloody war between capital and labor." As if that were not enough, the Bridgemen were also planning to undermine national security by damaging a lock section under construction for the Panama Canal, a job contracted to the anti union McClintic-Marshall Company. Like Allan Pinkerton, Burns spoiled for a fight with socialist revolutionaries even where they did not exist.[19]

What Burns wrote was hyperbole. The Los Angeles Times Building explosion led to a large loss of life because of the structure's exceptional physical characteristics compared with the Bridgemen's usual targets. Dynamite could usually cause little more than inconvenience. Compression difficulties meant it was difficult to cause serious explosive damage to open steel structures. McNamara and the Bridgemen dynamiters may have been unpleasant individuals, but they were neither revolutionaries nor deliberate mass murderers, and certainly not anti-American.

While the Los Angeles affair was a prominent success for Burns, he also continued to excel in other cases. In 1913, for example, he helped to clear Leo Frank of the murder of thirteen-year-old Mary Phagan in Atlanta, Georgia. This was in the face of an antisemitic campaign and of local prejudice that later resulted in the lynching of Frank. The specter of a great detective with principles who was stealing their thunder haunted the Pinkertons.

The leadership of the PNDA was far from inert in the face of the challenge. Back in 1909 Allan Pinkerton II had already proposed infiltration of the Burns agency. In the following decade the Pinkertons responded to the increasing prominence of their competitor by opening files on Bill Burns and his associates. They looked for ways in which the Burns agency might be discredited and denied a license to operate.

In March 1917 New York State had stepped into the breach left by the federal government's inaction regarding the licensing of detective agencies and decided on a licensing program of its own. The state comptroller's office estimated that by now there were 5,000 private detectives operating in New York. Some of them were confidence tricksters who, for example, induced Broadway and Fifth Avenue merchants to pay for antitheft security they did not deliver. Allan Pinkerton sneered that the comptroller's cautionary remarks "especially apply to the Burns case."[20]

The PNDA files bulged with items casting a poor light on the Burns agency. There was, for example, a deposition by Matthew J. Carroll, manager of the criminal department in the Burns agency, 1911–14, and thereafter superintendent of the O'Farrell agency, based in Boston. According to Carroll, the Burns agency acted for Walter S. Martin, a client in California, who believed his sister-in-law was behaving improperly. On investigation, it turned out that she was disporting herself in the upper-crust yachting milieu of Newport, Rhode Island, where she was "on intimate terms with the Duke of Mecklenburg." In the mean time, though, she had come to suspect that she was being followed. Like her brother-in-law, she turned to a well-known agency and hired a detective to ascertain if this was true. Carroll explained that in consequence the Burns agency "was handling both sides of the case."[21]

The Pinkertons would not accept divorce work. Their continuing reluctance to hire women as detectives likely went hand in hand with that. As late as 1935 a PNDA directive ordered, using language that might have been a direct rebuke to Kate Warne: "Female employees must not be employed permanently in any office in any position, excepting by permission of the General Management and IN NO CASE MUST A FEMALE BE EMPLOYED WHO HAS MADE APPLICATION DIRECT TO ANY OFFICE."[22]

The Pinkertons did overlook a genuine need. Women going through personal difficulties may well have found it difficult to confide in male detectives. Cora M. Strayer, advertising the services of her detective agency in the *Chicago Tribune* in 1905, made the following pitch: "Ladies: When in need of legal or confidential advice why not confer with one of your own sex?"[23]

Another Pinkerton scruple meant the agency was slow to resort to electronic eavesdropping. Competing agencies openly offered what one of them termed a "complete dictaphone service."[24] Burns was keen on prying technology. The PNDA learned that their rival had purchased almost a hundred "detectifones" from the Anderson Electric Corporation.[25] During the Indianapolis trial of the bombing Bridgemen, Burns had placed a secret dictograph in a jail cell in hope of obtaining incriminating evidence. He also bugged the office of Clarence Darrow, looking for evidence that the defense counsel had bribed a juror (Darrow was charged with this offense but found not guilty).

In 1916 Burns organized a break-in at the offices of the New York City law firm Seymour and Seymour and installed a listening device. This was on behalf of J.P. Morgan. The Wall Street finance house had acted for the French and British governments to secure the secret purchase of a million dollars' worth of armaments. Samuel Paul, a J.P. Morgan employee, had leaked the information. It was embarrassing for his employer because the arms deal breached the spirit of US neutrality toward the war in Europe. Burns detectives tried to find an evidential trail regarding the leak in the files of the Seymour firm. As a result of their efforts, when charged with the Seymour break-in offense Burns was able to plead superior motive. According to Burns documents obtained during his agency's Seymour break-in pointed to the complicity of Germany's ambassador, Count Johann Heinrich von Bernstorff, in leaking news of the controversial deal. In an added flourish, the Burns defense sought to show that the German authorities "were seeking information which would be of use in causing strikes, breakdowns and explosions in United States munitions plants and ships carrying munitions and supplies to the allies."[26]

Allan Pinkerton II wrote to the chief prosecution attorney in the Seymour case: "I have glanced through Burns' testimony and find nothing in same to in any way warrant his method of unlawful entry. There was no foreign government plot of any kind: simply an effort on his part to steal correspondence of commercial nature on behalf of Morgan and Company." The affair became a sensation. The New York legislature held hearings on the matter, and others joined the Pinkertons in a demand for the revocation of Burns's license. Yet the agitation fizzled out. Burns was charged and convicted over the Seymour break-in, but only on a lesser charge of burglary, as legislation had not yet caught up with the need to regulate wiretapping.[27]

The Pinkertons' most promising line of inquiry was into a rogue detective who worked for the Burns agency. Gaston B. Means was born in North Carolina in 1879. When as a child he stole $3 from his mother and blamed the maid, who lost her job, it was the start of a life of crime. He joined the Burns agency in 1914 and, at least until American entry into the war, sent reports on US ship construction to German officials and the Hamburg American shipping line. Then in 1917 Means took a wealthy widow on a shooting expedition on North Carolina. When he brought Maude King's dead body home, it had a bullet wound to the head. The absence of adjacent powder marks suggested she had not shot herself.[28]

In October of that year William Pinkerton wrote to his nephew Allan expressing satisfaction about the Means case. He recorded his recent conversation with BofI special agent C.B. Ambrose. Male and female BofI operatives had been tracking Means since well before the North Carolina murder. They had installed a dictaphone in his room at the Chicago Beach Hotel. It was apparent that Means worked for Germany from the start of the war in Europe. He had a reputation for bullying back in North Carolina. He had $80,000 of Maude King's money on his possession at the time of her death. The Justice Department was taking the matter forward.[29] From Ambrose's account, it looked as if things were going well for the uncle-and-nephew Pinkerton leadership team. However, a jury in Means's hometown acquitted him after deliberating for only fifteen minutes. A Justice Department document suggested most of the jury had decided on their verdict in advance, two had been intimidated, and one had been bribed.[30] With Means acquitted, the Burns agency kept its New York license.

Doggedly Allan Pinkerton II continued to look for dirt on the Burns agency. Disgruntled Burns employees wrote to him out of a spirit of revenge or to pitch for employment with the PNDA. In 1920 a former Burns operative wrote to him: "It is an old saying that a pitcher sent to the well too often gets broken. Liken this to Burns. He has been in a number of different messes in his career on account of frame ups and his crooked work but somehow he has managed to pull through. However he is bound to come to grief some time."[31]

After a while, these words would turn out to have been prophetic. Some people repent with the passage of time and become better citizens, but in Bill Burns's case, the direction of travel was downward.

In 1921 Burns became director of the Bureau of Investigation. His friend Harry Daugherty, attorney general in the newly elected administration of President Warren G. Harding, had appointed him. As director, Burns was progressive in some ways. If the BofI/FBI was indebted to the Pinkertons for some attributes, it also owed several of its practices to Burns. When BofI director, Burns imported a number of his private practices. He deployed dictaphones in rooting out corruption cases.[32] He centralized the pursuit of suspects. Until 1923 if agents in one BofI regional division suspected a person in another region, they would notify the superintendent of that other region to take up the case. But when M.H. Dinsmore embezzled $21,000 from Washington, DC, National Bank, he was pursued across the nation by a single BofI agent who finally had him arrested on Whibby Island, off Seattle. Burns agents, like the Pinkertons, had never been constrained by state or regional lines.[33]

A great deal less wisely, Burns hired Means as a BofI investigator. Means used his position to sell BofI information to criminals, forged alcohol permits during Prohibition, and blackmailed bootleggers. He had to be fired and was convicted of these offenses. Upon his release from prison, he would resume his life of crime. He embezzled thousands of dollars from a friend of Charles Lindbergh, the famous aviator whose son had been kidnapped and would later be found dead. Convicted of heartlessly promising nonexistent information as to the boy's whereabouts, Means died in prison in 1938.

Burns's career also came to a sticky end. In return for a bribe, Secretary of the Interior Albert B. Fall leased to two friends federal oil lands in Teapot Dome, Arizona. Daugherty obstructed the ensuing Senate inquiry. Burns used his position to harass investigating senators such as Robert M. La Follette, Sr., and to intimidate curious journalists. He hired operatives from his own agency to bully members of the jury once the Teapot Dome case came to trial. When all this began to come out, both Daugherty and Burns had to resign. Burns's departure ushered in the era of Hoover's BofI/FBI, confirming the Pinkertons' removal as America's national detective force. Yet in the immediate term, Burns's disgrace may have contributed to a relative revival in the Pinkertons' reputation that occurred in the 1920s.

CHAPTER 23

Of Harvard and Hammett

March 15, 1928, Cochran Field, Aiken, South Carolina. On this day, Red, White, and Blue polo teams slugged it out in contests that were close. Except the time the Whites beat the Reds by a clear margin of five to three.

Not that the Reds, astride their hard-ridden ponies, could be faulted for timidity. The absence of that attribute propelled a Vanderbilt into the embrace of a detective. In the words of a special report to the *New York Times*: "Cornelius Vanderbilt Whitney was thrown from his horse into the lap of Allan Pinkerton, a spectator, during the round-robin polo game . . . when the animal's feet struck against the side board as Mr. Whitney was hitting the ball. Mr. Whitney suffered a deep cut on a lip and the fracture of a finger. The horse bolted and several of the spectators were bruised."

A week later, the same newspaper recorded that the intrepid Whitney (a Yale alumnus) had won the trophy for Best Championship Pony with his "Reckless Lady." Allan Pinkerton (Harvard) handed out the prizes. The second prize in the Polo Pony class went to W. Averell Harriman (Yale). The little cameo over which Allan Pinkerton presided thus consisted of the descendants of two railroad magnates (Harriman and Vanderbilt) and a thoroughbred horse breeder (Whitney). Both prizewinners would go on to distinguished careers in business and federal government. The Pinkerton dynasty had, by any definition, arrived.[1]

The social privilege and milieu of the Pinkerton dynasty had changed since the early days of Allan Pinkerton. Yet at the beginning of the 1920s, the philosophy of the Pinkertons had still been recognizably that of the founder. This is clear from a document circulated in 1921 and prepared by George D. Bangs.

The Pinkerton general manager feared that there was still a chance that the labor lobby would "introduce legislation detrimental to our agency." It was why he prepared a statement "that must be read by every official."[2]

Bangs's circular to all offices ran to three and a half closely typed pages. He reminded his fellow Pinkertons that the agency was "the first of its kind" and "founded upon correct principles." Its success, with thirty-five offices in major US and Canadian cities, meant that "the name 'PINKERTON' to-day is a synonym for 'DETECTIVE.'" Bangs told his readers that the Pinkertons did no divorce work, never used "such disreputable methods as 'listening in' by tapping wires or the use of the dictograph" and refrained from providing strikebreakers.

Bangs's testament continued under the prominent subheading, "JUSTIFICATION FOR SECRET WORK UNDERTAKEN FOR EMPLOYERS AMONG EMPLOYEES." The agency helped businessmen who employed personnel in such large numbers that they could not know them individually and who for this reason had problems with the "shiftless and inefficient, to say nothing of the radical element, of our cosmopolitan population." Many labor union members were honorable. But their organizations harbored practitioners of violence and anarchy. Labor leaders should be aware that the Pinkerton spies were doing them a favor by rooting out such radicals, as well as by alerting employers to dangerous or unsanitary conditions in the workplace.[3]

It is not entirely clear that this continued emphasis on labor espionage was a good business decision for the Pinkertons. It has been estimated that industrial disputes declined in number by over 80 percent between the periods 1916–21 and 1926–30.[4] Yet in the 1920s the number of labor spies in American industry rose to an estimated 200,000. It meant more competition for a declining number of spying opportunities. There was, however, a countervailing factor. The 1917 Bolshevik takeover of Russia and the Red Scare of 1919–20 in the United States affected employers' mentality. They now employed labor spies in larger numbers not just for the usual reason, to suppress wages and enlarge profits, but also because they feared ideological challenge. This factor encouraged the belief that there was a market for the Pinkertons to exploit.

Paradoxically, another circumstance that played into the Pinkertons' hands was a reaction against government surveillance. The Red Scare of 1919–20 with its dragnet raids on supposed communists produced widespread revulsion because government agents had too often trampled on civil liberties—and because it soon became obvious that, in spite of the great panic, no Russian-style revolution was about to take place in the United States. This encouraged a considerable reduction in government espionage.

There was also a question hanging over the capabilities of government agents. Neither the Secret Service nor the BofI had been able to secure convictions in the wake of a wave of terrorist bombings on June 2, 1919. Additionally, government detectives (though also private eyes) drew a blank after an explosion on Wall Street on September 16, 1920 that killed 38 people.[5] On top of all this, there was a powerful urge to demobilize after the horrors of war. The government disinvestment in the military and associated federal activities was for pressing economic reasons. Government surveillance agencies, military as well as civilian, also experienced severe cuts in budgets and personnel.

The 1920s expansion of private labor espionage did not benefit the Pinkertons exclusively. There was competition from other detective agencies and from other quarters. One of World War I's legacies was that private individuals gathered data on people they regarded as suspect and passed to employers information about workers who might prove to be troublesome. During the war government agencies aided by private organizations like the American Protective League had compiled lists of citizens who were suspected of being antiwar, left wing, and/or supportive of independence movements in India and Ireland contrary to British war aims. At war's end President Woodrow Wilson had ordered the destruction of one such list, possibly swayed by the fact that some of his friends appeared on it. This was a roster of 105,000 suspects drawn up by the Navy Department. It was rumored to have survived the presidential edict and to have fallen into private hands.[6]

Ralph Van Deman (pronounced "demon") was the prime example of a private individual who kept tabs on persons he regarded as unpatriotic, radical, or industrial troublemakers. When the United States occupied the Philippines in the wake of the War with Spain and the Filipinos rebelled against their new masters, Van Deman compiled records on the freedom fighters for military intelligence, records that came to be regarded as a model for counterinsurgency. He subsequently served in Army intelligence in World War I and like his counterparts in the Navy opened files on fellow Americans who seemed to him to be potential saboteurs or otherwise worthy of suspicion.

After the war and the discrediting of the Red Scare, the Army showed a lack of interest in the continuation of Van Deman's antiradical work. He decided to go private with the techniques he had developed in the service of America's new empire. By the mid-1930s he was an authority on domestic radicals, including those who might organize strikes. Van Deman based himself in San Diego. At first he specialized on California, but he then expanded his activities to be nationwide. Federal agencies like the FBI would borrow from his files before, during, and after World War II. Van Deman was an ideologue, not in it for the money, a circumstance that in the eyes of some employers made him seem more trustworthy than private detectives. Such employers were keen recipients of Van Deman's lists of militant workers whom they could blacklist in the interest of industrial harmony and of profit.[7]

Another challenge to the Pinkertons as well as to other private detectives came directly from business. Several corporation executives concluded that private detectives conducted labor espionage only for their own profit. Their logic was that it would not pay such private detectives to destroy the labor movement or individual unions, as this would remove a vital source of income. That perception helped to explain why, in the 1920s, some major companies took labor espionage into their own hands.

One example is the Pennsylvania Central Railroad. During a strike in the spring of 1920, the company listed hundreds of workers who had withheld their labor, complete with their home addresses. No doubt using its own confidential sources of information, it also kept notes on particularly troublesome individuals such as Conductor C.E. Smith of 470 South Division Street, Buffalo, whose offense was that he "entered upon company's property at Ebenezer afternoon of Wednesday, April 7th, and persuaded a number of employes at that point to quit their work." Smith refused to leave the company's property until escorted off it by a "Company Patrolman." The railroad was by no means unique in having its own police force. A number of coal and steel industrialists had for some time made their own company police arrangements in the style of Coal and Iron Police known by their critics as the "Pennsylvania Cossacks."

In the case of the Pennsylvania Central Railroad, there was an additional twist—a twist of the type that made civil libertarians' hair stand on end. US Attorney General A. Mitchell Palmer, who had been the prime architect of the Red Scare of 1919–20, wrote to the railroad asking for the names of workers who had challenged corporate hegemony. Penn Central's vice president Richard O'Donnel complied with the request, supplying thousands of names. He apologized that he had not yet identified all the ringleaders of the strike, but promised that he soon would have the information and would send it on immediately.[8]

Henry Ford, pioneer of the assembly line method of manufacturing automobiles, was a prominent example of an industrialist who developed his own company's police and spies. He put Harry Bennett in charge of a company unit called the Service Department. A former boxer with connections to the underworld, Bennett favored a strong-arm approach to union busting. His "plug uglies" intimidated workers who were inclined to join a union. At the Rouge plant in Dearborn, Michigan, and then across the remainder of the Ford enterprise, Bennett deployed company spies. Some of these were sweepers, individuals who worked across the shop floor and were able to overhear snatches of conversation that they passed on to Bennett. In keeping with the precepts of "scientific" management, employees were timed when they went to the bathroom. Company spies peeped over the tops of toilet walls to ensure that the cubicle inhabitants were not protracting their absence from the workplace.[9]

The competition Pinkertons and other agencies faced was multisourced and extensive. They nevertheless persisted in the labor line of business. There were some longstanding reasons why they did not diversify. For example, although divorce work was undergoing a boom in the 1920s, it remained repugnant to the Pinkertons.[10] The emergence of city police detective departments locked the Pinkertons out of public service, just as the Anti-Pinkerton Act barred them from federal work. The Pinkertons also chose to refrain from wiretapping, which, while often controversial, was playing an increasing role in criminal investigation.

A leadership succession at the head of the agency also militated against change. William A. Pinkerton's death in the Hotel Biltmore in Los Angeles in December 1923 occasioned praise in far-flung obituaries. The British Sunday newspaper *Reynolds's News* spoke well of a man "who always played the game according to the rules," though it noted he could never be drawn to speak of the PNDA's role in labor disputes such as Homestead.[11] William had no male issue. His estate, initially estimated at $15 million, was filed in the Probate Court as $1,200,000. William had apparently made preemptive gifts to his family. He left the agency, valued at several millions, to his nephew Allan Pinkerton II, with the proviso that one-fifth of the annual income would go to each of his daughters, Margaret and Isabelle; the latter married to Joseph O. Watkins, the head of the Pinkerton Chicago office.[12]

Allan Pinkerton II had attacked the Burns agency for more than a decade in the interest of burnishing the Pinkertons' reputation, behavior that indicates intense loyalty to the family firm. However, he refrained from diversification and did not inherit the family commitment to enterprise. The idea of developing the Pinkertons' Rogues Gallery into a more methodical bureau of identification left him cold, no doubt one reason why that asset passed to Hoover's BofI in 1924. Ill health also weakened the leadership of the man now in charge of the Pinkertons. When the United States entered World War I in 1917, Allan had volunteered to serve his country. He ended the war with the rank of major in charge of the Paris-based criminal investigation division of the American Expeditionary Force. Before that, though, he had been stationed sufficiently near to the battle front to pick up a dose of gas poisoning. After the Armistice, he spent two years convalescing in Colorado and thereafter took generous summertime recuperative vacations. It did not cure him. The terrible aftermath of war never left Allan Pinkerton II. It sapped his strength and contributed to his death in 1930.[13]

A comparison of Allan Pinkerton's involuntary lethargy with the vigor of the (soon to be disgraced) William Burns indicated not just the contrast between the two men but also how the BofI was streaking ahead of private agencies in the field of detection even before the advent of the super-efficient J. Edgar Hoover. A born empire-builder, Burns at one stage schemed with Attorney General Daugherty to fuse all eight US investigative agencies into a single Secret Service, with himself as its chief. Frustrated in that ambition, he made the most of his current asset, the BofI. In March 1923 Burns undertook the first-ever nationwide inspection tour of the BofI's larger outposts. The purpose of this month-long trip to the South, California, and the Pacific Northwest, returning via the central states, was to acquaint himself with current cases and make assessments of personnel. In the same year he prepared the ground for the criminal identification unit that his successor J. Edgar Hoover would develop. Not content with this, he occupied himself with the exploitation of radio for the purpose of appealing to the public for information. To this end he pressed every police force in the United States to join in a radio communications network that he pioneered. Where the Pinkertons dragged their feet in the realm of new technologies, the BofI adopted them enthusiastically.[14]

In addition to competition from diverse sources, the PNDA faced rumblings of discontent about labor espionage. They were not serious enough to destabilize the agency in the Republican Decade but were a warning that Allan Pinkerton and his colleagues ignored at their peril. One indication of public concern was state-level investigations that followed the examples of the federal Homestead hearings and Commission on Industrial Relations reports. Following one such investigation in the early 1920s, Wisconsin adopted a licensing law that aimed to identify private detectives by name so that unionists would be able to spot them when they tried to infiltrate their organizations. As ever, such initiatives met with evasion. Detectives sidestepped the law by registering out of state—and further state hearings in Pennsylvania produced no legislation at all. Yet the initiatives were harbingers of things to come.[15]

Exposés of the labor spy industry meantime appeared. Jean E. Spielman, the author of one such study, was the secretary of the organization committee of the Minneapolis Trades and Labor Assembly. He issued a 240-page paperback revelation about the use of spies to destroy the local Flour Mill Workers Union as well as IWW unions in Minnesota. He estimated that, across the nation, three major detective agencies, Pinkerton, Burns, and Thiel, had 135,000 labor spies on their rolls. Labor spies made up 75 percent of the agencies' total number of operatives and pulled in a combined annual income of $65,000,000.[16]

Sidney Howard was the author of another critical study. Howard was a graduate of the University of California at Berkeley and had studied drama at Harvard. In World War I he served in a volunteer ambulance corps. Postwar, he was a budding playwright and published articles with the liberal/progressive *New Republic* magazine. These included a series on labor espionage, written under the direction of a Harvard professor, that resulted in a four-volume report, a pamphlet, and later a book. Introducing the series, *New Republic* editors declared, "There is very little room, if any, for private espionage in a republic." They stated that the practice was "100 percent un-American." The resulting pamphlet was a scathing indictment of the labor spy industry. It warned that spies were everywhere in American industry. Some detective agencies used fancy new names, such as "service corporations." They played both sides in industrial disputes and fomented ethnic discord—between, for example, Serbs and Italians. They were not, as they claimed, harmonizers but promoted unrest in the workplace.[17]

In Howard's book that appeared in 1924, he attacked not just the Pinkertons but all labor spy agencies—and took encouragement from the recent Burns–Daugherty scandal that had brought down the Pinkertons' greatest rival. In an erudite survey, Howard reminded his readers how federal investigators after Homestead and the *Los Angeles Times* explosion had found fault with detective agencies. He claimed that Scotland Yard, the United Kingdom's main police detective organization, held the US private detective agency business in contempt.[18]

In his conclusion Howard claimed that earlier editions of his work had "brought an avalanche of bills before state legislatures." But the bills had sunk into obscurity, just like the recommendations for federal and state legislation made by the Commission on Industrial Relations.[19] Had Howard timed his run later, he might have had a greater impact. He was on the cusp of glittering success and fame, ranging from the Pulitzer Prize he won in 1925 for the script of a play to his (posthumous) Oscar for the screenplay of the movie *Gone with the Wind*. As of 1924, however, his warning about labor espionage was no more than a hint of trouble on the horizon, and the Pinkertons remained unruffled.

A similar observation might be made about Dashiell Hammett, whose 1929 novel *Red Harvest* famously launched the hard-boiled detective genre. *Red Harvest* remains the most prominent literary work featuring the Pinkertons. The novel's Continental Op, a fictionalized Pinkerton operative, takes on murderers and other criminals in "Personville," a gang-ridden Montana mining town nicknamed Poisonville. It seems likely that in conceiving the Poisonville story Hammett had in mind the bloody struggle in Butte, Montana, between the Anaconda Copper Mining Company and the local IWW-led miners' union. In July 1917 Frank Little, a half-Quaker and half-Cherokee member of the IWW executive board, had arrived in Butte, limping painfully from a recent pounding administered by anti-union plug uglies. He rallied support for the union. To the delight of the large contingent of Irish workers in Butte, he condemned the war then raging in Europe, which the United States had recently joined. On August 1, a local vigilante gang that would never be apprehended abducted, tortured, and lynched Frank Little.

Hammett was a Pinkerton veteran who knew Butte at first hand. At the age of 13 he had left school and worked at sundry jobs for eight years before joining the PNDA. Except for an interval of ambulance service in World War I, he remained with the agency from 1915 to 1921. He worked out of the Continental Trust Building in Baltimore (hence "Continental" Op) and also in Butte, where he studied the labor struggles in that strongly unionized city. Like Damon Runyon he picked up the argot and outlook of a particular stratum of working-class stiffs in the bars that they frequented. Hammett much later confided to his lover, the playwright Lillian Hellman, that his experience of strikebreaking for the Pinkertons caused him to be singled out, in Butte, for a special mission. He told her that a Pinkerton official had tried to commission him to kill Frank Little prior to the Wobbly leader's lynching for the sum of $15,000. The offer shocked him and was a turning point in his life (he told Hellman) because it was predicated on the belief that he was the kind of man who would kill for money. It caused him to quit the agency in disgust.[20]

However, in public Hammett issued another story. Delegated to track down a cache of stolen dollars, he found the money on an ocean liner that was about to set sail. The timing was bad. He had hoped to succeed just a little bit later, thus necessitating more time on the ship and a free cruise. He was so disappointed with his premature success that, according to this sweetened, humorous version of what happened, he resigned from the agency for that reason—nothing to do with Frank Little's death.[21]

Red Harvest drew on stories Hammett had been contributing to *Black Mask*, a mystery magazine launched by the satirist H.L. Mencken in 1920. In the stories and resultant novel, Hammett painted a picture of the social structure of a monocultural mining community that witnessed severe industrial strife. One man, Elihu Willsson of the Personville Mining Corporation, "owned Personville, heart, soul, skin, and guts." He had in his pocket a US senator, a governor, two representatives, and most of the state legislature. He hired gunmen, national guardsmen, and federal troops to reduce the local IWW to the condition of a "used fire-cracker."[22]

The Continental Op operated as a loner. He incurred the disapproval of his agency's regional boss in San Francisco. This individualism would be a staple of future detective fiction. *Red Harvest* was not, however, a rebellious novel. It has even been said, if harshly, that Hammett whitewashed the Pinkertons.[23] Hammett's later reputation for radicalism—he went to prison for standing up to McCarthyism—indicates a left-wing disposition of the type that often rejects security surveillance. But to portray Hammett as a standard bearer of anti-Pinkertonism in the 1920s would be to read history backward. Hammett drew attention to the Pinkertons' labor work, that was all. At the end of the 1920s as at the beginning, to the undiscriminating eye the coast seemed clear for labor espionage.

The ailing Allan Pinkerton II did not attempt to change the agency's mission, but he did modify its administrative character. In 1925 he incorporated the firm. It meant that the capital of the company was now a loan from the Pinkerton family. Allan Pinkerton could benefit from dividends, from any salary that he chose to pay himself, and from paybacks of the loan.[24] He left governance largely in the hands of local managers.

Allan Pinkerton II devoted time to outside interests and to social advancement. He supported his son Robert Allan Pinkerton, but not in a way that prepared him to play a role in the PNDA. Having attended the elite St. Paul's boarding school in New Hampshire, Robert Pinkerton studied at Harvard University. There, he was a member of the exclusive "Hasty Pudding—Institute of 1770" social club. He was on the varsity polo team, 1924–27, and served as its captain for those three years. Robert's proud father consolidated his progress by making a gift of ten ponies to the Harvard Polo team. He ensured that his son should have a fitting home to return to in New York by buying a large Fifth Avenue apartment.[25]

Robert A. Pinkerton II was not, at first sight, ideally suited to improve on his father's performance at the PNDA. He was a bold sportsman who suffered injuries, one of which impaired his eyesight. It affected his studies, but he managed to graduate. In an attempt at recovery, he then embarked on a world cruise. On his return, he enrolled at Columbia Law School, from which he dropped out because "law was competing with a heavy romance." Then in the wake of the financial crash of 1929, he became a broker in a Wall Street firm controlled by his maternal uncle.[26]

In July 1930 Allan Pinkerton II went abroad "for a rest."[27] When he returned, the 54-year-old was so ill that he could not walk from the ship. On October 7, he died at New York City's Presbyterian Hospital. In a less than fulsome summation, the *New York Times* reported that the departed PNDA president had been "socially active in this city and Long Island." Allan left to his son Robert his entire estate with a declared value of just over $1,000,000, together with control of the PNDA.

Unlike previous generations of the Pinkerton family, the new boss had not served an apprenticeship at the agency. However, he did show a readiness to concentrate on his new responsibility. He gave up his brokering career and took seriously his role at the head of the PNDA. For example in 1935 he would emulate Burns at the BofI and undertake a tour of the agency's far-flung offices. But it was Robert Pinkerton's misfortune to be in charge at a time of major reckoning for labor espionage in the United States.[28]

CHAPTER 24

The La Follette Inquiry

Harvey C. Fruehauf was the president of a company that bore the family name. His Fruehauf Trailer Company was known for its pioneering technology. In 1935, for example, it emulated the freezer-equipped ships and trains of the previous century and began to market refrigerated trailers. They would be built at its plant in Detroit, Michigan, the nation's automotive capital. The company employed 700 workers, was the largest of its kind in the United States, and had annual sales of over $6 million. This would more than triple over the next five years, as steel-constructed articulated trucks became a common sight on the nation's expanding highways.[1]

In the summer of 1935 Fruehauf workers began to join a newly formed union. The AFL had in May of that year launched the United Auto Workers (UAW) in Detroit. Reflecting the widespread introduction of mechanization that diminished distinctions between skilled and unskilled workers, the UAW broke with the AFL craft-union tradition and took in all workers in the industry. It followed the IWW's One Big Union principle, but without the revolutionary ideology. Harvey Fruehauf, like other auto magnates, opposed the idea of labor unions whatever their character. The 177 Fruehauf employees who joined the UAW therefore did so in secret, as they feared reprisals. Because of this secrecy the boss approached the Pinkerton National Detective Agency. The result was that J.N. Martin, a Pinkerton operative, took a job at the plant. Martin worked alongside other employees for the standard hourly rate. The PNDA received £175 a month for his services. The spy ingratiated himself with union members and was elected treasurer of the UAW local. He was able to supply the company with the names of workers who had joined the union. Seven of them, the president of the local included, were fired.[2]

Given these circumstances, union members knew that a "stool pigeon" was at work. They suspected that Martin was the culprit. One unionist, John L. Peterson, set a trap. He took Martin aside and said he was going to resign from the UAW in the interest of keeping his job. The next morning, a superintendent greeted Peterson "with a smile" and said how pleased he was with the news. He rewarded the trap-setter with a pay rise of 5 cents an hour. There was only one way the superintendent could have known about Peterson's apocryphal intention. Now exposed, Martin had to resign. Peterson a little later related these events at the regional office of the National Labor Relations Board (NLRB). Established in 1933 under the auspices of the National Labor Relations Act, the NLRB's mandate was to ensure the right of labor unions to benefit from collective bargaining. When the company learned of Peterson's approach to the NLRB, it dismissed him.[3]

In the period since its creation in 1933 the NLRB had acquired a reputation for ineffectiveness. In the summer of 1935, however, Congress's passing of the National Labor Relations Act, also known as the Wagner Act after its sponsor Senator Robert F. Wagner, had increased its powers. The invigorated NLRB took up the trailer workers' cause. The *Detroit Free Press* noted that the case was "of such widespread interest that it is being covered by writers for New York publications."[4] In December the NLRB issued a ruling that required Fruehauf to reinstate the dismissed workers, pay them for the period of their dismissal, and abstain from labor espionage.[5] Fruehauf appealed. The Federal Court of Appeals in Cincinnati upheld his application and Harvey Fruehauf rejoiced that his firm would now revert to a system based on the "loyalty of our employees . . . free from interference by outside influences."[6] By now, the case was being closely followed as an indicator, together with a small cluster of parallel cases, of the fate of the reforming policies of the administration of President Franklin D. Roosevelt. On appeal from the NLRB, the Fruehauf case went to the US Supreme Court. By a five-to-four margin, the Court finally ruled in December 1937 that the Wagner Act did apply to Fruehauf and that the firm would have to rehire and compensate its UAW employees and refrain from labor espionage.[7]

The Fruehauf case and its outcome reflected a change in the mood of the nation. The financial crash of 1929 and ensuing depression had discredited, in the eyes of many voters, the Republicans' 1920s policy of minimally regulated business ascendency. The elections of 1932 swept into office a reforming Congress whose legislative initiatives would be supported by the sympathetic President Roosevelt, architect of the "New Deal." Taking heart from these political circumstances and from a surge in public sympathy, the labor movement surged forward, fueled by the growth of industrial unions like the UAW.

Further, more psychological factors lay at the root of a new determination to tackle labor espionage. There were (exaggerated) suspicions that the United States had been tricked into joining the Allies in World War I by a conspiracy of profiteering arms manufacturers and by financiers like J.P. Morgan. It was a blow to faith in transparency and to the prestige of American business. There were worries that those same secretive arms manufacturers were now putting an arsenal at the disposal of anti-union employers who wished to shoot down problematic workers. This was at a moment when the Roosevelt administration was embarking on a war on crime. The armed "goons" sent into action against union organizers seemed to be just as appropriate targets of federal action as "Machine Gun" Kelly Barnes and his fellow mobsters.

The time was opportune for a congressional investigation of labor espionage. Heber Blankenhorn, a special investigator for the NLRB, had witnessed the steel industry's deployment of labor spies during the disastrous 1919 steel strike and felt deeply about the matter. He lobbied Senator Robert M. La Follette, Jr. Sponsored by both the Republicans and the independent Progressive Party in Wisconsin, the senator came from a promising stable. His father, "Fighting Bob" La Follette, had been sympathetic to labor and had sponsored a law named after him, the La Follette Seamen's Act of 1915. That statute had been mercantilist in nature in that it aimed to ensure that American goods sailed in American bottoms manned by American crews, but at the same time it protected US sailors from cheap foreign labor competition. "Young Bob" was not just his father's son but also the representative of a reforming state. The university in Madison, Wisconsin, which was the alma mater of La Follette, Jr., had for years supported research into labor matters. Its industrial relations specialist John R. Commons had overseen research into labor espionage undertaken by the Research Division of the Commission on Industrial Relations. "Young Bob" La Follette had supported the Wisconsin law that required the licensing of every individual detective. He remembered how his father had suffered hostile surveillance at the hands of William J. Burns. He was ready to act, and in March 1936 he introduced Senate Resolution 266, authorizing the Committee on Education and Labor to launch "an investigation of violations of the rights of free speech and assembly and undue interference with the right of labor to organize and bargain collectively." In hearings on the desirability of the proposed investigation, Blankenhorn alleged that American industry employed more than 40,000 labor spies at an annual cost of $80,000,000. On June 6, the Senate approved Resolution 266.[8]

Once Congress had approved the investigation and he had been appointed the chair of a special investigative subcommittee, La Follette set about hiring staff. One of his main appointments was Marion Clinch Calkins. She was married to Charles Merrell, a businessman who also worked for a New Deal agency. However, for professional purposes she stuck to her maiden surname and, to remain gender neutral, dropped her first name to operate simply as Clinch Calkins. A published poet with a literary flair, Calkins had graduated from the University of Wisconsin in 1918. She had a good grasp of the complexities of the task that La Follette faced, and she would write the first official report that resulted from his inquiry.[9]

The La Follette inquiry investigated several abuses in different industries. It exposed the ruthless tactics—including the murder of union activists—used against the United Mine Workers of America (UMWA), founded in 1890 and America's first modern industrial union. It devoted hearings and an entire published volume to the munitions supplied to anti-union employers. However, it concentrated most heavily on employers' alleged use of private detectives and on the abuses said to flow from that practice. With limited if generous assets at its disposal, it concentrated on the biggest five detective agencies of the 1930s, the PNDA, the Burns agency, the National Corporation Service, the Railway Audit and Inspection Company, and the Corporations Auxiliary Company. Of these five, the Pinkertons received the most attention. They were the main target.

La Follette's special subcommittee sent out requests for information and for relevant documents and asked PNDA as well as other detective agency personnel to testify. Robert A. Pinkerton II's response was to order the destruction of documents and to instruct his colleagues not to appear before the La Follette subcommittee.

In response, Congress on July 13, 1936, passed a law making it illegal to fail to produce documents or to refuse to appear before a congressional inquiry.[10] Many in-house detective-agency statistics and accounts regarding labor espionage were nevertheless trashed, and thus lost to the subcommittee. However, inquiry officials resorted to a bit of espionage of their own. They raided the wastepaper baskets of the Railway Audit and Inspection detective agency, retrieved scraps of shredded paper, and reconstructed them. Then on September 21, a grand jury issued the first indictments under the new law, compelling officials of the same company to produce documents and appear in person upon pain of fines or imprisonment. The message could not have been clearer. The Pinkertons, too, had to think what they were going to say, because they were scheduled to testify imminently.[11]

Robert Pinkerton, like his grandfather and great uncle at the time of Homestead, would have to appear before a congressional committee. As he later said, it was a challenge for an executive who was only twenty-six years old when he took over the agency in 1930 and whose only training was "what I heard my father discuss at home." Writing from his business address in the towering Old Tribune Building, Nassau Street, New York City, he composed a preparatory statement for submission to the La Follette subcommittee. He defended his failure to appear before the committee in April: "we understood that appearance and testimony were voluntary." His firm had needed time to respond to the allegations of witnesses who were not testifying under oath. He objected to descriptors like "strike breaking agency" and "labor spy agency" when applied to his company. His investigators simply determined the loyalty of employees, an essential ingredient in any company's success. They countered "false propaganda" emanating from racketeers, the IWW, and the Communist Party, and they only assisted with labor cases when there was a danger of union enforcement of the closed shop. In further preparation, Pinkerton studied a newsletter issued by Chester M. Wright, formerly publicity officer for the AFL, who suggested there was reason to anticipate rising militancy and trouble because of the developing feud between the AFL and Committee for (later Congress of) Industrial Organizations (CIO) The CIO had been established on November 9, 1935, with a view to injecting urgency into the campaign to organize industry-wide labor unions—it became the umbrella organization for unions like the UAW, UMWA, and the Steel Workers Organizing Committee. Could this new militancy inspire rough tactics that might play into the Pinkertons' hands? Emulating his forbears, Robert Pinkerton arranged for the compilation of a two-folders-thick collection of accounts of alleged labor violence that had occurred so far.[12]

The La Follette inquiry compiled its own data in advance of hearings. Basing its findings on tax returns, inquiry staff estimated that the declared Pinkerton net-of-tax profit for the year ended December 31, 1933, was $76,760. Two years later, reflecting the labor turbulence that was gathering pace in the nation, the net-of-tax declared profit was $243,351.[13]

La Follette researchers compiled a list of firms known to be employing Pinkertons. Aside from the Fruehauf Trailer Company, there were many others. By

July 1938 the inquiry would find 309 clients. The entry for General Motors Corporation (GM) indicated that Pinkertons had infiltrated five of its subsidiaries. GM was the nation's largest corporation and Pinkertons' biggest customer in the 1930s. It engaged operatives to spy on charismatic UAW organizer Walther Reuther as well as on workers on the shop floor. The company's plant in Lansing, Michigan, was 100 percent UAW until the Pinkertons ensured that every member of the local UAW committee was a Pinkerton spy, which killed off the union. By February 1937 the auto firm had paid the Pinkertons $839,000, raising the question as to whether it might have been more profitable to recognize the UAW in the first place.[14]

In September 1936 the tall and slightly built figure of PNDA president Robert Pinkerton appeared before the La Follette Committee. Senator La Follette led the questioning. The subcommittee learned that Pinkerton owned 70 percent of PNDA company stock, the remainder equally divided between two aunts. PNDA by now owed Pinkerton $367,000, the balance that remained after earlier repayments of the company's borrowed capital, which the executive vaguely remembered as having been between $1 million and $1.5 million in 1925. Robert Pinkerton had not drawn a salary in the past year but had received $129,500 in dividends.[15]

La Follette proceeded to ask questions about labor espionage. Pinkerton was not forthcoming on the subject. From the evidence that had survived the paper purge, it became evident that a great deal of secrecy was involved. Invoices were written on blank pieces of paper, not on PNDA stationary. Even the overall agency budget was expressed on a single sheet of handwritten, lined paper.[16] Operatives who infiltrated unions were assigned code letters or numbers. Pinkerton explained that secrecy was necessary to all detective work.

When La Follette asked Pinkerton difficult questions, especially about the specifics of labor espionage, the company president denied any knowledge, saying it was a matter for his subordinates. He referred many questions to Asher Rossiter. This was an official who had been with the firm for forty-nine years, rising from the position of office boy to be vice president and general manager. In the past year, Rossiter had drawn a salary of $12,000, of which $2,000 represented bonuses. Supplying personal background, he said he was proud of his role in rounding up a gang that had robbed a train at Mud Cut, Nebraska, in 1909. He had otherwise had an administrative career and had taken to heart William A. Pinkerton's advice that "the ability to remain unseen" was a prime asset for detectives. Like his current boss, he blocked questions whenever he

Figure 24.1. Robert A. Pinkerton II (left) and his general manager Asher Rossiter testify before the US Senate's La Follette inquiry investigating strikebreaking on September 25, 1936. *Harris & Ewing Collection, Library of Congress*

could. Turning away from Rossiter, La Follette tried Pinkerton once more, this time with a general question. Would he agree that the recent expansion of labor unionism had coincided with and probably caused a boom in Pinkerton business? Pinkerton replied, "I am not familiar with it." Frustrated by the evasion, La Follette snapped, "I got the impression that you were at the head of this company."[17]

From Pinkerton employees who testified, the subcommittee built a picture of the agency, with further details supplied in collected evidential exhibits. The agency had 1,000 regular employees, spread over 27 offices. Between 5 and 10 percent of paid informers were women—but there was no mention of female or Black operatives, and the senators on the subcommittee did not ask. Company accounts were compiled in a manner that obscured what was going on. For example, a "picnic" at a GM subsidiary, the Fisher Body plant in Flint, Michigan, lasted for two years at a cost of $1,300. That sum had really gone to spying. Rossiter offered the undocumented guess that 30 percent of the company's undercover work was labor espionage. He justified it as a fight against communism.[18]

Events took a dramatic turn when, from the end of December 1936 until February 11, 1937, there occurred a sit-down strike by General Motors workers in Flint, Michigan. The La Follette investigation showed how Pinkerton labor espionage had provoked resentment among the GM workers in the three years preceding the sit-down. GM had responded to the 1930s spurt in unionization by saturating its plants with Pinkerton labor spies. With a view to prying, it even rented an office adjacent to the UAW's headquarters in Detroit's Hoffman Building. So worried were its managers that at one point they hired one Pinkerton to spy on another, who they feared was feeding confidential information to a commercial competitor. In the period of saturation, union membership declined from 26,000 to 120. According to the La Follette investigation, this was proof that espionage was the most efficient way to destroy unionism.[19]

The La Follette investigators reported on GM's efforts to cover its tracks once the auto manufacturer knew an inquiry was in progress. Only a few "sketchy" financial statements survived a general purge of documentation. The investigators did, however, have the advantage of information from a double agent. Arthur G. "Frenchy" Dubuc was a French Canadian on the books of the Pinkerton agency who had served as president of the federated local Chevrolet union in Flint, Michigan. He operated in elaborate secrecy. No doubt fearful of telephone intercepts, GM had asked Dubuc to report to them only from pay phones—and never to use the same pay phone more than once. However, Dubuc confessed his role as a Pinkerton spy to the UAW and to the La Follette investigators and thereafter kept them informed about the continuation of espionage during the sit-down strike—and about GM's efforts at concealment of evidence from congressional inquirers.[20]

The components manufactured in Flint were essential to GM subsidiaries like Buick and Chevrolet, so the sit-down work stoppage was an event of strategic importance. The company could not deploy strikebreakers as the workers were occupying its plants. When the police tried to enter and reoccupy Fisher Body 2 plant on January 11, 1937, firing their guns and using tear gas, the workers successfully resisted by throwing metal bolts and other missiles at the invaders. They ignored an injunction issued by a company-friendly judge. President Roosevelt refused to send federal troops and instead urged GM to recognize the union. Michigan's Governor Frank Murphy did send in troops, but with a difference. The Michigan national guard arrived to protect union supporters from company goons and strikebreakers. The upshot was that General Motors recognized the UAW, whose membership grew to 200,000 by the end of 1937, making the union a force in the land.

Against the background of these events, Pinkerton and several colleagues from the agency again testified to the La Follette subcommittee. There was further embarrassment for the Pinkertons when Senator Elbert D. Thomas, an influential Democrat representing Utah, reopened the questioning. William H. Martin, no relation of J.N. Martin discussed previously, testified about his experience as a Pinkerton labor spy from 1928 until his resignation on October 11, 1935. He recalled that he had been one of about twenty Pinkerton infiltrators in Flint's Fisher Body plant. However, what was more shocking to Senator Thomas was the fact that Martin had been assigned to spy on Edward McGrady. At the time, McGrady had been an NLRB conciliator; by the time of the hearing, he was US assistant secretary of labor. Martin and two colleagues had taken up positions in a room at the Secor Hotel, Toledo, Ohio, that was adjacent to McGrady's room. Still eschewing the eavesdropping equipment favored by the Pinkertons' rivals, Martin and his confederates had spent the evenings with their ears glued to the wall separating their room from McGrady's. Martin testified that only the Secor's good soundproofing frustrated the spying mission on this occasion.[21]

In the La Follette milieu, there was an incipient fear that the "eye that never sleeps" was becoming the optic of a surveillance society. On August 12, 1936, the die makers of Plant 3 of GM subsidiary Chevrolet had met in the plant's rest room not for the purpose of ablutions but to discuss in secret "the profits of General Motors Co." One of them, William Chumack, declared that "a few control all the wealth" and the Chevrolet workers should get the same bonuses as were paid in the Chrysler Co. The choice of venue had been in vain—a Pinkerton operative with the coded initials "H.J." was present and filed a report on the proceedings.[22] In the midst of such febrile revelations, Senator Thomas asked Pinkerton if his operatives were shadowing members of the investigative committee. Pinkerton thought not but was unsure. Rossiter was brought to the stand and denied that agency men had shadowed witnesses called by the subcommittee.[23]

In the same hearing, Harry W. Anderson, labor-relations director at General Motors, issued a declaration. He stated that he had instructed plant managers to discontinue employing Pinkertons for labor espionage purposes. The discontinuation would take effect on January 31, 1937. La Follette voiced his suspicion based on witness testimony that there would continue to be oral as distinct from written spy reports.[24] Soon, however, the Pinkerton agency likewise bowed to circumstances. Its board meeting on April 8, 1937, resolved that the Agency should not in the future "furnish information to anyone concerning the lawful attempts of labor unions or employees to organize and bargain collectively." This policy decision, the minute recorded, was at the urging of Robert Pinkerton, who was concerned about views held in Congress and by the public.[25]

Estimating public sentiment before the arrival of opinion polls in the later 1930s was never an easy task, but Robert Pinkerton does seem to have been right in his assessment. Congress approved the La Follette censure of labor espionage by a huge majority. The committee's revelations received extensive coverage in the press, mainly favorable to the inquisitors. A number of authors digested some or all of the fourteen volumes of the La Follette hearings and produced supportive books that summarized the revelations. Cinch Calkins, in her *Spy Overhead*, drew on her knowledge of the inquiry for which she had worked. She quoted from Robert's Pinkerton's testimony, representing him as squirming with embarrassment. Two other books appeared in the same year, 1937, dealing with the Pinkertons' roles as revealed in the first eight La Follette volumes: the eloquent socialist Leo Huberman's *Labor Spy Racket* (on sale for only 35 cents), and Robert Brooks's *When Labor Organizes*.[26] PNDA was not the only agency to recognize these signals of public opinion and proclaim an end to its labor work. The Corporations Auxiliary Company, which had been the subject of a dedicated La Follette hearing, chose to cease operations altogether.[27]

At least for the time being, the PNDA did give up labor work. Asher Rossiter tried to find a way back by arguing that the Pinkertons could operate against advocates of criminal violence such as communists. But in practice the PNDA appears to have lived up to Robert Pinkerton's promise and at a cost to its revenue. An in-house statement to mark the centenary of the agency's founding in 1950 estimated that on account of Robert Pinkerton's instruction it lost a sixth of its business at a stroke, and another sixth represented by pending contracts—as Rossiter had guessed at a La Follette hearing, this made a one-third loss of business.[28]

However, while the La Follette inquiry for a while affected opinion on anti-union industrial practices, it resulted in no legislation. In 1939 Senators La Follette and Thomas introduced a bill, S. 1970, which would have outlawed the use of spies, as well as other abuses such as the deployment of automatic weapons to intimidate pro-union workers. At first the bill had widespread support, but then changes in the political climate and context intervened. Public opinion, having previously been pro-unions, began to turn against Big Labor just as it had once been censorious of Big Business.[29] The National Association of Manufacturers launched a counteroffensive; the mid-term election results of 1938 were a setback for New Dealers in Congress; the House of Representatives established, under the chairmanship of conservative Virginia Democrat Howard W. Smith, a special committee to investigate the NLRB and the Smith deliberations undermined support for the New Deal; the war in Europe was increasingly a distraction. S. 1970 was first amended out of all recognition and then, in 1940, defeated in the House.

The Anti-Pinkerton Act of 1893 thus retained its uniqueness as an attempt to place federal limitations on the activities of private detective agencies. The failure to amplify federal restriction was a setback for reformers. Yet the fact that the 1890s statute survived the reactionary tide and remained on the statute book was still significant. Anti-Pinkertonism would remain a force on the land, even if the Pinkertons were past their heyday.

CHAPTER 25

A Corporate Era

Since the 1930s the Pinkertons have never been a major political issue. This does not mean that they were materially diminished. On the contrary, the firm grew and became more profitable. As it did so, it became more corporate in character in keeping with contemporary business trends. Meantime, anti-Pinkertonism enjoyed fluctuating fortunes.

The agency's loss of labor-spy income at first took its toll. The company's 1938 income of $1,224,661 was its lowest since 1921. However, the income volume changed with the nation's engagement in World War II. The Nazi spy cases of the 1930s had shown that US industry needed better security, and the Pinkertons stepped into the breach. War-plant protection contributed to the agency's gross of $4,089,969 in 1944. Once the Nazi foe was defeated, there was a danger of a postwar income slump. However, fears of Soviet espionage ensured the continuation of some security work.[1]

Labor espionage had little if anything to do with the Pinkerton revival. Regardless of Congress's failure to legislate against labor espionage, that kind of undercover activity had become a taboo practice. Public figures shied from any association with it. We can see this in the case of Wendell L. Willkie. In the fall elections of 1940, Willkie ran on the Republican ticket against the Democratic incumbent Franklin D. Roosevelt. Willkie had been a Democrat but turned against Roosevelt to combat what he saw as the twin evils of big government and big labor. He resented the development of the New Deal's vast, publicly owned Tennessee Valley Authority (TVA) project. TVA embraced hydroelectric and flood-control-irrigation initiatives. The public enterprise threatened to swallow up concerns like the Commonwealth and Southern Company, a private conglomerate headed by Willkie.

At the height of the 1940 presidential campaign the Democrats' national chairman, Edward J. Flynn, attempted to turn Willkie's private interests into a political liability. He charged that three Commonwealth and Southern subsidiaries had been Pinkerton clients. Willkie's Georgia Power Company alone spent $31,000 on Pinkerton labor spies. Willkie said this was "completely false." Whatever the truth of the matter, it is clear that both sides in the spat recognized the contaminating effect of any Pinkerton labor–spy association.[2]

The PNDA could not shake off its past. Journalists addressing the subject of the Pinkertons almost invariably mentioned Homestead. When opportunity arose, they would ask Robert A. Pinkerton II about his firm's labor work. His answer never varied. He regretted what his agency had done in the past, urged his interviewer to understand that labor work had been legal at the time when it was undertaken, and emphasized that the Pinkertons no longer spied on labor.[3] Once so antilabor, the PNDA was at one point on the cusp of being a union-recognizing company itself. The International Union of Plant Protective Employees in 1959 launched a campaign to unionize the nation's guards, including Pinkerton's 15,000 patrolmen. The 300-strong Boston district Pinkertons put union membership to the vote, with ninety-six in favor and eighty against. Unionization did not become commonplace, but a few decades earlier the very thought would have been sacrilegious.[4]

In harmony with dynastic tradition, Robert Pinkerton II continued the PNDA's public relations efforts. Attacks on the agency's labor record required that. Another spur was a chronic disposition, revealed in dime novels and movies, to portray the James brothers, Sundance Kid, and their like to be romantic, Robin Hood characters who justly fought against the oppressive PNDA. In 1939, for example, two movies appeared on the Jesse James theme, featuring leading actors of the day: Roy Rogers, Tyrone Power, and Henry Fonda. In one, the villain is a ruthless railroad detective. The other movie features a chronological inversion, with the Pinkerton firebomb thrown into the James home the cause of subsequent James mayhem and not the culmination of a long feud. To counter unfavorable representations, Robert Pinkerton engaged the services of true crime writer Alan Hynd, giving him exclusive access to Pinkerton files. In his consequent literary output, Hynd revived the eulogistic tone of earlier compliant writers and ignored controversial subjects like Homestead.[5]

A little later the Pinkertons offered similar privileges to James Horan. This New York journalist wrote articles and books on the Pinkertons casting them in a favorable light, and in 1955 supervised and partly scripted for television, then a charismatic new medium, a series on the Pinkertons called *Man Against Crime*. In a preface to one of Horan's books that appeared in 1962 Robert Pinkerton wrote, "In the last few years . . . numerous motion pictures, television shows, books and magazine articles on the life of the Jameses and Youngers and other Western outlaws have appeared. Many of them glorified the bandits as misjudged Robin Hoods." Horan was given access to Pinkerton files on western outlaws so that he could change the interpretive slant.[6]

Hynd articulated the modern Pinkerton creed. His PNDA operatives adhered to the ethics laid down by the agency's founder, Allan Pinkerton. They did no divorce work. They took on no labor cases. They always got their man. No doubt with the approval of Robert Pinkerton II, with his close interest in the agency's image, Hynd revised the nineteenth-century spin on the Pinkertons' role vis-à-vis public law enforcement. Allan Pinkerton had been at pains to contrast the upstanding character and competence of his own operatives with the shortcomings of city police forces. But according to Hynd/Robert Pinkerton II, "When the Pinkertons are called in on a major criminal case, they always work in close cooperation, never in opposition, with the public officials who are charged with the solution of the crime. The entrance of the Agency into a public crime picture does not imply failure on the part of those officials in whose jurisdiction the crime has been committed."[7]

The squeaky-clean image Hynd promoted does not stand up to scrutiny, as is evident in a story from 1952–53 that incidentally throws light on Pinkerton–police–FBI cooperation, indeed collusion. The story is set in the years of the Great Scare, or McCarthyism, when the nation was in thrall to a panic not just about communist spies and influence but also regarding the imaginary "Lavender" threat posed by homosexuals. Allegations centered on the governor of Illinois, Adlai Stevenson, who was the Democrats' choice as presidential candidate.

Stevenson, who would lose to the Republican Dwight D. Eisenhower in 1952 and then again in 1956, was smeared as a homosexual in a case that arose from illicit sporting activities. In the spring of 1952, members of the basketball team representing Bradley University, a private college in Peoria, Illinois, were accused of game fixing. During the investigation of these charges, local and New York police picked up rumors that David Owen, the president of Bradley University, was a homosexual—as was Governor Stevenson. The Bradley University governors, already shaken by the basketball scandal, suspended Owen and called in the Pinkertons. The agency investigated, and contributed to the whispering campaign when it concluded that Owen and Stevenson were gays, but that they could not produce any evidence to that effect that would stand up in court. Meantime the FBI, whose director J. Edgar Hoover was promoting both the current Red Scare and the parallel Lavender Scare, took up the case and noted with interest the part played by the Pinkertons.[8] David Owen never recovered from the innuendo. He resigned from his post and ended up the victim of a hotel room murder a few years later.

In 1961, when newly elected President John F. Kennedy proposed Stevenson as the US ambassador to the United Nations, Hoover resurrected the sexual smear against Stevenson. We know this because the index card on Stevenson from Hoover's Sex Deviates File survives. It is the only one of its kind that escaped destruction when, on the FBI director's death, his secretary destroyed almost all such evidence.[9] The Stevenson affair illustrated Pinkerton–FBI interaction and sat uneasily with the Pinkertons' carefully manufactured reputation for undertaking no dirty work.

By the 1960s Robert Pinkerton had steered the agency in the direction of becoming a modern corporation. In 1961 the poet and novelist Philip Benjamin painted a picture of the PNDA for *New York Times* readers. He wrote of an organization that had a shiny new glass-paned office at 100 Church Street, New York. Entering the suite, visitors walked across wall-to-wall carpeting to encounter a "good-looking" receptionist who sat beneath an oil painting of Robert A. Pinkerton, the son of the founder. The agency had 1.5 million index cards on persons of interest and a turnover of $28 million. There were 13,000 regular personnel spread across forty-five offices, 9,000 of whom were uniformed guards watching over factories, hospitals, banks, universities, museums, racetracks, and sports stadiums. When the rich partied, selected Pinkerton security men "looked good in white tie" and kept an eye on the silver. Sometimes Pinkerton guards carried guns, at other times they did not. The remaining 4,000 Pinkerton employees consisted of "investigators and supervisory personnel." Detection accounted for 20 percent of revenue. Because the FBI had taken up other aspects of criminal work, Pinkerton detectives (now called investigators) typically concerned themselves with store thefts and insurance cases and still served as the security arm of the Jewelers' Security Alliance. Howard W. Nugent, a Pinkerton vice president who had joined from the NYPD to oversee its investigative work, remarked that the agency "could not function" without police cooperation. The agency retained "lofty" principles regarding divorce work, plea bargaining, and strike breaking.[10]

Three years later another journalist reported that the PNDA had just grossed $43 million.[11] The agency remained the nation's largest private security enterprise. At this point, Robert Pinkerton, who took pride in his people skills, announced a major new contract. In 1964–65, Flushing Meadows-Corona Park in Queens, New York, was the site of a World's Fair. It was a show case for American and international businesses, with an emphasis on technology and the Space Age. Fifty-one million people would pass through its portals. The Pinkertons landed the guard contract, providing security. They would also look after fire protection, first aid, ambulance provision, traffic direction, parking, tourist guidance, and lost children. The contract would provide employment for an additional 2,200 to 4,500 Pinkerton personnel and earn the agency $9 million.[12]

In 1965 the PNDA changed its name to Pinkerton's Inc. Robert Pinkerton believed that was a more accurate description of the firm now that it concentrated less on detection and more on the provision of guards. Two years later Pinkerton revenues stood at $71 million. Regardless of where the agency stood in the culture wars, its owner and president had delivered dollar turnover. At this point, in March 1967, Robert Pinkerton took a step that would effectively end the history of the family dynasty. He sanctioned the first offering of Pinkerton stock on the Wall Street exchange, selling his own assets and those of other family members. The flotation was a success, with all shares snapped up at a premium. Pinkerton resigned as president and became chairman instead. The businessman and former naval officer Edward J. Bednarz became president and would remain in that position until 1979. Pinkerton was preparing the ground. His only child was a daughter, Ann, and there was still no expectation that a female could run the agency. He told one journalist somewhat ambivalently, "I'm sorry that the family name won't be carried on. I hope the name will still be around for many years to come."[13]

On October 11, 1967, Robert, the last male descendant of Allan Pinkerton, died at age 62 in a Long Island hospital not far from his home in East Islip. The *New York Times* meticulously noted his social credentials: educated at St. Paul's School, Concord, New Hampshire, captain of polo at Harvard, member of the Turf and Field Club and of the Racquet and Tennis Club, enthusiastic yachtsman. At the same time, though, the newspaper credited him with having greatly strengthened the business he had inherited.[14]

Robert Pinkerton's death did not extinguish the endless fascination with the agency's colorful past. The Hollywood movies *Butch Cassidy and the Sundance Kid* and *The Molly Maguires* appeared in 1969 and 1970, respectively (both were even-handed). But memories of past controversies did not impede the agency's continuing profitability. According to a 1973 report in the *Boston Globe*, a major expansion of business was under way. Pinkerton's (undefined) "growth" in the last two years was estimated to be between 20 and 25 percent. This compared with a 15 to 18 percent growth by what was still its closest competitor, Burns International Security Services. The *Globe* noted that the city police were sometimes troubled by the fact that private guards carried guns and used uniforms and cars similar to their own but without having the power to make arrests. However, the newspaper praised the Pinkertons for ensuring that their employees did not have criminal records. It also commented on the anomaly that Pinkerton anticrime business was expanding faster than crime itself. The FBI's Uniform Crime Report for 1972 indicated that crime overall had increased by only 1 percent in the past year. "Crime Pays—Those Who Fight It," the *Globe*'s headline declared.[15]

As in the past, the Pinkertons thrived on fear of crime as much as on crime itself, especially in times of social unrest—as is evidenced in the cases of the domestic protest against racism and against the war in Vietnam. There were sensational depictions, in the press and through the lips of politicians, of the degree of radicalism and violence involved. Such depictions were not in every case exaggerated—as shown, for example, in the 1974 kidnapping and subsequent brainwashing by the far-left Symbionese Liberation Army of Patricia C. "Patty" Hearst, granddaughter of the newspaper magnate William Howard Hearst. Fearing kidnappers, stars like Barbra Streisand and Elizabeth Taylor hired bodyguards for their children. Former Secret Service men were in demand for these jobs, but the Pinkerton and Burns agencies were also flooded with requests.[16]

As president, Edward Bednarz introduced further diversification. One innovation was significant because it illustrated how the nineteenth-century ban on the federal employment of Pinkertons was losing its force. In the 1980s the Federal Office of Personnel Management hired Pinkerton, Inc., and four other private firms to run background checks on 12,000 job applicants—ostensibly to clear a backlog, but in the eyes of critics to pursue President Ronald Reagan's privatization objectives.[17] Dropping one of the Pinkertons' previous scruples, Bednarz established a unit to investigate the merits of electronic eavesdropping devices. PNDA personnel advised the US Department of State on overseas security. Its first nondynastic head committed the agency to the manufacture and marketing of anti-intrusion devices (sophisticated burglar alarms). In a new twist to Allan Pinkerton's push for international recognition, Bednarz arranged for Pinkerton's, Inc., to be the sole US member of the London-based Ligue Internationale des Sociétés de Surveillance. Under Bednarz's leadership, the firm's financial performance put it in the top fifty US companies in terms of both return on assets and market value.[18]

In 1982 Bednarz facilitated the takeover of Pinkerton, Inc., by a holding company. Prior to 1966 American Brands had been known as the American Tobacco Company, but it had changed its name because a health-conscious nation had come to regard smoking as dangerous. American Brands still marketed Lucky Strike and other cigarettes but had diversified and was now interested in the services industry. Pinkerton's, which grossed $293 million in 1981, was an attractive acquisition. A spokesperson for Pinkerton's declined to explain the benefits for his company of absorption into American Brands but offered a clue when he remarked that competition in the security guard business was "cutthroat." That suggests that Pinkerton's, while in the business of selling security, itself needed the security offered by a larger financial umbrella.[19]

Early in 1999 Pinkerton's was once again acquired, this time by the Swedish-based security giant Securitas (in the following year, Securitas would also acquire Pinkerton's old rival, now known as the Burns International Services Corporation). Pinkerton's by this time had 250 offices and 48,000 employees distributed throughout North America, Europe, and Asia. Its 1998 sales were valued at one billion dollars. Following some stock dilution its shares, at $20, were not quite so buoyant as they had been but were attractive to a multinational firm that was already in the security business and wanted to consolidate its US foothold. From now on, Pinkerton's would be known as Pinkerton Consulting & Investigations. As part of the deal the Pinkertons engaged the services of Oxford University graduate Jane Adler to impose order on its archives in preparation for their transfer to the Library of Congress. The Pinkertons, in one sense at least, were now history.[20]

The Pinkertons may have declared themselves to be history in 1999, but the Pinkerton tradition lived on in diverse ways. One of these arose from explicit challenges to the 1893 federal Anti-Pinkerton Act, challenges that helped underpin the rise of the twenty-first century's privatized security state. In 1960 a House of Representatives measure to repeal the 1893 act failed. Three years later, Senator John L. McClellan introduced a repeal bill in the upper chamber. A Democrat from Arkansas, McClellan was known for his segregationist stance, and had chaired an investigation into corruption in the labor movement. In support of his bill, McClellan submitted a report from the Committee on Government Operations that summarized the 1892–93 congressional debate that had preceded passage of the Anti-Pinkerton Act. The summary noted that the act's framers had opposed the employment by government, but not private individuals, of a "Pinkerton force or any similar quasi-military organization." It contended that the 1893 law was anticompetitive as it excluded detective agencies from bidding for government contracts. It claimed that by now Pinkerton, Inc., was partly unionized, that federal laws offered organized labor plenty of protection, and that the repeal had support from sections of the labor movement.[21] The measure passed in the Senate, but the House voted it down.

Subsequent legislative attempts fared no better. Arguing for his 1971 bill "to authorize the hiring of employees of detective agencies for other than investigative services," Senator Jack Miller of Iowa, a Republican, repeated the argument that the 1893 law was an anachronism, and that labor was well looked after by federal legislation. His aim was to end the situation whereby "detective agencies may not provide protective or guard services for the Federal Government."[22] It was a tribute to the strength of the long-lasting feelings engendered by Haymarket, Homestead, and the La Follette revelations that Miller's efforts, like those of his predecessors, came to nothing.

However, laws may be rendered inoperative not just through repeal but also via judicial interpretation. In 1977 the Fifth US Court of Appeals issued a judgment in the case *Jacob Weinberger v. Equifax*. Equifax was a consumer credit rating company, and the case is of some interest because in the nineteenth century such companies had pioneered surveillance in a manner that would have been more controversial had it been performed for more nefarious purposes. Equifax met with a legal challenge when it took on government contracts and hired private detectives to perform some of its tasks. The *Equifax* ruling reviewed yet again the post-Homestead scene and congressional intent in 1893. It fixed on the idea that the real objection had been to the use of Pinkertons and similar for "quasi-military" purposes. As this was not Equifax's intention, the ruling held that Equifax was free to hire private detectives to do government work.[23] The far-reaching *Equifax* decision would be repeatedly endorsed in subsequent official communications and publications. For example, the 2004 edition of the Red Book, an official compilation of appropriations law, ran over the events of 1892–93 once again and referred to the *Equifax* decision as definitive. Prior to Equifax, the Red Book stated, there had been a good case for repeal of the Anti-Pinkerton law. However: "The statute is no longer a major impediment to legitimate guard service contracting, and certainly most would agree that the government should not deal with an organization that offers quasi-military armed forces for hire."[24]

The 9/11 attack of 2001 and consequent "War on Terror" prompted a shift in policy and a change in the complexion of the debate over the Anti-Pinkerton Act. Following the collapse of communism in Europe in the late 1980s, the US national security apparatus had been run down. Agencies like the CIA no longer seemed so necessary, and longstanding civil libertarian objections to spying and surveillance resurfaced. When the nation then found itself confronted by a terrorist threat, it was short of resources. By this time George W. Bush, Republican victor in the 2000 presidential election, was president. He and his governing team were committed to private enterprise. They massively increased investment in national security and, in effecting a quick expansion of personnel, resorted to the private sphere. The Department of Homeland Security, established in 2002, with 240,000 personnel by 2018, subcontracted half of its jobs to private firms, 60 percent in the case of intelligence-gathering functions. Firms like Blackwater, Palantir, and Booz Hamilton subcontracted to various government agencies. Some of the services they provided in conflicted zones and in embassies across the globe were investigative in nature, for example in the case of the interrogation of terrorist suspects. They also supplied armed guards, if not mercenaries. Pinkerton*ism*, if not the Pinkertons themselves, had at last benefited from federal employment, and on an extensive scale. By 2006, 70 percent of the $28 billion spent on national intelligence was spent on private contracts.[25]

Once again, the Anti-Pinkerton law became, if only briefly, a source of legal contention. The plaintiff in the *Brian X. Scott* case of 2006 was a contract bidder who claimed that his competitors were illegally offering "quasi-military armed forces for hire." The comptroller general, as director of the Government Accountability Office, dismissed the objection, arguing from *Equifax* and other legal precedent that the challenged private companies had supplied personnel who were individually armed and that this meant they were not an illegally constituted "quasi-military armed force."[26] In the anxious climate caused by the 9/11 attack and its aftermath, lawyers and government officials had ceased to regard the Anti-Pinkerton Act of 1893 as a significant or desirable impediment to the employment of Pinkerton-style companies on nonlabor work.

As for labor work, Robert Pinkerton II's policy of abstinence carried no legal or otherwise binding force, and the pendulum began to swing back to the practices of the founder, Allan Pinkerton. Within two decades of the Securitas takeover, the story was beginning to assume a familiar shape. In the spring of 2018 the telecommunications company Frontier Communications was in financial difficulties—it would file for bankruptcy on April 14. Possibly because they were keen to control costs, the managers were in no mood to deal with unions. Matters came to a head in Virginia and West Virginia in early March, with 1,400 members of the Communications Workers of America Local 142 going on strike. Frontier accused the striking workers of violence, axing its cables, and intimidation of strikebreakers. It hired Pinkerton Consulting and Investigations (also known as plain "Pinkerton") personnel to act as security guards.[27] The Securitas subsidiary made no secret of further services it provided. Its website publicity offered agents who would work "embedded or on-call," and one of its advertisements promised to monitor risks from "labor demonstrations." A *New Republic* journalist reached the conclusion that although "Pinkertons no longer kill workers," they "survived, and entered the 21st century intact largely on the strength of their ability to intimidate, surveil, and gather intelligence about workers."[28]

The Pinkerton firm's website in the 2020s offered a chronology of its past that did not mention Homestead. One of its brochures advertised its detection services in a way that perhaps reflected the purpose of Allan Pinkerton in the nineteenth century but in a twenty-first century wrapper. It marketed a digital Pinkerton Crime Index as part of its risk management services to modern businesses. The index "leveraged" police statistics in such a way that it helped firms to know where to locate, whether in US localities or abroad. This sophisticated descendant of the Rogues Gallery made no pretense at fighting crime other than crime that affected business. It boasted a 95 percent accurate predictive gauge of where firms might encounter criminal troubles—but did not mention unions specifically.[29]

CHAPTER 26

Who Was the Greatest Detective of Them All?

Who was the greatest detective of them all? And were America's Pinkertons and other private detectives superior to their public counterparts?

To address the question of who was the greatest detective, one must consider criteria. The practitioners defined one such set of principles. Famously articulated by Allan Pinkerton, it embraced the attributes of morality and incorruptibility. Pinkerton and other private detectives also promised the recovery of stolen assets and the arrest of suspected transgressors, suggesting the existence of measurable criteria.

Another set of criteria arises from public expectations. In the absence of opinion polls until the late 1930s, such expectations can be assessed from the language used by popular communicators who appealed to public opinion and mood. In the case of detective history, they are prominently reflected in popular detective fiction, especially its subgenre, hard-boiled stories and novels. "Hard boiled" refers to toughness in recorded action and speech. Practitioners of the mode have included Dashiell Hammett, Raymond Chandler, and—in a more recent genre revival—Walter Moseley. Hard-boiled fiction typically addresses the world of private detectives, not their public counterparts. Students of the genre agree that private detection is a distinctively American phenomenon.[1] Here, it is a mirror held up to the face of reality, for large-scale private detection is indeed distinctively American. To a degree, hard-boiled fiction represented American experience—Hammett had spent some years as a Pinkerton operative. Yet at the same time—and this is a puzzle in its own right—by the time it flourished in the 1930s, hard-boiled fiction was anachronistic and unrepresentative of American life, for by then city police forces were well established as was the publicly funded FBI. Though set in contemporary mean streets, the hard-boiled novels offered judgments based on historical criteria.

According to the American detective novel, especially its hard-boiled form, the private eye is typically (and, by extension, in principle) a maverick character who fights for justice, often in defiance of officialdom.[2] This fictional character is a descendant of the hardy individualists of the American frontier, of which Allan Pinkerton was, after all, a product. The fictional sleuth, typically male, owed a slice of his identity to the protagonists of James Fenimore Cooper's Leatherstocking tales portraying eighteenth-century pioneers.

The avoidance of dirty operations is a candidate for inclusion in our criteria for great detectives. Both the actual detective Allan Pinkerton and Chandler's fictional Philip Marlowe refused to undertake divorce work.[3] In each case, however, they implied they were in that way exceptional and that other private detectives did spy on errant spouses. In that sense Pinkerton and Chandler nodded to reality. Divorce work was an international phenomenon, as has been demonstrated in the case of the United Kingdom.[4] A much later novelist, one of the few French writers to look beyond *policiers* and address the private sector, noted that the end of the *in flagrante* avenue to divorce meant a slump in private eye revenue.[5] It was an acknowledgment of past profits made from sexual prying. Labor espionage, an even larger source of revenue than divorce for US private detective agencies and similarly seen as a dirty endeavor, met verbal rejection in the private profession at least in the 1930s and was rarely mentioned in spy fiction.[6] Whatever the reality, the enthusiasm with which private detection leaders professed their innocence of skullduggery means that the actual avoidance of dirty work must be a criterion for establishing greatness.

Looking beyond the prescriptions of practitioners and fiction writers, one might add further criteria that have operated in media discourse: truthfulness, avoidance of inflated claims, and dedication to the public good. These, in addition to morality, the avoidance of dirty work, incorruptibility, a willingness to defy authority and a record of securing justified arrests and convictions, make up our criteria.

Allan Pinkerton was America's most famous, but that did not necessarily mean greatest, detective. Pinkerton employed deception to trap criminals. One could excuse that on the ground of necessity—less so, however, his habitual self-inflation based on distorted data and his sweeping and mendacious assertion that the American labor movement was violent by its very nature. Pinkerton did enforce a moral code for his operatives, but there were questions about his personal sobriety and that of leading employees such as George Bangs and James McParland. Pinkerton promised fiscal rectitude and was not involved in financial swindles, but his exclusive embrace of rich paying customers could be regarded as its own form of corruption. He did succeed in placing in jail a string of criminals who belonged there, but his record of making arrests and securing safe convictions contained blemishes. Try as one can to find exceptional merit in Pinkerton as a detective, the verdict is ambivalent. His success came as a businessman and as a man who successfully projected a virtuous and heroic image. While he had his share of triumphs, he is also one of those figures who is famous for having been a celebrity.

Conan Doyle had a relationship with the Pinkertons and upheld their efforts against the Molly Maguires in his novella *Valley of Fear*. However, that relationship cooled, and Conan Doyle lent his imprimatur, instead, to the Pinkertons' greatest business rival, William J. Burns. A great persuader, in 1910 Burns wrested from the PNDA the American Bankers' Association contract. He was a gifted self-booster—for example, he conspired with the journalist Harvey O'Higgins to write ten adulatory articles about himself published in *McClure's* magazine in 1910–11.[7] As in the case of the Pinkertons, his reputation was to degree a synthetic one.

There were, however, some more convincing features of Burns's career that inspired the *New York Times* to dub him America's "greatest detective."[8] Both before and after he shot to fame as a private sleuth, Burns served as a public investigator. His commitment to the public sphere dwarfed Pinkerton's, whose role as a deputy sheriff in 1850s Chicago had been brief. One might argue that Burns the civil servant operated with bipolar morality, serving the nation well in his pursuit of land fraudsters when with the Secret Service, then bringing disgrace on the BofI in connection with the Teapot Dome Scandal. As a private detective, he displayed considerable skill, for example in bringing to justice the perpetrators of the Los Angeles Times Building explosion. The contrast with some of Pinkerton's celebrated cases is considerable—disabled, Pinkerton relied on the talents of his subordinates, whereas Burns did much of his own detective work. His contribution to the defense of Leo Frank in the Mary Phagan murder case illustrated Burns's willingness to defy prejudiced orthodoxy and to work against the grain. He had in that case worked in the interest of the public good.

Although the PNDA amounted to more than Allan Pinkerton, it is hard to find other Pinkerton agency figures with a claim to detective greatness. We can begin with the dynasty. Allan Pinkerton's sons, Robert and William, were both able proprietors, but neither had a claim to being a great detective. Allan Pinkerton II falls into the same category and, like his grandfather in the stroke-affected last years of his life, had to place his trust in subordinates on account of ill health. Robert Pinkerton II, the last of the dynasty, saved the PNDA from possible demise on the wake of its loss of labor work. The agency prospered as never before under his presidency, and he had a claim to be the most successful businessman of the four Pinkerton generations. However, he made no pretense of being a detective and sought to refocus the PNDA onto security as distinct from detective contracts.

Turning to prominent Pinkertons outside the family, George Bangs Sr. and Jr. were administrators, not detectives. James McParland conceived of himself as driven by a morality that derived from his strong commitment to Catholicism, but his habit of serving only the rich and seeking to imprison men not for their crimes but because of what they stood for disqualified him from serious consideration as a worthy detective. Just as Allan Pinkerton had placed his trust in McParland, so his sons had a high regard for George S. Dougherty, the colleague who left the agency for the NYPD for a short spell before setting up his own private agency. Dougherty was able but also showed that he had learned the Pinkerton trick of finessing his reputation. In 1922 he regaled the American press with a story in the wake of his recent trip to post-Kaiser Germany. He wrote of how the Berlin commissioner of police, William Richter—a socialist and former saloonkeeper—complained of being unable to hunt down a gang of precious medallion thieves. Dougherty rode to the rescue. According to his account, he posed as a prospective buyer of medallions. Rather improbably, he claimed to have won the confidence of the robber gang (he needed an interpreter) and had them all arrested. The story flagged the presence of yet another publicist rather than a great detective.[9]

Looking beyond senior members of the Pinkertons, there were several operatives, for example Kate Warne and Frank Dimaio, who succeeded in particular cases or who, like the tracker Tom Horne, had special skills. There were also numerous non-Pinkerton private detectives with claims to distinction. Among these was Seymour Barmore, who in the 1860s joined the Ku Klux Klan in Tennessee with a view to exposing its terrorist activities against Black freedmen and their sympathizers. Barmore might be thought to have had morality on his side and to be a candidate for due reverence. He did proclaim himself to be "the greatest detective in the world."[10] But he was motivated by private gain, not ideals. Also, the Klan saw through Barmore from the beginning and killed him before his investigation had any effect.

Of greater merit was Grace Humiston, who operated as a private detective independently of any agency. Humiston (neé Winterton) came from a middle-class background, completed a law degree at New York University, and was called to the bar in 1903. She offered legal counsel to poor people and immigrants who could not afford it or who could not understand the language of the courts. To that end, in 1905 she established the Poor People's Law Firm. Arising from her legal vocation, she took on investigative work.

By the time Humiston took up the case of Ruth Cruger in 1917, she was 46 years old and had distinguished herself by investigating neoslavery in the turpentine industry of the American South. The New York Police Department had encouraged the press to hint that when 18-year-old Cruger went missing, she had, perhaps voluntarily, entered the "white slavery" trade, or prostitution. Humiston acted on the challenging premise that Gruger had fallen victim to an NYPD trusty, Alfredo Cocchi. She thus epitomized that popular trope, a private investigator with personal integrity who takes on the established police. She found Cruger's "ripped" body in Cocchi's cellar and accused the NYPD of a corrupt cover-up. She later joined NYPD as a special investigator and founded the Morality League of America. Humiston may not have been a household name, but in other respects she met some of the essential criteria we have set for the great detective.[11]

Prominent Black detectives are mainly notable for their absence—except in the persons of fictional characters like Walter Mosley's Easy Rawlins.[12] And characteristically absent from the public scene, especially by comparison with Kate Warne and Grace Humiston in the private sphere, are women.

Because public policing at first lagged behind private policing in America, most of our public candidates date from the 1930s onward, but there is a prominent exception. Hiram C. Whitley, US Secret Service chief from 1869 to 1875, was the son of a Glasgow-born medical doctor. In 1871 the federal government gave his Secret Service the mission of penetrating the Ku Klux Klan. Whitley worked with newly enfranchised Black citizens who supplied information about the Klan. These Black informal detectives risked their lives for a cause, not for gain—and no African American undercover operative was rewarded with the status of Secret Service special agent. Whitley did an impressive job. US marshals arrested the Klan's ringleaders and many rank and file members. Whitley was undoubtedly effective, even if he operated at a distance and not in the field like his Black detectives. The task he undertook was moral in character. If our assessment stopped there, Whitley would qualify as a great detective, even if he did not defy authority—his bosses, the Radical Reconstructionists, were at the time in charge of the nation. Yet although Whitley undertook a moral mission, he was a pragmatist and not a morally committed detective. A poacher turned gamekeeper, he had been a slave catcher before the war—and soon after his success against the Klan, Whitley was accused of using dirty tricks in one of the complex scandals that blighted the presidency of Ulysses S. Grant.[13]

Leon Turrou was an able criminal investigator for the FBI. Soon after Turrou joined what was then still called the Bureau of Investigation, a senior inspector asserted that he was "the best investigator of criminal violations in the Bureau." Six years later, by the time the BofI had become the FBI in 1935, Turrou had worked over 2,000 cases. One of them was the investigation into the kidnap and murder of Charles Lindbergh Jr. In March 1932 Bruno Richard Hauptmann climbed into the 20-months-old infant's bedroom near Hopewell in New Jersey, abducted him, and sent a ransom note to the father of the child, the world-famous aviator Charles A. Lindbergh. By the time the Bureau caught up with Hauptmann the little boy was dead. Fearing retribution, the murderer proved a hard nut to crack. Turrou sat with Hauptmann for hours. The killer knew he should not supply an example of his handwriting that could be compared with that on the ransom note. Yet Turrou persuaded him, against his better judgment, to write out passages from the *Wall Street Journal*. Hauptmann went to the electric chair. In 1935 J. Edgar Hoover's trusted confidant, Clyde Tolson, observed that Turrou had "an uncanny knack of securing information."[14]

In 1938 Turrou investigated a Nazi spy ring after a tip-off from British intelligence. He identified the members of the ring. The case was to prove controversial. Instead of hastening to make arrests—a mantra of the FBI as well as one of our chosen criteria—he let his suspects run to see where they would take his inquiry and to give him time to maximize the information at his disposal. McParland and Burns would have understood his tactic. But as a result, leading Nazi agents like Ignatz Griebl, who had been a useful informer, escaped to Germany. Only minor figures in the spy ring went on trial in the fall of 1938.[15]

Turrou later used his disclosures to launch a campaign against the Nazis that helped persuade Americans to abandon their mid-1930s neutrality. His handling of the case and avoidance of early arrests made him, in this one instance, more of a counter-spy than a detective. His articles in the *New York Post* and the Warner Brothers movie about his exploits, *Confessions of a Nazi Spy*, transformed him from Hoover's blue-eyed boy into the director's bogeyman. Turrou's spectacular falling out with Hoover placed him firmly into the anti-authoritarian mold. It remains the case that Turrou failed to maximize his arrests and was a publicity seeker who tended to exaggerate his own brilliance. In other respects, he meets our criteria for being a great detective.[16]

Further examples of public detective proficiency abound. Not every celebrated case meets our criteria. Melvyn Purvis was a contemporary of Turrou's in the Bureau of Investigation. He was the BofI's special agent in charge in mobster-ridden Chicago. On the evening of July 21, 1934, he lit a cigar outside the city's Biograph movie theater, an act that made him a household name. It was the signal to his men to open fire. The notorious bank robber John Dillinger, who had been tracked to the theater, dropped dead. The Purvis-centered publicity arising from this was too much for Hoover, who sidelined his agent just as he would Turrou. Purvis, like many an American lawman, was brave. But his cognitive skills did not compare with Turrou's. When he wanted a confession he beat his suspect to a pulp rather than putting them at ease, Turrou-style, by offering a cigarette.[17]

Policemen who took on their own hierarchies tended to win a place in American esteem. That this happened in reality, as well as in fiction, we see from an incident in January 1938. In that month, Los Angeles Police Department officers paid a lethal compliment to their colleague Harry Raymond. His investigation of police corruption had been too effective for their liking. Earl Kynette of the LAPD's Intelligence Squad was ultimately convicted in connection with the murder-by-bomb that silenced Raymond. The assassinated detective met at least some of our criteria.[18]

Years later Frank Serpico became legendary for similar rebelliousness. When he was shot in the face during a drug raid in Brooklyn, New York, on February 3, 1971, it was widely assumed the assault was a police setup because of his whistleblowing about NYPD corruption in the 1960s and 1970s. The movie *Serpico* (1973) starred Al Pacino in the lead role and honored the courageous officer's undercover work. A major reform of the NYPD followed. The moral pursuit of justice and honesty characterized both Raymond and Serpico.

Here it should be noted that hype could affect city police forces as well as private agencies and Hoover's FBI. Dave Toschi worked at the homicide detail of the San Francisco Police Department between 1966 and 1978. His loud bow ties, tasteless suits, and vulgar hairstyles made him a darling of the media, as did his quick-draw gun-in-shoulder-holster. His work on the Zodiac killings especially boosted his profile. The Zodiac serial murderer was responsible for five confirmed deaths, and he or she claimed to have dispatched thirty-seven in aggregate. Early on, a Toschi-inspired film, *Dirty Harry*, featured Clint Eastwood. Then the 2007 movie *Zodiac* injected new life into the Toschi celebrity cult. Toschi failed the modesty test with flying colors, as he did the competence test, for the Zodiac killer was never apprehended.

In the absence of a convenient comparative guide to real-life American detectives with a claim to greatness, I asked around for suggestions. John Fox, the FBI's official historian, drew my attention to a point I had overlooked. Technology was already improving back in the days of Allan Pinkerton and William Burns. In the twentieth century, the methodology of detection grew ever more sophisticated. Many crime cases were now cracked in the modest seclusion of the laboratory. Fox drew attention to the earlier work of forensic experts like Calvin Goddard (from the 1920s, a New York City pioneer of ballistics and blood sampling), August Vollmer (a Berkeley, California, police chief who took an interest in genetic aspects of criminal personality and hired both Black and female colleagues in the years 1919 to 1925), and Frances Glessner Lee (she pioneered the miniature recreation of crime scenes and in 1931–38 helped establish the Department of Legal Medicine at Harvard University).[19]

Psychological work has also become more important over the years. John E. Douglas of the FBI's Investigative Support Unit, whose interviewing skills compared with those of Turrou, patiently listened to the cult leader and serial murderer Charles Manson, who was permanently behind bars after 1971. He looked for personality traits and behavioral patterns that would help with the identification of criminals who were still at large. An authority on criminal psychology, he helped pioneer the technique of the criminal profile, a conceptual portrait of the likely characteristics of the perpetrator of a particular crime.[20] The technique ultimately attracted criticism for its vulnerability to stereotyping and racial bias. The work of both forensic scientists and psychologists is thus unavoidably open to challenge in particular cases. However, the practitioners in these fields did contribute to the solving of criminal cases and meet some of our criteria.

The FBI's Carlos T. Fernandez demonstrated a further range of skills, skills appropriate to a new threat to America—organized international terrorism. From the late 1990s Fernandez combated Al Qaeda and similar groups. He faced organizational challenges. There was a history of bickering and misunderstanding that got in the way of information flows in a way that America could ill afford. In the face of global terrorism, there was additionally a need for international cooperation. Fernandez worked on these issues as head of the New York Joint Terrorism Task Force. He also showed an appreciation of the principle that it is not always best to arrest a suspect (for example, young militants in Afghanistan). Sometimes, it is best to follow and to listen. Like

Turrou, Fernandez can be defended against the charge that he did not arrest people quickly enough.[21]

From the foregoing examples, it can be concluded that it would be invidious to single out one candidate or even group of candidates without bending criteria in a subjective manner. Second, for all their business success and fame, Allan Pinkerton, his descendants, and their senior operatives were not outstanding detectives when considered in a comparative light. It would be tempting to go further and to say that, as they served only the interests of the rich, private detectives as a species came second best to detectives on public police forces. If the truth was inconvenient to the bottom line, private detectives were tempted to ignore it.

That would be, however, too sweeping a conclusion. William Burns, a private detective in the years of his prime, would stand comparison with most public detectives. Grace Humiston, another private detective, stands shoulder to shoulder with any of her publicly financed peers. Historically, there has been little to choose between the detection capacities of private and public detectives. The main difference was institutional: a public servant is in principle, and mostly in reality, too, committed to the public good.

Conclusion

Two propositions tie together the themes of this book. The first relates to the life of Allan Pinkerton. The famous detective is generally held to have changed his attitude to industrial relations on crossing the Atlantic, allowing him to spy on organized labor in ways that were at odds with the Chartist beliefs he expressed in Scotland. However, previous accounts have been wrong to dwell on his revolutionary commitment and participation in the Newport Rising of 1839. He simply was not there. On the contrary, it is likely that by the time of his valedictory voyage down the river Clyde, he had already absorbed the deeply ingrained Scottish preoccupation with informing. Furthermore, the evidential gap about his activities in the two years prior to his emigration in 1842 may well exist not because he was in hiding from the police, but, as his great grandson Robert A. Pinkerton II inadvertently stated, because "the Chartists were breathing down his neck."

Our first thesis, therefore, is that Allan Pinkerton remained in thrall to a darker side of his Scottish heritage and was in that sense more consistent than has hitherto been allowed. The cosmetic enhancement of his radical and abolitionist past to boost his own stature became a feature of his career once he had arrived in the United States. He projected a distorted image of his youthful radicalism, just as he later did of some of his American achievements.

The second proposition arising from this book is that Allan Pinkerton, his successors, and their detractors collectively left a series of legacies, some of which still affect America today. They range from hostility to the left and to labor unionism with an emphasis on the dangers of conspiratorial inner circles to the recent trend toward the privatization of security. The legacies and their long-lasting effects invite encapsulation in this final chapter.

Allan Pinkerton was instrumental in establishing the prominent role in American life of private detectives, one of the distinctive features of US society. His initiative was not unique—other private eyes set up in business before he did. But it was the way in which Pinkerton's detective skills combined with his commercial acumen that made "Pinkertonism" virtually synonymous with private detection in America and a profitable sector of business.

The rise of private detection did not stem solely from the efforts of one individual. Other causative factors included the western expansion of nonindigenous people in the frontier era, an expansion so rapid that the apparatus of public law enforcement could not keep up, giving private operators an opportunity. In addition, America's federal polity meant a dispersal of law enforcement provision between counties, cities, states, and the federal government, leaving gaps in provision that the Pinkertons could fill—Max Weber's thesis equating the state to the governmental monopoly of the deployment of force did not apply in post–Civil War America, in spite of the triumph in that struggle of the principle of federal union. Finally, as Pinkerton persuasively argued, corruption in public law enforcement too often made the police unreliable, creating a further opportunity for private operators. Factors such as these facilitated Allan Pinkerton's success.[1]

However, that success would not have occurred had Allan Pinkerton not been a talented individual with a particular mindset. One can acknowledge his achievements without bending a knee to the army of sycophants who have devalued his reputation by blowing too hard on the trumpet. Pinkerton's contributions as a detective and as an advocate of the art of detection included a stress on morality and avoidance of shady commissions such as divorce work. They further embraced the issuance of a code of practice with an emphasis on probity, the development of identification files capped by a Rogues' Gallery, and a convincing demonstration, in the context of the plausible Baltimore plot to kill Abraham Lincoln, of the need to protect presidents-elect and sitting presidents from assassination.

The founder of Pinkerton's National Detective Agency additionally advanced the cause of feminism. He appointed Kate Warne to be an operative in 1855. Agreeing with Warne's logic that women had special gifts in the art of detection, he then appointed further female colleagues. Warne continued to enjoy Pinkerton's confidence. She served his agency until she died of pneumonia in 1868, her remains interred in Pinkerton's special plot in the Graceland cemetery, Chicago.

It is true that there were limits to Pinkerton's feminist enlightenment. Arguably, he married Joan Carfrae when she was a very young orphan because he wanted to control her just as he would attempt to control his daughter, also called Joan. Daughter Joan was not brought up to entertain any expectation that she would help run the family business after the founder's demise—that was left to her brothers Robert and William. Allan Pinkerton did have a controlling personality regardless of gender, but that disposition was more clearly evident in his treatment of female family members. Furthermore, when Allan Pinkerton died in 1884 he failed to bequeath a legacy of female employment. When his sons took over the management of the PNDA they refrained from hiring women. Despite these various cavils, it is still undeniable that Pinkerton was years in advance of the great majority of his male peers in entrusting female colleagues with responsible tasks.

Present-day law enforcement agencies as well as espionage entities like the CIA acknowledge, if sometimes more in principle than in practice, that diversity in their work force is not only just but also a wise practical measure. It means that they can recruit from a wider reservoir of talent, deploy undercover agents who can remain undetected because they look and sound like the targets of their surveillance, and command wider public support for their endeavors. Such enlightenment was rare in the 1850s, but, in that decade, the radical minority known as the abolitionists did prepare the way for greater racial tolerance. Allan Pinkerton aligned himself with the abolitionists of Illinois. He then deployed Black spies like John Scobell and W.H. Ringgold during the Civil War. It was a pioneer effort in advance of its time. In the next half century there were few examples of Black detectives. US Secret Service chief Hiram Whitley used Black informers in fighting the 1870s Ku Klux Klan, and in 1917 Chief A. Bruce Bielaski of the Bureau of Investigation employed African American John E. Hawkins to investigate the phenomenon of Mexican immigration into the United States. These were sparse examples, and progress was slow. J. Edgar Hoover's FBI (1924–72) became and remained a byword for racially biased recruitment.[2]

Pinkerton's own racial enlightenment had its limits. He used his abolitionist background for career advantage. He blew hot and cold on the issue depending on the direction of the political wind. He employed Scobel only in a menial role, as the groom to Carrie Lawton, one of his female spies in Civil War Richmond (in his defense, though, Scobel would otherwise have stood out a mile in Virginia's racially stratified society). Like other supposedly progressive citizens, Pinkerton used racially freighted vocabulary, notably in belittling Black strikers and their families in the 1870s. To conclude: on balance, Pinkerton's stance on racial issues can still be said to have been less questionable than his stance on Chartism back in Scotland. If, as some maintain, racial control has been at the root of US public policing from its nineteenth-century origins to the present day, Allan Pinkerton's private model appears to have stood apart from, and above, the general trend. Furthermore because historians have unfailingly mentioned his abolitionism, consciousness of his stance survives to the present day and can be regarded as one of his legacies even if he did show signs of ambivalence.[3]

Turning to a tragic aspect of Pinkerton's career, he and General George McClellan concocted inflated estimates of Confederate military strength. Their estimates, an example of politicized intelligence, deceived the commander in chief, President Lincoln. They may well have deprived the Union's Army of the Potomac of an opportunity to land a decisive blow early in the 1861–65 conflict—and there can be few things worse than a long-drawn-out civil war. While Pinkerton was not the prime instigator of order-of-battle distortion, it is still relevant to ask: Was the estimative profligacy that he helped legitimize a legacy bestowed on future generations? The fixing of estimates to make them conform to presuppositions would indeed be a recurring cause of controversy in future decades. General Dwight D. Eisenhower's critics, ranging from the Soviets to the Free French leadership, accused him of being overcautious and too afraid of enemy strength to authorize the counterinvasion of Nazi-occupied Europe earlier than he did. In the case of the Vietnam War, General William Westmoreland constantly complained about not having enough men to combat enemy manpower.[4] Yet it is implausible to argue that Pinkerton established what was to be an unfortunate trend. The mere fact that a later phenomenon resembles an earlier one does not indicate causation. Rather, war of its nature generates subjective estimates. Pinkerton's predisposition to exaggerate is no more than a chapter in the story.

Threat exaggeration was nevertheless embedded in Allan Pinkerton's operational style. The bottom line of his commercial activities depended on his success on exaggerating the threat that organized labor posed for employers. Pinkerton and his colleagues would not raise a finger except for money paid by those employers willing and gullible enough to believe their tales. Their vendettas against the James brothers and Sundance were partial exceptions to this rule but did not typify the Pinkertons' work against bank robbers, work that was intrinsically a service to the rich and powerful based on the successful marketing of fear. In serving the Napoleonic ambitions of men who were already rich, the Pinkertons did not serve society and were inferior to public police forces.

Through their labor espionage, Allan Pinkerton and his colleagues contributed to the development of a surveillance society. According to one historian, until the late twentieth century Americans feared private intrusions into their privacy far more than state prying.[5] However, private detectives provided just one strand of the story. The surveillance conducted by the Pinkertons led to the pernicious practice of blacklisting but was not nearly as widespread as another private form of surveillance, the credit industry. Firms like R.G. Dun listed, and sold for a fee, the credit ratings of hundreds of thousands of businessmen (in the case of Dun, 800,000 of them by 1880).[6] Dun-like surveillance was benevolent in nature, unlikely to generate the resistance that Pinkerton spying did, and for this reason gave respectability to the mass gathering of personal information. It should further be noted that after the passage of the Anti-Pinkerton law of 1893, the Pinkertons offered their services only to private customers. The surveillance *state* was not one of Allan Pinkerton's legacies.

Pinkerton labor espionage did, however, contribute to a significant element in American paranoia. Allan Pinkerton's more alarmist views had been shaped in the crucible of Scottish class struggle. The Tory Sir Archibald Alison had spoken of a "secret committee" that ran the 1837 Glasgow spinners' strike and plotted murder. Just so, Pinkerton and his lieutenant James McParland insisted that "inner circles" ran terrorist campaigns on behalf of the Molly Maguires, the Western Federation of Miners, and, by explicit extension, the whole of the labor movement. Allan Pinkerton elaborated on such themes in his writings. It was a short step for him to warn of the threat that scheming, violent communists posed to the security of America. Legacies that flowed from that claim included conservative political rhetoric in the years to come. Reactionary populist scaremongering focusing on real or imaginary threats from targeted minorities owed some of its inebriation to Pinkerton's brew of panic for profit.

Allan Pinkerton's emphasis on labor violence and his equation of that with communism had a further consequence. To shield itself from Pinkerton-style populist opprobrium, organized labor shrank into a shell of political conservatism. This had a major consequence. In other countries, more assertive labor movements pressed with considerable success for social welfare programs like universal medical care. America had to make do with less. Arguably, Pinkerton-style labor spies also inflicted long-term damage on unionism—America has a relatively small proportion of union members.

Some of Pinkerton's legacies were indirect, even accidental. Pinkerton the anticommunist could not have foreseen that anti-Pinkertonism would take hold on the political left in a way that reinforced American democracy. An international comparison illustrates the point. The influential French socialist Georges Sorel saw espionage against domestic targets as, characteristically, an activity of the state, even in nations where parliamentary socialists influenced politics. His recipe for purification was antistatist and antidemocratic. He proposed that industry and society should be run by workers' syndicates (America's IWW had a similar outlook, though there is no evidence of French tuition).

America's Robert Hunter offered a contrasting analysis. Hunter was an Indiana carriage manufacturer who had won fame, through his 1904 book *Poverty*, by introducing the notion of a "poverty line" into US discourse. He was a supporter of the Socialist Party of America (SPA), founded on democratic principles in 1901 and destined to be the most successful socialist party in the nation's history. Hunter demonstrated in a book published in 1914 that oppressive espionage against domestic targets in the United States was the work not of state spies as postulated by Sorel but of private agencies epitomized by Pinkertons. The answer to such malpractices, in Hunter's analysis, lay not in violence or physical revolution but in democratic action. The reform of America lay in the hands of American voters. The Hunterian point of view contrasted strongly with Sorel's. His argument was distinctively American just as private detection was. It defeated challenges to the SPA and to American values from the totalitarian left.[7]

Hunter's anti-Pinkertonism was one facet of widespread opposition to Allan Pinkerton's aspirations. That opposition consolidated after his death. The Anti-Pinkerton Act of 1893, though the labor movement thought it feeble, left a decades-long legacy of opposition to the idea that public policing should be privatized. Not until the administration of George W. Bush (2001–09) did the privatization of state security achieve ascendency. That long delay stemmed in part from legal inhibitions generated by the 1893 legislation and reflected an ideological opposition to the privatization that the Pinkertons had championed in the nineteenth century.

Changing ideologies and the "culture wars" lay behind fictional and filmic depictions of the role of private detectives in the American past and behind memorialization. The first sculpture dedicated to the Haymarket martyrs was unveiled in Chicago's Forest Park in 1893. The sentiment it represented has gathered renewed force in recent decades. The Forest Park Haymarket martyrs' monument was designated a National Historic Landmark in 1997. Seven years after that, a further Haymarket Memorial was dedicated. This was at the site of the speakers' wagon on the day of the fateful bomb attack in 1886 that led to allegedly false Pinkerton testimony against Chicago's anarchists. In the more recent past, Mahoney City, Pennsylvania, dedicated a Molly Maguire Park complete with a statue of an unjustly convicted miner. The hood worn by the miner inadvertently lent substance to Allan Pinkerton's rhetoric, as it referenced secrecy.

The memorialization events just mentioned could be described, at least approximately, as gestures by the American left against conservativism, with Allan Pinkerton and his heirs cast as members of the conservative camp. However, the statuary message is more complex than that. In our current century, monuments to Confederate heroes and slave owners have been brought tumbling down in large numbers. Such actions might be seen as the left demonstrating against the right, with Pinkerton this time on the left of the spectrum. For the topplings revived the spirit of the abolitionists—of whom Allan Pinkerton was one. Pinkerton and the causes he espoused are remembered in complex ways.

One accidental legacy of Pinkerton history was a contribution to the whistleblowing tradition. Today we tend to associate the word "whistleblowing" with leakers of secret data about actual or alleged government malpractices. However, the term first gained currency at a time of revelations about private malpractices. Ralph Nader utilized industry whistleblowers' information when he exposed the shortcomings of automobile manufacturing. His book *Unsafe at Any Speed* (1965) was in the tradition of "muckraker" journalists who had attacked the policies of the great "trusts" that dominated the US economy by the early years of the twentieth century—Ida M. Tarbell's exposé of John D. Rockefeller's Standard Oil Company is an example.[8] Morris Friedman's *The Pinkerton Labor Spy* (1907) occupied a place within the genre, written as it was by an insider with firsthand experience of the behavior he wished to expose. Charles Siringo's *Two Evil Isms: Pinkertonism and Anarchism* (1915) fell into the same category, as did Dashiell Hammett's *Red Harvest* (1929) and the testimony of disillusioned Pinkertons operatives during the La Follette inquiry. Unintentionally, through the reactions they provoked, the Pinkertons contributed to the often healthy, if sometimes problematic, American tradition of whistleblowing.

Though a private agency, the PNDA had an institutional impact on city and government policing. As we saw in Chapter 21, several characteristics of the BofI and FBI echoed, and to a degree must have sprung from, Pinkerton traits. J. Edgar Hoover's self-publicizing obsession could have been modeled on Allan Pinkerton's example. The same could be said of Hoover's puritanism—though not his intolerance of women and Black people. The PNDA operated on an interstate scale, which would be one of the FBI's advantages, too. The FBI's "Ten Most Wanted" approach to publicizing top criminals continued the tradition of Pinkerton's Rogues' Gallery. The roots of American anticommunism are many, but there is still a meaningful resemblance between Allan Pinkerton's rhetoric and that of J. Edgar Hoover.

Modern police excesses cannot be definitively traced to the Pinkertons' influence. Such excesses have stemmed from domestic issues such as racism and from the importation of counterinsurgency tactics used overseas.[9] However, the Pinkertons did leave their imprint. Their infiltration of labor and radical organizations is a precedent to FBI practices that culminated in its notorious COINTELPRO penetration of Black Power, antiwar, and other radical groups in the 1950s and 1960s. The similarity between the Pinkerton and FBI policies arose partly because they reacted to similar causative stimuli. However historically ingrained habits also performed a continuing role.[10]

The Pinkerton experience foreshadowed aspects of the history of the CIA. Whistleblowing, for example, regularly embarrassed the CIA from the 1960s on. The suppression of unwelcome opinion was another point in common. In 1947 CIA officers sought to buy up the supply of printing ink in France, releasing the ink they had accumulated only to friendly scribes—who were trying to overcome the communists' efforts to buy up all the printing presses.[11] The effort is reminiscent of the way in which the PNDA bought up the entire print run of Siringo's *Two Evil Isms* to protect its reputation.

That illustration shows not that CIA officers were students of Pinkerton history, but that some of the CIA's actions were less unusual or un-American than they might have seemed. Extraordinary rendition is another case in point. This was the CIA's implementation of a policy, in the administrations of George W. Bush and Barack Obama (2001–17), of capturing suspected terrorists in foreign countries and "rendering" (transporting) them to locations where they could be interrogated. The policy skirted the laws of the foreign countries concerned and of the United States. The warrantless apprehension of Moyer, Haywood, and Pettibone and their secret "rendition" from Colorado to Idaho to be questioned and put on trial was a Pinkerton precedent for the policy, even if it flouted domestic state laws as opposed to federal or foreign statutes.

There is another more directly relevant—and legally binding—example of Pinkerton precedent. This is Pinkerton operative Henry Julian's pursuit of Frederick Ker, who in January 1883 stole $55,000 from a Chicago bank. Julian tracked his man to Lima in Peru. The South American nation had an extradition treaty with the United States. However, Chile had invaded Peru and occupied Lima, making it impossible to extradite. Undeterred, Julian had Ker uplifted, kept on a US naval ship without access to legal advice, then removed to the United States. There, Ker was convicted and received a ten-year prison sentence. In December 1886, in the appealed *Ker v. Illinois* case, the US Supreme

Court upheld the principle of *male captus, bene detentus* (wrongly captured, properly detained), meaning that a fugitive from US justice captured abroad could not appeal against a domestic conviction on the ground of violations of the US Constitution or American laws and treaty obligations in the course of his original capture.

According to historian Katherine Unterman, the FBI "utilized the same sort of legal rationales as the Pinkertons, particularly its reliance on the *Ker v. Illinois* precedent to justify international abductions and other forms of irregular rendition."[12] The legal ground was thus prepared when the CIA launched its controversial rendition program. The Pinkertons had helped to establish the principle that America, though famed for its "litigious" mentality ever since the days of Crèvecoeur, was ready to disrespect its own legal principles in some cases.[13] Unterman observed that the Pinkertons did so to favor the rich. The FBI and CIA differed in that they acted in the name of the US public interest.[14] The Pinkerton precedent nevertheless prepared the way for federal agencies with their wider agenda.

Thomas Carlyle (1795–1881), Allan Pinkerton's approximate contemporary, was a native of Ecclefechan, a village seventy-five miles south of the Gorbals. He was a historian who wrote on the principle that great men make history.[15] Since Carlyle's day there have been many different schools of history. Carlyle's approach has been both admired and criticized. Historiography has moved on since Carlyle, yet biography retains its practitioners, not to mention readers. Decades ago, spies were arguably an exception to the biographic legacy. One US historian, Richard Rowan, remarked in 1938 how biographers had refrained from studying spies. They were repelled by "the character of spies, the nature of their work, and the often unsavory motives of those who have been the chief beneficiaries of espionage and the intrigues of political secret agents. Spies, in short, are a veritable insecticide upon the Great-Man treatment of history."[16]

By the time of his remark, Rowan had taken steps to remedy the situation. He had already written a history of the Pinkerton dynasty that incorporated a biography of Allan Pinkerton. Almost a century after the appearance of Rowan's *Pinkertons*, espionage is a popular subject and spy biographies (of women as well as men) proliferate. Biographies of famous detectives are beginning to appear.

A purely biographical approach would not tell the whole story of the Pinkertonian legacy. But it is still pertinent to ask the biographical question, what made an influential man like Allan Pinkerton tick? In answer, not just the Gorbals and not just Chartism, but also some less salubrious aspects of Scottish radical history shaped the young emigrant who headed for the New World in 1842. So did the frontier experience once he got there, and his encounter with antislavery personalities, including Abraham Lincoln. And what were the essential consequences of Pinkerton—the man, his philosophy, and his agency? They may be summed up as a liberal approach to social issues such as slavery, feminism, and carceral reform. The consequences also included political distortion, labor spying, and the American reaction against that dirty practice. A final consequence was the large-scale privatization of national security—interrupted, however, by the Pinkerton Pause that ran from the Anti-Pinkerton Act of 1893 to the loosening of restrictions following the *Equifax* case of 1977.

Primary Source Archives and Abbreviations Used in the Notes

ABIR	American Bureau of Industrial Research, Manuscript Collections on the Early American Labor Movement, 1862–1908, WL
APII	Allan Pinkerton II
ARPS	Albert R. Parsons Scrapbook, ABIR
BC	Bridgemen's Union Correspondence (Walter Drew notes on), UM
CHS	Chicago Historical Society
CIR	U.S. Commission on Industrial Relations materials, NA and WL
CM	Charles McCarthy Papers, WL
FBIT	FBI file on Leon Turrou, obtained via FOIA, Request No. 1366027–000.
GRDJ	General Records of the Department of Justice, RG60, NA2.
HADC	Haymarket Affair Digital Collection, CHS
HL	Houghton Library, Harvard University, Cambridge, Massachusetts
JAM	Materials made available to the author by Jane Adler, Pinkerton's National Detective Agency archivist
JI	Joseph Ishill Papers, HL.
JL	Joseph A. Labadie Collection, SCRC
JVF	James V. Forrestal Papers, SGM
LD	Legislative Division, NA
MADH	Manuscripts and Archives Division, Hagley Museum, Delaware
NA	National Archives, Washington, D.C.
NA2	National Archives, College Park, Maryland

OR	United States War Department, *The War of the Rebellion: A Compilation of the Official Records of the Union and Confederate Armies*
PNDA	Pinkerton's National Detective Agency Records, Manuscript Division, Library of Congress, Washington, D.C.
PQ	Accessed via ProQuest
PR	Philadelphia and Reading Railroad Collection, MDH
RAP	Robert A. Pinkerton
RAPII	Robert A. Pinkerton II
SCRC	Special Collections Research Center, University of Michigan, Ann Arbor
SFDJ	The Strike Files of the U.S. Department of Justice, Part 1, 1894–1920, PQ
SGM	Seeley G. Mudd Manuscript Library, Princeton University, New Jersey
TAL	The Anarchist Library online
UM	Bentley Historical Library, University of Michigan, Ann Arbor
WAP	William A. Pinkerton
WD	Walter Drew Papers, Bentley Historical Library, UM
WL	State Historical Society Library, Madison, Wisconsin

Notes

Acknowledgments

1. The 130-year span referred to ran from Chicago's Great Fire of 1871 to 2000, the year when the Library of Congress accepted the surviving Pinkerton papers. Pinkerton still exists as an entity within the Securitas umbrella. An inquiry about twenty-first-century Securitas/Pinkerton records prompted the reply, "Unfortunately, we do not have any historians or archivists to answer questions": Aimee Monk, global manager director, marketing and communications, Pinkerton, email to author, July 12, 2023.

2. Mrs. Adler said that the Pinkerton agency had weeded the files but had been "surprisingly liberal" and there were still "plenty of clues": Adler, telephone interview with the author, September 14, 1998.

Introduction

1. Lavine, *Pinkerton*, 10; Rowan, *Pinkertons*, 15; Horan, *Pinkertons*, 10–11; Morn, *Eye*, 19. For more questioning views, see Mackay, *Pinkerton*, 49, and O'Hara, *Inventing*, 7, 15.

2. In her book on the history of UK female detectives, Caitlin Davies gives isolated examples of women performing private detection roles in Victorian England. In an echo of Allan Pinkerton's skepticism about public police, she mentions *Punch*'s 1840s reference to the Metropolitan Police (established in 1829) as a "Defective Force." But her female sleuths' work related mainly to matrimonial cases, and Davies concedes that the UK had no woman detective to match the Pinkerton star Kate Warne: Davies, *Private Inquiries*, 24, 26, 31, 37, 61ff.

3. The claims are in Pinkerton, *Spy of the Rebellion*, 292. The historian Edwin C. Fishel shows how Pinkerton's claims inspired widespread disbelief up through the 1980s. He argues that while Pinkerton got his sums wrong, his influence may not have been decisive, and Fishel indicates that historical opinion on the subject of Pinkerton's estimates was beginning to change by the 1990s: Fishel, "Pinkerton and McClellan," 115, and Fishel, *Secret War*, 615–6n1.

4. If, as the sociologist Max Weber and others have argued, the monopolization of force is a defining characteristic of the state, do we conclude that America for many decades was a weak state—or, conversely, that Weber's definition does not apply to America? See Weber, *Rationalism*, 136.

5. See David, *Haymarket Affair*, and Wolff, *Lockout* [Homestead] for accounts that are sympathetic to the radicals and workers involved. There has been a reaction against the assumption that workers in violent disputes were innocent and without agency, a reaction that is reminiscent of Welsh historians' repudiation of David Williams's portrayal of Chartist innocence in *Frost*—for example Jones, *Last Rising*. The historiography of the Mollies has veered violently between Pinkerton hagiography and improbable exculpations of the coal patch terrorists. For a balanced appreciation of the historiography on this subject, see Kenny, *Molly Maguires*, 3–6. Allan Pinkerton and his successors made a sales point of their assertion that, unlike their competitors, they rendered to their clients' daily accounts of their financial outgoings. The detective firm manifested a contrasting coyness when it came to publicizing aggregated incomes streams. An exception to this coyness is the circa 1950 public statement by Pinkerton general manager Asher Rossiter revealing that labor work made up one-third of the Pinkerton income prior to its abandonment in the later 1930s: Rossiter undated statement celebrating the centenary of the Pinkerton agency's founding in 1850: Box 25, PNDA.

1. The Gorbals Man

1. Pinkerton, letter to [borderline illegible but seems to be David Gallagher] of Gordon Street, Glasgow, 12 September 1872, Letterbooks, Box 8, PNDA.

2. Smith, *Gorbals*, I, 29.

3. Buchan, *Huntingtower*, 204.

4. The figure is for the 1850s: Devine, *Scottish Nation*, 340.

5. A genealogical account of the Pinkerton family cites a claim by Allan Pinkerton's son, William A. Pinkerton, that his mother Joan Carfrae Pinkerton gave birth to nine children (others estimated eight or ten), with the comment that official records reveal only six names, the inference being that three died before, during, or shortly after being born: "The Pinkerton Genealogy" (undated but containing data up to 1940), Box 6, PNDA. Only three survived to adulthood.

6. Dallas L. Jones in his doctoral study of Scottish emigrants' letters home from America in the years 1815–1861 noted their "predominantly optimistic" tone: Jones, "Background and Motives," 134. In her study published two years later than the certification of Jones's thesis, Charlotte Erickson detected a more discouraged trend in private letters penned by English and Scottish emigrants to America, but her Scottish sample is much smaller than that of Jones: Erickson, *Invisible Immigrants*, 5.

7. "Allan Pinkerton: Great Detective Was Once a Poor Cooper," *Boston Daily Globe*, March 31, 1895.

8. Wakeman, "Allan Pinkerton: Reminiscences of the Early Life of a Great Detective," *Philadelphia Evening Star*, September 21, 1889. Wakeman, a respected US journalist, posted this account from Glasgow, where he was doing further research into Alan Pinkerton's Gorbals days.

9. Lavine, *Pinkerton*, 10.

10. Chance, "Pinkerton," 126.

2. The Revolutionary

1. Wakeman, "Allan Pinkerton Reminiscences," Philadelphia *Evening Star*, September 21, 1889. Wakeman mistakenly gave the year of the Newport Rising as 1838.

2. Horan, *Pinkertons*, 8.

3. See Rowan, *Pinkertons* (1931); Lavine, *Pinkerton* (1963); Horan, *Pinkertons* (1967 rework of a 1951 publication), 5–8; and Mackay, *Pinkerton* (1996), 37–43. Frank Morn chose to ignore the legend: Morn, *Eye* (1982). Another scholar, Paul O'Hara, made no mention of Newport and stated that the extent of Pinkerton's "radical activities" in Scotland was uncertain: O'Hara, *Inventing* (2016), 15.

4. Johnston, *History of the Parliamentary Franchise*, 1.

5. O'Neill, *Woman Movement*, 18.

6. At the trial of John Frost, the leader of the Newport Rising, the defense pointed out that there was no direct mail service between the Welsh town and Birmingham: Cole, *History of the British Working Class*, 105.

7. Frost quoted in Williams, *Frost*, 128.

8. Michie, *Alison*, 65.

9. Frost quoted in "Great Radical Demonstration at Glasgow," *The Chartist*, June 16, 1839. On the significance of Frost's hostage threat, see Williams, *Frost*, 168.

10. Chase, "Allan Pinkerton," 132; O'Hara, *Inventing*, 15.

11. Pinkerton to Alex M'Donald, January 27, 1869, published in the *Glasgow Sentinel*, March 6, 1869, and reproduced in Gutman, "Five Letters," 389–91.

12. Pinkerton to Mrs. Alex Campbell, September 7, 1873, in Letterbooks, Box 8, 414, PNDA.

13. Fraser, *Taylor*, 55, 59.

14. Wilson, *Chartist Movement in Scotland*, 105–7.

15. Fraser, *Chartism in Scotland*, 72; W. Hamish Fraser, email to the author, September 6, 2021; Cole, *History of the British Working Class*, 98; Horan, *Pinkertons*, 8. The Londoner Harney was a gifted orator. He spoke several times in Glasgow and was briefly married to an Ayrshire woman.

16. Horan, *Pinkertons*, 8, 517n1, 518n3. Horan specifies letters to Robert dated May 22, 1879, and April 28, 1883, in note 1 without being specific about the source of the quotation in note 3, which should have documented the remark.

17. Mackay, *Pinkerton*, 43, 241n7. Mackay apparently collapsed Horan's endnotes, above, to create his own reference.

18. Alan Pinkerton to Robert Pinkerton, May 22, 1879, in Letterbooks, Box 48, 222–26, PNDA; Alan Pinkerton to Robert Pinkerton, April 28, 1883, in Letterbooks, Box 48, 309–16, PNDA.

19. Two searches of the Letterbooks did not find a letter containing the passage quoted. The first of these searches was by the author. The second was kindly undertaken by Dr. Michelle A. Krowl, Civil War and Reconstruction specialist, Manuscript Division, Library of Congress: Krowl email to author, April 3, 2022.

20. The Newport Rising was the sole focus of John Frost's obituary in the *Boston Daily Advertiser*, August 14, 1877. However, Frost's death was not widely reported in America.

21. See Wilks, *South Wales and the Rising of 1839*. Wilks as well as Jones, *The Last Rising*, challenges the view promoted in earlier work by David Williams (notably, in *Frost*) that the Newport Rising leaders were innocent martyrs.

22. Neither Angela John nor Les James mentions Pinkerton in relation to the Newport Rising. John and James have come across no references to him in the course of their research: Angela John, email to the author, September 8, 2021; Les James, email to the author, September 15, 2021. I am grateful to Dr. Elin Jones, author of a history of Wales (*Hanes yn y Tir* [Llanrwst: Gwasg Carreg Gwalch, 2021]) for putting me in touch with these scholars. On John and her work on Chartism, see www.angelavjohn.com. James, an adviser on the Monmouthshire Hall Chartist Project and the Chartist exhibition at Newport Museum and Art Gallery, is the author of *Render the Chartists Defenceless: John Frost's Voyage with Dr McKechnie to Van Dieman's Land in 1840* (Newport: Three Impostors, ca. 2015).

23. See, for example, the observation by one of Andrew Carnegie's biographers: "Pinkerton, whose very name was to become the symbol of labor oppression in the late nineteenth century, had, curiously enough, a Radical background": Wall, *Carnegie*, 547. Pinkerton's fellow Chartist immigrant, Matthew Mark Trumbull, served as a Union general in the Civil War and later campaigned for a pardon for the anarchists convicted for the Chicago bomb tragedy of 1886, comparing the episode to the Newport Rising. He condemned his former comrade as a mercenary oppressor of American labor who was a disgrace to the Chartist movement: Trumbull, *Was It a Fair Trial*, 2; Trumbull, "Current Topics," *Open Court*, 6 (1892), 3316, cited in Boston, "Trumbull," 172–73.

3. Escape to America

1. "Obituary, Mrs. Joan Pinkerton," *Chicago Inter Ocean*, 22 January 1887.

2. National Records of Scotland, 'What Was and Is the Minimum Age for Marriage in Scotland?' (website accessed on May 3, 2022). According to Mackay, *Pinkerton*, 50, Joan Carfrae was "under age" at the time of her marriage, when she "claimed to be eighteen."

3. Allan Pinkerton letter to his wife, Chicago, March 28, 1878, in Letterbooks, Box 7, 141, PNDA.

4. Horan, *Pinkertons*, 11.

5. The source of this particular myth appears to have been the Pinkertons' daughter Joan Pinkerton Chalmers: Mackay, *Pinkerton*, 54.

6. Typewritten letter, Pinkerton to R. W. Dewe, Post Office Inspector, Toronto, Ontario, n.d. but probably in 1862/3, dispatched from Washington, DC, in Box 4, folder 1, PNDA. Spelling is as in the original—including the correct spelling, in this instance, of "Birmingham."

7. See the poet Charles Fitzgeffrey's lines in praise of Sir Francis Drake in 1596:

> And bold and hard adventures t'undertake,
> Leaving his country for his country's sake.

Oxford Dictionary of Quotations, 8th ed. (2014), online.

Cf. the verse (from the same source) penned by Henry Carter for the mainly convict transportee actors at the opening of the Sydney Playhouse, New South Wales, 16 January 1796:

> True patriots we; for be it understood,
> We left our country for our country's good . . .
> And none will doubt that our emigration
> Has proved most useful to the British nation.

8. Wakeman, "Allan Pinkerton Reminiscences," Philadelphia *Evening Star*, September 21, 1889.

9. "Pinkerton, Allan," in *National Cyclopedia of American Biography*, III.

10. Hamish Fraser, email to the author, May 25, 2019.

11. William A. Pinkerton, letter to Mrs. Carrie Pinkerton McEwen of Tulsa, OK, dated Chicago, June 10, 1908, in Box 6, folder 3, PNDA.

12. Adler, letter to the author on Pinkerton Archives stationary, dated September 16, 1998. The author is grateful to Mrs. Adler for bringing the Pinkerton–McEwen letter to his attention.

13. Rice, *Scots Abolitionists*, 111. See also Murray, *Advocates of Freedom*, and Roper, *Narrative*.

14. Pinkerton, *General Principles* (1873), 7.

15. Robert A. Pinkerton, "A Detective on Ex-Convicts," Chicago *Daily Inter Ocean*, September 18,1887. The term "stool pigeon" referring to police informers who received special protection from prosecution predated the industrial strife of later years and had been in use in America since at least the 1840s. See, for example, "Stool Pigeons," an article about police corruption in New York City, in *Saturday Evening Post*, June 20, 1840.

16. Porter, *Plots and Paranoia*, 50.

17. Ellis, *Scottish Insurrection of 1820*, 22, 35.

18. Court of Special Commission, Scotland, indictment against Wilson reproduced in Mackenzie, Peter, *Trial of James Wilson*, 4. Writing about English working-class history, E.P. Thompson challenged the "Whig" view that there was no serious revolutionary intent in 1817 and that agents provocateurs made it all up: Thomson, *Making of the English Working Class*, 713.

19. Johnston, *History Working Classes in Scotland*, 238.

20. Mackenzie, *Trial of James Wilson*, *Exposure of the Spy System*, and *Reply to Kirkman Finlay*. See also Ellis, *Scottish Insurrection of 1820*, 286–88.

21. Thomis, *Threats of Revolution in Britain*, 67–70; Wilson, *Chartist Movement in Scotland*, 105.

22. Archibald, *Some Account of My Life*, 378.

23. *Scots Times*, January 13, 1838, quoted in Michie, *Enlightenment Tory*, 71.

24. Charles F. Bourke, "Story of the Pinkertons," *Leslie's Monthly Magazine*, LIX (April 1905), 6.

25. Jones, *Last Rising* (citing editorials in the *Northern Star*), 183

26. Robert A. Pinkerton to Peter Whitman of Johnson & Higgins, Wall Street, New York, NY, 4 May 1962, Box 6, PNDA.

4. Pinkerton & Co.

1. The historian Ray Boston found that of the 76 immigrant Chartists for whom there is reliable information, just 17 traveled west of the Appalachians: Boston, *British Chartist in America*, Appendix A. The historian Irma Dupré offered no supporting figures when she observed that the Pinkertons "had avoided the city of New York [which was] the most important of the New World cities because of its superior advantages as a seaport": Dupré, "The Canny Cooper" (page 48), an unpublished biography of Allan Pinkerton sent to his grandson under cover of a letter, Irma Dupré to Robert A. Pinkerton, June 14, 1937, Box 2, PNDA.

2. Extract from *Past and Present of Kane County, Illinois* (Chicago: William le Baron, Jr, and Co, 1878) in Box 3, PNDA; Dupré quotations from pages 52 and 85, Dupré, "The Canny Cooper." Irma Dupré was the author of a book later revised and published as *Romance of Dundee Township* (1985).

3. Pinkerton, *Professional Thieves*, 19

4. Pinkerton, *Criminal Reminiscences*, 12.

5. Morn, *Eye*, 21–22.

6. Pinkerton, *Professional Thieves*, 36.

7. "Allan Pinkerton: Great Detective Was Once a Poor Cooper," *Boston Daily Globe*, March 31, 1895.

8. It is unclear what Pinkerton called his agency in 1850, but a subsequent letter of his headed "North-Western Police Agency" carried also, as a reminder, the older title "Pinkerton & Co." (the "Co." referred to a co-founder, the lawyer Edward A. Rucker, who appears to have been a sleeping partner): Pinkerton to Harry E. Hunt, October 2, 1856, Box 4, folder 1, PNDA. The Chicago city directory for 1855–1856 listed "Pinkerton and Company, Detective Police Agency." It was said to be the first directory to list the Pinkerton detective agency: summary of research carried out by K.W. Wadsworth for the PNDA, January 25, 1949, in Box 13, folder 7, PNDA.

9. Miller, *History of Private Policing*, 86.

10. *Chicago Tribune*, February 3, 1854.

11. I am grateful to the PNDA archivist, the late Jane Adler, for drawing to my attention the widespread use of the human eye symbol by Pinkerton's early rivals: author's interview with Jane Adler, September 14, 1998.

12. Weiss, "Private Detective Agencies," 89; Morn, *Eye*, 17–18.

13. Davis Cummings, a burglar with five known aliases, was No. 1589 in the NYPD's Rogues Gallery: *New York World*, January 29, 1891.

14. Lavine, *Pinkerton*, 22; Bedore, *Dime Novels*, 186n3.

15. Pinkerton, *Spy of the Rebellion*, 84.

16. Pinkerton, *Expressman*, 95. See also Pinkerton, *Somnambulist*, 144–45.

17. Pinkerton related in his *Expressman and the Detective* how one of his female staff ran an effective sting operation leading to the arrest of a white-collar criminal. For further examples, see Bedore, *Dime Novels*, 92.

18. The suspicions of Allan Pinkerton's son, Robert, are recorded in Morne, *Eye*, 54–55, 216n3. PNDA archivist Jane Adler was adamant that Kate Warne became Allan Pinkerton's mistress: author's interview with Jane Adler, September 14, 1998.

19. "Obituary, Mrs. Joan Pinkerton," *Chicago Inter Ocean*, January 22, 1887. According to another newspaper, Joan gave birth to eight children: *New York Herald*, July 2, 1884.

20. Monkonnen, *Police*, 45; Morne, *Eye*, 27–29; *Chicago Tribune*, June 26, 1857.

21. Quoted in Rowan, *The Pinkertons*, 41.

22. Wagoner, "About a Grand Old Man: A Denver Man's Recollections of John Brown," *Denver Times*, August 3, 1889.

23. Lavine, *Pinkerton*, 38; Rowan, *Pinkertons*, 29, 73; Horan, *Pinkertons*, 37–42; Mackay, *Pinkerton*, 9–10, 63, 81–82.

24. Lewis, "Lincoln and Pinkerton," 376.

25. Pinkerton to Harry E. Hunt, October 2, 1856, Box 4, folder 1, PNDA.

26. Pinkerton, *Strikers, Communists*, 379–80. "Aunt" Dinah was a cook in Harriet Beecher Stowe's *Uncle Tom's Cabin* (1852).

5. The Baltimore Plot to Assassinate Lincoln

1. Pinkerton to Lincoln's former law partner William H. Herndon, Aug. 23, 1866, in Cuthbert, ed., *Baltimore Plot*, 11; notes taken by Herndon on an "interview with Norman B. Judd," n.d. (circa 1866), Box 23, PNDA.

2. Extracts from letters written in December 1860 and originally published in the *Cincinnati Commercial*, together with a quoted passage from the *New York Sun*, in "The Plot to Assassinate Mr. Lincoln—Production of 'the Documents'," *Baltimore Sun*, March 1, 1861.

3. Pinkerton, *Spy of the Rebellion*, 60.

4. Pinkerton, *Spy of the Rebellion*, 89.

5. Pinkerton to Herndon, Aug. 23, 1866, in Cuthbert, ed., *Baltimore Plot*, 4–10. Further details of Pinkerton's account are taken from Pinkerton, "History and Evidence," 299 and Pinkerton, *Spy of the Rebellion*, 81–113. See also "Man Who Saved Lincoln's Life," *Boston Globe*, February 12, 1933.

6. *Chicago Democrat*, March 5, 1861, quoted in Morn, *Eye*, 41; *New York Times*, n.d., quoted in Mackay, *Pinkerton*, 243n10; Greenhow, *My Imprisonment*, 12; *Vanity Fair*, March 9, 1861.

7. Pinkerton to Herndon, August 5, 1866, in Cuthbert, ed., *Baltimore Plot*, 2.

8. Lincoln's letter reproduced in Cuthbert, ed., *Baltimore Plot*, xv–xvi.

9. Cuthbert, ed., *Baltimore Plot*, xvii, 114–15; Pinkerton, *Spy of the Rebellion*, 61.

10. Morn, *Eye*, 47–49, citing Lossing, *Pictorial History of the Civil War*.

11. Extracts from Lamon, *Life of Lincoln*, 512–13.

12. Notes and excerpts from Moffett article in *McClure's*, November 1894, and Herndon, *Abraham Lincoln*, II, 201–2 in Box 23, PNDA. Popular author Cleveland Moffett, a Yale alumnus, wrote extensively about the achievements of Allan Pinkerton and the PNDA. A collection of his robbery tales appeared in Moffett, *True Detective Stories: From the Archives of the Pinkertons* (New York: G.W. Dillingham, 1897).

13. Robert A. Pinkerton to Howard Swiggett, August 12, 1950, Box 63, PNDA.

14. See, for example, Wise, *Detective Pinkerton and Mr. Lincoln*, and Larry Newman, "A Century Later, the True Story of the First Attempt to Kill Lincoln," *Boston Globe*, February 7, 1965.

15. Sears, ed., *Civil War Papers*, 617.

16. Decipher of telegram, Pinkerton to Stanton, April 19, 1865, in Folder 1, Box 4, PNDA.

17. Lincoln's statement to Benson J. Lossing on the Baltimore plot, 1864, in Box 1, PNDA.

6. A Secret Service

1. Pinkerton to Lincoln, n.d. (circa April 13, 1861), copy in Box 25, PNDA.

2. Morn, *Eye*, 42–3; O'Hara, *Inventing*, 13; Horan, *Pinkertons*, 31, 36.

3. Pinkerton, *Spy of the Rebellion*, 292.

4. "Extract, embracing the 'First Period,' from Maj. Gen. George B. McLellan's report of the operations of the Army of the Potomac from July 27, 1861, to November 9, 1862" (August 4, 1863), in Series 1, Vol. V, *OR*, 51–52.

5. Morn, *Eye*, 39.

6. Greenhow gave an account of her successes in her memoir *My Imprisonment*, but the timeliness and accuracy of some of the information that she sent to the South has been disputed. Her messages to Beauregard's adjutant have never been located. For this and the Pinkerton quotation, see Fishel, *Secret War*, 59.

7. Greenhow, *My Imprisonment*, 11, 54.

8. Quotation from Markle, *Spies of the Civil War*, 162.

9. Greenhow quoted in "The War Day by Day: Fifty Year Ago," *Boston Globe*, August 23, 1911.

10. Markle, *Spies of the Civil War*, 162. According to another account, woollen balls were delivered to Greenhow, who then knitted them into message containers: Horan, *Pinkertons*, 95.

11. Markle, *Spies of the Civil War*, 163.

12. Greenhow, *My Imprisonment*, 204.

13. "War Secret Service; Daring Deeds Performed by Operatives," an article originally commissioned by the *Chicago Evening Post* and consisting almost entirely of William Pinkerton's narrative, in the *Boston Globe*, July 9, 1898.

14. Pinkerton, *Spy of the Rebellion*, 590–93.

15. Horan, *Pinkertons*, 327.

16. Bridgeman obituary with comments by William A. Pinkerton in the *Chicago Times*, December 20, 1894.

17. Fishel, *Secret War*, 117–18.

18. Grant, *War for a Nation*, 95.

19. "The War Day by Day: Fifty Year Ago," *Boston Globe*, June 20, 1912.

20. For a list of historians making this judgement prior to 1988, see Fishel, "Pinkerton and McClellan," 115. For a further list together with indications of how historical opinion was beginning to change by the 1990s, see Fishel, *Secret War*, 615–6n1.

21. Fishel, *Secret War*, 102–3. Fishel in another publication advanced a similar argument with different statistics: Fishel, "Pinkerton and McClellan," 116.

22. Fishel, *Secret War*, 102.

23. Pinkerton quoted in Fishel, *Secret War*, 105. Italics added.

24. "The War Day by Day: Fifty Year Ago," *Boston Globe*, June 20, 1912.

25. Fishel, *Secret War*, 585.

26. McClellan quoted in Grant, *War for a Nation*, 122.

27. Figures from online source, National Park Service, Antietam National Battlefield Maryland, "Antietam Casualties by Type." McClellan acknowledged that "Allen" was with him "up to the time I was relieved of my command." However, Pinkerton's stock was declining along with that of his commander with the result that the detective had to operate with diminished resources. Fishel noted that Pinkerton had seven operatives in the service of McClellan at the time of Antietam, half the number present during the earlier Peninsula campaign. See "Extract," 52, and Fishel, *Secret War*, 215.

7. *The* Secret Service

1. For an assessment of the Proclamation's impact on morale, see Grant, *War for a Nation*, 127–28.

2. Pinkerton to McClellan, August 23, 1862, in Box 4, folder 1, PNDA.

3. Pinkerton to McClellan, September 22, 1862, in Box 4, folder 1, PNDA.

4. Pinkerton to McClellan, October 7, 1862, in Box 4, folder 1, PNDA.

5. Allan Pinkerton to Robert Pinkerton, April 28, 1883, in Letterbooks, 309–16, Box 48, PNDA.

6. Morn, *Eye*, 45.

7. Pinkerton to Andrews, April 12, 17, and May 24, 1865, Box 4, PNDA.

8. E.J. Allen to Stanton, April 19, 1865, Box 4, PNDA.

9. Stanton to E.J. Allen, April 24, 1865, Box 25, PNDA.

10. Fishel, *Secret War*, 24–28; O'Toole, *Honorable Treachery*, 128.

11. Fishel, *Secret War*, 2.

12. Leonnig, *Zero Fail*, 12.

13. Whitley's instruction paraphrased in his report, January 1872, 100, Letters Received, Source Chronological Files, 1871–1884, Treasury, GRDJ.

14. Jeffreys-Jones, *FBI*, 26, 30.

15. Monkonnen, *Police in Urban America*, 49–64 and *Murder in New York City*, 159–60; Jeffreys-Jones, *FBI*, 17–38, 61, 79–80.

8. Labor Violence a New Source of Income

1. On the *Sentinel* (until 1857 called the *Glasgow Sentinel*), see Fraser, *Alexander Campbell*, 141–42, 153. The second working-class newcomer in the House of Commons in 1874 was another miners' leader, Thomas Burt from Northumberland.

2. Allan Pinkerton, National Police Agency, 92 and 94 Washington Street, Chicago, January 27, 1869, to Alex. M'Donald, Esq., Holytown, Scotland, originally in

Glasgow *Sentinel*, March 6, 1869, and reproduced in Gutman, "Five Letters," 389, 390, 391. In a covering letter to the *Sentinel*, Macdonald observed that, while Pinkerton had "all the feelings of a son of toil yet," he was ignorant of the fact that the home country had changed since the future detective's departure; "the principle of arbitration is taking deep root in our minds": Gutman, "Five Letters," 388n8.

3. This is the theme of Jeffreys-Jones, *Violence and Reform in American History*.

4. Joint statement of Robert and William Pinkerton, December 3, 1892, in "Investigation in Relation to the Employment," *Senate Report*, 242.

5. "Riots of June 3, 1875: Shenandoah, Hazelton, Mahoney City," anonymous, undated report written from the perspective of the PNDA, in Box 140, PNDA.

6. Kenny, *Making Sense*, 192; McParlan [*sic*] and Kerrigan, *Among the Assassins*, 4; summary of Gomer case and testimony of James McParland at the trial of Thomas Hurley, Pottsville, PA, August 17, 1876, in Box 140, PNDA.

7. Table 1 in Kenny, *Making Sense*, 8.

8. Pinkerton, *General Principles*, 7, and see Chapter 3.

9. Exhibit A, statement, acknowledged to be genuine by Allan Pinkerton's sons Robert and William, on the advantages of the "Pinkerton Preventive Patrol," being the undated text of a circular that was also printed as an advertisement in newspapers, reproduced in "Investigation in Relation to the Employment for Private Purposes of Armed Bodies of Men," 60. The circular was submitted in the course of a Senate investigation into the Homestead disturbance of 1892 and it is unclear when the PNDA originally adopted the text.

10. Gowen quoted in *The Nation*, May 25, 1871, 352; Pinkerton quoted in Broehl, *Molly Maguires*, 144. See also Aurand, *Molly Maguires and United Mine Workers*, 99.

11. Franklin quoted in Kenny, *Making Sense*, 154.

12. Pinkerton, *Molly Maguires*, 13–14.

13. Pinkerton, *Molly Maguires*, 16.

14. Horn, *Invisible Empire*, 108; "The Kuklux: Discovery of the Remains of Detective Barmore," *New York Times*, February 27, 1869. The historian David Silkenat drew my attention to the Barmore case. He argues in a forthcoming book that opposition to the Klan was widespread in the South.

15. Bulik, *Sons of Molly Maguire*, 268.

16. Pinkerton, *Molly Maguires*, 17.

17. Thomas Hanley quoted in Bulik, *Sons of Molly Maguire*, 269

18. Pinkerton, *Molly Maguires*, 24; Anon., "Brief History of James McParland, Famous Detective," n.d., Box 30, folder 1, PNDA; Riffenburgh, *Pinkerton's Great Detective*, 46; Grant, *Spies*, 96.

19. The Orange Order was so named because its members upheld the right to rule of the successors to adherents of the Netherlands's House of Orange, the Protestant

dynasty imposed on Ireland (as on England, Scotland, and Wales) following the deposition of the Catholic King James II in the "Glorious Revolution" of 1688.

20. McParland quoted in Riffenburgh, *Pinkerton's Great Detective*, 48.

21. McParland to George D. Bangs, Jr., February 10, 1914, Box 172, PNDA.

22. Since McParland's report, debate has raged over the true nature of the Mollies. Among the many publications portraying the Mollies as pure evil were McParlan [*sic*] and Kerrigan, *Among the Assassins* (1876), Dewees, *Molly Maguires* (1877), and famously Conan Doyle, *Valley of Fear* (1915). Ethnic explanations fell short because other Irish immigrants, such as the more skilled miners from southeast Ireland, engaged in fewer clashes. The fragmentation and internecine conduct of the anthracite miners undermines the class conflict explanation, even if Gowen and his ilk could be regarded as upper-class conscious. The "frontier" explanation—that society in Schuylkill County was as undeveloped and anarchic as points much further West—may have some merit. More accurately one could point to the fact that the mining "patches" of communities were isolated monocultures with no mediating middle classes, as the latter were to be found in Pottsville, away from the smoke and grime of the coal workings. Other explanations focus on the Mollies as adherents to preindustrial values or archaic Irish cultures that had powerful consequences but little bearing on the new, American environment. For an analysis of the Irish origins of the Molly Maguires and of the historiography of that subject, see Kenny, *Making Sense*, 18–44.

9. McParland Tilts at the Molly Maguires

1. On McParland's life-story inventions, see Riffenburgh, *Pinkerton's Great Detective*, 46–58.

2. Riffenburgh, *Pinkerton's Great Detective*, 51.

3. McParlan [*sic*] and Kerrigan, *Among the Assassins*, 3. The journalist H. B. Hanmore, in Gowen's pay for information he supplied about the miners, similarly thought that workers who set fire to the shaft at the East Norwegian mines did so to "'get square' with the Company on general principles," even if they were drunk at the time: Hanmore to Gowen, April 4, 1875, Box 979, Folder 3, PR.

4. The title of the ballad is as sung by the Dubliners and other groups in recent years and may have changed over time.

5. Quotation from Riffenburgh, *Pinkerton's Great Detective*, 54.

6. Quoted in McParlan [*sic*] and Kerrigan, *Among the Assassins*, 9. William Ewart Gladstone was UK prime minister, 1868–1874. He supported Home Rule and bowed to Irish Catholic opinion by disestablishing the Protestant Church of Ireland, but his government also implemented repressive measures.

7. Monkonnen, *America Becomes Urban*, 105–7.

8. McParlan, *Among the Assassins*, 5.

9. Gowen quoted in Riffenburgh, *Pinkerton's Great Detective*, 143.

10. Trial quotation in Criminal Case File, Box 140, PNDA.

11. Trial quotation in Criminal Case File, Box 140, PNDA.

12. Quotation from prosecution materials, Criminal Case File, Box 140, PNDA.

13. Bedore, *Dime Novels*, 96; Kenny, *Making Sense*, 232.

14. Quotations from Gowen's address to the court and jury at the trial of Thomas Munley, June 28 to July 1, 1876, Criminal Case File, Box 140, PNDA.

15. Plaque inscription quoted in O'Hara, *Inventing*, 168.

16. O'Hara, *Inventing*, 4.

17. William A. Pinkerton to C.V. Hatter, 19 May 1919, folder 1, Box 30, PNDA. For further information on the Pinkerton–Conan Doyle spat, see Owen Dudley Edwards, "Introduction," in Conan Doyle, *Valley of Fear*, xxxiii–xxxiv.

10. Inventing Anticommunism

1. Historians who portray the Bolshevik revolution of 1917 as the starting point of US anticommunism and for this reason make little reference to Allan Pinkerton, as he died in 1884, include Richard G. Powers, in his book *Not Without Honor* and Klehr et al., *Secret World*. Michael J. Heale in his study of American anticommunism adopts a broader definition of the phenomenon and takes the story back to 1830. He also notes the Pinkertons' role in nineteenth-century social history, though without giving special attention to Allan Pinkerton's propaganda: Heale, *American Anticommunism*, 30, 32, 34, 38. A forthcoming book by Dolores E. Janiewski, provisionally titled "Inventing UnAmericans: Media, Surveillance Capitalism and Reactionary Americanism, 1871–1957," affords Allan Pinkerton a greater role.

2. JAM and author's interview with Jane Adler, September 14, 1998.

3. Pinkerton, *Strikers, Communists*, 66.

4. On American reactions to the Paris Commune, see Heale, *American Anticommunism*, 23–29.

5. The historian Richard White depicts the expansion of America's railroads as hasty and predatory: White, *Railroaded*.

6. Stowell, "Railroad Strikes," 1172–74. On the upheavals of 1877, see Bruce, *1877* and Foner, *Great Labor Uprising*.

7. Marx, "A Contribution to the Critique of Hegel's Philosophy of Right: Introduction" (1844), in Marx, *Early Political Writings*, 57. A qualification here is that Marx's comment on religion became well-known only in the 1930s. However, communism's link with atheism had long before become a staple of anticommunist rhetoric.

8. Pinkerton, *Strikers, Communists*, 79.

9. Pinkerton, *Strikers, Communists*, 93.

10. Godkin, "Sex in Politics," *Nation*, 20 (April 1871), cited in Janiewski, "Inventing UnAmericans," supplied by kind permission of the author.

11. See O'Neill, *Woman Movement*, 28–29.

11. Inventing Private Detection

1. Quotations from Morn, *Eye*, 70–71.

2. Printed letter heading, facsimile of letter by Allan Pinkerton to the president of Western Union warning of the dangers of wiretapping, December 3, 1867, reproduced from Chicago Historical Society collections in Horan, *Pinkertons*, 152.

3. Pinkerton, *General Principles*, 5. Pinkerton's argument about the virtue of regular pay for his operatives appeared in the 1867 edition of *General Principles*: O'Hara. *Inventing*, 28

4. McWatters, *Knots Untied*, 643.

5. Pinkerton, *General Principles*, 6, 9–12.

6. Pinkerton, *General Principles*, 12.

7. Pinkerton, *General Principles*, 5.

8. Morn, *Eye*, 76–7.

9. *Manhattan Yellow Pages* (1979), 987–90.

10. Chandler, *Lady in the Lake*, 10.

11. Pinkerton, *Somnambulist*, 145–46; review, *Boston Daily Globe*, November 6, 1875.

12. Morn, *Eye*, 54–55 and 216n3. Pinkerton archivist Jane Adler declared herself "maddened" by Morn's unspecific citation methods (Adler letter to author, October 22, 1998). But she herself saw Allan Pinkerton as having been in the grip of nineteenth-century "masculine" opinions, as someone who failed to protect his wife from multiple pregnancies, and (like Morn) as a person who used his power to take advantage of several concubines: author's interview with Adler, September 14, 1998. Adler sent the author facsimiles of several items from the archives but no evidence in support of her contention about Pinkerton's infidelity.

13. Bangs obituary, *New York Times*, September 15, 1883.

14. Allan Pinkerton report, September 2, 1872, Box 7, PNDA.

15. Jane Adler told the author (without pointing to documentation) that Allan Pinkerton drank heavily throughout his life and that she found his condemnation of George Bangs's drinking to be "hilarious": author's interview with Adler, September 14, 1998.

16. "Allan Pinkerton Dead: The Great Detective Breaths His Last at Chicago," New York *World*, July 2, 1884.

17. General R.B. Marcy, "Detective Pinkerton," *Harper's New Monthly Magazine*, no. 281 (October 1873), 720–27; Wakeman, "Detective Allan Pinkerton: Story of his Early Struggles; The Tribute Paid by an Ardent Admirer," *Springfield Republican*, September 22, 1889.

18. Moffett, How Allan Pinkerton Thwarted the First Plot to Assassinate Lincoln," *McClure's Magazine*, 3 (November 1894); and "The Overthrow of the Molly Maguires," *McClure's Magazine*, 4 (December 1894).

19. "Pinkerton on Guard; The Man and his Winchesters," Chicago *Sunday Herald*, November 7, 1886.

20. Bourke, "Story of the Pinkertons," *Leslie's Monthly Magazine*, LIX (April 1905), 6.

21. "Pinkerton's," *London Gazette*, August 19, 1907.

22. The author is grateful to his former colleague at Edinburgh University's history department, Owen Dudley Edwards, for the ideas and data behind this line of thought: many conversations with Edwards, Edwards email to the author, October 4, 2022, Edwards, *Quest for Sherlock Holmes*, 14. See also Josephson, *Robber Barons* and (for a compilation of investigative articles published in journals), Weinberg and Weinberg, *Muckrakers*.

23. Alan Bilansky argued that the Pinkerton agency helped ensure that the "surveillance state" would be "other-then-public": Bilansky, "Pinkerton's," 81. Stephen Robertson regarded Allan Pinkerton's insistence on his labor spies' rendering of daily reports as a cornerstone of the surveillance state, though he also noted that in practice Pinkerton operatives were not so scrupulous: Robertson, "The Pinkertons and the Paperwork of Surveillance," 125.

24. Jeffreys-Jones, *We Know All About You*, 15.

25. The Library of Congress Manuscript Room archivist Michele Krowl points out, however, that agent reports were not filed with the PNDA papers, suggesting they may not have been routinely copied to headquarters: email, Michelle Krowl to author, October 24, 2022, citing also Rhodes and Streeter, *Before Copyediting*. A comparison might be made with the FBI's filing system under its Library of Congress-trained director (1924–72), J. Edgar Hoover, thanks to which special agents' reports are preserved for posterity.

12. Jesse James as Robin Hood

1. *Kansas City Times* quoted in John Herbers, "Special Introduction," Graham and Gurr, *History of Violence in America*, xiii.

2. Quotations from Stiles, *James*, 208, 215

3. Jesse James quoted from the text of his interview with Major Edwards, published in John Edwards, "A Terrible Quintette," *St. Lous Dispatch*, November 22, 1873, reproduced in Stephens, *Wildest Lives*, 216–29 at 223.

4. Davis, "Jesse James' Legend Lives On," *Boston Globe*, February 12, 1989.

5. Davis, "Legend Lives On."

6. Roosevelt, foreword dated "Cheyenne Aug 28th 1910" in Lomax, comp., *Cowboy Songs*.

7. Quotations from Anon, "Special to Elks Magazine: Butch Cassidy's Five Mistakes," n.d., and James D. Horan, "The Jungle Robin Hoods," both in Box 89, PNDA;

8. Quoted in Stephens, *Wildest Lives*, 210, Jesse James's claim "we are bold robbers [who] rob the rich and give to the poor" was in an anonymous letter attributed to him.

9. Settle, *James*, 44ff and Michael Fellman introduction to Love, *Rise*, vii.

10. Herbers, "Special introduction," above.

11. Pinkerton, *General Principles*. The prison reform views of Allan Pinkerton and his two sons are further discussed in Chapter 14, "Odyssey of the Sons."

12. Geiger, *Fraud and Guerrilla Violence*, 1–3.

13. See, for example, Stephens, *Wildest Lives*, 210, 230–35.

14. Younger quoted in Stephens, *Wildest Lives*, 256.

15. Allan Pinkerton letter to Patrick Henry Woodward, chief special agent of the Post Office secret service, January 27, 1875, Box 119, PNDA.

16. Robert A. Pinkerton to J.H. Schumacher, PNDA superintendent in Kansas City, November 11, 1898. Emphasis in the original. Initials at the top of the letter indicate that copies went to, among others, William A. Pinkerton and George D. Bangs—testifying to RAP's concern, and also to the efficient office practices being introduced the PNDA's New York office. One copy of the letter went to the *Kansas City World*, which published it on November 19, 1898, with a footnote challenging its accuracy.

17. William E. Lewis, "That Sad Old Bomb Fake," New York *Morning Telegraph*, March 2, 1915. Lewis, who claimed to have known Frank James, was writing in response to an article in the previous day's edition of the *Telegraph* in which his fellow-journalist Julian Street gave credence to the bomb story.

18. Cole Younger account of the attempted Northfield Bank robbery, Chicago *Sunday Record-Herald*, May 2, 1909.

19. Frank James quoted in the *St. Louis Republican*, October 6, 1882.

20. H.I. Cleveland, "Shall the Youngers Be Pardoned? Story of their Crime," Chicago *Sunday Record-Herald*, February 19, 1899.

21. Former Attorney General Wallace B. Douglas quoted in New York *World*, May 8, 1901.

22. Crook, *Robin Hood*, 258.

23. Hilton, "Origins of Robin Hood," 30.

24. Early contributions to the James mythology included *The Life, Ties and Treacherous Death of Jesse James, Bank and Train Robbers of the West, Frank and Jesse James; The Younger Brothers*; Joseph A. Dacus, *Life and Adventures of Frank and Jesse James*; and, by "one who dare not now disclose his identity," *Jesse James, the Life and Daring Adventures*. The literature scholar Pamela Bedore remarked that there was a "symbiotic literary partnership" between the popular fiction on Allan Pinkerton and that on Jesse James: Bedore, *Dime Novels*, 99.

25. *The Assassination of Jesse James by the Coward Robert Ford* was a Warner Brothers film starring Brad Pitt. It was based on a 1983 novel of the same title by Ron Hansen—whose research led him to concede that the James brothers never gave their

money away. On media attention devoted to the James brothers since 1908, see Geiger, *Fraud and Guerrilla Violence*, 137. See also Bedore, *Dime Novels*, 100.

13. Death of the Founder

1. Horan, *Pinkertons*, 182. James Horan based his account on Pinkerton's own narration of events in a letter to a friend dated February 3, 1872, deposited in the Chicago Historical Society, now incorporated in the Chicago History Museum.

2. According to an undated inventory of the purchase and development of The Larches, the initial cost was $91,074.62. This and other Larches information from miscellaneous items in Folder 11, Box 4, PNDA.

3. Allan Pinkerton to Robert Pinkerton, May 22, 1879, Letterbooks 222–26, Box 48, PNDA. This letter is also on Reel 3 of the microfilmed correspondence but is largely illegible there. The author is grateful to Dr. Michelle Krowl of the Library of Congress's Manuscript Division for sending him a readable facsimile of the original.

4. Inis Weed, "Summary of Report in Violence," n.d., 20 in CIR; Jeffreys-Jones, "Problem", 261–62.

5. Pinkerton quoted in Horan, *Pinkertons*, 322–23.

6. Allan Pinkerton to Robert Pinkerton, April 28, 1883, Letterbooks 309–316, Box 48, PNDA.

7. "Obituary: Mrs. Joan Pinkerton," *Chicago Inter Ocean*, January 2, 1887.

8. "Allan Pinkerton," *Chicago Tribune*, July 4, 1884.

9. "Allan Pinkerton's Death," *New York Times*, July 2, 1884; "Allan Pinkerton Dead," *New York Herald*, July 2, 1884.

10. "Obituary: Mrs. Joan Pinkerton," *Chicago Inter Ocean*, January 2, 1887; Mark Twain, *The Gilded Age: A Tale of Today* (1873).

11. "Death of Robert Pinkerton, Country's Greatest Detective," York, Pennsylvania, *Gazette*, August 19, 1907.

12. Although American obituaries referred to Pinkerton's world fame, his death was little heeded in the United Kingdom. Even in his native Scotland, the *Aberdeen Journal*'s death notice was an exception to the general rule: "Death of a Famous Detective," *Aberdeen Journal*, July 5, 1884.

13. "Allan Pinkerton Dead," New York *Sun*, July 2, 1884.

14. Odyssey of the Sons

1. "Pinkerton's Death Mourned by Ex-Crooks He Befriended," *Buffalo Evening News*, December 12, 1923; "A Kind Hearted Foe to Crooks Who Won Fame and Millions," *Kansas City Times*, December 13, 1923.

2. 1874 correspondence quoted in Morn, *Eye*, 60.

3. *South Wales Daily News*, August 19, 1907; quotations from headlines in Lincoln, Nebraska *Evening News*, August 19, 1907.

4. "Pinkerton, Robert A.," biographical note, folder 1, Box 9, PNDA.

5. *Chicago Examiner*, August 18, 1907.

6. Musser, *Before the Nickelodeon*, 286.

7. *Chicago Examiner*, August 18, 1907.

8. "Pinkerton's Great Detective Career," *New Haven Register*, August 19, 1907.

9. Miller, *History of Private Policing*, 95.

10. Robertson, "Pinkertons and Paperwork," 125.

11. "Memorandum dictated by Mr. Bangs and given to Dr. Farrar Sept, 3rd, 1907," folder 1, Box 9, PNDA.

12. W.A. Pinkerton to Messrs Durham Bros, Onarga, Illinois, February 6, 1906, and R.A. Pinkerton to W.A. Pinkerton, June 7, 1906, both in folder 1, Box 12, PNDA.

13. Headline, *New York Mail*, August 19, 1907. See also Morn, *Eye*, 112.

14. The quotation is from the *Kansas City Times*, December 13, 1923.

15. Robert to Allan Pinkerton, March 11, 1905, folder 2, Box 16, PNDA

16. W.A. Pinkerton to H.D. Bailey, April 12, 1908, folder 6, Box 16, PNDA.

17. Pinkerton, *General Principles*, 8, 12–13.

18. Robert A. Pinkerton, "A Proposal for the Formation of a National Prison Reform Society," *Chicago Daily Inter Ocean*, September 18, 1887, and "Do Professional Criminals Reform?" *New York Post*, February 13, 1898. See also Robert Pinkerton, "Ex-Convicts and Reform," *Chicago Sunday Herald*, April 3, 1887, and letter dated April 30, 1887, *The Journal of Prison Discipline and Philanthropy* (January 1987): 186–94.

19. Frank Stockbridge, "Is There is Criminal Class? William Allan Pinkerton Says No," *Hampton Magazine*, May 1, 1912.

20. See, for example, Monkonnen, *Police*, and Gurr, *Rogues*, neither of which mentions the Pinkertons. Lawrence Friedman, a law professor at Stanford University, did make fleeting mention of Allan Pinkerton in a seminal work but did not credit the three Pinkertons discussed in the present chapter with being reformers: Friedman, *Crime and Punishment*, 207–8.

21. *Denver News*, August 17, 1907; *Kansas City Post*, December 12, 1923; *New York Tribune*, December 12, 1923, *New York Times*, December 12, 1923.

22. *New York Telegraph*, September 6, 1907.

15. Pinkertons in the Haymarket Trial

1. Ginger, *Altgeld's America*, 47–48.

2. "Chicago Jurist Dead; Judge Julius S. Grinnell, a Noted Lawyer, Suddenly Expires," *New York Times*, June 9, 1898.

3. Grinnell quoted in David, *Haymarket Affair*, 253.

4. Carpenters quoted in Avrich, *Haymarket Tragedy*, 159.

5. Messer-Kruse, *Trial*, 6.

6. Avrich, *Haymarket Tragedy*, 368; Howells quoted in Green, "Haymarket Affair," 580. Howells wrote a novel based on the Haymarket episode, *A Hazard of New Fortunes* (1889).

7. Foner, *Autobiographies*, 61, 97, 160.

8. Tucker (from Boston) to Labadie (in Detroit), June 5, 1886, Joseph Ishill additional papers, MS Am 1614.1, (293), Box 5, JI. *Labor Leaf* was a workers' periodical that insisted on the innocence of all the accused: David, *Haymarket Affair*, 215. Emphasis in the original.

9. *Arbeiter Zeitung* editorial of December 28, 1885, cited in O'Hara, *Inventing*, 70.

10. 'We believe firmly that the bomb was thrown by a Pinkerton,' *Workingmen's Advocate*, May 14, 1887, quoted in Avrich, *Haymarket Tragedy*, 437.

11. *Chicago Tribune*, July 25, 1886.

12. Cohen, *Conspiracy*, 43.

13. O'Hara, *Inventing*, 75.

14. *A.R. Parsons' Appeal to the People of America*, from prison cell number 29 (Chicago, IL, September 21, 1887), in ARPS.

15. *Parsons' Appeal.*

16. *Chicago Tribune*, July 25, 1886.

17. Thomas Nast, "What's in a Name?" *Harper's Weekly*, April 24, 1886.

18. *Illinois v. August Spies et al.* trial transcript, vol. K, HADC, 12–13.

19. For examples in the context of a chapter on "Workers and Violence, 1886–1912," see Jeffreys-Jones, *Violence and Reform*, 47–48.

20. John P. Altgeld, "Reasons for Pardoning Fielden, Neebe & Schwab, The Haymarket Anarchists," June 26, 1893, TAL.

21. E.V. Debs, "The Martyred Apostles of Labor," *New Time* (February 1899), 38. Cather's character is Rodney Blake in her novel *The Professor's House* (1925), excerpted in Cather, *Five Stories*, 22. The Dreyfus Affair affected French politics, 1894–1906. Because of antisemitic prejudice, Captain Alfred Dreyfus was wrongly convicted of spying for Germany. After a long, divisive campaign, he was cleared of the alleged crime and vindicated.

22. In 2011 the historian Timothy Messer-Kruse reviewed the literature. He challenged the orthodox view, arguing that the Chicago anarchists had a fair trial "by the standards of the day." See Chicago Public Art Program's online "The Haymarket Memorial" and Messer-Kruse, *Trial*, 4–5, 8.

23. Gould quoted in O'Hara, *Inventing*, 11.

24. Section 2, Article 1 of the Pennsylvania constitution of 1874 quoted in *Journal of United Labor* (published by the Knights of Labor), March 7, 1889; *Journal of*

the Knights of Labor (formerly *Journal of United Labor*), August 21, 1890; Powderly, "Strikers, Stand Ready! Powderly's Proclamation to the People," *Journal of the Knights of Labor*, August 28, 1890; "Powderly on Pinkerton" and "New York Central Strike . . . Memorials to Congress Demanding the Suppression of Pinkerton's Assassins," both in *Journal of the Knights of Labor*, September 4, 1890; "Push Labor Legislation" in *Journal of the Knights of Labor*, October 30, 1890.

16. Homestead Lockout and the End of Legitimacy

1. Montgomery, *Fall of the House of Labor*, 41.

2. H.C. Frick testimony, in "Investigation of Employment of Pinkerton Detectives," 3.

3. Carnegie, *Gospel of Wealth*, 98. The essay in which the passage originally appeared was Carnegie, "An Employer's View of the Labor Question."

4. Montgomery, *Fall of the House of Labor*, 35; Powderly's reply to a question by Congressman Charles J. Boatner (D, Louisiana), in "Investigation of Employment of Pinkertons," 231.

5. Cf the interpretation in Josephson, *Politicos*, 508–9.

6. Montgomery, *Fall of the House of Labor*, 37.

7. Principles of August 1876 quoted in Wright, "Amalgamated," 418.

8. Case, "Homestead," 612.

9. Table supplied by H.C. Frick in "Employment of Pinkerton Detectives," xxxi.

10. All quotations from Frick to Pinkerton, Exhibit C, "Investigation in Relation to the Employment," 161.

11. Frick letter quoted in Warren, *Frick*, 84.

12. Carnegie had used Pinkertons in 1887 at Pittsburgh's Edgar Thomson Steel Works to enforce wage cuts in the teeth of opposition from the Amalgamated and the Knights of Labor: Case, "Homestead," 612. In 1884 Frick hired Pinkertons to facilitate the strikebreaking activities of Hungarians and Slavs who displaced workers of northern European heritage; when the Hungarians and Slavs rebelled, he deployed Italian Americans to similar ends: Weiss, "Private Detective Agencies," 92. On the Homestead workers' postulated failure to anticipate the arrival of Pinkertons in 1892: Pinkertons' joint statement, above, 240; Burgoyne, *Homestead*, 57.

13. Oates, Curtis, and Powderly, "Homestead Strike," 360. US Congressman Oates was a Confederate general who would also serve in the War of 1898. He led a committee of inquiry into events at Homestead. The accuracy of his estimate of numbers of mortalities is borne out from multiple sources in "List of 76 Strikes Giving Rise to Mortalities, 1890–1909," in Jeffreys-Jones, "Problem of Industrial Violence," 317–19.

14. Marchand, "Homestead Strike," document #38.

15. Correspondence from the Frick papers in Pittsburgh, July 11–14, 1892, cited in Warren, *Frick*, 86

16. Marchand, "Homestead Strike," document #39.

17. Kahan, *Homestead Strike*, 90; Montgomery, *Fall of the House of Labor*, 38

18. Louis M. Lyons, "America's Great Steelmakers Set for Showdown with Labor," *Boston Globe*, July 12, 1936.

19. Carnegie quoted in Montgomery, *Fall of the House of Labor*, 40.

20. See Wall, *Carnegie*, 571.

21. Carnegie, *Autobiography*, 232.

17. Anti-Pinkerton Legislation

1. *Boston Globe*, May 4, 1888; *Louisville Courier-Journal*, January 31, 1889. On railroad corporations' deputization of private detectives, see White, *Railroaded*, 339.

2. These were Massachusetts (1879), Maine and Nebraska (1885), and Colorado and Pennsylvania (1887): Morn, *Eye*, 237n97.

3. "A Man Shot in Albany," *Philadelphian Inquirer*, August 17, 1890. The railway unions accused the New York Central of employing "Pinkerton thieves, thugs, and murderers, vile wretches from the slums and brothels of New York and other cities, to kill workingmen because they dared to . . . strike for their rights": Eugene V. Debs, "The Strike on the New York Central," *Locomotive Firemen's Magazine*, 14 (September 1890), 804. See also Morn, *Eye*, 107.

4. William Pinkerton's remarks on March 1, 1892, reported in *Chicago Tribune*, March 3, 1892; *New York Times*, March 3, 1891.

5. *New York Tribune*, February 9 and March 3, 12, 1891.

6. *New York Tribune*, February 5, 1892.

7. "Against Pinkerton Men," *New York Tribune*, February 17, 1892; "Passage of the Anti-Pinkerton Bill," *New York Tribune*, March 3, 1892.

8. William Pinkerton's remarks on March 1, 1892, reported in *Chicago Tribune*, March 3, 1892.

9. "An Anti-Pinkerton Memorial in the Senate," *Los Angeles Times*, August 30, 1890; petition, April 12, 1892, LD.

10. Watson quoted in Woodward, *Watson*, 205.

11. *Congressional Record—House*, May 12, 1892, 4222–25; "The Pinkerton Agency, An Investigation Ordered by the House of Representatives," *Detroit Free Press*, May 13, 1892.

12. Knoles, "Populism," 296.

13. People's Party National Platform (July 4, 1892), in Tindall, *Populist Reader*, 90–96.

14. Watson was the vice-presidential candidate of the People's Party in 1896, a year when the Populists joined the Democrats in endorsing William Jennings Bryan's unsuccessful run at the White House (the Democrats ran their own vice-presidential candidate). The combined Democrat–Populist vote reached five and a

half million, 40 percent of the ballots cast. Watson received only a quarter of the vote of the Democratic vice-presidential candidate—still a significant number (217,000) but fewer than Weaver's total in 1892, when the Homestead issue burned hot.

15. Josephson, *Politicos*, 512, Wolff, *Lockout*, 221, Moore and Hale, *Harrison*, 143. The historian Robert W. Cherny takes the view (email comment on author's draft, April 22, 2022) that "Homestead was one of many factors that defeated Harrison. Before Homestead, in the 1890 off-year elections, the Dems had done very well by campaigning mostly against the McKinley Tariff." See also Cherny, *American Politics in the Gilded Age*, 105, 106, 108. Cherny's view compares with that of Homer E. Socolofsky: *Presidency of Benjamin Harrison*, 198. Post-Homestead, the steel employers were able to impose their own unchallenged system of governance on the industry until the advent of government regulation in World War I, for example by accelerating the introduction of mechanization, meaning that skilled workers were no longer so irreplaceable: See Brody, *Steelworkers in America*, 58.

16. Watson remarks in Congress, July 1892, quoted in Woodward, *Watson*, 206–7.

17. *Congressional Record—House*, July 7, 1892, 5865–67.

18. "Investigation of the Employment of Pinkerton Detectives," 33, 238.

19. *Congressional Record—House*, August 5, 1892, 7119–22, and Appendix, 468.

20. *Congressional Record—Senate*, July 7, 1892, 5823, 5827.

21. *Congressional Record—Senate*, July 26, 1892, 6782, August 2, 1892, 7005–6.

22. *Congressional Record—House*, August 5, 1892, 7120.

23. "Employment of Pinkerton Detectives," 8, 14, 15.

24. "Investigation in Relation to the Employment for Private Purposes of Armed Bodies of Men," 2, 4, 13, 15.

25. 27 Stat. 368 amended to ch. 208, 27 Stat. 591, now found at 5 USC ch 31 3108: *Principles of Federal Appropriations Law* ["Red Book"] (US Government Accountability Office, January 1, 2004).

26. Morn, *Eye*, 107; Kahan, *Homestead Strike*, 104–5.

27. R. Dudley, letter to Robert A. Pinkerton II (the son of Allan Pinkerton II, who died in 1930), by this time principal of the PNDA, February 19, 1937, folder 7, Box 13, PNDA.

18. Sundance and the Setting of the Western Sun

1. Poster, n.d., Box 88, PNDA. The main source for the opening narrative in this chapter is the Philadelphia *Public Ledger*, June 21, 1903. The PNDA poster's account of the Montana robbery differs slightly from the *Ledger*'s account, stating that two bandits boarded the train in Malta and that a further two waited under a bridge for the arrival of the highjacked train. Other contemporary newspaper reports also

varied in matters of detail: Salt Lake *Herald*, July 7, 1901; Los Angeles *Herald*, July 7, 1901; *New York Times*, July 5, 6, 1901.

2. "Harry Longbaugh, Train & Bank Robber," report giving Sundance's age as thirty-five, and remarks in the hand of Pinkerton detective Francis Dimaio extracted from his notebook dated "1900" (in error, as Dimaio was active on the Sundance case only from 1903), both in Box 92, PNDA.

3. Philadelphia *Public Ledger*, June 21, 1903.

4. See Owen Wister, *The Virginian* (1902), Zane Grey, *Riders of the Purple Sage* (1912), and Jack London, *The Call of the Wild* (1903).

5. *New York World*, March 15, 2003.

6. W.D. Haywood, *A Detective* (n.d.), JL.

7. Holbrook, *Rocky Mountain Revolution*, 147–50.

8. Whatever the mythology, Hole in the Wall personnel were unlikely class warriors. One of their number, J.B. Hubbard, shot dead a Seamen's Union picket in San Francisco in 1907, just as Farley was intervening in the streetcar strike. The scenario is discussed in the *Coast Seamen's Journal*, 20 (June 19, 1907), 6.

9. Mercer, *Banditti*, 14, 20, 26, 52.

10. William Pinkerton quoted in *Weekly Nevada State Journal*, October 10, 1891; Henry, *Horn*, 190.

11. See, for example, Box 57 on Sundance, Boxes 88 and 91 on the Hole in the Wall gang, and Box 89 on both Sundance and Butch Cassidy. Boxes 89–93 contain biographical material on various criminals listed alphabetically, but not daily reports of a type associated with the US Secret Service and, later, the FBI.

12. Siringo, *Two Evil Isms*, 2–3.

13. Siringo, *Pinkerton's Cowboy Detective* (galleys of the original unexpurgated 1910 edition labeled "disputed publication" in Box 18, PNDA), 343, 379, 499; Morn, *Eye*, 161–62; Lamar, *Siringo's West*, 201–2; O'Hara, *Inventing*, 128.

14. "Harry Longbaugh, alias Harry Alonzo, alias Frank Jones, alias Sundance Kid, alias 'Kid' Longbaugh, alias Harry E. Place, Hold Up Robber," note for circulation to all offices, July 29, 1902, Box 92, PNDA.

15. Undated PNDA poster offering a $6,500 reward in connection with the Great Northern robbery of July 3, 1901, stating "it had been determined" that the robbers were Cassidy, Curry, and Sundance, Box 89, PNDA; several copies of undated information sheet on Harry Longbaugh, with the deletion on just one of them, in Box 92, PNDA.

16. *Denver Republican*, March 25, 1904.

17. Above note for circulation to all offices, July 29, 1902, Box 92, PNDA.

18. Morn, *Eye*, 156. The full, if embroidered, New Orleans story is in a chapter called "Operative Dimaio: 'The Raven,'" in Horan, *Pinkertons*, 418–41.

19. "Appendix 'A,'" an undated PNDA account of Dimaio's activities in Argentina, Box 89, PNDA.

20. Some details in this account are from Buck and Meadows, "Neighbors on the Hot Seat," 10. On the anti-imperialist sentiments of the Welsh Argentinians and the survival of their sense of national identity, see Baur, "Welsh in Patagonia," and Williams, "Social Conflict and Change within the Welsh Colony in Patagonia."

21. The American researchers Anne Meadows and Dan Buck discovered an account of the episode in the local newspaper *El Industrial.* Following up, they found the relevant judicial report in the Chilean national archives. See Uki Goñi, "New documents detail deadly chapter in Butch and Sundance's escape to Chile," *Guardian*, December 17, 2022.

22. PNDA poster dated February 4, 1907, Box 89, PNDA.

23. The Washington, DC, lawyer turned historian Anne Meadows questioned the (otherwise standard but never proven) account of the final hours of Butch and Cassidy. On the basis of her research in Bolivia, including the exhumation of a grave purporting to contain the remains of the two outlaws, she speculated that the American pair used the famous shootout to fake their deaths: Meadows, *Digging Up Butch and Cassidy.*

24. Note in Box 69, PNDA.

25. Roosevelt, *Autobiography*, 94.

19. The Trial of the Wobblies

1. On Steunenberg's assassination, see Lukas, *Big Trouble*, 15–56 especially 50–51.

2. McParland to Bangs, March 5, 1901, Box 30, PNDA. For his part in the Union Pacific robbery Bob Lee, a member of the Wild Bunch, was arrested in Cripple Creek, Colorado, and served a long prison sentence.

3. McParland reports, January 9, 10, 1906, Box 172, PNDA.

4. McParland notes on first meeting with Orchard, January 22, 1906, in William Allan Pinkerton report to Governor Gooding in the Idaho State Archives, quoted in Riffenburgh, *McParland*, 269

5. McParland to W. Pinkerton, February 3, 1906, Box 172, PNDA. In 1907, the New York publisher McClure issued an edition of Orchard's confession under the assassin's real name, Albert E. Horsley.

6. Editorial, *New York Times*, May 20, 1899; editorial, "The Imprisoned Men at Wardner," *American Federationist*, 6 (July 1899), 105; "Labor Troubles in Idaho," 3; Root to Steunenberg, September 28, 1899, quoted in "Coeur d'Alene Mining Troubles," 17.

7. John M. O'Neill, editor of the WFM's *Miners' Magazine*, quoted in the *Idaho Daily Statesman*, June 28, 1906.

8. Jury verdict quoted in *New York Times*, June 11, 1904.

9. Horsley, *Confessions*, 128–40, 196.

10. 106 men lost their lives in coal mining disputes in the years in question, when 309 mortalities occurred altogether: "List of 76 Strikes Giving Rise to Mortalities, 1890–1909," in Jeffreys-Jones, "Problem of Industrial Violence," 317–19.

11. Benjamin McKie Rastall had been a student at Colorado College in Colorado Springs at the time of the later Cripple Creek troubles. His MA thesis perhaps showed, in its emphasis on frontier individualism in the early 1890s, the influence of Frederick Jackson Turner, the great frontier historian who was at the University of Wisconsin until he accepted a professorship at Harvard in 1910. Rastall's advisor when he moved to Wisconsin for his PhD was, however, the distinguished labor economist John R. Commons, who oversaw Rastall's work on the later period. See, respectively, Rastall, *An Enquiry*, and Rastall, *Labor History*, 61–2.

12. McParland to Bangs, March 4, 1915, Box 172, PNDA.

13. Colorado Mine Operators' Association, comp., *Criminal Record of the Western Federation of Miners*; *Reply of the Western Federation of Miners*.

14. Brace, *Dangerous Classes of New York*, 25; Bellamy, *Looking Backward*, 18.

15. Haywood, "Socialism the Hope of the Working Class," 467.

16. Roosevelt quoted in Lukas, *Big Trouble*, 394.

17. Gooding to WAP, February 10, 1906, WAP to Gooding, February 13, 1906, and Gooding to McParland, November 28, 1906, all in Box 30, PNDA.

18. WAP to Edward S. Gaylor, a Pinkerton manager in Chicago, May 22, 1907, McParland to Gaylor, May 30, 1907, and RAP to McParland, June 8 1907, all in Box 30, PNDA.

19. RAP to McParland, May 15, 2006, Box 30, PNDA.

20. Lukas, *Big Trouble*, 290, 329.

20. The Verdict

1. Lukas, *Big Trouble*, 510; Riffenburgh, *Pinkerton's Great Detective*, 3, 23.

2. Lukas, *Big Trouble*, 453

3. John W. Carberry, "Defence the Active Force," *Boston Daily Globe*, May 12, 1907.

4. Carberry, "Detective Spies in Miners' Unions," *Boston Daily Globe*, June 30, 1907.

5. Friedman, *Pinkerton*, 53.

6. Darrow quoted in Lukas, *Big Trouble*, 710.

7. Darrow quoted in O'Hara, *Inventing*, 132.

8. Lukas, *Big Trouble*, 748.

9. Gustavus J. Hasson to P.K. Ahern (general superintendent, Seattle), April 2, 1908, WAP to McParland, April 6, 1908, and McParland to George D. Bangs, April 6, 1908, all in Box 172, PNDA. Orchard died in 1954.

10. Friedman, *Pinkerton*, 7, 22, 23, 178.

11. Friedman, "Pinkertonism in the Conspiracy," *The Industrial Union Bulletin*, June 1, 1907.

12. Siringo, *Two Evil Isms*, 37, 78–9, 95–7. The copy of *Two Evil Isms* in the Pinkerton files is marked "Lawsuits: Disputed Publications": Box 61, PNDA. See also Lamar, *Siringo*, 266–71, and O'Hara, *Inventing*, 135–41.

21. The BofI: Challenge and Succession

1. Jeffreys-Jones, *FBI*, 48–9.

2. WAP quoted in *Boston Daily Globe*, September 12, 1901.

3. RAP, "Detective Surveillance of Anarchists," *The North American Review* (November 1901), 173.

4. *Congressional Record*, May 1, 1908, 5558. Slightly muddled, Congressman Fitzgerald mentioned the New York State law of 1893, which had been aimed at prohibiting the use of Pinkertons in labor disputes. He and his congressional colleagues really had in mind the federal anti-Pinkerton law of the same year, which prohibited the *federal* employment of (generic) Pinkertons.

5. *Denver Daily News*, December 24, 1908.

6. Pliley, "Mann Act," 299; "Wilkie Talks of Secret Service: Chief of Great Bureau Tells of the Kind of Men He Uses and What They Do and How," *Philadelphia Record*, January 24, 1909; "Wilkie Knows No 3d Degree; Secret Service Chief Says It Exists in the Minds of Dramatists," *New York Sun*, November 23, 1910, clippings in Box 24, PNDA.

7. *New York Times* obituary of Bangs, September 15, 1883.

8. For a number of examples, see Morn, *Eye*, 169–70.

9. APII to WAP, December 24, 1909, Box 28, PNDA.

10. WAP to Bangs, May 3, 1911, Box 28, PNDA.

11. New York *World-Telegram*, July 25, 1928. See Dougherty, *The Criminal as a Human Being* (1924).

12. On the bequeathing of fingerprints, Joseph E. Wolfe (great-nephew of George Dougherty) to FBI, April 27, 1949 Box 28, PNDA. William Pinkerton had from 1894 promoted the work of the National Bureau of Criminal Identification, contributing criminal biographies, photographs, and a separate bank of fingerprinting expertise. These, according to an in-house narrative in the Pinkerton archives, were the files handed over to the BofI in 1924: Box 2, PNDA. See also Morn, *Eye*, 126–27.

13. Hochman, *Listeners*, 64, 296n45.

14. According to one historian, Hoover explicitly admired Allan Pinkerton for the nationwide scale of his operations and his opposition to organized labor and radicalism, as well as for being "the public face of a professional detective industry, and for

promoting the Pinkertons with dime novels and innovative publicity campaigns": Cohen, *Conspiracy*, 226.

15. Hoover introduced the FBI's "Ten Most Wanted Fugitives List" on March 14, 1950, but the Bureau had been sending lists of nationally wanted criminals to local police departments since approximately 1910, calling them in the 1930s "Public Enemy Number 1," "Public Enemy Number 2," and so on. See Charles, "Most Wanted," 314–15.

22. Private Rivals

1. *Los Angeles Times*, October 1, 1910.

2. Pearson, *Reform or Repression*, 217.

3. Drew pamphlets, *Closed Shop Unionism* (New York: National Association of Manufacturers, 1910), 5; and *Labor Unions* (n.p., n.d.), 10–11. Drew was an apostle of the open shop movement both within and beyond his own industry. See Fine, *Without Blare*, 50.

4. On the parenthetical theme, see Pearson, *Reform or Repression*, 2

5. Jeffreys-Jones, *Violence and Reform*, 13, 155–97. Cf. Adams, *Age of Industrial Violence*, 27–29.

6. *Final Report*, 11, 152, 154, 355.

7. Phillips, "Treason of the Senate . . . the 'Millionaires' Club.'"

8. O'Regan finding cited in Inis Weed, "The Industrial Causes of Violence," n.d., 4 Parts, II, 1, in CIR, NA.

9. William J. Burns to Charles McCarthy, February 16, 1915, CM.

10. William Leiserson to Charles McCarthy, November 30, 1914, CM; O'Regan to Basil M. Manly, June 29, 1914, CIR, NA.

11. "Employment of Pinkerton Detectives," 193.

12. "Private Police Equals [New York police commissioner William G.] McAdoo Force in Numbers," *New York Times*, January 22, 1905.

13. Burns, *Masked War*, 11; Lincoln Steffens quoted in Hunt, *America's Sherlock Holmes*, Chapter 9, unpaginated website copy.

14. Typewritten copy of Slattery resolution, BC; front-page tribute to Slattery in *Nassau Daily Review*, October 14, 1929. The Slattery resolution was in notes kept by Drew, and unsurprisingly did not appear in the union's published proceedings: Fine, *Without Blare*, 92.

15. Cohen to Drew, October 26, 1910, WD.

16. Fine, *Without Blare*, 102.

17. Blum, *American Lightning*, 159–63; Jeffreys-Jones, *Violence and Reform*, 71.

18. Quoted in Caesar, *Incredible Detective*, 17.

19. Burns, *Masked War*, 299.

20. *New York Evening Journal*, March 14, 1917; APII to Meier Steinbrink (the state's leading attorney in a prosecution of the Burns agency later in the year), March 15, 1917, Box 63, PNDA.

21. Sworn deposition of Matthew J. Carroll, May 9, 1917, Box 63, PNDA.

22. "Order 110—Employees," quoted in "Pinkerton's National Detective Agency, Inc.," 6079.

23. Strayer advertisement reproduced in Walton, *Legendary Detective*, 50.

24. Advertisement for the A.J. Kane Detective Agency in the San Francisco City Directory for 1920, reproduced in Walton, *Legendary Detective*, 61.

25. Handwritten note on letter, Burns to Anderson Electric Corporation, June 6, 1917, confirming "we have used your secret service appliances as you know in considerable quantities," together with Anderson promotional materials, all in Box 63, PNDA.

26. Paraphrase of defense case in *Wichita Daily Eagle*, January 26, 1917. See also *New York Times*, January 23, 1917.

27. APII to Meier Steinbrink, February 26, 1917, Box 63, PNDA; Hochman, *Listeners*, 61–63; Morn, *Eye*, 177.

28. Charles, "Means," 311; "Burns' Loyalty Questioned in Hun Plot Quiz [US Senate inquiry led by Knute Nelson of Minnesota]," *Indiana Daily Times*, January 7, 1919.

29. WAP to APII, October 17, 1917, Box 63, PNDA.

30. Justice Department chronology cited in Hoyt, *Spectacular Rogue*, 106.

31. Undated letter sent by unidentified sender enclosed in APII to Steinbrink, June 11, 1920, Box 63, PNDA.

32. Burns detectives used dictaphones leading to the indictment of several Ohio politicians. Ultimately, he would fall from grace because of his own connections with the corruption of the "Ohio gang," politicians from President Harding's home state. See Perceval Segrue, "How Burns Used Dictaphones and Obtained Indictments of 11 Ohio Legislators in Graft Cases," *St. Louis Star and Times*, March 22, 1922.

33. "Detective Bringing Bank Employee Back," *Washington Evening Star*, August 13, 1923.

23. Of Harvard and Hammett

1. Foregoing quotations from the *New York Times*, March 16, 23, 1928.

2. Bangs to WAP, APII, and all offices, June 1, 1921, Box 13, PNDA.

3. Memorandum entitled "Legislation," New York, June 1, 1921, enclosed with Bangs letter, above, in Box 13, PNDA.

4. Extrapolated from indexed statistics in Bernstein, *Lean Years*, 89. Bernstein (87–9) sees the anti-union activities of employers as one of six factors accounting for the decline and docility of organized labor in the 1920s. The other factors were the

heterogeneity of the labor force, the adverse ideological climate, the migration of industry to non-union locations, the obsolescence of craft unionism in an age of mechanization, and the adverse legal system.

5. Gage, *Day Wall Street Exploded*, 1, 129.

6. Rowan, *Spy Menace*, 156.

7. Olmsted, "Anticommunism," 95–100.

8. O'Donnel to Palmer, April 15, 1920, with enclosed notes and lists, SFDJ.

9. Norwood, *Strikebreaking*, 176–81.

10. According to Bureau of the Census figures, there were 201,000 divorces in the United States in the years 1927–29, compared with 158,000 in 1921–23. The number and incidence of divorces would escalate further in future decades. See "Table 1: Number and Rate of First Marriages, Divorces, and Remarriages: United States, Three-Year Averages, 1921 to 1974," in Norton and Glick, "Marital Instability," 6.

11. "Big Bill Pinkerton," *Reynold's News*, December 16, 1923.

12. *New York Times*, December 12, 20, 1923.

13. "Allan Pinkerton Dies of War Gas," *New York Times*, October 8, 1930. See also Morn, *Eye*, 184.

14. "U.S. 'Sleuths' of All Kinds Plan to Consolidate," *Pittsburgh Daily Post*, April 1, 1921; *New York Times*, April 1, 1921; "Chief Burns on Tour," Washington, DC, *Evening Star*, March 16, 1923; "Government to Use Radio for Check on Crime; William J. Burns, Head of Federal Bureau of Investigation, Gives Plans," *Oakland Tribune* (California), January 13, 1923; "Arrested by Radio," *Johnston County Journal* (Nebraska), March 22, 1923.

15. Luff, "Spies, Labor," 1314.

16. Spielman, *Stool Pigeon*, cited by Howard, *Labor Spy*, 17.

17. "The Labor Spy" (editorial introduction), *The New Republic*, February 16, 1921, 338; summary of Sidney Howard's pamphlet in *Current Opinion*, 71 (September 1921), 378. Howard's collaborator Robert W. Dunn explained the background to their report in a book review in *Science and Society*, 2 (January 1938), 135–39.

18. Howard, *Labor Spy*, 18, 112, 178, 182.

19. Howard, *Labor Spy*, 199–200.

20. Hammett's daughter Josephine ("Jo") challenged Hellman's account, stating that he was in Butte in 1920 and not 2017. For an inconclusive review of the evidence both ways, see Crowley, "*Red Harvest* and Dashiell Hammett's Butte."

21. O'Hara, *Inventing*, 155.

22. Hammett, *Red Harvest*, 10–11.

23. As charged in Zumoff, "Politics," 84, citing Goulart, *Dime Detectives*, 36.

24. "Labor Espionage: Pinkerton's National Detective Agency, Inc.," 475–6.

25. *Harvard Nineteen Twenty-Seven Class Album*, 129; *New York Times*, March 29, 1927.

26. Class notes dating from the 1930s written by RAPII, Box 14, PNDA.

27. Quotation from *New York Times*, October 8, 1930.

28. *New York Times*, October 17 (quotation), November 4, 1930; class notes above; G.L. Packard, Pinkerton divisional manager, Chicago, to A.E. Arvedson, December 12, 1935, Box 13, PNDA.

24. The La Follette Inquiry

1. "Bargain offered in refrigerators," *Detroit Free Press*, October 6, 1935; *National Labor Relations Board v. Fruehauf Trailer Co.*, 301 U.S. 49, 57 S.Ct. 642, 81 L.Ed. 918.

2. Louis Stark, "Hired Detective in Trailer Plant," *New York Times*, November 8, 1935. Stark was the *New York Times* labor correspondent and had recently researched the effects on jobs of mechanization in the Detroit auto industry. See also "Labor Espionage and Strikebreaking: Pinkerton's National Detective Agency," 515–16.

3. Louis Stark, "Say Union Trapped Plant's Detective," *New York Times*, November 9, 1935.

4. Clarence E. McConnell, "Wagner Law Fight Opened," *Detroit Free Press*, November 7, 1935.

5. For the decision and its background see Exhibit 331, "Labor Espionage and Strikebreaking: Pinkerton's National Detective Agency," 683–90.

6. Fruehauf quoted in *Detroit Free Press*, July 1, 1936.

7. *National Labor Relations Board v. Fruehauf Trailer Co.*, 301 U.S. 49, 57 S.Ct. 642, 81 L.Ed. 918. The case took as its precedent *National Labor Relations Board v. Jones & Laughlin Steel Corporation*, 301 U.S. 16, 57 S. Ct. 615, 81 L. Ed.

8. Auerbach, "La Follette Committee," 439–41.

9. Biographical Note, "Finding Aid," Clinch Calkins Papers, Georgetown University Archival Resources, and information kindly supplied to the author by Dolores Janiewski.

10. Clarification of section 104, Revised Statutes, USC Title II, sec 194, reproduced in Box 13, PNDA

11. *Boston Globe*, September 21, 22, 1936.

12. Pinkerton quoted in Walter Carlson, "Pinkerton Force Is a Family Affair," *New York Times*, August 16, 1964; undated submission to the La Follette inquiry together with other items in Box 13, PNDA.

13. The sociologist John Walton indicated that, in 1935, 53 percent of PNDA income came from labor work, while historian Dolores Janiewski found that the Pinkertons made $6 million "by alarming corporations with warnings about communism": Walton, *Legendary Detective*, 63–4; Janiewski, "From Labor Rights," 379.

14. Norwood, *Strikebreaking and Intimidation*, 18; *Boston Globe*, February 19, 23, 1937; Louis Stark, "La Follette Committee Explores 'Little Steel,'" *New York Times*, July 31, 1938.

15. "Labor Espionage and Strikebreaking: Pinkerton's National Detective Agency," 474–75.

16. "Pinkerton's National Detective Agency, Inc.," Exhibit 2497, Memo, 1935, giving "total bills" as $205,574.59, 5929.

17. "Ace Sleuth Ends 60-Year Career," *New York Times*, 6 June 1947; "Labor Espionage and Strikebreaking: Pinkerton's National Detective Agency," 497.

18. "Labor Espionage and Strikebreaking: Pinkerton's National Detective Agency," 478, 482, 485–87, 491–92, 507.

19. Fine, *Sit-Down*, 37–9, 41.

20. Fine, *Sit-Down*, 40, 349n66.

21. "Labor Espionage: Pinkerton's National Detective Agency, Inc.," 1513.

22. "Pinkerton's National Detective Agency, Inc.," Exhibit 2632 dated 12 August 1936, 6140.

23. "Labor Espionage: Pinkerton's National Detective Agency, Inc.," 1525.

24. "Labor Espionage: General Motors Corporation," 1894, 1897.

25. "Pinkerton's National Detective Agency, Inc.," Exhibit 2797 dated 29 July 1937, 6294–95.

26. Meyer Levin's novel *Citizens* (1940) was a further work in the same category. It drew on the subsequent six volumes arising from the La Follette inquiry and focused on the later events covered therein, notably the Republic Steel strike and Chicago's notorious Memorial Day Massacre of May 30, 1937. Levin advanced the unlikely hypothesis that fascists were behind the Massacre, and his novel had little relevance to the history of the PNDA.

27. Auerbach, *Labor and Liberty*, 99n7.

28. Rossiter circular to all offices, New York, 16 June 1937, Box 13, PNDA; anonymous undated typescript, Box 25, PNDA.

29. Schickler and Caughey, "Public Opinion, Organized Labor," 163.

25. A Corporate Era

1. Horan, *Pinkertons*, 510–11.

2. "Flynn Challenges Willkie on Labor," *New York Times*, September 3, 1940; "Willkie Denies Labor Spies Story," *New York Times*, September 4, 1940.

3. See, for example, RAPII's remarks quoted in Walter Carlson, "Pinkerton Force Is Family Affair," *New York Times*, August 16, 1964.

4. Wilfrid D. Rogers, "Ex-Enemy Pinkertons Win Right to Unionize," *Boston Globe*, October 18, 1959.

5. O'Hara, *Inventing*, 162–3. The films referred to are *Days of Jesse James* (with Roy Rogers) and *Jesse James*, starring Tyrone Power as Jesse and Henry Fonda as Frank. Hynd's articles on the Pinkertons included "With the Pinkertons Through the Labyrinth of Death," *True Detective Magazine* (November 1940) and at least fifteen further contributions to the same magazine: index in Box 140, PNDA.

6. "TV Show to Look at 'Private Eyes': Pinkerton Detective Agency Will Be Subject of Series Filmed by Desilu Concern," *New York Times*, October 12, 1955; quotation from Robert Pinkerton's preface to James Horan, *Desperate Men: Revelations from the Sealed Pinkerton Files* (New York: Doubleday, 1962), quoted in O'Hara, *Inventing*, 164–65.

7. Hynd quoted in O'Hara, *Inventing*, 162. Alan Hynd's *Pinkerton Case Book* appeared in 1948. Horan's first book on the subject, *Pinkerton Story*, was published three years later.

8. Alan Belmont to D. Milton Ladd, memo, January 6, 1953, folder 143, Adlai Stevenson, Hoover Official and Confidential file, copy kindly supplied to the author by Douglas M. Charles.

9. Facsimile, Charles, *Hoover's War on Gays*, 184.

10. Benjamin, "'They Never Sleep': Pinkerton's 'Private Eyes' Have Been on Duty for More Than a Hundred Years," *New York Times* (Sunday Magazine), August 27, 1961, and, on Benjamin, *New York Times*, April 19, 1966.

11. Walter Carlson, "Pinkerton Force Is Family Affair," *New York Times*, August 16, 1964.

12. *New York Times*, February 25, 1961, March 29, 1967.

13. Pinkerton quoted in *New York Times*, August 16, 1964.

14. *New York Times*, October 12, 1967.

15. Paul Langer, "Crime Pays—Those Who Fight It," *Boston Globe*, July 29, 1973.

16. *Boston Globe*, 29 July 1973, April 28, 1974.

17. Miller, *History of Private Policing*, 123.

18. Harvard Business School, "Great American Business Leaders of the 20th Century: Edward J. Bednarz" (online).

19. Tamar Lewin, "Pinkerton's Is Being Acquired," *New York Times*, December 8, 1982.

20. Securitas, "Securitas and Pinkerton to Form World Leader in Security," press release published online, February 22, 1999; Javers, *Broker*, 59.

21. "Repealing that Portion," 4, 8.

22. *Congressional Record*, Senate, 2 October 26, 1971, 37484.

23. 557 F.2D 456 (5th Cir. 1977). On June 7, 1978, the US General Accounting Office circulated the heads of all federal departments and agencies alerting them to follow the Equifax decision in awarding all future contracts: B-139965, Jun. 7, 1978, 57 Comp. Gen. 524.

24. *Principles of Federal Appropriations Law*, 3rd ed., Vol I (Washington, DC: US Government Accountability Office, January 1, 2004), 175.

25. Miller, *History of Private Policing*, 128; Keefe, "Privatized Spying," 297.

26. Elsea et al., *Private Security Contractors*, 34.

27. *Charleston Gazette-Mail*, March 15, 2018.

28. All quotations from Sarah Jones, "The Pinkertons Still Never Sleep," *The New Republic*, March 23, 2018.

29. "Pinkerton Crime Index," online, accessed in July 2023.

26. Who Was the Greatest Detective of Them All?

1. Grella, "Literature of the Thriller," 52; Winks, *Modus Vivandi*, 98.

2. See Miller, *Private Policing*, 83. Sean McCann makes the point that Hammett, the champion of beyond-the-pale mavericks, was himself an outsider—although well-read, he never completed high school: McCann, *Gumshoe America*, 91.

3. Chandler, *Lady*, 10.

4. See the examples given in Davies, *Private Inquiries*.

5. Despentes, *Apocalypse Now*, 93.

6. Chandler was an elitist who found no room for the poor or for Blacks in his work: Winks, *Modus Vivandi*, 114.

7. Hunt, *America's Sherlock Holmes*, 172, 268.

8. *New York Times* quoted in Caesar, *Incredible Detective*, 17.

9. The story's by-line identified Dougherty not as a private detective but as a former deputy police commissioner of New York: George S. Dougherty, "My Most Thrilling True Detective Story: The Berlin Police and the Rare Medallions," *The Salt Lake Telegram*, August 6, 1922.

10. Barmore quoted in Horn, *Invisible Empire*, 108.

11. Abbot, "Mrs. Sherlock Holmes." See also Blackmon, *Slavery by Another Name*.

12. Chester Himes (1909–84), who pioneered hard-boiled Black detective fiction, was a precursor to Mosley (1952–), if less well known.

13. Lane, *Freedom's Detective*, 43, 250–56; Jeffreys-Jones, *FBI*, 17–34.

14. Quotations from D. Milton Ladd, Inspector report on Turrou, April 1, 1929, and Tolson, "L.G. Turrou . . . remarks," November 6, 1936, both in FBIT File 1, Section 2, Serial number 1.

15. See Jeffreys-Jones, *Nazi Spy Ring*.

16. Turrou was the main character in the author's book *Nazi Spy Ring*. For a biographical treatment, see Bareford, "Turrou," 463–64.

17. Powers, *Secrecy*, 193; Stockham, "Purvis," 385–86. These remarks and others below draw on Jeffreys-Jones, "Turrou."

18. Raymond's biographer also presents a darker side to his nature: Jenning, *Long Winding Road*.

19. See Lee, "Legal Medicine."

20. With the help of co-authors, Douglas wrote sixteen nonfiction works explaining his work and methods.

21. Benjamin Mueller, "FBI Official Who Investigated Major Attacks for Decades Is Stepping Down," *New York Times*, June 29, 2017. Further information on Fernandez and on other notable detectives in the public sphere kindly supplied to the author by John Fox of the Bureau's History office. The interpretation in this chapter is the author's and should not be imputed to Dr. Fox.

Conclusion

1. Miller, *History of Private Policing*, 2, 85. For a list of federal policing deficiencies, see, Friedman, *Crime and Punishment*, 262.

2. Jeffreys-Jones, *FBI*, 26–7. The information on Hawkins comes from the draft of a new book on the history of the FBI by Douglas Charles, his reference being Report, John E. Hawkins, April 16, 1917, In Re: Chicago Defender-German Neutrality, Old German File, file 5911, NA. According to Charles, William J. Burns as BofI chief, 1921–4, also hired Black Americans, but his successor J. Edgar Hoover reversed the policy: author's correspondence with Charles. Hawkins was hired as a "special employee," giving him a lower status than that of special agent. Charles estimates that, during the directorship of J. Edgar Hoover (1924–72), "white men comprised 98 percent of the FBI": Charles, "Special Agent," 430.

3. Morn, *Eye*, 44. Micol Seigel is a scholar who has examined the background to the 1960s and 1970s "disparity of police-caused Black death—a rate consistently nine times greater than for whites." He notes that private detective agencies like Pinkerton and Burns "were less displaced than absorbed into the FBI," and states that they were paid by the state indirectly via federal government grants. However, he concedes that the privatization of security is a modern phenomenon. The Anti-Pinkerton Act of 1893 delayed privatization for decades. See Seigel, *Violence Work*, 2, 74–5, 83.

4. At the same time, there arose a different type of "numbers" controversy, as, in the wake of the Viet Cong's briefly effective Tet offensive in 1968, Westmoreland appeared to have *under*estimated enemy capability. The success of the ensuing US counteroffensive failed to erase the image of a general who invented numbers out of thin air. See Adams, *War of Numbers*, and Wirtz, "Intelligence to Please."

5. Hochman, *Listeners*, 9, 296. Hochman notes that the Pinkertons claimed to eschew electronic eavesdropping in the early twentieth century but practiced it in the 1930s and by the early 1950s gave their operatives at least a pale green light in the matter.

6. Jeffreys-Jones, *We Know All About You*, 15.

7. See Georges Sorel, *Reflections on Violence* (1908), and Robert Hunter, *Violence and the Labor Movement* (1914). As the titles of these publications indicate, both

authors, like Allan Pinkerton, focused on the problem of violence in industrial and class relations. For contextual discussion, see Jeffreys-Jones, *Violence and Reform*, 36–7.

8. Tarbell, *The History of the Standard Oil Company* (1904).

9. Schrader, *Badges Without Borders*, 2, 273. On the importation of antiradical tactics honed in the US counterinsurgency campaign in the Philippines, see Olmsted, *Right Out of California*, 152–57.

10. For other reflections on the FBI's debt to the Pinkertons, see "From the Pinkertons to the FBI," which is Chapter 7 in Unterman, *Uncle Sam's Policemen*, 183ff.

11. William Donovan (CIA advocate) to James Forrestal (US Secretary of the Navy), August 14, 1947, Box 73, JVF.

12. Unterman, *Uncle Sam's Policemen*, 185.

13. Crèvecoeur, *Letters from an American Farmer* (1783), 166–68.

14. However, Unterman argues that the FBI was still disposed to protect property interests: *Uncle Sam's Policemen*, 185.

15. Carlyle, *On Heroes*, 1–2.

16. Rowan, *Story of Secret Service*, 1.

Bibliography

Abbot, Karen. "'Mrs. Sherlock Holmes' Takes on the NYPD." *Smithsonian Magazine*, August 23, 2011. Online.

Adams, Graham. *Age of Industrial Violence, 1910–1915*. New York: Columbia University Press, 1966.

Adams, Samuel A. *War of Numbers: An Intelligence Memoir*. South Royalton: Steerforth Press, 1994.

Adler, William M. *The Man Who Never Died: The Life, Times, and Legacy of Joe Hill, American Labor Icon*. New York: Bloomsbury, 2011.

Alison, Sir Archibald. *Some Account of My Life: An Autobiography*. Edited by Lady Jane R. Alison. Edinburgh: William Blackwood, 1883.

Arnesen, Eric, ed. *Encyclopedia of U.S. Labor and Working Class History*, 3 vols. New York: Routledge, 2007.

Auerbach, Jerold S. *Labor and Liberty: The LaFollette Committee and the New Deal*. New York: Bobbs-Merrill, 1966.

Auerbach, Jerold S. "The La Follette Committee and the CIO." *Wisconsin Magazine of History* 48 (Autumn 1964): 3–20.

Auerbach, Jerold S. "The La Follette Committee: Labor and Civil Liberties in the New Deal." *Journal of American History* 51 (December 1964): 435–59.

Aurand, Harold W. *From the Molly Maguires to the United Mine Workers: The Social Ecology of an Industrial Union*. Philadelphia: Temple University Press, 1971.

Avrich, Paul. *The Haymarket Tragedy*. Princeton: Princeton University Press, 1984.

Baker, La Fayette C. *History of the United States Secret Service*. Philadelphia: L.C. Baker, 1867.

Bank and Train Robbers of the West, Frank and Jesse James, The Younger Brothers. Chicago: Belford, Clarke, 1884.

Bareford, Richard C. "Turrou, Leon George (1895–1986)." In *The Federal Bureau of Investigation: History, Powers, and Controversies of the FBI*, edited by Douglas M. Charles and Aaron J. Stockham, I: 463–464. Santa Barbara: ABC-CLIO, 2022.

Baur, John E. "The Welsh in Patagonia: An Example of Nationalistic Migration." *The Hispanic American Historical Review* 34 (November 1954): 468–92.

Bedore, Pamela. *Dime Novels and the Roots of American Detective Fiction*. London: Palgrave Macmillan, 2013.

Bellamy, Edward. *Looking Backward, 2000–1887.* Boston: Ticknor & Company, 1888.

Bernstein, Irving. *The Lean Years*. Boston: Houghton Mifflin, 1960.

Berthoff, Rowland T. *British Immigrants in Industrial America, 1790–1950*. Cambridge: Harvard University Press, 1953.

Bilansky, Alan. "Pinkerton's National Detective Agency and the Information Work of the Nineteenth-Century Surveillance State." *Information and Culture* 53, no. 1 (2018): 67–84.

Bimba, Anthony. *The Molly Maguires*. New York: International Publishers, 1932.

Blackmon, Douglas A. *Slavery by Another Name: The Re-Enslavement of Black Americans from the Civil War to World War II*. New York: Anchor, 2009.

Blum, Howard. *American Lightning: Terror, Mystery, Movie-Making and the Crime of the Century*. New York: Crown, 2008.

Bonaninga, Jay. *Pinkerton's War: The Civil War's Greatest Spy and the Birth of the U.S. Secret Service*. Old Saybrook: Lyons Press, 2011.

Boston, Ray. *British Chartists in America, 1839–1900*. Manchester: Manchester University Press, 1971.

Boston, Ray. "General Matthew Mark Trumbull, Respectable Radical." *Journal of the Illinois State Historical Society* 66 (Summer 1973): 159–176.

Brace, Charles L. *Dangerous Classes of New York and Twenty Years Among Them*. New York: Wynkoop & Kallenbeck, 1872.

Brody, David. *Steelworkers in America: The Nonunion Era*. Cambridge: Harvard University Press, 1960.

Broehl, Wayne G. *The Molly Maguires*. Cambridge: Harvard University Press, 1964.

Brooks, Robert R. R. *When Labor Organizes*. New Haven: Yale University Press, 1937.

Bruce, Robert V. *1877: Year of Violence*. Chicago: Quadrangle Books, 1959.

Buchan, John. *Huntingtower*. Edinburgh: Polygon, 2012 [1922].

Buck, Daniel, and Anne Meadows. "Neighbors on the Hot Seat: Revelations from the Long-Lost Argentine Police File." *Washington Office on Latin America Journal* 5 (Spring–Summer 1996): 6–15, 59–60.

Buck, Simon. "The University of Edinburgh Dialectic Society: Debating American Slavery and Abolition, 1856–1870." Paper delivered to the University of Edinburgh American history workshop, October 5, 2023.

Buhle, Mari Jo, Paul Buhle, and Dan Georgakas, eds. *Encyclopedia of the American Left*. Urbana: University of Illinois Press, 1992.

Bulik, Mark. *The Sons of Molly Maguire: The Irish Roots of America's First Labor War.* New York: Fordham University Press, 2015.

Burgoyne, Arthur G. *Homestead: A Complete History of the Struggle of July, 1892, Between the Carnegie Steel Company, Limited, and the Amalgamated Association of Iron and Steel Workers.* Pittsburgh: Rawsthorne, 1893.

Burns, William J. *The Masked War: The Story of a Peril that Threatened the United States by the Man Who Uncovered the Dynamite Conspirators and Sent Them to Jail.* New York: George H. Doran, 1913.

Caesar, Gene. *Incredible Detective: The Biography of William J. Burns.* Englewood Cliffs: Prentice-Hall, 1968.

Calkins, Marion Clinch. *Spy Overhead: The Story of Industrial Espionage.* New York: Harcourt, Brace, 1937.

Carlyle, Thomas. *On Heroes, Hero-Worship, and the Heroic in History.* London: Chapman and Hall, 1840.

Carnegie, Andrew. *Autobiography of Andrew Carnegie.* Boston: Houghton Mifflin, 1920.

Carnegie, Andrew. *The Gospel of Wealth and Other Timely Essays.* Cambridge: Belknap/Harvard University Press, 1962 [1900].

Carnegie, Andrew. "An Employer's View of the Labor Question," *Forum,* I (April 1886): 114–25.

Case, Teresa. "Homestead Strike (1892)." In *Encyclopedia of U.S. Labor and Working-Class History,* edited by Eric Arnesen, 611–614. New York: Routledge, 2007.

Cather, Willa. *Five Stories.* New York: Vintage, 1956.

Chance, Sue. "Allan Pinkerton: A Psychobiographical Sketch." *American Imago* 42 (Summer 1985): 131–42.

Chandler, Raymond. *The Lady in the Lake.* Harmondsworth: Penguin, 1971 [1944].

Charles, Douglas M. *Hoover's War on Gays: Exposing the FBI's "Sex Deviates" Program.* Lawrence: University Press of Kansas, 2015.

Charles, Douglas M. "Means, Gaston B." In *The Federal Bureau of Investigation: History, Powers, and Controversies of the FBI,* edited by Douglas M. Charles and Aaron J. Stockham, I: 311–312. Santa Barbara: ABC-CLIO, 2022.

Charles, Douglas M. "Most Wanted Fugitives Program." In *The Federal Bureau of Investigation: History, Powers, and Controversies of the FBI,* edited by Douglas M. Charles and Aaron J. Stockham, I: 314–315. Santa Barbara: ABC-CLIO, 2022.

Charles, Douglas M. "Special Agent." In *The Federal Bureau of Investigation: History, Powers, and Controversies of the FBI,* edited by Douglas M. Charles and Aaron J. Stockham, II: 428–430. Santa Barbara: ABC-CLIO, 2022.

Charles, Douglas M., and Aaron J. Stockham, eds. *The Federal Bureau of Investigation: History, Powers, and Controversies of the FBI*, 2 Vols. Santa Barbara: ABC-CLIO, 2022.

Chase, Malcolm. *Chartism: A New History*. Manchester: Manchester University Press, 2007.

Cherny, Robert W. *American Politics in the Gilded Age*. Hoboken: Wiley-Blackwell, 1997.

Churchill, David, Dolores Janiewski, and Pieter Leloup, eds. *Private Security and the Modern State: Historical and Comparative Perspectives*. London: Routledge, 2020.

Churchill, Ward. "From Pinkertons to the PATRIOT Act: The Trajectory of Political Policing in the United States, 1870 to the Present." *CR: The New Centennial Review* 4 (Spring 2004): 1–72.

"Coeur d'Alene Labor Troubles." *House Report 1999*. 56th Cong., 1st sess., 1900.

"Coeur d'Alene Mining Troubles. Correspondence Regarding the Miners' Riots in the State of Idaho not Included in Report of Brig. Gen. H.C. Merriam." *Senate Document 142*. 56th Cong., 1st sess., 1900.

Cohen, Michael. *The Conspiracy of Capital: Law, Violence, and American Popular Radicalism in the Age of Monopoly*. Amherst: University of Massachusetts Press, 2019.

Cohen, Steven R. "Steelworkers Rethink the Homestead Strike of 1892." *Pennsylvania History* 48 (April 1981): 155–57.

Cole, George D. H. *A Short History of the British Working-Class Movement, 1789–1947*. London: George Allen & Unwin, 1948 [1925].

Colorado Mine Operators' Association, comp. *Criminal Record of the Western Federation of Miners: Coeur d'Alene to Cripple Creek, 1804–1904*. Colorado Springs: MOA, 1904.

Conan Doyle, Arthur. *The Valley of Fear*. Oxford: Oxford University Press, 1993 [1915].

Crèvecoeur, J. Hector St. John de. *Letters from an American Farmer*. Harmondsworth: Penguin, 1986 [1783].

Crowley, John ("Jack") J. "*Red Harvest* and Dashiell Hammett's Butte." *The Montana Professor* 18 (Spring 2008). Online.

Crook, David. *Robin Hood: Legend and Reality*. Woodbridge: Boydell Press, 2020.

Cuthbert, Norma B., ed. *Lincoln and the Baltimore Plot, 1861: From Pinkerton Records and Relating Papers*. San Marino: Henry E. Huntington Library and Art Gallery, 1949.

Dacus, Joseph A. *Life and Adventures of Frank and Jesse James, the Noted Western Outlaws*. St. Louis: W.S. Bryan, 1879.

David, Henry. *The History of the Haymarket Affair*. New York: Russell and Russell, 1936.

Davies, Caitlin. *Private Inquiries: The Secret History of Female Sleuths*. Cheltenham: The History Press, 2023.

Despentes, Virginie. *Apocalypse Now*. Translated by Siân Reynolds. London: Profile, 2013 [2010].

Devine, Thomas M., ed. *Recovering Scotland's Slavery Past: The Caribbean Connection*. Edinburgh: Edinburgh University Press, 2015.

Devine, Thomas M. *The Scottish Nation: A Modern History*. London: Penguin, 2012 [1999]).

Dewees, Francis P. *The Molly Maguires*. Philadelphia: Lippincott, 1877.

Dougherty, George S. *The Criminal as a Human Being*. New York: Appleton, 1924.

Dubofsky, Melvyn. *We Shall Be All: A History of the Industrial Workers of the World*. New York: Quadrangle, 1989.

Dupré, Irma. *Romance of Dundee Township*. Carpentersville: Crossroads Communications, 1985.

Durie, Bruce. *The Pinkerton Casebook: Adventures of the Original Private Eye*. Edinburgh: Mercat, 2007.

Edwards, Owen Dudley. *The Quest for Sherlock Holmes: A Biographical Study of Sir Arthur Conan Doyle*. Edinburgh: Mainstream, 1983.

Eggert, Gerald G. *Railroad Labor Disputes: The Beginnings of Federal Strike Policy*. Ann Arbor: University of Michigan Press, 1967.

Ellis, P. Beresford. *The Scottish Insurrection of 1820*. London: Pluto, 1989 [1970].

Elsea, Jennifer K., Mishe Schwartz, and Kennon H. Nakamura. *Private Security Contractors in Iraq: Background, Legal Status, and Other Issues*. Washington: Congressional Research Service, 2008.

"Employment of Pinkerton Detectives." *House Report No. 2447*. 52nd Cong., 2nd sess., 1893.

Erickson, Charlotte. *Invisible Immigrants: The Adaptation of English and Scottish Immigrants in Nineteenth-Century America*. Ithaca: Cornell University Press, 1990 [1972].

Ernst, Donna. *The Sundance Kid: The Life of Harry Alonzo Longabaugh*. Norman: University of Oklahoma Press, 2009.

Feuer, Rosemary, and Chad Pearson, eds. *Against Labor: How US Employers Organized to Defeat Union Activism*. Urbana: University of Illinois Press, 2017.

Final Report of the Commission on Industrial Relations. Washington: 1915.

Fine, Sidney. *Sit-Down: The General Motors Strike of 1936–1937*. Ann Arbor: University of Michigan Press, 1969.

Fine, Sidney. *Without Blare of Trumpets; Walter Drew, the National Erectors' Association, and the Open Shop Movement, 1903–57*. Ann Arbor: University of Michigan Press, 1995.

Fishel, Edwin C. "Pinkerton and McClellan: Who Deceived Whom?" *Civil War History* 34 (June 1988): 115–42.

Fishel, Edwin C. *The Secret War for the Union: The Untold Story of Military Intelligence in the Civil War.* Boston: Houghton Mifflin, 1996.

Foner, Philip S., ed. *The Autobiographies of the Haymarket Martyrs.* New York: Monad Press, 1969.

Foner, Philip S. *The Great Labor Uprising of 1877.* New York: Monad Press, 1977.

Fraser, W. Hamish. "Alexander Campbell, 1796–1870." *Scottish Labour History Society Journal* 31 (1996): 35–38.

Fraser, W. Hamish. *Alexander Campbell and the Search for Socialism.* Manchester: Holyoake Books, 1996.

Fraser, W. Hamish. *Conflict and Class: Scottish Workers 1700–1838.* Edinburgh: John Donald, 1988.

Fraser, W. Hamish. *Dr. John Taylor, Chartist: Ayrshire Revolutionary.* Ayr: Ayrshire Archaeological and Natural History Society, 2006.

Friedman, Lawrence M. *Crime and Punishment in American History.* New York: Basic Books, 1993.

Friedman, Morris. *The Pinkerton Labor Spy.* New York: Wilshire, 1907.

Gage, Beverly. *The Day Wall Street Exploded: A Story of America in Its First Age of Terror.* Oxford: Oxford University Press, 2009.

Gara, Larry. "A Glorious Time: The 1874 Abolitionist Reunion in Chicago." *Journal of the Illinois State Historical Society* 65, no. 3 (Autumn 1972): 280–292.

Geiger, Mark W. *Financial Fraud and Guerrilla Violence in Missouri's Civil War, 1862–1865.* New Haven: Yale University Press, 2010.

Ginger, Ray. *Altgeld's America: The Lincoln Ideal versus Changing Realities.* Chicago: Quadrangle, 1965 [1958].

Goulart, Ron. *The Dime Detectives.* New York: Mysterious Press, 1988.

Graham, Hugh D., and Ted R. Gurr. *The History of Violence in America.* Report of the Task Force on Historical and Comparative Perspectives, National Commission on the Causes and Prevention of Violence. New York: Bantam/New York Times, 1969.

Grant, Hamil. *Spies and Secret Service: The Story of Espionage, its Main Systems and Chief Exponents.* New York: Frederick A. Stokes, 1915.

Grant, Susan-Mary. *The War for a Nation: The American Civil War.* New York: Routledge, 2006.

Green, James. "Haymarket Affair (1886)." In *Encyclopedia of U.S. Labor and Working-Class History*, edited by Eric Arnesen, 577–580. New York: Routledge, 2007.

Greenhow, Rose. *My Imprisonment and the First Year of Abolition Rule at Washington.* London: Richard Bentley, 1863.

Gregory, Anthony. *American Surveillance: Intelligence, Privacy, and the Fourth Amendment*. Madison: University of Wisconsin Press, 2016.

Grella, George. "The Literature of the Thriller: A Critical Study." PhD diss., University of Kansas, 1967.

Grella, George. "Murder and the Mean Streets: The Hard-Boiled Detective Novel." *Contempora* 1, no. 1 (March 1970): 6–13.

Gurr, Ted R. *Rogues, Rebels, and Reformers: A Political History of Urban Crime and Conflict*. London: Sage, 1976.

Gutman, Herbert G., ed. "Five Letters of Immigrant Workers from Scotland to the United States, 1867–1869: William Latta, Daniel M'Lachlan, and Allan Pinkerton." *Labor History* 9 (1968): 384–408.

Gutman, Herbert G. "Review of Wolff, Lockout." *The Pennsylvania Magazine of History and Biography* 90 (April 1966): 273–76.

Gutman, Herbert G. "Work, Culture and Society in Industrializing America, 1815–1919." *American Historical Review* 78 (June 1973): 531–88.

Hammett, Dashiell. *Red Harvest*. London: Pan, 1975 [1929].

Haywood, William D. "Socialism the Hope of the Working Class." *International Socialist Review*, 12 (February 1912): 467.

Henry, Will, ed. *I, Tom Horn*. London: Corgi, 1976 [1904].

Heale, Michael J. *American Anticommunism: Combating the Enemy Within, 1830-1970*. Baltimore: Johns Hopkins University Press, 1990.

Herndon, William. *Abraham Lincoln*, 2 vols. New York: D. Appleton & Co., 1896 (1892).

Hilton, Rodney H. "The Origins of Robin Hood." *Past and Present* 14 (November 1958): 30–44.

Hobsbawm, Eric J. *Labouring Men: Studies in the History of Labour*. London: Weidenfeld and Nicolson, 1968 [1964].

Hochman, Brian. *The Listeners: A History of Wiretapping in the United States*. Cambridge: Harvard University Press, 2022.

Hoerder, Dirk, ed. *'Struggle a Hard Battle': Essays on Working-Class Immigrants*. DeKalb: Northern Illinois University Press, 1986.

Hofstadter, Richard. *The Paranoid Style in American Politics and Other Essays*. New York: Knopf, 1965.

Hogg, J. Bernard. "Public Reaction to Pinkertonism and the Labor Question." *Pennsylvania History* 11, no. 3 (July 1944): 171–99.

Holbrook, Stewart H. *The Rocky Mountain Revolution*. New York: Holt, 1956.

Holtzer, Harold. *Lincoln President-Elect: Abraham Lincoln and the Great Secession Winter 1860–1861*. London: Simon & Schuster, 2009.

Horan, James D. *The Pinkertons: The Detective Agency that Made History*. New York: Crown, 1967.

Horan, James D., and Howard Swiggett. *Pinkerton Story*. New York: Putnam, 1951.

Horn, Stanley F. *Invisible Empire: The Story of the Ku Klux Klan, 1866–1871*. New York: Gordon Press, 1972 [1939].

Horsley, Albert E. (alias Harry Orchard, alias Tom Hogan). *The Confessions and Autobiography of Harry Orchard*. New York: McClure, 1907.

Howard, Sidney. *The Labor Spy*. New York: Republican Press, 1924.

Howells, William Dean. *A Hazard of New Fortunes*. Edinburgh: D. Douglas, 1889.

Hoyt, Edwin P. *Spectacular Rogue: Gaston P. Means*. Indianapolis: Bobbs-Merrill, 1963.

Huberman, Leo. *The Labor Spy Racket*. New York: Modern Age, 1937.

Hunt, William R. *America's Sherlock Holmes: The Legacy of William Burns*. Guildford: Lyons Press, 2019.

Hunter, Robert. *Poverty*. New York: Macmillan, 1904.

Hunter, Robert. *Violence and the Labor Movement*. New York: Macmillan, 1914.

Hyde, Charles K. "Undercover and Underground: Labor Spies and Mine Management in the Early Twentieth Century." *Business Studies Review* 60 (Spring 1986): 1–27.

Hynd, Alan. *Pinkerton Case Book: Great Modern True Crimes from the Archives of the World's Leading Detective Agency*. New York: New American Library, 1948.

"Investigation of the Employment of Pinkerton Detectives in Connection with the Labor Troubles at Homestead, PA." *House Miscellaneous Document No. 335*. 52nd Cong., 1st sess., 1892.

"Investigation in Relation to the Employment for Private Purposes of Armed Bodies of Men, or Detectives, in Connection with Differences between Workmen and Employers." *Senate Report No. 1280*. 52nd Cong., 2nd sess., 1893.

James, Les. *Render the Chartists Defenceless: John Frost's Voyage with Dr. McKechnie to Van Dieman's Land in 1840*. Newport: Three Impostors, 2015.

Janiewski, Dolores E. "Through a Glass Darkly: The NLRB, Employer Counteroffensives, Investigative Committees, and the CIO." In *Against Labor: How US Employers Organized to Defeat Union Activism*, edited by Rosemary Feuer and Chad Pearson, 129–158. Urbana: University of Illinois Press, 2017.

Janiewski, Dolores E. "From Labor Rights to the Right to Work: Constituting and Resisting Social Citizenship, 1932–1953." *Journal of Policy History* 34, no. 3 (2022): 371–402.

Javers, Eamon. *Broker, Trader, Lawyer, Spy: The Secret World of Corporate Espionage*. New York: Harper, 2010.

Jeffreys-Jones, Rhodri. "Allan Pinkerton: Informed Scot or Scottish Informer?" *Journal of Scottish Historical Studies*, 42/2 (2022): 197–216.

Jeffreys-Jones, Rhodri. "The Defictionalization of American Private Detection." *Journal of American Studies* 17 (August 1983): 265–74.

Jeffreys-Jones, Rhodri. *The FBI: A History*. New Haven: Yale University Press, 2007.

Jeffreys-Jones, Rhodri. "Leon Turrou: The Greatest Detective of Them All?" *Strand Magazine*, online, September 10, 2020.

Jeffreys-Jones, Rhodri. *The Nazi Spy Ring in America: Hitler's Agents, the FBI, and the Case that Stirred a Nation*. Washington, DC: Georgetown University Press, 2020.

Jeffreys-Jones, Rhodri. "The Pinkerton Pause: How Opposition to Pinkertonism Delayed the Advent of the Private Security State." *Intelligence and National Security*, 39, no. 6 (2024): 1067–1075.

Jeffreys-Jones, Rhodri. "The Problem of Industrial Violence in the United States, 1899–1909." PhD diss., Cambridge University, 1969. EP Microform 1978.

Jeffreys-Jones, Rhodri. *Violence and Reform in American History*. New York: New Viewpoints, 1978.

Jeffreys-Jones, Rhodri. *We Know All About You: The Story of Surveillance in Britain and America*. Oxford: Oxford University Press, 2017.

Jenning, Patrick. *The Long Winding Road of Harry Raymond: A Detective's Journey Down the Mean Streets of Pre-War Los Angeles*. Santa Monica: Bay City Press, 2021.

Jensen, Vernon H. *Heritage of Conflict: Labor Relations in the Nonferrous Metals Industry to 1930*. Ithaca: Cornell University Press, 1950.

Jesse James, the Life and Daring Adventures of This Bold Highwayman and Bank Robber and His No Less Celebrated Brother. Cliffside Park, NJ: W.F. Kelleher, 1951 (1896).

Joh, Elizabeth E. "The Forgotten Threat: Private Policing and the State." *Indiana Journal of Global Legal Studies* 13 (Summer 2006): 357–389.

Johnson, Loch K., ed. *The Oxford Handbook of National Security Intelligence*. Oxford: Oxford University Press, 2010.

Johnston, Neil. *The History of the Parliamentary Franchise*. Research Paper 13–14. House of Commons Library. March 1, 2013.

Johnston, Thomas. *The History of the Working Classes in Scotland*. Glasgow: Forward Publishing, 1920.

Jones, Dallas L. "Background and Motives of Scottish Emigration to the United States of America in the Period 1815–1861, with Special Reference to Emigrant Correspondence." PhD diss., Edinburgh University, 1970.

Jones, David J.V. *The Last Rising: The Newport Insurrection of 1839*. Oxford: Clarendon Press, 1985.

Josephson, Matthew. *The Politicos 1865–1896*. New York: Harcourt, Brace, 1938.

Josephson, Matthew. *Robber Barons: The Great American Capitalists, 1861–1901*. New York: Harcourt, Brace, 1934.

Kahan, Paul. *The Homestead Strike: Labor, Violence, and American Industry*. New York: Routledge, 2014.

Keefe, Patrick R. "Privatized Spying: The Emerging Intelligence Industry." In *Oxford Handbook of National Security Intelligence*, edited by Loch K. Johnson, 296–309. Oxford: Oxford University Press, 2010.

Kenny, Kevin. *Making Sense of the Molly Maguires*. New York: Oxford University Press, 1998.

Klehr, Harvey, John E. Haynes, and Fridrikh I. Firsov. *Secret World of American Communism*. New Haven: Yale University Press, 1995.

Knoles, George H. "Populism and Socialism, with Special Reference to the Election of 1892." *Pacific Historical Review* 12 (September 1943): 295–304.

Krause, Paul. *The Battle for Homestead, 1890–1892: Politics, Culture, and Steel*. Pittsburgh: University of Pittsburgh Press, 1992.

Krause, Paul. "Labor Republicanism and 'Za Chlebom': Anglo-Americans and Slavic Solidarity in Homestead." In *Struggle a Hard Battle*, edited by Dirk Hoerder, 143–169. DeKalb: Northern Illinois University Press, 1986.

"Labor Espionage: General Motors Corporation." *Hearings Before a Subcommittee of the Committee on Education and Labor, United State Senate*. 75th Cong., 1st sess., pursuant to S. Res. 266, February 15–19, 1937.

"Labor Espionage: Pinkerton's National Detective Agency, Inc." *Hearings Before a Subcommittee of the Committee on Education and Labor, United State Senate*. 74th Cong., 1st sess., pursuant to S. Res. 266, February 8–12, 1937.

"Labor Espionage and Strikebreaking: Pinkerton's National Detective Agency." *Hearings Before a Subcommittee of the Committee on Education and Labor, United States Senate*. 74th Cong., 2nd sess., pursuant to S. Res. 266, September 24–25, 1936.

Lamar, Howard R. *Charlie Siringo's West: An Interpretive Biography*. Albuquerque: University of New Mexico Press, 2005.

Lamar, Howard R., ed. *The New Encyclopedia of the American West*. New Haven: Yale University Press, 1998.

Lamon, Ward. *The Life of Abraham Lincoln from his Birth to his Inauguration as President*. Boston: J.R. Osgood, 1872.

Lane, Charles. *Freedom's Detective: The Secret Service, the Ku Klux Klan and the Man Who Masterminded America's First War on Terror*. Toronto: Hanover Square Press, 2019.

Lavine, Sigmund Arnold. *Allan Pinkerton: America's First Private Eye*. New York: Dodd, Mead, 1963.

Lee, Frances G. L. "Legal Medicine at Harvard University." *Journal of Criminal law and Criminology* 42 (Winter 1952): 674–78.

Leonnig, Carol. *Zero Fail: The Rise and Fall of the Secret Service*. New York: Random House, 2021.

Levin, Meyer. *Citizens*. New York: Viking, 1940.

Lewis, Lloyd. "Lincoln and Pinkerton." *Journal of the Illinois State Historical Society* 41, no. 4 (December 1948): 367–82.

The Life, Ties, and Treacherous Death of Jesse James, dictated to Frank Triplett by Mrs. Jesse James (wife) and Mrs. Zerelda Samuel (mother). St. Louis, MO: J.H. Chambers, 1882.

Line, Michael J. *The Baltimore Plot: The First Conspiracy to Assassinate Abraham Lincoln.* Yardley: Westholme, 2008.

Lomax, John A., comp. *Cowboy Songs and Other Frontier Ballads.* New York: Macmillan, 1929 [1910].

London, Jack. *The Iron Heel.* New York: Macmillan, 1907.

London, Jack. *War of the Classes.* New York, Macmillan, 1905.

Lossing, Benson J. *Pictorial History of the Civil War in the United States of America*, 3 vols. Philadelphia: George W. Childs, 1866.

Love, Robertus. *The Rise and Fall of Jesse James.* Lincoln: University of Nebraska Press, 1990 [1926].

Luff, Jennifer. "Spies, Labor." In *Encyclopedia of U.S. Labor and Working-Class History*, edited by Eric Arnesen, 1312–1325. New York: Routledge, 2007.

Lukas, J. Anthony. *Big Trouble: A Murder in a Small Western Town Sets Off a Struggle for the Soul of America.* New York: Simon & Schuster, 1997.

Mackay, James. *Allan Pinkerton: The Eye Who Never Slept.* Edinburgh: Mainstream, 1996.

Mackenzie, Peter. *An Exposure of the Spy System Pursued in Glasgow, During the Years 1816-17-18-19 and 20.* Glasgow: Muir, Gowans, 1832.

Mackenzie, Peter. *Reminiscences of Glasgow and the West of Scotland*, 3 vols. Glasgow: John Tweed, 1865–1866.

Mackenzie, Peter. *Reply to Kirkman Finlay, Esq. On the Spy System.* Glasgow: Muir, Gowans, 1833.

Mackenzie, Peter. *The Trial of James Wilson for High Treason.* Glasgow: Muir, Gowans, 1832.

Manhattan Yellow Pages. New York: New York Telephone Co./Bell Atlantic Yellow Pages Company, 1979.

Marchand, Roland. "The Homestead Strike of 1892." *The History Project.* University of California, Davis, 2015.

Markle, Donald E. *Spies and Spymasters of the Civil War.* New York: Hippocrene, 1994.

Marx, Karl. *Early Political Writings.* Edited by Joseph J. O'Malley and Richard A. Davis. Cambridge: Cambridge University Press, 1994.

McCann, Sean. *Gumshoe America: Hard-Boiled Crime Fiction and the Rise and Fall of New Deal Liberalism.* Durham: Duke University Press, 2000.

McDougall, Ian, ed. *An Interim Bibliography of the Scottish Working Class Movement*. Edinburgh: Society for the Study of Labour History, 1965.

McParlan, James and Jimmy Kerrigan. *Among the Assassins! The Molly Maguires and Their Victims; Full Report of the Evidence of Detective McParlan, Jimmy Kerrigan, and Others at the Celebrated Molly Maguire Trials, at Pottsville*. Pottsville: Miners' Journal, 1876.

McWatters, George S. *Knots Untied, or, Ways and By-Ways in the Hidden Life of American Detectives*. Hartford: J.B. Burr and Hyde, 1871.

Meadows, Anne. *Digging Up Butch and Sundance*. New York: St. Martin's Press, 1994.

Melville, Herman. *The Confidence-Man: His Masquerade*. New York: Dix, Edwards, 1857.

Mercer, Asa S. *The Banditti of the Plains, or The Cattlemen's Invasion of Wyoming in 1892. The Crowning Infamy of the Ages*. Cheyenne: A.S. Mercer, 1894.

Messer-Kruse, Timothy. *The Trial of the Haymarket Anarchists: Terrorism and Justice in the Gilded Age*. New York: Palgrave Macmillan, 2011.

Michie, Michael. *An Enlightenment Tory in Victorian Scotland: The Career of Sir Archibald Alison*. Montreal and Kingston: McGill-Queen's University Press, 1997.

Miller, Wilbur R. *A History of Private Policing in the United States*. London: Bloomsbury, 2019.

Moffett, Cleveland. *True Detective Stories from the Archives of the Pinkertons*. New York: Doubleday and McClure, 1897.

Monkonnen, Eric H. *America Becomes Urban: The Development of US Cities and Towns 1780–1980*. Berkeley: University of California Press, 1988.

Monkonnen, Eric H. *Police in Urban America, 1860–1920*. Cambridge: Cambridge University Press, 1981.

Monkonnen, Eric H. *Murder in New York City*. Berkeley: University of California Press, 2001.

Montgomery, David. *The Fall of the House of Labor: The Workplace, the State, and American Labor Activism, 1865–1895*. New York: Cambridge University Press, 1987.

Moore, Anne C., and Hester A. Hale. *Benjamin Harrison*. New York: Nova Science, 2009.

Morn, Frank. *"The Eye That Never Sleeps": A History of the Pinkerton National Detective Agency*. Bloomington: Indiana University Press, 1982.

Mortimer, Gavin. *Double Death: The True Story of Pryce Lewis, the Civil War's Most Daring Spy*. New York: Walker, 2010.

Moss, Marissa. *The Eye That Never Sleeps: How Detective Pinkerton Saved President Lincoln*. New York: Abrams Books for Young Readers, 2018.

Murray, Hannah-Rose. *Advocates of Freedom: African American Transatlantic Abolitionism in the British Isles*. Cambridge: Cambridge University Press, 2020.

Musser, Charles. *Before the Nickelodeon: Edwin S. Porter and the Edison Manufacturing Company*. Berkeley: University of California Press, 1991.

Nasaw, David. *Andrew Carnegie*. New York: Penguin, 2006.

National Cyclopedia of American Biography, Being the History of the United States. New York: Jas. T. White & Co., 1893.

National Records of Scotland, "What Was and Is the Minimum Age for Marriage in Scotland?" Online.

Norton, Arthur J., and Paul C. Glick. "Marital Instability: Past, Present, and Future." *Journal of Social Issues* 32 (January 1976): 5–20.

Norwood, Stephen H. *Strikebreaking and Intimidation: Mercenaries and Masculinity in Twentieth-Century America*. Chapel Hill: University of North Carolina Press, 2002.

Oates, William C., George T. Curtis, and Terence V. Powderly. "The Homestead Strike." *The North American Review* 155 (September 1892): 355–75.

O'Hara, S. Paul. *Inventing the Pinkertons: Or, Sleuths, Mercenaries, and Thugs, being a Story of the Nation's Most Famous (and Infamous) Detective Agency*. Baltimore: Johns Hopkins University Press, 2016.

Oliver, Willard. *The Birth of the FBI: Teddy Roosevelt, the Secret Service, and the Fight over America's Premier Law Enforcement Agency*. Lanham: Rowman and Littlefield, 2019.

Olmsted, Kathryn S. "British and American Anticommunism Between the Wars." *Journal of Contemporary History* 53 (January 2018): 89–108.

Olmsted, Kathryn S. *Real Enemies: Conspiracy Theories and American Democracy, World War I to 9/11*. Oxford: Oxford University Press, 2009.

Olmsted, Kathryn S. *Right Out of California: The 1930s and the Big Business Roots of Modern Conservatism*. New York: The New Press, 2015.

O'Neill, William L. *The Woman Movement: Feminism in the United States and England*. London: George Allen and Unwin, 1969.

Orchard, Harry. See Horsley, Albert E.

O'Toole, George J. A. *Honorable Treachery: A History of US Intelligence, Espionage, and Covert Action from the American Revolution to the CIA*. New York: Atlantic Monthly Press, 1991.

Packard, Vance. *The Status Seekers: An Exploration of Class Behavior in America*. Harmondsworth: Penguin, 1961 [1959].

Parry, David M. *The Scarlet Empire*. Indianapolis: Bobbs-Merrill, 1906.

Past and Present of Kane County, Illinois. Chicago: William le Baron, Jr, and Co, 1878.

Pearson, Chad. *Reform or Repression: Organizing America's Anti-Union Movement*. Philadelphia: University of Pennsylvania Press, 2016.

Pelling, Henry. *A History of British Trade Unionism*. Harmondsworth: Penguin, 1963.

Phillips, David Graham. "The Treason of the Senate: Aldrich, the Head of It All—The "Millionaires' Club."" *Cosmopolitan* (March 1906): 628–638.

Pinkerton, Allan. *Criminal Reminiscences and Detective Sketches.* Freeport: Books for Librarians Press, 1970 [1878].

Pinkerton, Allan. *The Expressman and the Detective.* Chicago: W.B. Keene, Cooke, 1874.

Pinkerton, Allan. *General Principles of Pinkerton's National Detective Agency.* Chicago: Fergus, 1873.

Pinkerton, Allan. "History and Evidence of the Passage of Abraham Lincoln from Harrisburg to Washington, February 22–23, 1861." *The Magazine of History* 8, no. 32 (1914).

Pinkerton, Allan. *The Molly Maguires and the Detectives.* New York: G.W. Dillingham, 1877.

Pinkerton, Allan. *The Detective and the Somnambulist.* Chicago: W.B. Keen, Cooke, 1875.

Pinkerton, Allan. *The Spy of the Rebellion: Being a True Story of the Spy System of the United States Army.* Lincoln: University of Nebraska Press, 1989 [1883].

Pinkerton, Allan. *Strikers, Communists, Tramps, and Detectives.* New York: G.W. Carleton, 1878.

Pinkerton's National Detective Agency, Inc. *Hearings Before a Subcommittee of the Committee on Education and Labor, United State Senate.* 74th Cong., 2nd sess., pursuant to S. Res. 266, November 18, 1937.

Pinkowski, Edward. *Lattimer Massacre.* Philadelphia: Sunshine Press, 1950.

Pliley, Jessica R. "Mann Act/White Slave Traffic Act of 1910." In *The Federal Bureau of Investigation: History, Powers, and Controversies of the FBI,* edited by Douglas M. Charles and Aaron J. Stockham, I: 298–301. Santa Barbara: ABC-CLIO, 2022.

Porter, Bernard. *Plots and Paranoia: A History of Political Espionage in Britain 1790–1988.* London: Routledge, 1989.

Powers, Richard G. *Not Without Honor: The History of American Anticommunism.* New York: The Free Press, 1995.

Powers, Richard G. *Secrecy and Power: The Life of J. Edgar Hoover.* New York: The Free Press, 1987.

Rastall, Benjamin M. *An Enquiry into the Cripple Creek Strike of 1893.* Colorado Springs: Board of Trustees of Colorado College, 1905.

Rastall, Benjamin M. *The Labor History of the Cripple Creek District.* Madison: University of Wisconsin, 1908.

Ray, Gerda W. "Pinkerton Detectives." In *Encyclopedia of U.S. Labor and Working-Class History,* edited by Eric Arnesen, 1088–1089. New York: Routledge, 2007.

"Repealing that Portion of the Act of March 3, 1893, which Prohibits the Employment, in any Government Service or by any Officer of the District of Columbia, of any Employee of the Pinkerton Detective Agency of any Similar Agency." *Senate Report No. 447.* 88th Cong., 1st sess., 1963.

Reply of the Western Federation of Miners to the "Red Book" of the Mine Operators' Association (Denver: WFM, 1904)

Rhodes, Barbara and William Wells Streeter. *Before Copyediting: The Art and History of Mechanical Copying, 1780–1938.* New Castle, Delaware: Oak Knoll Press, 1999.

Rice, C. Duncan. *The Scots Abolitionists 1833–1861.* Baton Rouge: Louisiana State University Press, 1981.

Richardson, Lewis F. *Statistics of Deadly Quarrels.* Edited by Quincy Wright and C.C. Lienau. Pittburgh: Boxwood Press, 1960.

Richmond, Alexander B. *Narrative of the Conditions of the Manufacturing Population and the Proceedings of Government which led to the State Trials in Scotland.* Glasgow: 1824.

Riffenburgh, Beau. *Pinkerton's Great Detective: The Amazing Life and Times of James McParland.* New York: Viking, 2013.

Robertson, Stephen. "The Pinkertons and the Paperwork of Surveillance: Reporting Private Investigation in the United States, 1855–1940." In *Private Security and the Modern State: Historical and Comparative Perspectives*, edited by David Churchill, Dolores Janiewski, and Pieter Leloup, 117–134. London: Routledge, 2020.

Roediger, Dave. "Haymarket Incident." In *Encyclopedia of the American Left*, edited by Mari Jo Buhle, Paul Buhle, and Dan Georgakas, 295–297. Urbana: University of Illinois Press, 1992.

Roosevelt, Theodore. *An Autobiography.* New York: Macmillan, 1913.

Roper, Moses. *A Narrative of the Adventures and Escape of Moses Roper, from American Slavery.* Philadelphia: Merrihew & Gunn, 1838.

Ross, Peter. *The Scot in America.* New York: The Raeburn Book Company, 1896.

Rowan, Richard W. *The Pinkertons: A Detective Dynasty.* London: Hurst & Blackett, 1931.

Rowan, Richard W. *The Spy Menace.* London: Thornton Butterworth, 1934.

Rowan, Richard W. *The Story of Secret Service.* London: John Miles, 1938.

Schickler, Eric, and Devin Caughey. "Public Opinion, Organized Labor, and the Limits of New Deal Liberalism, 1936–1945." *Studies in American Political Development* 25 (October 2011): 162–89.

Schrader, Stuart. *Badges Without Borders; How Global Counterinsurgency Transformed American Policing.* Berkeley: University of California Press, 2019.

Sears, Stephen W., ed. *Civil War Papers of George B. McClellan: Selected Correspondence, 1860–1865.* New York: Ticknor & Fields, 1989.

Seigel, Micol. *Violence Work: State Power and the Limits of Police*. Durham: Duke University Press, 2018.

Seiple, Samantha. *Lincoln's Spymaster: Allan Pinkerton, America's First Private Eye*. New York: Scholastic Press, 2015.

Siringo, Charles A. *Pinkerton's Cowboy Detective: A True Story of Twenty-Two Years with Pinkerton's National Detective Agency*. Chicago: W.B. Conkey, 1910.

Siringo, Charles A. *Two Evil Isms: Pinkertonism and Anarchism: By a Cowboy Detective Who Knows, as He Spent Twenty-Two Years in the Inner Circle of Pinkerton's National Detective Agency*. Chicago: Charles A. Siringo, 1915.

Settle, William A., Jr. *Jesse James Was His Name*. Columbia: University of Missouri Press, 1966.

Slavishak, Edward. "Working-Class Muscle: Homestead and Bodily Disorder in the Gilded Age." *The Journal of the Gilded Age and Progressive Era* 3 (October 2004): 339–68.

Smith, Robert P. A. *The Gorbals of Old. Vol. 2 of The Gorbals and Oatlands: A New History*. Catrine: Stenlake, 2014.

Smith, Shannon M. "'They Met Force with Force': African American Protests and Social Status in Louisville's 1877 Strike." *Register of the Kentucky Historical Society* 115 (Winter 2017): 1–37.

Socolofsky, Homer E. *The Presidency of Benjamin Harrison*. Lawrence: University Press of Kansas, 1987.

Sorel, Georges. *Reflections on Violence*. Translated by T. E. Hulme and J. Roth. New York: Collier, 1912 (in 1906 published as articles in *Mouvement Socialiste*; 1908 book as *Réflections sur la violence*).

Spielman, Jean E. *The Stool Pigeon and the Open Shop Movement*. Minneapolis: The American Publishing Company, 1923.

Stephens, John R. *Wildest Lives of the Frontier: America Through the Words of Jesse James, George Armstrong Custer, and Other Famous Westerners*. Guildford: TwoDot, 2017.

Stiles, T.J. *Jesse James: Last Rebel of the Civil War*. New York: Knopf, 2002.

Stockham, Aaron J. "Purvis, Melvin (1903–1960)." In *The Federal Bureau of Investigation: History, Powers, and Controversies of the FBI*, edited by Douglas M. Charles and Aaron J. Stockham, II: 384–385. Santa Barbara: ABC-CLIO, 2022.

Stowell, David O. "Railroad Strikes (1877)." In *Encyclopedia of U.S. Labor and Working-Class History*, edited by Eric Arnesen, 1172–1174. New York: Routledge, 2007.

"Strikebreaking Services." *Violations of Free Speech and Rights of Labor, Senate Report*. 76th Cong., 1st sess., pursuant to S. Res. 266, January 26, 1939.

Tarbell, Ida M. *The History of the Standard Oil Company*. New York: McClure, Phillips, 1905.

Thomis, Malcolm I. *Threats of Revolution in Britain, 1789–1848*. London: Macmillan, 1977.

Thompson, Edward P. *The Making of the English Working Class*. Harmondsworth: Penguin, 1968 [1963].

Tindall, George B., ed. *A Populist Reader*. New York: Harper & Row, 1966.

Trelease, Allen William. *White Terror: The Ku Klux Klan Conspiracy and Southern Reconstruction*. London: Secker and Warburg, 1972.

Trumbull, Matthew M. *Was It a Fair Trial? An Appeal to the Governor of Illinois*. Chicago: Lucy E. Parsons, 1886.

Twain, Mark (Samuel Langhorne Clemens). *The Gilded Age: A Tale of Today*. Hartford: American Publishing Company, 1873.

United States War Department. *The War of the Rebellion: A Compilation of the Official Records of the Union and Confederate Armies*. 70 vols. Washington, DC: Government Printing Office, 1880–1901.

Unterman, Katherine. *Uncle Sam's Policemen: The Pursuit of Fugitives Across Borders*. Cambridge: Harvard University Press, 2015.

Veblen, Thorstein. *The Theory of the Leisure Class*. New York: Viking, 1931 [1899].

"Violations of Free Speech and Right of Labor." *Senate Interim Report*. 75th Cong., 3 sess., pursuant to S. Res. 266, January 5, 1938.

Wall, Joseph F. *Andrew Carnegie*. New York: Oxford University Press, 1970.

Walton, John. *The Legendary Detective: The Private Eye in Fact and Fiction*. Chicago: Chicago University Press, 2015.

Warren, Kenneth. *Triumphant Capitalism: Henry Clay Frick and the Industrial Transformation of America*. Pittsburgh: University of Pittsburgh Press, 1996.

Weber, Max. *Rationalism and Modern Society*. Edited and translated by Tony Waters and Dagmar Waters. New York: Palgrave Macmillan, 2015.

Weinberg, Arthur, and Weinberg, Lila. *The Muckrakers, 1902–1912*. New York: Simon & Schuster, 1961.

Weiss, Robert P. "Private Detective Agencies and Labour Discipline in the United States, 1855–1946." *The Historical Journal* 29, no. 1 (March 1986): 87–107.

White, Ahmed. *Under the Iron Heel: The Wobblies and the Capitalist War on Radical Workers*. Berkeley: University of California Press, 2022.

White, Richard. *Railroaded: The Transcontinentals and the Making of Modern America*. New York: Norton, 2011.

Wilks, Ivor. *South Wales and the Rising of 1839: Class Struggle as Armed Struggle*. Urbana: University of Illinois Press, 1984.

Willett, Ralph. *Hard Boiled Detective Fiction*. Keele: British Association for American Studies, 1992.

Williams, David. *John Frost: A Study in Chartism*. Cardiff: University of Wales Press, 1939.

Williams, Glyn. "Social Conflict and Change within the Welsh Colony in Patagonia." *Anthropological Quarterly* 44 (April 1971): 78–93.

Wilson, Alexander. *The Chartist Movement in Scotland.* Manchester: Manchester University Press, 1970.

Winks, Robin. *Modus Vivandi: An Excursion into Detective Fiction.* Boston: David R. Godine, 1982.

Wirtz, James J. "Intelligence to Please? The Order of Battle Controversy during the Vietnam War." *Political Science Quarterly* 106 (Summer 1991): 239–63.

Wise, William. *Detective Pinkerton and Mr. Lincoln.* New York: E.P. Dutton, 1964.

Wolff, Leon. *Lockout: The Story of the Homestead Strike of 1892: A Study of Violence, Unionism, and the Carnegie Steel Empire.* London: Longmans, 1965.

Woodward, C. Vann. *Tom Watson: Agrarian Rebel.* New York Oxford University Press, 1963 [1938].

Woodward, Patrick H. *The Secret Service of the Post-Office Department.* Hartford: Dustin, Gilman, 1886.

Wright, Carroll D. "The Amalgamated Association of Iron and Steelworkers." *Quarterly Journal of Economics* 7 (July 1893): 400–432.

Young, Arthur H. *The Best of Art Young.* New York: Vanguard Press, 1936.

Zumoff, Jacob A. "Politics and the 1920s Writings of Dashiell Hammett." *American Studies* 52, no. 1 (2012): 77–98.

Index

Note: Page numbers followed by "*f*" refer to figures.

About the Author

Born in Wales, Rhodri Jeffreys-Jones was educated at the universities of Aberystwyth, Michigan, Harvard, and Cambridge, where he obtained his PhD. He held postdoctoral fellowships at Harvard, the Free University of Berlin, and the University of Toronto. He is now professor emeritus of American history at the University of Edinburgh and honorary president of the Scottish Association for the Study of America. Among his books are *Changing Differences: Women and the Shaping of American Foreign Policy, 1917–1994* (1995), *The American Left: Its Impact on Politics and Society since 1900* (winner of the Neustadt Prize in 2013), *The Nazi Spy Ring in America: Hitler's Agents, the FBI, and the Case that Stirred a Nation* (2020) and *A Question of Standing: The History of the CIA* (2022).